PREFACE

This book is the first of two volumes containing
papers prepared for the Second International Congress
for the Study of Child Language, held August 9-14, 1981
in Vancouver, British Columbia. The Congress was
sponsored by the International Association for the
Study of Child Language and the University of British
Columbia.

We judge the Congress to have been a particularly
successful one, due to several contributing factors.
More than one hundred papers represented research from
eighteen countries on a wide range of language
acquisition topics. Vancouver was at its scenic best,
with sunshine by day and meteor showers by night. The
local organizing committee worked very hard; thanks go
to Deborah Gibson, John Gilbert, David Ingram, Carolyn
Johnson, Ken Reeder, Carol Thew (Chair), Darcy Dybhavn,
Maura O'Melinn, and many other individuals and agencies,
including the Province of British Columbia.

As editors, our primary concern was to make the
Congress proceedings available as soon as possible.
Accordingly, Volume I contains the first camera-ready
papers in each research area that we received. Volume II,
to be published shortly, will include the remaining
papers submitted, completing the sections Phonology,
Morphology and Syntax, Semantics, Pragmatics and
Discourse, Mother-Child Interaction, and Language
Development in Exceptional Children. Two additional
topics addressed in Volume II are Cognition and Language
Development, and Bilingualism.

Carolyn Echols Johnson
School of Audiology and Speech Sciences
University of British Columbia

Carol Larson Thew
Department of Language Education
University of British Columbia

iii

TABLE OF CONTENTS

PRESPEECH

PHONOLOGY

MORPHOLOGY AND SYNTAX

SEMANTICS

PRAGMATICS AND DISCOURSE

MOTHER-CHILD INTERACTION

THE SPECIFICITY OF INFANT BABBLING IN THE LIGHT OF CHARACTERISTICS OF THE MOTHER TONGUE

Bénédicte de Boysson-Bardies

Laboratoire de Psychologie
C.N.R.S.

Most current work on prelanguage and first language is based on the idea that language acquisition is constrained by strong biological dispositions. From this point of view, the linguistic environment provides structures that the receiving organism analyses according to its own structures, its degree of maturation, and the type of perceived information. For speech development, recent knowledge about discriminatory capacities and capacities of early categorisation of linguistic stimuli allows us to hypothesize that the perceived information can at a very early stage influence the infant's selection of vocal targets. In the first months, vocal productions are fairly strictly dependent upon the infant's physiological equipment. Such motoric and respiratory constraints account for the equivalence of cooing in all infants below four months. They also account to a large extent for similarities found in later productions, as well as in phonological universals of first language development. But from five or six months onward, the differences found in babies' vocal productions suggest that strict restrictions on articulatory and phonational capacities are being lifted.

Our hypothesis is that at the same time as the child's productions begin to be more controlled, a selection of certain specific characteristics of the infant's linguistic environment can be found in his vocalizations. In this paper we present the first of a series of experiments whose purpose is to determine at what point in vocal development an interpretation in terms of selection of aspects of the mother tongue must be added to the interpretation in terms of physiological constraints. We especially want to establish, in the light of the characteristics of the target language, which elements will tend to be selected. To study this point we use an intercultural approach. This approach includes experiments with adults' perceptual judgments in a babbling identification task, as well as acoustic analysis of this experimental material. This material is composed of samples of babbling from four, six, eight and ten-month-old babies from different linguistic communities. From the babies' productions, we think it will be possible to specify which phonetic and intonational parameters carry phonological and metaphonological information and which are most salient and easily reproduced by the babies.

We have few valid homogeneous descriptions of the different parameters specifying the prosody of different languages. The absence of uniformity in the description of acoustical data and the absence of precise knowledge of the perceptual value of the data generally prevent a direct comparison between acoustic analyses of languages and babbling. For this reason it is useful to do babbling identification experiments with adults. These imply judgment of the compatibility or incompatibility of instances of babbling with the phonology and prosody of the language of adults in the same community. These judgments allow us to establish whether perceptual correlates of dimensions such as intonation, rhythm, and voice quality of a given language exist in the babbling of the babies from that linguistic community.

Research done using the babbling discrimination or identification paradigm has not provided reliable data. Tervoort (1966) found identification of babbling in six to seven-month-old Dutch babies, and Weir (1966), in pilot studies, suggests the possibility of discriminating between Chinese and American babies at six months. However neither Atkinson, MacWhinney & Stoel (1970), using Weir's samples, nor Olney & Scholnick (1976), using samples from six, twelve and eighteen-month-olds, found identification. We used this paradigm, but made the following modifications:
    1. Vocal productions at eight and ten months differ in structure. At eight months babbling is characterized by strongly intonated patterns. At ten months a stage appears which is marked by more segmented -- often mono- or bisyllabic -- less intonated productions. Obviously adults should use different cues for distinguishing between different types of babbling. Since they may be more or less sensitive to the characteristics of the various stages, and given that rapid changes take place in the last half of the first year, we chose to select samples of babbling with intonation patterns spreading over the whole breath group.

2. The characteristics of individual languages play a fundamental role. We hypothesize that parameters such as timbre, rhythm, duration, f_o contour, and voice quality will be among the relevant cues in the mother tongue selected by babies. We expect that when a language relies heavily on a particular set of such parameters, babbling will reflect this. Two languages relying on very different sets of parameters will give rise to very different kinds of babbling.

Our first experiment involves vocal productions of eight and ten-month-old babies belonging to linguistic communities whose languages are differentiated by the presence or absence of a stress system, the presence or absence of systematic phonetic contrasts involving different voice qualities, and whether or not the language is a tone language. The languages also involve different phonetic repertories and syllable structures. Tunisian Arabic is differentiated from French mainly by the presence of a particular voice quality -- faucalized voice (Laver 1980) -- and a stress system based on syllable weight (Hyman 1977). Cantonese is a tone language.

We collected our data in the countries of origin. Samples of 15 seconds duration were extracted from the corpuses. Samples from eight and ten-month-old infants were presented to the judges in two separate blocks. Each block included eight pairs of samples. Each pair contained a sample from a French baby and a sample from either an Arabic or a Chinese baby. Each French sample occurred once with an Arabic, once with a Cantonese sample. The judges, who did not know the linguistic origin of the non-French samples, were required to designate the samples they thought were from French babies. Forty subjects participated in the experiment: two groups of women -- one of mothers and one of nonmothers-- and one group of men. Table 1 gives the percentages of correct identification of French babbling samples for the two types of pairs: French-Arabic and French-Cantonese. An analysis of variance indicates that for the factor linguistic community, $F(1,14)=10.38$, significant at $p<.01$, and for age, $F(1,14)=6.76$, $p<.01$. No difference existed between the subject groups. All subjects found discriminations easier with eight-month-old babies.

Results are very coherent for the French-Arabic comparisons: in seven out of eight pairs, the French babbling sample was correctly identified by the majority

3

TABLE 1. PERCENTAGES OF CORRECT IDENTIFICATION
OF FRENCH BABBLING SAMPLES FOR FRENCH-ARABIC
AND FRENCH-CANTONESE PAIRS

PAIR TYPE	AGE	
	8 months	10 months
French-Arabic	78,75*	74,37*
French-Cantonese	69,37*	31,89*

---

* $p < .001$

of subjects ($p < .01$). They are less coherent for the
French-Cantonese comparison, since Cantonese samples
were selected as French by the majority of the judges.

We will now consider the acoustic analysis of these
samples.

French
    Direction of air flow is always expiratory. Voice
quality remains clear. Productions are voiced throughout, with mainly front articulation and smooth vocalic
ingress. F_0 contours of two types are found: a) long
and flat in the medium frequency range with some smooth
pitch glides and flat or falling terminal contours, and
b) starting high and then falling, ending medium or low
with more variations of pitch. Pitch and loudness tend
to covary, i.e. rises and falls in f_0 contours correspond to rises and falls in loudness. There are cases
of variations of pitch or loudness without corresponding
variations in loudness or pitch. Variations of loudness
are generally not very great in the same breath group.
With reference to temporal organisation, productions are
long; the median is 1000ms for the eight-month samples.
No systematic contrasts in pitch or in loudness between
consecutive segments are found. Duration of terminal
syllables are very often much longer; babies let the
sound continue until the end of expiration. The phonetic features front, low, unrounded are preferred over
the features back, high and rounded. Vocalic sounds are
various. At eight months voiced labial or dental fricatives are found in all the samples. At ten months there
are mainly voiced and voiceless stops. Syllables are
mainly open V or CV and there are sequences of the form
VCV.

4

Arabic (Tunisian)

Inspiratory and expiratory directions of air flow
are frequently found, with alternated production of
ingress and egress breathing cycles. Phonation types
show a wide range of variation from breathy to tense.
Vocal ingress is very often abrupt at the beginning of
the production. All parameters can move more briskly
than they can in French. Productions are mainly short;
the median at eight months is 450ms. The main characteristic is variation with sharp contrasts in both pitch
and loudness. Rises and falls, including initial rises
and falls, are both characterized by sharp slopes.
Pitch and loudness tend to covary, but dissociations can
be found. Variations in loudness are often large within
a single breath group. Temporal configuration is characterised by typical binary organisation, with sharp
"stress" or phonetic correlates of stress on the first
part. The accent is marked by strong laryngeal activity
and sometimes different kinds of respiratory activity.
This involves increases of pitch and loudness, so that
productions form rhythmical series with contrasts of
phonation, pitch, loudness and/or duration. Few types
of vocalic sounds are found in our samples. Consonants
are mainly stops, with many aspirated released stops,
glottal stops and a sound resembling the voiced laryngeal fricative of Arabic. Syllables are often closed,
with final stop consonants strongly aspirated.

Cantonese

As far as Cantonese is concerned, the main difference with French found for eight-month-old babblers is
the frequency of rising intonation contours and high
pitch modulations. The judges' inability to discriminate among ten-month-olds is perhaps related to the fact
that both French and Cantonese have a mainly demarcative,
often phrase-final, stress system.

Discussion

This first experiment suggests that from eight
months, children's vocal productions show characteristics
which are "linguistic" in the sense that adults can
judge the compatibility of these productions with the
melodic contours and sound patterns of their own language. However adults listen globally, and their judgments are coherent only when they can detect some set of
very specific characteristics which are either obviously
compatible or obviously incompatible with the characteristics of their own language. This was the case in the

French-Arabic comparison, where adults were able to
reject outright the Arabic infants' babbling as incompatible with French.

However the types of samples presented to the
judges are determinants of discrimination. In a subsequent experiment we used the same kind of samples for
eight-month-olds as extracted from the dominant productions at this age. For ten-month-olds we selected only
reduplicated babbling. In this case we found correct
discrimination for eight-month-olds but not for ten-
month-olds.

The most obvious characteristics for adult judges
in this experiment were not segmental cues, but more
general features such as phonation types, backness of
articulation, vocal ingress and variations in pitch and
amplitude. These dimensions are the first specific
dimensions found in infants' vocal productions. This
can be explained because these parameters have strong
differential perceptual weight depending on the language.
This is particularly true for French and Arabic. In
addition, these dimensions are fundamental to speech
production. Dimensions of voice quality, i.e. laryngeal
set (which is responsible for phonation), as well as
supralaryngeal setting, are at the base of the production of the speech signal. The mastery of these aspects
is a prerequisite for fine articulatory control. For
eight-month-old children, such parameters seem, at a
level independent of segmental production, already under
a certain amount of control. Thus a rhythm which is
marked by the succession of strong/weak distinctions on
consecutive segments seems very frequent in Arabic
babbling, although this contrast involves putting to
work a large variety of phonatory and glottal mechanisms,
as well as control of duration.

The productions of eight and ten-month-old babblers
have, however, basic similarities across languages.
These similarities show up in the fact that common intonation patterns and phonetic preferences are found
across language backgrounds for given ages.

The study we have presented shows the way in which
we have tried to investigate how specific dimensions of
the mother tongue are added to common intonational
dimensions and phonetic preferences found in infants'
vocal productions. Selection, as well as the mode of
processing the different speech dimensions found in
languages in general and in the mother tongue in

particular, should help us to develop a model of the representations the child uses as a basis for the development of speech.

REFERENCES

Atkinson, K., McWhinney, B. & Stoel, C. (1970). An experiment on the recognition of babbling. Papers and Reports on Child Language Development 1. Stanford University.

Hyman, L. (1977). On the nature of linguistic stress. Southern California Occasional Papers in Linguistics 4.

Laver, J. (1980). The phonetic description of voice quality. Cambridge: Cambridge University Press.

Olney, R. & Scholnick, E. (1976). Adult judgments of age and linguistic differences in infant vocalization. Journal of Child Language 3. 145-156.

Tervoort (1966). Cited in General discussion, Weir presentation. F. Smith & G. Miller (eds), The genesis of language: a psycholinguistic approach. Cambridge, Mass.: MIT Press.

Weir, R. (1966). Some questions on the child's learning of phonology. F. Smith & G. Miller (eds), The genesis of language: a psycholinguistic approach. Cambridge, Mass.: MIT Press.

A Young Baby's Prosodic Differentiation Between
a Person and a Toy

Diane Fujitani
University of California, Berkeley

Patricia M. Greenfield
University of California, Los Angeles

James Argiro
North Hollywood, California

ABSTRACT

This study investigated whether or not a baby, boy
two to three months old, differentiated his vocalizations to a person and to a toy. The baby interacted vocally with an adult in the Person condition
and responded vocally to a noisemaking toy in the
Toy condition. At two months, the baby's vocalizations to the toy were generally prosodically less
varied. Toy vocalizations were more monotone in
pitch; successive sounds were less detached in the
Toy condition, and rhythmic variability in duration
was greater in the Person condition. These comparisons were not significant for the baby's three-
month-old data. These results suggest there was
reflexive imitation of the stimuli at two months,
which disappeared with neurological development at
three months.

Our study investigated whether or not a 2-
month-old baby, Brian, would vocalize differently
to a person and to a toy. In the Person condition,
Brian vocally interacted with an adult, and in the
Toy condition, he responded vocally to a noisemaking toy. His vocalizations in the two conditions
were compared for differences in intonation and
other suprasegmental features. The study explored

8

whether there would be differences in prosody to the Person and Toy stimuli.

Research shows that as early as their newborn period, infants differ in orientation to people and to things presented to them visually. Bower (1979) argues that newborns have different sets of coordinated responses to their social and physical worlds. For example, they can make the general gesture of opening and closing the hand in the presence of either a person or an object, but this gesture is actually part of more complex responses which are vastly different toward these two types of stimuli. In the presence of an adult who is modelling this hand gesture, the infant produces his or her own version in imitation of the model (Bower, 1979). The sight of an object, however, stimulates opening and closing of the hand as a part of the overall response of reaching and grasping for the object (Bower, 1972).

Newborns also respond on an auditory level to differences between social and nonsocial stimuli. Condon and Sander (1974) found that babies 1-day-old respond differently to rhythm in language and nonspeech sounds. When hearing an adult speaking, they move their limbs in synchrony with the rhythm of the speech input. This kind of gestural imitation does not occur, however, to the sound of regular tapping noises.

There is some evidence that very young babies vocalize differently to a person and an object. For example, Proctor (1982) found that babies in their first six months of life have a higher rate of vocalization with the mother than with an object, and a greater amount of silence with the object. Also, at times these babies had different types of vocalization with person and object (Proctor, personal communication).

Also, in a longitudinal study of infants from 5 weeks
to 15 months old, Delack compared vocalization patterns
produced in three situational contexts: being alone, being
with an adult who's just been speaking, and being with a
toy or blanket. He reports, 'that, given changes of
situation, the infants generally did not alter their
intonation patterns; and even when they did they did so
inconsistently (with respect to a given context), and performance did not improve with age' (Delack 1976:67).
However, there are also exceptions to this general finding,
indicating that situational context could influence
intonation, and this could happen as early as 5 weeks.
Perhaps this evidence for the influence of context would
have been stronger if the infants had been more involved in
their interactions with the adult and the object.

Our study explored whether a baby as young as 2 months
old would vocalize differently to a person and a toy if he
were actively interacting with the stimulus in a turn-
taking manner. The baby's patterns of prosody were what
was looked at since later in infancy these become the
earliest proto-linguistic structures.

In order to study prosody, a system of transcription
using musical notation was developed. Musical symbols
were used to transcribe such features as pitch, rhythm and
volume change. The resulting musical score provided the
raw data for chi square comparisons between the infant's
responses to the person and the toy. Part of the score is
provided in Figure 1. These are 15 vocalizations to the
toy at 2 months.

Method

The method we used was basically a naturalistic one.
Both the Person and Toy conditions were naturalistic,
except for the restriction of turn-taking. The sessions
were run in the home with the baby lying in his crib,
watching the stimulus which was about 2 feet in front of
him. In the Person condition, the researcher first smiled
and greeted him, and then became quiet and still until he
responded vocally. The adult was generally silent throughout the infant's turn, and then took her turn, making it
last until the baby seemed ready to respond back. This

10

Figure 1. Vocalizations to the toy at 2 months

turn-taking interaction continued until the baby became tired or fussy.

The Toy condition was similar with the toy held still and silent during the baby's turn, and shaken in an active and noisy manner during its turn. The toy used was either a hand-sized plastic squeeze toy, or a small plastic puppet with several moving parts.

Both sessions were run on the same evening. The Person and Toy conditions were run again in a similar manner when the baby was 3 months old.

The audiotape of the baby's vocalizations was transcribed by a musician who had an ear for absolute pitch. The transcriber was blind to the conditions of the study. To prevent biasing of the transcription, the Person and Toy sounds were manually edited from the original tape. Also, if part of a vocalization of the baby's either overlapped with the stimulus sound or was difficult to hear, the entire vocalization was deleted. Altogether, for the 2-month data, 10 vocalizations in the Person condition and 39 vocalizations in the Toy condition were transcribed. In the transcribed 3-month data, there were 11 vocalizations to the person, and 17 to the toy. A tape of the sessions is available to persons interested in hearing the original vocalizations.

When considering the response categories used for our data analysis, intra-rater reliability was 76% (.76) for pitch and .71 for connectedness. It was somewhat lower for rhythm, .67. Reliability was also calculated for absolute values of these aspects of sound. For absolute pitch within the range of about 18 Hz (or a half step), it was .73; and for connectedness, .71.[1] It was somewhat lower for for absolute values of duration. Within the range of 17 hundredths of a second, it was .64. Reliability for volume was fairly low. It was .60 when using our data categories and .52 when using absolute values.

Transcription of typical vocalizations to the person and toy at 2 months are provided in Figure 2. The vocalization to the Person is on the left, and the Toy vocalization on the right. Each vocal sound is represented

Figure 2. Typical vocalizations

at 2 months

Person   Toy

by a musical note. An approximate, subjective
phonetic transcription of the vocal sound is
written in English sound symbols below the note.

Each sound was transcribed for pitch, rhythm,
relative volume change, and degree of connectedness with adjacent sounds. The position of the
solid notehead on the musical staff indicates
absolute pitch. The higher the position, the
higher the pitch. The "X" notehead indicates
untranscribable deviation from the line or space
on the staff.

Rhythm was transcribed by coding how long
each sound lasted. Table 1 provides the key to
the code for duration values. Here the values are
given in seconds.

Table 1. Key for duration values

symbol	duration (seconds)	symbol	duration (seconds)
	<.171		.512
	=.171		.682 (88 per min.)
	.257		1.023
	.341		1.364

13

The durations of sounds are as indicated except that any sound which was shorter than a sixteenth note (♪) was written as a "grace note" (or ornamentation) without indication of its exact length. These grace notes contain slashes through their stems (♪). In some vocalizations where the sound did not fall exactly on a beat or on a reasonable fraction of a beat, the vocalization was arbitrarily "moved over" to the nearest beat or fraction of a beat. This was done consistently and so it did not affect analyses of the data. Moreover, the differences in question are in the realm of extremely small durations of time.

Rhythm was judged against a metronome ticking at 88 beats per minute. At this beat, the rate of the quarter note was 88 per minute. Surprisingly, all of the vocalizations fit this beat. In a sense, the baby's vocalizing had a beat to it.

Volume changes are more general in transcription. There are symbols for a gradual increase or decrease across successive sounds, and symbols for stress on individual sounds. An example of each of these is in the Toy vocalization in Figure 2. The sideways "V" below the staff marks a gradual decrease in loudness, whereas the smaller similar mark above the first sixteenth note indicates stress on that one particular sound.

Degree of connectedness between sounds is indicated by markings for definite connectedness, or "slurring," between notes and also by symbols for silence or pauses between sounds. An example of a mark for clearly connected sounds is in the Toy vocalization. It is the curved line going from the second to the third note.

One of the symbols for silence between sounds is in the Person vocalization. The dot above the last note indicates that a brief pause separates this sound from any sound following it. Notes which do not have either of these types of symbols are "normal" in degree of connectedness.

14

Results

Chi square tests showed that at 2 months, Brian's vocalizations to the person generally varied to a greater extent from sound to sound than did his vocalizations to the toy. Table 2 provides chi squares for differences in patterns of vocalizations. At 2 months, there are significant differences between the Person and Toy vocalizations, but at 3 months, there are no differences. At 3 months, the vocalizations to the person generally became less varied, and so they looked more like the vocalizations to the toy.

Table 2. Chi square values for differences in variability between Person and Toy vocalizations

	pitch	rhythm	volume change	connectedness
2 months	4.89*	3.97*	3.07	4.82*
3 months	0.05	1.62	0.04	1.37

$p < .05$

The differences at 2 months between the Person and Toy vocalizations, in both pitch and rhythm, held only for patterns of successive vocal sounds. The pattern[3] considered was a pair of successive sounds. Within this pattern, variability was defined as amount of change from one sound to the next.[4]

The baby's vocalizations to the person at 2 months tended to be somewhat varied in pitch and his Toy vocalizations more monotone. The examples in Figure 2 show that the Person vocalization has greater change in pitch, from one vocal sound to the next. In the Person condition, the change in pitch was often greater than about 40 Hz (or 1 whole step), while in the Toy condition, the extent of change tended to be about 40 Hz or less.

Similarly, rhythmic variability was greater in the Person condition, with more changes in duration from sound to sound. In contrast, two successive sounds in the Toy condition tended to have the same duration with 17 hundredths of a second. This can also be seen in the examples in Figure 2. In the Person vocalization, each sound has a different duration, while the Toy vocalization has two successive sounds having the same duration.

Table 3. Proportion of absolute pitches

PITCH		2 months		3 months	
musical note	# Hz	Person	Toy	Person	Toy
above G	392.00+	0	.02	.02	.09
G	392.00	0	.02	.02	.02
F	349.23	0	.08	.08	.10
E	329.63	.04	.18	.06	.13
D	293.66	.40	.28	.41	.27
middle C	261.63	.36	.26	.34	.23
B	246.94	.12	.10	.05	.09
A	220.00	.04	.04	.02	.06
G	196.00	.04	.01	.02	.01
below G	< 196.00	0	.01	0	0

Finally, there was some difference between the two conditions in proportion of connected pairs to disconnected pairs of successive vocal sounds. A greater proportion of consecutive sounds tended to be connected in the Toy condition. Again, the examples in Figure 2 show this difference.

There was no difference between conditions in volume pattern. This was probably related to the low reliability of coding for volume.

16

These differences between Person and Toy vocalizations disappeared when only unpatterned absolute frequencies[5] of the pitch or duration of individual sounds were considered. Table 3 gives the proportion of absolute pitches represented by the vocal sounds in both conditions. It shows that the pattern of proportions is similar for both the Person and Toy conditions. Likewise, Table 4 shows that both conditions have similar proportion of durations of individual sounds.

Table 4. Proportion of duration values

at ♩ = 88 per minute

DURATION	2 months		3 months	
	Person	Toy	Person	Toy
♬	.04	.06	.03	.10
♪	.32	.47	.63	.40
♪.	0	0	0	.01
♩	.32	.37	.22	.38
♩.	.04	.01	.06	.09
♩	.28	.08	.06	.03
♩.	0	.01	0	0

Discussion

Although an interactive element could have been operating in the prosodic differentiation between a person and a toy at 2 months, the most likely interpretation of this differentiation is imitation of the stimuli, since the adult's utterances were distinguishably more varied than the toy sounds, in both pitch and rhythm. Also, the adult's utterances seemed to be less connected, having more pauses between sounds. It has been shown that babies 8 weeks old imitate the pitch of an adult model. Wolff (1969) found that when presented with speech sounds which are part of the infant's repertory, the baby attempts to copy the pitch of the model. It seems likely, then, that differences in Brian's vocalizations at 2 months occurred through imitation.

Why the differentiation of vocalization to person and toy present at 2 months disappears a month later is a bit mysterious. However, this result fits with the growing body of findings indicating that a number of newborn abilities, originally under reflexive control, temporarily disappear, to reappear later in development, this time in the form of voluntary behavior (e.g., Bower, 1976). Our hypothesis is that the imitation of prosodic relations, present at 2 months in Brian's vocalizations, could constitute a reflexive basis for the later use of prosody in the development of voluntary or intentional communication.

References

Bower, T.G.R. (1979) Human development. San
    Francisco: Freeman.

Bower, T.G.R. (1976). Repetitive processes in
    child development. Scientific American
    235. 38-47.

Bower, T.G.R. (1972). Object perception in
    infants. Perception 1, 15-30. Developing
    in infancy. San Francisco: Freeman.

Condon, W.S. & Sander, L. (1974). Neonate move-
    ment is synchronized with adult speech:
    Interactional participation and language
    acquisition. Science 183. 99-101.

Delack, J. (1976). Infant vocalizations. In
    W. von Raffler-Engel & Y. Lebrun (eds),
    Baby talk and infant speech. Amsterdam:
    Swets & Zeitlinger B.V.

Proctor, A. (1982). Effects of social context
    on vocalization and hand gesture in early
    infancy. Paper presented at the Second
    International Congress for the Study of
    Child Language, 1981. Published this
    volume, pp. 29-42.

Wolff, P.H. (1969). The natural history of
    crying and other vocalisations in early
    infancy. In B.M. Foss (ed.), Determinants
    of infant behavior, Vol. 4, London: Methuen.

Footnotes

We are especially indebted to Bob Opaluch for his advice
on categorization of the data and results analysis.
We'd also like to thank Nancy Rader for her helpful
comments. And, last but not least, our appreciation
goes to our subject, Brian.

[1] The _absolute values_ of duration were measured in terms
of fractions of a second (see Table 1), whereas the _data
categories_ used for duration were "change" or "no change"
in duration from one vocal sound to the next.

[2] The contingency tables for the chi square values in
Table 2 are provided below.

2 Months

PITCH

	person	toy
>1 whole step	8	12
≤1 whole step	8	46

VOLUME CHANGE

	person	toy
change	5	33
no change	11	26

RHYTHM

	person	toy
same duration	5	33
different duration	10	20

CONNECTEDNESS

	person	toy
connected	8	43
not connected	7	10

Footnotes, continued

3 months

PITCH   RHYTHM

	person	toy		person	toy
> 1 whole step	13	19	same duration	34	49
≤ 1 whole step	39	76	different duration	17	39

VOLUME CHANGE   CONNECTEDNESS

	person	toy		person	toy
change	21	37	connected	29	41
no change	31	58	not connected	22	40

[3]This pattern needed to be adjusted for long periods of silence between some successive sounds in the 3-month data. Wherever two consecutive sounds were separated by at least a half-note rest (1.365 sec), they were considered too far apart in time to be a "pair." Any consistency or change between these particular successive sounds was therefore not included in the results analysis.

(The adjustment did not affect the overall pattern of results for the 3-month data, however, When large gaps of silence were overlooked and all pairs of successive sounds included in the results, all chi square values remained insignificant.)

[4] Turns consisting of a single vocal sound were not included in the results for rhythm variability or for connectedness. However, these single-note vocalizations <u>were</u> counted as monotone "pairs" in the chi squares for pitch since all such single-sound turns were long enough in duration to have either changed in pitch or remained monotone.

Single-note vocalizations were also included in the tallies for volume change since a single vocal sound could have either changed in volume or maintained the same volume throughout the note.

[5]"Unpatterned absolute frequencies" refers to the tally of individual vocal sounds regardless of any context of pattern, or sequence, of vocal sounds.

PERCEPTUAL AND ACOUSTIC ATTRIBUTES OF INFANT DISTRESS VOCALIZATIONS

Nina Petrovich-Bartell, Nelson Cowan,
and Philip A. Morse

University of Wisconsin, Madison

As a step toward becoming an adult, a human being must at some time begin the process of vocal communication. An early beginning exists in infancy, with the modulation of voice in a way that allows the expression of a variety of emotions. We have focused on vocalizations that convey distress, because previous work has demontrated that infants are capable of subtle voice modifications that appear related to the type and intensity of distress. The main purpose of our work is to examine mothers' sensitivity to specific acoustic information within infant calls of distress, and to define this acoustic information in terms of physical parameters commonly used to describe speech sounds.

An important distinction within distress vocalizations, and one that organizes the present research, is the distinction between "cries" and "fusses". Emde (1976) has suggested that unlike the infant "cry", which may signal specific needs such as thirst, hunger, or pain, the infant "fuss" is an unexplained cry that is not related to specific physiological needs. Stark, Rose, and McLagen (1975) have characterized fusses as discomfort sounds involving a different configuration of behavior than cries. Specifically, discomfort sounds are accompanied by a cry face, but less stiffening of limbs and more movement than occurs with crying. Furthermore, fusses are shorter and more intermittent than cries.

Given this combination of vocal and nonvocal distress behaviors, it is hypothetically possible that mothers are able to use only nonvocal cues to diagnose the specific state of their infants.

We attempted to rule out that possibility by providing situations in which mothers would judge
infant vocalizations with all nonverbal cues removed.

The subjects were five primiparous mothers,
23-28 years of age, who had healthy three-to-four
month old infants. Two infants were male and
three were female. All recording and testing was
done on two separate home visits. For the first
15 minutes of the first visit, the baby's voice
was recorded with the mother present, with the
baby in a slightly uncomfortable position and at
a time when it was expected to be fussy. Distress
vocalizations obtained from these recording
sessions were selected for subsequent use only
if they contained no silent breaks longer than
1 second and were separated from other vocalizations by at least 2 seconds. Each baby yielded
12 to 13 of these vocalizations, which were recorded onto a second tape recorder by the experimenter in another room. Approximately 30 minutes
after the termination of the initial recording
session, the experimenter emerged with a tape to
be played back to the mother. This tape contained the 12 or 13 selected sounds produced by
the infant in their original serial order. The
mothers used a five-point rating scale for each
sound, with the values, "definitely fuss",
"probably fuss", "don't know", "probably cry",
and "definitely cry".

After the first home visits were completed,
a single master tape was constructed that contained the 12 or 13 vocalizations from each
infant, randomized across infants. Each vocalization appeared on the master tape three times,
for a total of 62 x 3 or 186 sounds. This master
tape was presented to each mother 3 weeks after
the first visit. Presumably, the nonverbal contextual cues present in the first session were
minimized in this situation, and the mothers were
forced to rely almost entirely upon acoustic cues
in judging the vocalizations of their own infants

as well as infants unfamiliar to them.

Lastly, each of the 62 unique vocalizations was analyzed spectrographically with a computer speech analysis program that examined the waveform of each sound in digital form. The output of the speech analysis program yielded 14 acoustic measures related in various ways to the frequency, duration, and intensity of the sounds. These acoustic parameters were then correlated with the results of the mothers' ratings.

The results indicated that mothers were indeed able to differentiate fusses and cries reliably and with substantial agreement between mothers. When each mother's visit two ratings of her own baby's vocalizations were compared with ratings of her baby's vocalizations by other mothers, the resulting correlation across all of the vocalizations was .85. However, there were some discrepancies between the ratings of individual mothers in home visits one and two. The most extreme example of this pattern of results was a mother whose visit one and two ratings of her own infant were negatively correlated, r = -.74, even though her visit two ratings of her own infant were correlated +.45 with ratings of her infant by the other mothers on visit two.

Differences between the results of visits one and two may be due to the use of nonverbal cues on visit one. Recall that on visit one, each mother was only asked to judge the vocalizations of her own infant, 1/2 hour after those vocalizations were produced. This procedure may have allowed the mother to recall the accompanying nonverbal behavior of her infant. On visit two, however, vocalizations of all infants were presented in random order three weeks after the initial recording, and judgments presumably could not be based only upon acoustic features of the sounds. The data suggest that judgments based on acoustic vs. nonacoustic information may in some cases differ. Mothers displayed somewhat more certainty in their ratings on visit one, when nonacoustic cues were available. They almost never used the "don't know" category, and the "definitely fuss" and "definitely cry" categories were by far the most often used. On visit two, with nonacoustic information removed, judgments were somewhat less certain. The "don't know" category was used 12% of the time, for example. Nevertheless, the agreement between mothers was high. For example, Figure 1 depicts each mother's mean rating of sounds produced by each infant. On the vertical axis, "5" represents "definitely cry" and "1" represents "definitely fuss". Notice that the rank order of the five infants' vocalizations was almost identical for each mother, resulting in five lines that intersect only rarely. An analysis of variance confirmed that the difference between infants was significant, $F(4,57) = 9.10$, $p < .001$.

The remaining analyses were carried out to determine the critical acoustic differences between fusses and cries. Out of 14 acoustic parameters, only 5 were significantly correlated with the visit two fuss/cry ratings: sound duration, mean intersity, peak intensity, mean second formant frequency, and the ratio of the average frequencies of Formant 1 to Formant 2. Further inspection of the data revealed that the most distinctly different acoustic parameters occurred with the upper quartile of the 62 vocalizations judged most cry-like along the fuss-cry continuum. These well-defined cries were substantially louder and longer than the other, more fuss-like vocalizations. Furthermore, the second formant was lower in frequency and the Formant 1 to Formant 2 ratio was higher for the cries. These formant values are related to the vowel quality of the infants' vocalizations. Fusses apparently are made with the tongue body extended as in the front vowel /I/, whereas cries are made with the tongue body retracted as in the back vowel /U/.

In conclusion, this study demonstrates that mothers can use acoustic information in a consistent manner in their judgment of infant distress vocalizations. These acoustic cues are not primarily idiosyncratic to each infant, but are such that mothers' ratings of infant vocalizations exhibit substantial agreement. Furthermore, we have determined some of the specific acoustic parameters distinguishing vocalizations labeled as "fusses" vs. "cries". However, judgments based solely upon acoustic information may differ somewhat from judgments based upon a richer source of information that includes nonverbal, contextual behaviors. The present results contribute to our understanding of the perceptual consequences of vocal modifications that occur as infants tell us of their dissatisfactions both large and small.

References

Emde, R. Emotional expression in infancy. In H. J. Schlesinger (Ed.), Psychological Issues (Vol. X, No. 1). New York: International University Press (1976).

Stark, R., Rose, S., & McLagen, M. Features of infant sounds: the first 4 weeks of life. Journal of Child Language, 1975, 2, 250-221.

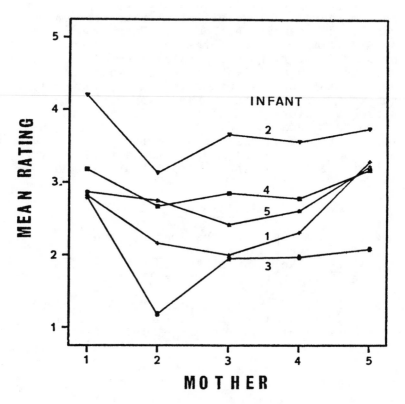

Figure 1. Mean visit two ratings of each
infant by each mother (5 = definitely
cry, 1 = definitely fuss).

Effects of Social Contexts on Vocalization and
Hand Gesture in Early Infancy. Adele Proctor, Sc.D.

Concurrent with child language research, there
has been an increased interest in defining infant
communicative systems, delineating components of
this system and attempts to determine whether infant
behavioral signals function as precursors, or at
least intercursors, to the speech and language acquisition process. Studies of prelinguistic communication have shown that infant behavioral signals
have considerable communicative value and are functions of the various channels of communication. That
is, vision, touch, audition, vocalization, facial
expression and body movement occur simultaneously
and with regularity to formulate the infant communicative package (Stern, 1977). Consequently, both
vocal and gestural (kinesic) behaviors modulate
portions of the interactive process with the caregiver and often regulate the infant's own behavior.

Child language researchers also found that different contexts affect preschoolers' communicative
competence and some see the child's early speech as
a means of socialization, having a direct relationship to the context in which socialization occurs,
and characterize the speech as conversational or
dialogic. Similarly, infant researchers found behavioral differences in babies, and their parents,
when subjects were placed in contrasting situations
in home and laboratory settings. Moreover, concepts
of adult conversation have been modified to treat
vocal turn-taking in the mother-infant dyad (Bateson, 1975; Bullowa, 1979) and the notion of early
communicative exchanges or reciprocity, based on
conversational or dialogic models, has become an
accepted phenomenon.

Although several investigators (Delack, 1978;
Lewis & Freedle, 1973; Nakazima, 1972) discussed
effects of different situations on infant vocal
behavior, few have explored the effects of social
contexts on two components of infant expressive
behavior. There is a need to explore the function
of more then one component of the infant communica-

29

tive systems, and situations in which they occur, since it is through the combined use of these constituents that infants adjust and regulate their own behavior and that of others. Further, it is during the prelinguistic period that infants appear to learn rules of interaction or prerequisites for later communicative competence (Bruner, 1975).

Others (Sugarman-Bell, 1978; von Raffler-Engel, 1981) suggest that further study of more than one component of infant behavioral packages, in different settings, may assist in clarifying the relationship between preverbal patterns and communication in the presence of language. Since vocalization and hand gestures are key features in communicative acts and share joint activity during communication, early observers of the language acquisition process (cf. Sully, 1896) reported the co-occurrence of speech and gesture during the first two years of life. de Laguna (1927) and others later discussed explicit relationships between the use of gesture and speech in the language learning child. Recently, a number of theoretical and empirical studies (Bates, 1976) of language acquisition emphasized verbal and nonverbal behaviors as well as contextual influences on these expressive behaviors.

At the prelinguistic stage, however, only a few directly investigated the relationship between hand movement patterns and vocal production. Fogel (1979), Lar (1976) and Trevarthen et al. (1974a, 1974b, 1975, 1977) studied normal infants in home and laboratory settings. Results of their research suggest: (1) certain movements appear to signal onset of vocalization; (2) stereotypical arm and hand movement patterns are closely synchronized with vocalization; (3) both behaviors are differentially used in response to people vs. objects and; (4) there is a regular reoccurrence of patterned behaviors that are used gesturally and signal readiness to communicate.

From a developmental perspective, then, infant communicative patterns contribute to establishing routines of social interaction. These elaborate and

30

repetitive routines between infant and caregiver serve as a basic framework upon which later speech and language are developed. Infant communicative signals occur in a behavioral package and include the various channels of communication. Vocalization and hand gesture are two components of this package and may be adapted for communicative use very early in life. Although the presence of some relationship between vocalization and gesture is frequently inferred, there is limited data that directly relates these patterns of activity during the early sensorimotor stages. Therefore, the purpose of this exploratory investigation was to determine if selected types of vocalization and hand gesture were influenced by four different social situations during the first six months of life.

Definitions: Since infants differ from adults in a variety of ways, terms used to describe adult communicative interaction must be defined when applied to infant functioning. Infant communication and infant communicative acts are typically described as they relate to infant and maternal behaviors and are differentiated from the terms as they are employed when speaker and hearer use language. Because the infant does not have the means to express sign and/or symbolic representations, behavioral expressions produced by the infant are considered signals. Almost any signal produced by the infant may be viewed as communicative by the mother. Infant communicative acts involve any interactive behaviors to which the mother is likely to respond and maternal acts are any interactive behaviors to which the infant is likely to respond (Bakeman & Brown, 1977). Both vocal and gestural behaviors co-occur during infant communication and are interpreted by caregivers as cues to initiate interaction.

Crystal's (1975) definition of vocalization served as a guiding principle for intitial identification of infant sounds and types of vocalization were further defined through modification and recombination of systems proposed by Stark et al. (1974), Strain (1975) and Young & DeCarie (1977). Table 1 illustrates definitions for nondistress vocalizations described as comfort and neutral.

Gesture was defined as movement patterns of upper limbs and, specifically, movements of arms, hands and fingers. Through pilot work (Proctor, 1979), it was determined that features common to hand movements, despite age, were proximity/area, intensity/rate and direction/vector. A gestural system, developed for this study, classified hand gestures based on these shared features. Type of gesture was classified as slight, moderate or exaggerated. The circled areas in Illustrations 1, 2 and 3 show the range of motion for each type of hand gesture.

Social contexts were defined in broad, interactive terms, i.e., who or what the infant played with during observations. Specific social contexts were defined in relation to infant and maternal behaviors and included: (1) infant alone; (2) infant with mother only; (3) infant with object only and; (4) infant with mother and object. Table 2 is representative of specific definitions for social contexts.

METHOD
Subjects: Two first born singletons, one male and one female, reared in monolingual English speaking environments were video taped on a weekly basis from 2 weeks to 24 weeks of age. Controls were instituted to monitor postnatal development and additional data were collected on subjects' overall development. Mothers were primary caregivers for the subjects.

PROCEDURE
Recording of each session was initiated in the home when subjects were in alert, awake states, as judged by the mother. Attempts were made to begin observations with infants in a semi-upright, supported position. Mothers were given instructions concerning the desired situations, but were not told how to achieve these conditions. Sessions were terminated when mothers indicated that infants were experiencing fatigue.

32

Table 1. Definition of Two Types of Infant Vocalization

Sound Type	Facial Expression	Gaze Behavior	Mother or Adult's Comments
Comfort (CFS)	--Happy face	--Usually directed toward adult, toy or part of self (e.g. feet)	"Good Girl!"
Auditory Characteristics	--Smiling face		"Good Boy!"
--vowel-like sound of low to moderate intensity	--Shy smile	--Intermittent looking away from primary point of focus, but intent on interaction and exploration.	"You're Mommy's little cuddle bunny."
-- lax, voiced vocalization	--Semi-smile face		"You're pretty, yea! You are. You're a pretty girl."
	--Attentive face		"You're handsome."
--consonant - vowel- like sounds	--Shy face	--Eyes may be periodi- cally directed downward, sideways or both.	"You're funny."
--vowel - consonant- like sounds			"You're silly."
--usually smooth onset consonant-like sound			
Neutral (NV)	--Detached face	--Usually not directed although baby may or may not be alone	Usually does not respond verbally to this vocalization.
Auditory Characteristics	--Passive face		
--grunts (may be short, soft grunts or medium- pitched grunt of louder intensity)	--Stare face		
	--No real interest expressed facially in object and/or person		
--vowel-like sounds			
--little short sounds			
--usually produced on fairly short expiration			
--Panting (and heavy breathing)			

33

ILLUSTRATION 1

SLIGHT HAND GESTURES

ILLUSTRATION 2

MODERATE HAND GESTURES

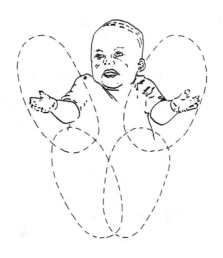

ILLUSTRATION 3

EXAGGERATED HAND GESTURES

34

Table 2. Type of Social Context: Mother-Infant Interaction

Setting

Can be any room in the home

Infant Behaviors

State: May be alert, awake, inactive/active sleepy, drowsy.

Posture: May be prone, supine, semi-upright, sitting.

Facial Expression: May vary from mostly bright, positive, play face to attentive or perplexed face to pout, sad or tremble face.

Visual Attention: Direct looks at person; mutual regard, major focus of attention on other person within reach.

Proximity: Within a few inches of other person; often in face-to-face interaction.

Vocalization: May or may not produce sounds.

Tactile/Vestibular: Hands may swipe across clothes or objects in close proximity; passive physical contact of hands in relation to nearby objects, clothes or toys.

Maternal Behaviors

Facial Expression: Smiling, laughing; making faces, actively trying to get infant's attention; may be frowning when trying to soothe infant.

Visual Attention: Major focus of attention on baby; mutual regard; directed looks at infant.

Proximity: Within reach of infant; may be within 10 feet.

Verbalization: Attempts to elicit vocalization; actively encouraging motor skills, e.g., sit up; sustained imitation in response to baby's vocalizations; encourages smiling; sings to baby; uses non-speech sounds to baby, e.g., whistling, tsk-tsk, goo-goo; vocalizes to soothe infant following distress sounds from infant; encourages baby to look; frequent use of baby talk.

Tactile/Vestibular: Actively touches and manipulates baby; holds hands, tries pat-a-cake type games; moves parts of baby, e.g., picking up, righting baby when leaning; rocking or jiggling baby, holding to soothe baby; active physical contact.

35

Results of pilot data had shown that control for: (1) duration and change of social context; (2) time of day and day of week of observation; (3) length of exposure time to inanimate objects; (4) amount and degree of interaction with mother and; (5) order of presentation of stimuli should be mother-infant determined. Therefore, duration, rate of change and sequential order of contexts, type of stimuli and mother-infant interaction were determined by mothers' impressions and interpretations of infants' actions.

Data Analysis: Both fixed and real time were used to analyze the continuously recorded video taped data. Five second intervals were used as a means of obtaining small units of time in which to score the complex and rapidly changing behaviors. When 5 second intervals were used to establish inter-observer agreement each interval was considered a discrete category. Reliability measures and subsequent analysis of presence or absence of vocalization, presence or absence of hand gesture and type of social contexts involved the use of 5 second intervals. Types of vocalization and hand gesture were determined in real time based on explicit recognition rules defined in terms of onset and offset of action.

After original data were coded with 5 second intervals, six different pairs of adult judges independently scored five behavioral categories. Table 3 presents inter-observer reliabilities for each of the five behavioral categories.

Table 3. Inter-Observer Reliabilities

Behavioral Categories	Mean Percent Agreement (%)	
	Subject A	Subject B
Presence/Abs. Voc.	93.4	92.4
Presence/Abs. Hnd. Ges.	97.6	90.3
Type Soc. Context	89.2	86.3
Type Vocalization	82.4	81.6
Type Hand Gesture (at onset of Vocalization)	83.3	80.5

Frequency distributions and rates of occurrence were determined for vocalized and silent intervals in different contexts, effects of age and contexts on vocal-gestural behavior and the relationship between selected types of vocal (comfort & neutral) and gestural (slight, moderate & exaggerated) behaviors in different contexts. Frequency data were converted to proportional data to adjust for the variable time base of observations and to compare subjects.

RESULTS

Over the six month period, Subject A was recorded for a total of 18 sessions yielding 5,183 five second intervals. Subject A, the male, vocalized in 1,326 intervals and was silent in 3,856. Subject B, the female, was observed for a total of 23 sessions resulting in 7,085 intervals. Subject B vocalized in 2,087 intervals and was silent in 4,998. Of these numbers, 4,875 and 6,914 intervals were analyzed for Subjects A and B, respectively.

Frequency distributions, supported by proportional data, demonstrated a relationship between the presence of vocalization and the presence of hand gestures. For Subject A, 99% of all vocalized intervals were accompanied by hand gestures and for Subject B, 100% of all vocal intervals were accompanied by gesture. During the first six months of life, both subjects produced hand gestures at a higher rate when they vocalized than when they were silent.

Both subjects consistently exhibited a higher rate of vocalization in interaction with mother only than in any other context. Both spent more time with mothers and proportionately vocalized at the same rate when with their mothers. Since gestures consistently accompanied vocalization, hand gestures were produced at a higher rate when in interaction with mother only. The male vocalized the least in the mother and object context and the female vocalized the least when alone. When infants were in some type of interaction with objects a higher rate of silence-no gesture was found for the six month mean.

Despite age or type of social context, neutral sounds and slight gestures emerged earlier than comfort sounds, **moderate and exaggerated gestures·** Over time, however, the vocal gestural pattern of comfort-exaggerated gesture exhibited a higher rate of occurrence than any other vocal-gestural pair. The highest rate of comfort-exaggerated gesture was found for both subjects in interaction with mother and object. Table 4 shows rates of vocalized and silent intervals with and without hand gestures as classified by social context.

Table 4. Rate of Vocalized & Silent Intervals With and Without Gesture by Social Context (%)

	Subject A				Subject B			
	Social Contexts[a]							
	I	II	III	IV	I	II	III	IV
Vocal Interval W/ Ges. $\bar{X}$ per 6 months	11	20	12	7	7	22	11	11
Silent Int. W/ Ges. $\bar{X}$ per 6 months	9	17	13	10	16	34	27	24
Vocal Int. W/out Ges. $\bar{X}$ per 6 months	0	0	.004	0	0	0	0	0
Silent Int. W/out Ges. $\bar{X}$ per 6 months	34	17	39	8	39	13	43	3
Vocal Int. W/ Ges. $\bar{X}$ Interval/Context	22	41	24	14	13	44	22	21
Silent Int. W/ Ges. $\bar{X}$ Interval/Context	19	33	27	21	16	34	27	24

[a]I: S alone; II: Mother only; III: Object only; IV: Mother & object

DISCUSSION
     In this study, infants in the first six months of life were found to vocalize and produce hand gestures at a higher rate during interaction with

mother only than during three other social contexts. These data are contrary to at least two other reports in the literature which specifically studied acoustic features of infant vocalization. Delack (1978) and Nakazima (1972) found a higher rate of occurrence of vocalization in their subjects when infants were alone. Several procedural and methodological variables may account for differences found in this study and other results.

Both Delack and Nakazima observed vocalization for a longer period than the first six months. In the second half of the first year of life, infants are more vocally active. After the first six months, mothers feel more comfortable leaving their infants alone. The definitions of alone and mother-infant interaction vary and become a primary factor influencing results of each study. Here, 5 second intervals were used for analysis, while Delack and Nakazima counted breath units. There was also variability in the weighting of silence in each of the studies. Since other cross sectional studies of infant vocal activity (e.g., Jones & Moss, 1971) reported higher rates of vocalization during maternal absence, what mother does when present may be a deciding factor influencing rate of vocalization. The two subjects in this study spent more time in face-to-face communication with mothers.

These data suggest that vocalization and hand gesture co-vary in different interactive situations. The nature of the co-variance can best be documented at this time in terms of presence or absence of vocal and gestural activity. This is consistent with previous research (Brazelton et al., 1974; Crystal, 1973a, 1973b, Trevarthen, 1977) which discussed infants' differential interaction with people and objects. Despite discrepancies about vocalization rates, what stands out is that the mother-infant dyad and the alone situations require further study and more specifically defined parameters for social contexts. At later ages, i.e., after 4 months, the mother and object context becomes another important condition for further investigation.

In searching for a relationship between selected
types on noncry and hand gestures, no systematic
relationship was found when data were analyzed in
the manner used in this study. Additional observations of these infants' vocal-gestural combinations,
however, revealed occurrences of vocal-gestural
clustering requiring further study. For example,
mother's approach elicited a different type of vocal
and gestural combination than those observed in en
face communication. The mothers' approach was often
greeted with exaggerated waving of arms and hands
and were usually accompanied by long, loud comfort
sounds. Yet, during protoconversations, soft comfort
or neutral sounds of short duration were accompanied
by slight gestures. These behaviors were first observed around 8 weeks and continued in each of the
subjects thereafter. This suggested that initial
differentiation of hand gestures may first be found
during interaction with mother. Objects tended to
elicit cessation of vocal-gestural activity and increased visual scanning.

Further inspection of subjects' video tapes
showed: (1) vocal and gestural combinations were
clustered differently dependent on type of interaction with mother, e.g., approach vs. en face; (2)
simultaneous clustering of certain vocal-gestural
combinations at onset of vocalization; (3) clustering of certain types of hand gestures preceding
vocal onset; (4) clustering of certain types of
hand gestures following termination of vocalization;
(5) clustering of certain vocal-gestural combinations
in time with one another and; (6) clustering of
certain vocal-gestural combinations used in people
vs. object interaction. These observations are consonant with previous research on infants in this
age range and would require a microanalytic procedure if additional studies are carried out.

In summary, the present study suggests that
social contexts affect the nature of vocal and gestural interaction during the first six months of
life. While certain contexts, e.g., en face interaction with mother, appear to be facilitators of
communication, others, such as object interaction,

reduce or suppress vocal and gestural behavior during the first six months of life. The frequency with which vocalization and hand gestures co-occur when in interaction with mothers lends support to the notion that infant signals, feeding into routines of social interaction, assist in laying the groundwork for later communicative competence when the child uses language. Finally, hand gestures and vocalization are viable units of study in deciphering the developing communicative process.

REFERENCES

Bakeman, R. & Brown, J.V. Behavioral dialogues. Child Dev., 1977, 48, 195-203.
Bates, E. Lang. & context. N.Y.: Acad. Press, 1976.
Bateson, M.C. Mother-infant exchanges. Ann. N.Y. Acad. Sci., 1975, 263, 101-113.
Brazelton, T.B. et al. The origins of reciprocity. In M. Lewis & L. Rosenblum (Eds.), The effect of the infant on its caregiver. N.Y.: Wiley, 1974.
Bruner, J. The ontogenesis of speech acts. J. Chld. Lang., 1975, 2, 1-20.
Bullowa, M. (Ed.), Before speech. Cambridge: Cambridge University Press, 1979.
Crystal, D. Non-segmental phonology in language acquisition. Lingua, 1973a, 32, 1-45.
Crystal, D. Linguistic mythology and the first year of life. Brit. J. Com. Dis., 1973b, 8, 29-36.
Crystal, D. The English tone of voice. London: Edward Arnold, 1975.
Delack, J.B. Aspects of infant speech dev. in the first year of life. In L. Bloom (Ed.), Readings in language develop. N.Y.: Wiley, 1978.
de Laguna, G.A. Speech: Its function and development. New Haven: Yale University Press, 1927.
Fogel, A. Peer vs. mother directed behav. in 1- to 3 mo. old infants. Infant Behav. & Dev., 1979, 2, 215-226.
Jones, S.J. & Moss, H.A. Age, state & maternal behav. associated with inf. vocalizations. Chld. Dev., 1971, 42, 1039-1051.

Lar, R. Movement behavior & preverbalization of
    five infants. In W. von Raffler-Engel & Y.
    Lebrun (Eds.), Baby talk and infant speech.
    Amsterdam: Swets & Zeitlinger, 1976.
Lewis, M.M. & Freedle, R. Mother-infant dyad. In
    P. Pliner et al. (Eds.), Communication & affect.
    N.Y.: Academic Press, 1973.
Nakazima, S. A comparative study of speech develop.
    Studia Phonologica, 1972, VI, 1-37.
Proctor, F.A. Vocalizations and hand gestures in
    early infancy. Unpublished doctoral dissertation.
    Johns Hopkins University, 1979.
Stark, R.E. et al. Classification of infant vocali-
    zation behavior. Paper presented at Amer. Sp. &
    Hearing Asso., Las Vegas, 1974.
Stern, D. The first relationship. Cambridge, Ma.:
    Harvard University Press, 1977.
Strain, B.A. Early dialogues. Unpublished doctoral
    dissertation. George Peabody College, 1975.
Sugarman-Bell, S. Some organizational aspects of
    preverbal communication. In I. Markova (Ed.),
    The social context of lang. N.Y.: Wiley, 1978.
Sully, T. Studies of childhood. N.Y.: Appleton, 1896.
Trevarthen, C. The psychobiology of speech develop.
    In E.H. Lenneberg (Ed.), Language & Brain, 1974a,
    12, 570-585.
Trevarthen, C. Conversations with a 2 mo. old. New
    Scientist, 1974b, 2, 230-233.
Trevarthen, C. Early attempts at speech. In R. Lewin
    (Ed.), Child alive.London: Temple Smith, 1975.
Trevarthen, C. Descriptive analysis of infant
    communicative behavior. In H. R. Schaffer (Ed.),
    Studies in mother-infant interaction. N.Y.:
    Academic Press, 1977.
von Raffler-Engel, W. Developmental kinesics.
    Infant Mental Health, 1981, 2, 84-94.
Young, G. & DeCarie, T.G. An ethology based cata-
    logue of facial/vocal behavior in infancy.
    Animal Behavior, 1977, 25, 95-107.

Dominant Consonants in Non-Language Vocalization as Preparation for the First Words of Language

David Woods
Howard University

Ida Stockman
Howard University
Center for Applied
Linguistics

At the end of the first year of life, the child is expected to have developed a minimum capacity for speech. While it is generally assumed that a relationship exists between speech development and infants' nonlanguage vocalizations prior to and following the earliest words, much remains to be learned about this initial capacity for speech. This study is among those that have focused on the segmental aspect of this initial capacity in relation to early speech. It assumes that the segmental content of nonlanguage vocalizations develops in a systematic way and is preparatory to the onset of language. Specifically, the <u>purpose</u> of the study was to determine if those consonant-like segments,[1] which are <u>dominant</u> in prelanguage vocalization, are more likely to be used in the first words of language. The term <u>dominance</u> is used here to refer to habitual and routinized articulatory patterns of early vocal output as measured by their frequency of occurrence. Based on frequency criteria, a developmental model of dominant nonlanguage consonants at monthly intervals was proposed and then compared to the sounds used in the earliest words of language as reported by several authors (Ferguson and Farwell, 1975; Shibamoto and Olmsted, 1978; Leonard, et al, 1980). Thus the study extends previous work that has examined the relationship between nonlanguage and language segments (cf. Crutten-den, 1970; Oller et al.,1976; Boysson-Bardies et al., 1981).

Deriving the Developmental Model
of Dominant Non-Language Segments

Description of Data

The nonlanguage data consisted of three linguists' transcriptions of one female child's segments in 600 vocalizations, evenly distributed at the ages of 7 to 12, 15, 16, 20, and 21 months. For child FS, the total number of segment tokens transcribed by the three linguists was 10,450, which consisted of 5,504 vowels and 4,946 consonants.

For the data analysis of this study, only the consonant segments were considered. The 4,946 consonant tokens were distributed across the linguists as follows: Judge 1, 1,556; Judge 2, 2,014; and Judge 3, 1,376. The segmental data from FS constitute a subset of a larger data base that includes three other children: child SW (months 9 to 11), child NH (months 11 to 14), and child CA (months 14 and 15). Refer to Stockman, Woods, and Tishman (1981) for the details of the methods for data collection.

Method for Deriving Consonant Dominance

  Frequency Criteria for Establishing Consonant Dominance. The transcribed segments attributed to FS' vocalizations by the three judges presumably represented a sampling of her developing articulatory capability. The number of different consonant types noted by the judges ranged from a low of eight (Judge 1, month 7) to a high of 24 (Judge 2, month 16) and averaged, in each of the 10 months, 17 for Judge 1, 20 for Judge 2, and 14 for Judge 3. In order to reveal the dominant articulations of each month, the consonants were first rank-ordered separately for each judge according to their raw frequencies of transcription. The raw frequencies were than added, starting with the most frequently transcribed consonant and continuing until the cumulative total reached 75% of the total number of all consonant tokens transcribed. Those consonants in the top 75% for at least two judges[2] constituted the dominant consonants of a given month. A subset of the dominant consonants, meeting a more stringent 50% criterion, was also found for each month. The consonants meeting the 75% and the 50% criteria were then arranged hierarchically to model FS' developing articulatory skill from months 7 to 12 and additionally in months 15, 16, 20, and 21.

  Construction of the Dominance Hierarchy. Figure 1 displays the dominant consonants for each month of the data collected on FS. For month 7, it shows just two dominant consonants, [ʔ] and [h] . This means that their combined frequencies made up more than 75% of all consonant tokens transcribed in that month for at least two of three judges. The frequencies of the remaining 15 consonant types [l w p b d k g m n r j z ɸ β ɣ], transcribed in the same month, were very low by comparison.

The horizontal rows of the figure can be scanned further for the consonants that met the dominance criteria in each subsequent month of sampled data. By applying a dominance criterion, an average of 61% of the transcribed consonants was eliminated in any given month.

A branching hierarchical model was chosen to display the dominant consonants because it can be used to represent a developmental pattern which "unfolds" from general to specific categories. The branching at a given age represents the development of new articulatory possibilities within a previously established phonetic class. For example, the obstruent class, represented by glottal [ʔ] at month 7, is differentiated into glottal and lingual obstruents in month 8, represented by the still dominant glottal [ʔ] and the newly dominant lingual [d t g ɣ] . Thus the branching represents the empirically observed increasing range of dominant articulatory types. Consonants were positioned in the hierarchy according to their shared phonetic content. New branches, labeled with the name of a phonetic feature, were established when a consonant met the most stringent 50% criterion for the first time (cf. [j] and [d] at 9 and 10 months, respectively). Such consonants were continued on a separate branch in subsequent months on the assumption that previously dominant articulations continued their dominance in subsequent months. In general, this assumption was justified, but empty brackets indicate observed exceptions. The remaining one or more consonants, not accorded a separate branch by the 50% criterion, were bracketed together according to their phonetic content. In some cases, several consonants are bracketed (cf. lingual [d t g ɣ] in month 8); in other cases, they became singletons (cf. labial [b] in month 11, which, being non-lingual and non-glottal, had to be placed under a new branch). To distinguish between such singletons and those meeting the 50% criterion, the latter are starred (*). The resulting structure can be viewed as a hypothesis about the developing well-practiced consonant articulations in nonlanguage vocalization.

Results of the Study of Consonant Dominance

Figure 1 reveals that the number of consonants that met the dominance criteria ranged from as few as two in month 7 to as many as 10 in months 15 and 21. The hierarchy suggests

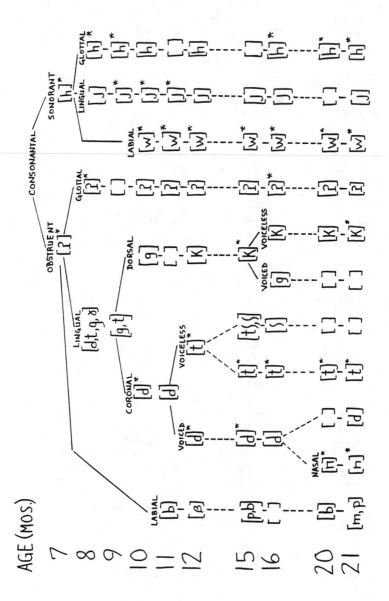

Figure 1: Dominance Hierarchy: Nonlanguage Consonants (Child FS)

46

a systematic expansion of the repertoire of well-practiced consonants between months 7 and 12 and to a lesser extent in post-language samples in months 15, 16, 20, and 21 of FS. The expansion appears to be parallel in obstruents and sonorants.[3] In our data, the earliest dominant consonants are glottal ([ʔ h]). Certain lingual consonants become dominant in month 8 ([d t g j ɣ]), but none achieves the top 50% subset until months 9 ([j]) and 10 ([d]). The expansion proceeds anteriorly to include labials [w] and [b] in months 10 and 11 respectively. Voicing is first used to distinguish the coronal obstruents [t] and [d] when both are found in the top 50% subset in month 12. Thus by the end of the first year, 11 consonants are included in the dominance hierarchy, eight of them remaining dominant in month 12 itself. The dominant consonants have developed from glottis to lips in comparable patterns of expansion among obstruents and sonorants. Of the eight obstruents noted, six are stops. One voicing distinction is noted among stops.

The data of the two later periods (months 15-16 and 20-21) add to the dominant consonants, two sibilants [tʃ ʃ], two nasals [m n] , and the voiceless labial stop [p] .

Dominant Consonants and the First Words

The question asked in this section of the investigation was whether FS' frequently practiced or dominant consonant articulations in nonlanguage vocalization were likely to be used in the earliest words of language.

Source of Language Data

Since no record of FS' earliest words was kept, the language data of other children were utilized. Specifically, the data consisted of consonants used in the earliest words of seven children whose phonological development has been previously described in the context of phone tree analysis by several writers (Ferguson and Farwell, 1975; Shibamoto and Olmsted, 1978; Leonard et al.,1980). Table 1 summarizes the ages of the children at the beginnings of the studies and the time span in which approximately the first 50 words were observed.

47

Table 1. Subjects' Ages and Time-Spans of Studies.

Child	Age	Time Span	Study
T	0;11	13 weeks	Shibamoto and Olmsted Ferguson and Farwell
K	1;2	13 weeks	Shibamoto and Olmsted Ferguson and Farwell
H	1;0	6 months	Shibamoto and Olmsted Ferguson and Farwell
S11	1;7	4 months	Leonard et al.
S12	1;7	4 months	Leonard et al.
S13	1;9	7 weeks	Leonard et al
F	1;2	8 months	Shibamoto and Olmsted

The modeling of these children's early phonological development in terms of phone tree representation of consonant segments deemphasizes "...the separation of phonetic and phonemic development..." (Ferguson and Farwell, 1975, p. 437) by using words as the primary units of analysis. Broad classes or sets of consonant segments are formed in relation to their use in word pronunciation. This approach represents a major methodological breakthrough in the study of early phonemic development in that it does not rely on distributional criteria, used to derive phonemic segment contrasts, but difficult to apply to early child language data.

Method for the Comparison of Nonlanguage to Language Data

All consonant types recorded in the phone trees of the earliest words of the seven children were arranged in three subsets of consonants that reflected different frequencies in FS' nonlanguage data: (1) the 16 dominant consonants which constituted the top 75% of all consonants transcribed in any given month. Refer to the dominance hierarchy in Figure 1; (2) an additional nine sporadic consonants, transcribed at least twice by two judges in one or more months of the nonlanguage vocalization data; and (3) nine rare consonants, which did not even meet the criterion for sporadic consonants or, for the most part, never occurred at all, but were noted in the

language data. Thus, only the dominant and sporadic consonants of the nonlanguage vocalization data could be said
to form a pool of articulatory possibilities for the observed
child FS; some of the consonants in the pool were articulated
frequently and presumably became well practiced and automatic,
hence dominant, while others were noted often enough by more
than one judge to support our confidence that they were
really produced by FS and were not a momentary aberration of
a judge's perception as may have been the case with some of
the rare consonants.

Results of the Comparison of Nonlanguage to Language Data

Figure 2 shows the distribution of consonants that
were observed in the nonlanguage and language data. The
columns, labeled by the name code used in the original
study, identify the consonants observed in the earliest
words of each of the seven children. The rows represent the
34 consonants observed in the nonlanguage and/or language
data. The parenthesized number next to the dominant and
sporadic consonants indicates the month in which that consonant first met the minimal criterion for sporadic consonants (i.e. observed at least twice by two judges in the
same month) in FS' nonlanguage data. The asterisks identify
those consonants that were articulated with sufficient
frequency in FS' nonlanguage vocalizations to meet the dominance criteria before 12 months. A plus sign (+) in a cell
at the intersection of a child's column and a consonant's
row indicates the presence of a given consonant in one of
the child's first words.

The density of the plus signs suggests a correlation
between the relative frequency of consonants in FS' nonlanguage vocalization and their occurrence in the first words
of language. The children's earliest words were more likely
to include consonants found among FS' dominant nonlanguage
vocalizations than those found among the sporadic or rare
vocalizations. Each child used an average of 75% of the
dominant consonants, 41% of the sporadic consonants, and
22% of the rare consonants.

Inasmuch as the sizes of the children's consonant
inventories varied, (they ranged from a low of 11 for S13
to a high of 27 for T), few nonlanguage consonants were
observed in the earliest words of all seven children. In

49

CONSONANTS USED IN
FIRST 50 WORDS BY

		T[1,3]	K[1,3]	H[1,3]	SI1[2]	SI2[2]	SI3[2]	F[3]
p	(11)	+	+	+	+	+	+	+
*b	(8)	+	+	+	+	+	+	+
*t	(8)	+	+	+	+	+	+	+
*d	(7)	+	+	+	+	+	+	+
*k	(8)	+	+		+	+		+
*g	(7)	+	+	+	+	+		+
*ʒ	(7)	+	+	+				+
β	(8)	+	+		+			
ʃ	(11)	+	+	+	+	+		+
*ʒ̆	(7)							
*h	(7)	+	+	+	+	+	+	+
tʃ	(11)	+				+		
*w	(7)	+		+	+	+	+	+
*j	(7)	+		+	+			+
m	(8)	+	+	+	+	+	+	+
n	(11)	+	+	+		+	+	+
f	(21)	+	+			+	+	
s	(15)	+	+		+	+		+
ʒ	(15)	+	+					
dʒ	(11)	+				+		+
l	(7)	+	+	+				
x	(9)	+			+	+		
λ	(8)	+						
φ	(21)	+						+
r	(20)							
z			+			+	+	+
ŋ			+	+				
v							+	
θ								+
ɤ		+						+
c		+						
ʕ		+						
ʄ		+						
w̥								+

DOMINANT (IN HIERARCHY) FIGURE 1

SPORADIC

RARE OR NON-OCCURRING

Figure 2: Comparison of Nonlanguage and Language
Consonant Types.

[1] Ferguson and Farwell (1975. [2] Leonard et al. (1980).
[3] Shibamoto and Olmsted (1978).

fact, only six consonants ([p b t d h m]) appeared
in the language data of all seven children. Note that
each of these six consonants was among FS' dominant nonlanguage consonants before 12 months of age.

More detailed observation of segment classes reveals
that the seven stops [p b t d k g ʔ], all of which were
included among FS' dominant nonlanguage consonants, were
found in the earliest words of at least half the children.
In comparison to [p b t d] , however, [g] and especially [k] and [ʔ] were observed less often in the language data.

Among nasals, the dominant nonlanguage consonants,
[m n] , occurred in the early words of all children
with one exception (S11). The [ŋ] , on the other hand, was
rare in the nonlanguage data and used by just two children
in their early words.

Among the liquids and glides, the early dominant
[h w j] nonlanguage consonants were observed in the
early words of a larger number of children (seven, six and
four, respectively) than were the sporadically occurring
[l] (3 children) and the non-English [ʎ] (1 child); the
remaining English liquid [r] was not noted in the first
words of any child and it even appeared late (20 months) in
FS' nonlanguage data. Because of its relative openness of
articulation, [h] was interpreted in this study as
a sonorant or glide, especially since it often seemed
to be an unvoiced onglide or offglide to an adjacent vowel
in the nonlanguage data.

Fricatives[4] in general were less frequent in the nonlanguage data and in the language data compared to stops.
Of the four that appeared among FS' dominant nonlanguage
consonants [β ʃ ɣ tʃ], [ʃ] was the most frequently observed segment in early language data whereas [ɣ], a
non-English allophone, was never observed in the language
data and even disappeared from the dominance hierarchy altogether after its one appearance in month eight. Though its
voiceless counterpart, [x] , was never dominant in the nonlanguage data, it was noted in three children's words.

Of the remaining fricatives, all of which were either
sporadic or rare nonlanguage consonants ([f s z v] dʒ

51

ɸ ɵ ð꜡), only [f s z] were observed in the language data of more than two children.

Discussion

Continuity between Nonlanguage and Language Data

The picture that emerges from this study, which traces nonlanguage consonantal vocalizations from well before the onset of language (month 7) to after the onset of language (month 21), is one in which a relatively small number of consonantal types stand out each month as high frequency or dominant types. The number of dominant consonants increases over time in a systematic way, starting with a predominance of glottal articulations and expanding to include first lingual and then labial consonants. This expansion develops in parallel among sonorants (e.g., from [h] to [j] to [w]) and obstruents (e.g., from [ʔ] to [d] to [b]). Distinctions are also seen in voicing and in manner of articulation. The differentiation is such that, by about 12 months, the child has ample phonetic resources to support his first words. But just as leg movements continue to differentiate after the onset of walking, so too does the pool of phonetic resources continue to expand, adding to the range of confidently articulated consonantal types.

The fact of an expanding consonantal repertoire as well as a general back to front direction of expansion have also been reported by others (e.g., Irwin, 1947 and Cruttenden, 1970). There is even a rough concurrence between our nonlanguage vocalization data from months 15, 16, 20, and 21 and the data on the late babbling of a 16-18 month French boy (Boysson-Bardies, 1981). Thus, the use of the notion of dominance to characterize a developing pattern of consonantal articulations has not yielded substantially different results from previous research. However, in focusing on the most frequently articulated sounds, the dominance principle may provide an explanatory basis for which consonants are likely to be used in the first words of language.

With respect to motor behavior in general, it has long been recognized that skilled movement patterns are more likely to become routinized and automatic when they are constantly repeated and practiced. Our data, like those of previous studies, revealed a restricted range of babbled sounds. But, the use of a segment dominance principle suggests that even within this restricted range of babbled sounds, not all segments may be equally relevant to subsequent use in speech. It was assumed that the most frequently articulated consonantal types were becoming routinized and automatic in the pre-language repertoire of articulations and, therefore, most likely used by children in their first words. This expectation was borne out by our finding of a close correspondence between the dominant or frequently occurring consonants of nonlanguage vocalization and those used in the earliest words of language. This finding adds to the growing evidence which favors the hypothesis that there is continuity between nonlanguage and language behavior. (Cf. Cruttenden, 1970; Oller et al., 1976; Boysson-Bardies et al.,1981; Olney and Scholnick, 1976). Except for Cruttenden (1970), however, previous studies have not focused on the relationship between language and nonlanguage behavior with respect to the inventory of specific segments. The present study extends Cruttenden's work by applying a quantitative dominance principle to yield a more precise descriptive and explanatory analysis of this relationship.

One could argue on the basis of our findings and those of Cruttenden's, that the child brings to the task of learning the speech code, a particular store of well practiced phonetic routines. Intuitively, such prior learning would ease the pronunciation task. Still, whether such a pre-language store of phonetic content should be conceptualized strictly in terms of specific segments, classes of segment features or both is not entirely clear. In this paper, the use of particular dominant segments as exemplars of segment or feature classes is an interesting notion since it presumably would allow specific comparison of the order of emerging phonetic content across languages that have differing segment types. To the extent that the emerging sequence of nonlanguage segment features or classes can be accounted for by corresponding changes in physiological and anatomical features, universal tendencies might be hypothesized. For example, the frequent observation that fricatives occur much less often than do stops in nonlanguage data suggests that the same kind of segment preferences are shown in nonlanguage as in language data. This point has been amply supported by findings of Oller et al. (1976). Stops and fricatives may differ in perceptual saliency and such differences may relate to developing myelination in the central nervous system.

Discontinuity between Nonlanguage and Language Data

While there is substantial support for viewing early language in relation to nonlanguage vocal output and thus to argue for the continuity hypothesis, there is evidence for discontinuity as well. This point has been made by Oller (1977) and is supported by data of this study. For example, we observed that one dominant nonlanguage consonant ([ɣ]) was not used by any of the seven children in their first words. Conversely, the nine rare consonants of Table 2 were, generally, not found in nonlanguage data, but were noted in the words of at least one child. Among these, the consonant [z] , used by four children, did not even meet the pool criterion in the nonlanguage data.

Several possible explanations for discontinuity may be put forth. On the one hand, when data from different studies are compared in which different transcribers have been used, the discontinuity may be an artifact of the methodology (see the discussion of transcriber bias in Stockman et al.,1981). On the other hand, when data from different children are compared across language and nonlanguage data, the lack of continuity may be due to differences in the individuals themselves. Such differences could arise from the use of varying strategies for processing and producing vocal output and/or from the differences in the structure of speech input that the child is exposed to in his environment. (Cf. discussion of individual variation in Cruttenden, 1970 and Ferguson and Farwell, 1975.)

Future Research

Obviously, many issues must be empirically addressed before the nature of early vocal behavior and its relationship to spoken language is understood. Insight is likely to be facilitated by studies that provide for comparative segment analysis of nonlanguage and language data on the same child. This would, furthermore, control for one dimension of discontinuity, noted above. Given the variability that has been observed among young children, more than one child should be studied in order that findings do not reflect just idiosyncratic tendencies. Using such strategies, the present research can be expanded in at least three ways: (1) the dominance principle could be applied to the study of vowel relationships in nonlanguage and language data; (2) a comparative acoustic analysis of the features of non-language and language segments transcribed with identical phonetic symbols could be conducted; (3) parallel studies on data collected from children raised in different linguistic environments could be conducted to test the possible universality of the developmental pattern displayed in the dominance hierarchy, in which certain phonetic features emerge before others.

[1] The term "consonant-like" reflects our view that non-language and language segments are probably not isomorphic. However, for simplicity of reference, we use the term consonant instead of consonant-like when referring to such segments in the nonlanguage data.

[2] Given the differences among judges in the total number and types of segments transcribed as in the description of the data, it was not surprising that the rank orderings of the judges were never identical for any given month. The methodological problem of listener agreement has been discussed in Stockman, Woods, and Tishman (1981). The study revealed substantial disagreement among the judges on the precise segments to be attributed to a given vocalization of the child. For this study, we observed, however, that despite disagreements on the precise segments attributed to a given vocalization of the child, the judges' distributions of transcribed segments in terms of relative frequencies of occurrence were often strikingly similar. For example, [ʔ] and [h] of FS month 7, were transcribed more frequently than other segments by all three judges though the judges' agreement on the location of [ʔ] and [h] segments in particular vocalizations never exceeded 60%.

[3] [h] is treated here as sonorant because of the presumed openness of its articulation which opposes it to the maximum closure of obstruent [ʔ] . (Cf. also Chomsky and Halle, 1968, p. 303, who list [h] as sonorant.)

[4] Affricatives are grouped with fricatives for presentation simplicity.

References

Boysson-Bardies, Bénédicte de; Sagart, Laurent; and Bacri, Nicole. 1981. Phonetic analysis of late babbling: a case study of a French child. J. of Child Language 8. 511-524.

Chomsky, Noam and Halle, Morris. 1968. The Sound Pattern of English. New York: Harper and Row.

Cruttenden, A. 1970. A phonetic study of babbling. British J. of Disorders of Communication 5. 110-118.

Ferguson, Charles, and Farwell, C. B. 1975. Words and sounds in early language acquisition. Language 51. 419-439.

Irwin, O. C. 1947. Infant speech: consonantal sounds according to place of articulation. J. Speech Disorders 12. 397-401.

Leonard, L. B.; Newhoff, M.; and Mesalin, L. 1980. Individual differences in early child phonology. Applied Psycholinguistics 1. 7-30.

Oller, D.; Wieman, L.A.; Doyle, W.J.; and Ross, C. 1976. Infant babbling and speech. J. Child Language 3. 3-12.

Oller, D. K. 1977. Infant vocalization and the development of speech. Presented at the Milwaukee Conference on Early Intervention with Infants and Young Children (U. of Wisconsin).

Olney, R. L. and Scholnick, E. K. 1976. Adult judgments of age and linguistic differences in infant vocalization. J. Child Language 3. 145-156.

Salus, Peter H. and Salus, Mary W. 1974. Developmental neurophysiology and phonological acquisition order. Language 50. No. 1. 151-160.

Shibamoto, J. S. and Olmsted, D. L. 1978. Lexical and syllabic patterns in phonological acquisition. J. Child Language 5. 417-456.

Stockman, I.; Woods, D.; and Tishman, A. 1981. Listener agreement on phonetic segments in early infant vocalizations. J. of Psycholinguistic Research 10. 593-617.

THE EFFECT OF WORD FAMILIARITY ON PHONEMIC RECOGNITION IN
PRESCHOOL CHILDREN AGED 3 TO 5 YEARS

Harold Clumek, Northwestern University

1. Introduction

There has been a long history of attempts to investigate
children's ability to discriminate perceptually among speech
sounds in minimal word pairs. Initial attempts focused
mostly on the question of the order of acquisition among
phonemic contrasts and the relative degree of perceptual difficulty among them, (Shvachkin, 1973; Garnica, 1973; Edwards,
1974). The general method employed in these studies was to
teach children the nonsense names for various objects and to
use these names as stimuli in minimal word pairs: a child
was therefore presented with two objects whose names were
minimally different from each other and was then asked to
perform actions with one or the other of the objects. The
issue of a perceptual order of acquisition was the question
first posed by Barton (1976) when he began a study using a
picture-pointing task in which the stimulus items were pairs
of real words, as opposed to nonsense names used in the earlier work. Rather than discovering a perceptual order of
acquisition, Barton found that a child between 2 and 3 years
of age is much more dependent upon how familiar the test
items are than upon the actual phonemes in the contrast being
tested.

It should be emphasized that the tasks reported in these
studies do not test mere auditory discrimination, i.e. the
child's ability to differentiate between two different acoustic signals. Since the tasks call for the child to make responses by choosing either from a set of three-dimensional
objects or a set of pictures, the question has to do with
phonemic recognition, or identification, i.e. does a child
of a given age interpret acoustically-different sounds as
signaling differences in meaning in a systematic and consistent way?

Barton's study thus showed a major difference between
2-to-3-year-old children and adults in the ability to recognize phoneme contrasts, namely, that 2-to-3-year-old children rely heavily on knowledge of the test words before being
able to identify a contrast consistently, whereas adults,
presumably, would recognize phonemic differences regardless
of how familiar they might be with the test items.

58

The purpose of this study was to investigate further the role of word familiarity in children's identification of phoneme distinctions, and to use a picture-pointing task in order to study children older than those in earlier studies, that is, children between 3 and 5 years of age. The question raised here is in what ways do these older preschool children differ from both younger children and from adults in their ability to recognize phonemic contrasts in minimal word pairs? What developmental changes can be observed in children as they pass from an age of being very dependent upon word familiarity toward a more adultlike ability in phoneme recognition?

2. Method

2.1. Subjects

Subjects were 31 children, 16 boys and 15 girls, ranging in age from 3;1 to 5;10, and all from middle-class monolingual English-speaking families. The children were screened for articulation with the Goldman-Fristoe Test of Articulation and for receptive vocabulary with the Peabody Picture Vocabulary Test (Form B). Articulation was judged to be age-appropriate for all subjects. The mean percentile score on the Peabody was the 80th percentile, with half of the subjects scoring at or above the 90th percentile; the range was from the 27th to the 100th percentile. In addition, the children's hearing was measured by pure tone and speech reception thresholds, and middle ear function was assessed by tympanometry. Hearing levels were all within normal limits. Of the 31 subjects, ten exhibited some middle ear dysfunction in either one or both ears, such as negative pressure or slightly reduced amplitude. These dysfunctions were mainly due to the children's recovering from recent colds, and, furthermore, the subjects with abnormal tympanograms behaved no differently in the experimental task than those with normal middle ear function.

2.2. Stimulus materials

2.2.1. Word list

The word list used for the study is presented in Table I. It consists of 19 minimal pairs of monosyllabic real words. Seven pairs are of words differentiated by the feature of voicing, nine pairs contain words distinguished by place of articulation, two contain the contrast between /l/

TABLE I
WORD LIST

	MINIMAL PAIR		DISTRACTOR
1.	bear	pear	cup
2.	robe	rope	horse
3.	deer	tear	car
4.	beets	beads	cow
5.	goat	coat	shoe
6.	bag	back	tree
7.	vase	face	dog
8.	pie	tie	bird
9.	spool	stool	brush
10.	map	mat	duck
11.	soup	suit	fish
12.	peas	keys	flower
13.	pouch	couch	pig
14.	tape	cape	sock
15.	towel	tower	horse
16.	feet	seat	car
17.	mouth	mouse	shoe
18.	glass	grass	tree
19.	wing	ring	hand

and /r/, and one contains the distinction between /w/ and /r/. Twelve pairs have the contrast in word-initial position, and seven word-finally; in sixteen pairs, the contrast occurs in a singleton consonant, and in three pairs within a cluster.

Selection of pairs used in this word list was made in accordance with several factors: 1) an attempt to test a variety of the consonantal contrasts of English, in both initial and final positions; 2) the desire to restrict the length of the list so as not to make the testing sessions too long for the children; and 3) the necessity of having both familiar and unfamiliar words in the list, and the difficulty of finding picturable nouns whose names would be unfamiliar to children at the upper end of the age range being tested.

In addition to the 19 minimal pairs, the word list contained a number of monosyllabic real words commonly known to 3-year-olds, such as cup, car, and bird, which were meant to serve as distractors during the experimental portion of the study.

2.2.2. Picture stimuli

Black and white line drawings for the items in the stimulus list and for some other items used in a pilot study were drawn on 5" x 5" cards which were then laminated. Before the study began, the drawings were tested to see how well they worked as exemplars of the stimuli with which they were to be associated. This was done by showing the pictures to eight children with normal speech and hearing between the ages of 3 and 5 years, and who were not subjects for the main study. At each session, the child was first asked to say what was in each picture. If the intended stimulus word was not elicited for a given picture, the picture was later placed in front of the child within a group of other pictures not previously seen by the child, and the child was asked, "Do you see a ___?" In almost all cases, the children had no difficulty in associating the verbal stimuli with the pictures receptively, while some pictures had to be slightly revised.

Four additional children, one boy and three girls aged between 3;2 and 4;6, participated in a second pilot study

61

which was, like the main study, a picture-pointing task using both picture stimuli and taped verbal stimuli.[1]

A very useful result of these pilot tests was that they yielded good expectations for which specific words in the stimulus list were likely to be familiar or unfamiliar to the children who participated in the main study.

2.2.3. Recorded stimuli

The list of minimal pairs was arranged into two different random orders of presentation. Each word pair was to be tested on a block of fifteen trials, five trials for each of the two members of the minimal pair, and five trials for the distractor. Five different random orders of fifteen were selected and assigned to the different word pairs. There were therefore two different orders of presentation of the stimuli, differing in two ways: 1) the order in which the word pairs were presented was different, and 2) the order of the fifteen trials within each block differed for each minimal pair in the two orders of presentation. Of the 31 subjects in the study, one of the orders of presentation was assigned to 16 subjects, while the other order was assigned to the remaining fifteen.

The two different orders of presentation of the stimuli were recorded in a sound-proof booth by a female speaker (recordings were made using an Ampex 350 and Western Electric 640AA microphone with Condenser Microphone Complement). With 19 pairs, and 15 trials for each pair, there were therefore a total of 285 stimuli for each order of presentation. Each stimulus was recorded within a sentence frame such as "Point to the ___." or "Show me the ___." During recording, the volume of the speaker's voice was monitored on the VU meter of the recorder in order to maintain roughly equal intensity for all stimuli.

After the recording, a panel of four adults unfamiliar with the project listened to the tapes and were asked to write down the words which they heard. Any tokens for which there was no unanimous agreement were re-recorded.

2.3. Experimental procedure

At the beginning of each testing session, the child was seated at a small table in front of a loudspeaker (Ampex

Model AA-620, Amplifier/Loudspeaker). The speaker was connected to a large recorder (Ampex AG440) where the experimenter sat and could control all movements of the tape. The
volume of the recorder was set at a level such that when
the child's head was 4 feet away from the speaker, the intensity of the stimuli from the speaker was approximately
60 to 65 dB SPL.

The three pictures for the first minimal pair (the two
members of the pair and one distractor) were placed before
the child with the instructions that someone's voice coming
from the speaker would ask him or her to point to one of the
pictures, and that the voice would be asking several times.
The child's pointing responses were then recorded on a scoring sheet, and imitation of stimuli as well as any comments
on the part of the child were also noted. Following completion of the first block of testing, the next set of pictures
for the second minimal pair were placed before the child, and
so forth.

During each session, experimenter and child took a few
breaks to work on puzzles or play games. Generally, three
to four sessions of about 45 minutes each were necessary to
complete the testing, and there was little problem in keeping the children motivated to perform the task. For 27 of
the 31 subjects, all testing took place within a time period
of less than ten days; of the remaining four subjects, three
completed testing within two weeks, while the last took
nearly a month because of illness and an intervening holiday.

When a child had completed the testing, a check was made
to determine which items in the word list had previously been
unfamiliar to the child. There were two steps to this process, expressive and receptive. The expressive part involved
showing to the child in random order the pictures for those
word pairs where the child had failed to identify the contrast, as well as pictures for any pairs in which the child
had succeeded but that contain items often unfamiliar to
children of this population, and then the child was asked to
say what was in the picture. If the child produced the intended stimulus word for a given picture, no further question
was asked. If, on the other hand, the child either did not
know what the object in the picture was, or if the child provided a word other than the intended stimulus, these pictures
were then used for the receptive part.[2] In this part, each

of the pictures was placed before the child within a small group of other pictures which the child had never seen before. At this point, the child was asked, "Do you see a ___?"

Following the check for familiarity, another check was made for auditory discrimination. The purpose of this was to ensure that failure to recognize a distinction had not been due to failure to perceive the acoustic differences between the two items of a word pair in the first place. For this, the experimenter told the child that he would say a few words and asked the child to say them back exactly as they had been said. The experimenter then covered his mouth and produced in random order the words from those pairs where the child had failed to identify the distinction.

2.4. Analysis

2.4.1. Recognition of the contrasts

The following criteria were used to determine whether or not a child was recognizing a contrast:

1. If the child correctly answered the first five trials for the items in the minimal pair, it was assumed that the child was making the identification (p approximately .03), according to Barton (1976). At that point, the testing for that pair stopped, and the child went on to the following pair.

2. If the child missed one or more of the first five trials, the full ten trials for the items in the minimal pair were completed. If the child answered correctly nine trials out of ten, it was assumed that the contrast was being identified ($p < .05$); if the child answered correctly on only five trials or fewer, it was assumed that the distinction was not being recognized. In both cases, the child went on to the following minimal pair.

3. If, however, the child answered correctly on either 6, 7, or 8 trials out of the first ten, the tape was wound back, and the pair was tested a second time, so that the child was given a total of 20 trials for that minimal pair. In this case, it was determined, following Barton's criteria, that 15 correct trials out of 20 were necessary (p

approximately .02) in order to conclude that the contrast had been identified.

2.4.2. Familiarity

The question of determining which words were familiar or unfamiliar to a child was sometimes difficult, and the criteria for making decisions about familiarity were slightly different for different-aged children. If a child failed both expressive and receptive portions of the familiarity check for a given word, it was judged that the word was unfamiliar. This was obviously a criterion used for all the children, and the cases were very clear-cut, especially for the younger ones.

If, on the other hand, a child failed the expressive part but succeeded on the receptive part, or if a child succeeded first on the expressive part, then it was possible that the child had either been at least partially familiar with the word before the testing had begun, or had become familiar with the word during testing. This was especially true of the children who were roughly 4-1/2 years of age and older. In many cases, a variety of clues were available to help determine if the child had been unfamiliar with the word prior to testing. It was judged that the word had been unfamiliar if, in the expressive part of the check, the child responded by giving a close phonological approximation of the test word but not the exact form, indicating an effort to recall what the word had been. (One child even admitted, on seeing one picture, "I forget what the word was.") Most often, the best clue to the child's prior lack of familiarity was a reaction to hearing the unfamiliar word for the first time during testing, such as the child's saying, "What's that?" or "Where's that?"

3. Results

Results for all 31 subjects are given in the three parts of Table II. Phoneme recognition in Table II is defined solely in terms of the children's pointing responses. A plus mark appears where a child successfully identified a contrast, and a minus mark indicates that a child failed to recognize the distinction. Some spaces are left blank, meaning that either not enough trials were completed to determine whether or not the child was making the identification, or else, more

TABLE II
PART 1 - 3-YEAR-OLDS

					SUBJECTS AND THEIR AGES			
		1	2	3	4	5	6	7
CONTRASTS		3;1	3;2	3;6	3;7	3;10	3;10	3;10
1.	bear, pear	+	+	+	+	+	+	+
2.	robe, rope	-			-	-		
3.	deer, tear	-	+	-	+	+		+
4.	beets, beads	-	-	-	-	-	-	
5.	goat, coat	+	+	+	+	+	+	+
6.	bag, back	+	+	+	+	+	+	+
7.	vase, face			+	+	+	+	+
8.	pie, tie	+	+	+	+	+	+	
9.	spool, stool	-	+	-	-	-	+	+
10.	map, mat	-	-	-	-	-	-	-
11.	soup, suit	+		-	+	+	+	-
12.	peas, keys	+	+	+	+	+	+	+
13.	pouch, couch	-	-	-	-	-	-	-
14.	tape, cape	+	+	+	+	-	-	
15.	towel, tower		+	+	+	+*	+	-
16.	feet, seat	+	+	+	+	+	+	+
17.	mouth, mouse		+	+	+	+	+	+
18.	glass, grass	+	+	+	+	+	+	+
19.	wing, ring	+		+	+	+	+	

Some spaces are left blank either because not enough trials were completed to determine if the child was recognizing the contrast, or because the child had misinterpreted the representation in the picture.

*Subject #5 answered correctly on 20 trials out of 20, and, for 9 out of 10 trials in which she was asked to point to the tower, she pointed to the base of a sink in another picture.

TABLE II
PART 2 - 4-YEAR-OLDS

		SUBJECTS AND THEIR AGES						
	8	9	10	11	12	13	14	15
CONTRASTS	4;1	4;2	4;3	4;3	4;5	4;5	4;5	4;5
1. bear, pear	+	+	+	+	+	+	+	+
2. robe, rope	+	+	+	-	+	+	-	-
3. deer, tear	+	+	+	+	+	+	+	+
4. beets, beads	+	-	+	-	-	-	-	-
5. goat, coat	+	+	+	+	+	+	+	+
6. bag, back	+	+	+	+	+	+	+	+
7. vase, face	+		+	+	+	+	+	-
8. pie, tie	+	+	+	+	+	+	+	+
9. spool, stool	+	+	+	+	-	+	+	
10. map, mat	-	-	+	+	-	-	+	-
11. soup, suit	+	+	+	+	+	+	-	+
12. peas, keys	+	+	+	+	+	+	+	+
13. pouch, couch	-	+**	+*	+	-	-	-	+
14. tape, cape	-	+	+	+	+	+	+	-
15. towel, tower	+	+	+	+	+	+	+	+
16. feet, seat	+	+	+	+	+	+	+	+
17. mouth, mouse	+	+	+	+	+	+	+	+
18. glass, grass	+	+	+	+	+	+	+	+
19. wing, ring	+	+	+	+	+	+	+	+

*Subject #10 was correct on 10 out of 10 trials, but when she was asked to point to a pouch, she pointed to the stomach of a pig in another picture.

**For subjects #9 and #19, there were too few correct responses to say statistically that they recognized the contrasts, but they were recognizing them more consistently by the end of testing.

TABLE II
PART 2 - 4-YEAR-OLDS (cont.)

		SUBJECTS AND THEIR AGES							
		16	17	18	19	20	21	22	23
CONTRASTS		4;6	4;7	4;7	4;8	4;8	4;9	4;10	4;10
1.	bear, pear	+	+	+	+	+	+	+	+
2.	robe, rope	+	-	+	+**	-		-	+
3.	deer, tear	+	+	+	+	+	+	+	+
4.	beets, beads	-	+	+	-	+	-	-	+
5.	goat, coat	+	+	+	+	+	+	+	+
6.	bag, back	+	+	+	+		+	+	+
7.	vase, face	+	+	+	+	+	-	+	+
8.	pie, tie	+	+	+	+	+	+	+	+
9.	spool, stool	-	+	+	+	-	-	-	+
10.	map, mat	+	+	+	+	-	+	+	+
11.	soup, suit	+	+	+	+	+	+	+	+
12.	peas, keys	+	+	+	+	+	+	+	+
13.	pouch, couch	-	+	+	+	+	+	+	+
14.	tape, cape	+	+	+	+	+	+	+	+
15.	towel, tower	+	+	+	+		+	+	+
16.	feet, seat	+	+	+	+	+	+	+	+
17.	mouth, mouse	+	+	+	+	+	+	+	+
18.	glass, grass	+	+	+	+	+	+	+	+
19.	wing, ring	+	+	+	+	+	+	+	+

TABLE II
PART 3 - 5-YEAR-OLDS

		SUBJECTS AND THEIR AGES							
CONTRASTS		24 5;3	25 5;3	26 5;4	27 5;4	28 5;7	29 5;8	30 5;9	31 5;10
1.	bear, pear	+	+	+	+	+	+	+	+
2.	robe, rope	+	+	+	+	+	+**	+	+
3.	deer, tear	+	+	+	+	+	+	+	+
4.	beets, beads	-	-	+	+	+	+	+	+
5.	goat, coat	+	+	+	+	+	+	+	+
6.	bag, back	+	+	+	+	+	+	+	+
7.	vase, face	+	+	+	+	+	+	+	+
8.	pie, tie	+	+	+	+	+	+	+	+
9.	spool, stool	+	-	-	-	+	+	+	+
10.	map, mat	+	+	+	+	+	+	-	+
11.	soup, suit	+	+	+	+	+	+	+	+
12.	peas, keys	+	+	+	+	+	+	+	+
13.	pouch, couch	+	-	+	+	+	+	+	+
14.	tape, cape	+	+	+	+	+	+	+*	+
15.	towel, tower	+	+	+	+	+	+	+	+
16.	feet, seat	+	+	+	+	+	+	+	+
17.	mouth, mouse	+	+	+	+	+	+	+	+
18.	glass, grass	+	+	+	+	+	+	+	+
19.	wing, ring	+	+	+	+	+	+	+	+

*Subject #30 was correct on 9 out of 10 trials, but when she was asked to point to the cape, she pointed to a tape-holder.

**For subject #29, there were too few correct responses to say statistically that she recognized the contrast, but she was recognizing it consistently by the end of testing.

rarely, because it was discovered during the familiarity check after testing that the child had misinterpreted the intended representation of the picture.

Three plus marks in the table appear with one asterisk, namely in the columns for subjects #5, 10, and 30. This single asterisk indicates that the child was recognizing the contrast consistently but pointing to an incorrect object for one member of the test pair. For example, when subject #30 was being tested on the pair tape, cape, she pointed consistently to the tape portion of the picture of Scotch tape when she was asked to point to the tape, but pointed to the tape-holder in the same picture when asked to point to the cape.

Another three plus marks in the table appear with two asterisks, and these are in the columns for subjects #9, 19, and 29. The double asterisks indicate that there were not quite enough correct responses out of 20 trials to say statistically that the child was recognizing the contrast, but most of the child's errors were made during the first half of the testing, and correct responses were being made consistently toward the end.

It can be seen from Table II that the younger children failed to make many more identifications than the older children. With all 31 subjects taken together, there were a total of 569 instances of testing for phoneme recognition. Of these, 78, or roughly 13.7%, were cases in which the children failed to recognize the phoneme contrast.

In breaking down this total into three parts, namely for the 3-year-olds, 4-year-olds, and 5-year-olds, it was found that the percentage of failure to recognize phonemic distinctions is correlated with age: the percentage was 28.8% for 3-year-olds, 12.37% for 4-year-olds, and 4.6% for 5-year-olds. Furthermore, age is also correlated with familiarity as shown in Table III and Figure 1. For the 3-year-olds, there was a total of 32 instances of testing in which the test pair contained an unfamiliar item. The children failed to recognize the contrast in 29 of these 32 cases, or approximately 90% of all cases. The 4-year-olds failed to recognize about 64% of those contrasts containing an unfamiliar word, while the 5-year-olds failed to recognize only 30%. The differences among all three groups were

TABLE III

PERCENTAGE OF CONTRASTS WITH AN
UNFAMILIAR WORD WHICH WERE NOT IDENTIFIED

3-year-olds:	90%	(29 out of 32 instances)
4-year-olds:	64%	(31 out of 48 instances)
5-year-olds:	30%	(6 out of 20 instances)

PERCENTAGE OF CONTRASTS WITH
FAMILIAR WORDS WHICH WERE NOT IDENTIFIED

3-year-olds:	3.5%	(3 out of 86 instances)
4-year-olds:	2.4%	(6 out of 251 instances)
5-year-olds:	0.76%	(1 out of 132 instances)

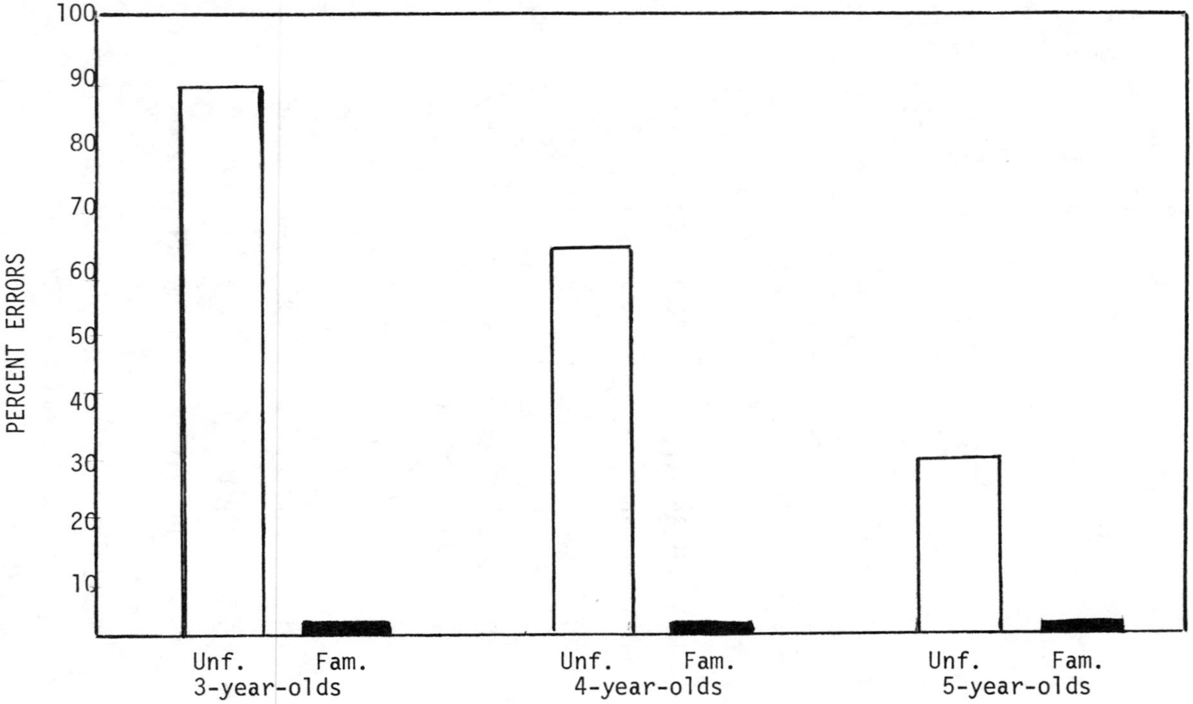

PERCENT ERRORS

Figure 1: Percentage of familiar vs. unfamiliar contrasts which the children failed to identify.

72

significant, according to chi-square (p < .01).

On the other hand, the number of contrasts with only familiar words which were not identified was very low: for 3-year-olds, the percentage was about 3%, for 4-year-olds, it was about 2%, and for 5-year-olds, it was less than 1%. None of these differences was found to be significant, according to chi-square.

These figures clearly show age-related differences in the effect of word familiarity on children's ability to recognize phoneme contrasts, namely, for the youngest children, lack of familiarity with the test items resulted in failure to recognize a contrast, whereas with the oldest children, an unfamiliar item in the test pair made little difference in the child's ability to identify the distinction.

More interesting were the differences in responding patterns which the children of different ages exhibited when faced with a test pair containing an unfamiliar item. The 3-year-olds, and some of the younger 4-year-olds, almost always pointed to the picture whose name was the familiar word, regardless of whether the stimulus for a given trial was the familiar or the unfamiliar word. In doing so, they never showed an unfavorable reaction to the unfamiliar word. One girl, aged 3;2 who was a subject in the pilot study, pointed consistently to the picture of a couch when she heard either couch or pouch. Her mother, who was sitting behind her during this session, noticed this pattern of responding, and, when the last trial of pouch was over, asked her daughter, "What did the lady say?" The girl, having already pointed to the couch, turned around and answered calmly, "She said to point to the pouch."

This pattern of ignoring the unfamiliar in favor of the familiar was the most common one whenever a child failed to exhibit recognition of a phonemic contrast. In fact, of the 78 instances of failure to identify a contrast, biased responding was the pattern in 68 of them, or approximately 87%. The remainder showed random responding.

The children who were roughly 4-1/2 years of age often continued this pattern of pointing to the familiar item, but, even while doing so, they sometimes showed a negative reaction to the unfamiliar word whenever they heard it. For example, one boy, aged 4;6, also a subject in the pilot study, was being tested on the pair couch, pouch where pouch was the unfamiliar word. When he was asked to point to the couch, he did so, but when he was asked to point to the pouch, he refused to respond on the first two trials, and finally on the third trial, he decided to point to the couch, saying, "She means couch, but she's saying it wrong." Another child, a girl aged 4;10, was being tested on the pair stool, spool where spool was the unfamiliar item. When she heard stool, she pointed to the picture of the stool, and when she heard spool, she pointed to the same picture but said, in a rather suspicious tone, "She said spool." After the testing was done, this child was asked why the voice had been saying spool, and her reply was, "She's making a mistake." A third child, aged 4;5, pointed to the familiar map when he heard that stimulus item, but when he heard mat for the first time, he stared briefly at the picture of the mat, whispered to himself, "This is the rug," then pointed back to the picture of the map. He continued pointing to the map for the remaining trials. Still another child, a boy aged 4;6, who was shy and less extroverted than some of the others, never made any verbal protests but showed his reaction on hearing an unfamiliar word by hesitating for a long time before finally choosing the familiar item.

Finally, there were other children, mainly older than 4-1/2 years, who were surprised by the unfamiliar word but who then reasoned that the word must be referring to the item in the remaining picture. One girl, aged 4;7, was being tested for couch, pouch where pouch was the unfamiliar item, and when she first heard the word pouch, said, "There is no pouch. That must be the pouch," (pointing to the correct picture). Another girl, aged 4;7, had been unfamiliar with the word spool yet pointed correctly on all the trials for the pair stool, spool. When she was asked afterward why she had pointed to the picture of the spool whenever she had heard that word, she responded, "I knew the lady wasn't trying to say stool."

4. Discussion

The different kinds of responding patterns exhibited by children of different ages show changes in the degree of dependence upon word familiarity for recognizing phoneme

distinctions. Clearly, more is involved in this kind of
testing than phonemic recognition alone. The children see
that three pictures are placed in front of them for any
given block of trials, and the oldest of them may reason
that they should eventually be pointing to all three. The
younger children, however, were also reasoning a little in
this way: they frequently failed to recognize a contrast
as they were pointing only to the familiar item of a given
pair, and when they saw the pictures being taken away at
the end of the block of trials, they would often remark, in
reference to the picture of the unfamiliar item, "She never
said that one!"

In addition to revealing differences in reasoning
strategies, many of the older children's reactions to and
comments on unfamiliar words show that defining phonemic
recognition only in terms of pointing responses is inadequate: children who fail to recognize a contrast while
pointing, and yet indicate that one of the stimuli sounds
"wrong" to them, are clearly identifying the contrast
phonemically, even though they may not be responding in an
adultlike way. The results thus indicate aspects of the
development of metalinguistic awareness. Specifically, the
children's various reactions to unfamiliar words are said
to be indicative of metalinguistic awareness insofar as the
children were essentially formulating judgments about the
relative appropriateness or inappropriateness of linguistic
forms being presented to them, even though they were never
explicitly asked to make such judgments. Two of the metalinguistic skills listed by Clark (1978:34) accurately describe the behavior of the children in this study: 1) check-
ing the result of an utterance, including commenting on
and correcting the utterances of others, and 2) testing for
reality, that is, deciding whether a word works or not, and
if not, trying another. As has already been illustrated,
some of the children commented explicitly on what they
thought were incorrect pronounciations of certain words,
whereas other children decided that the unfamiliar phonological form they heard did not "fit" their internal representation of the word for the familiar item, so that they
then had to make it fit the object in the other picture.

Not all children used the same strategy for all word
pairs. One striking example was a boy, aged 5;4, who had
been unfamiliar with the words pouch and spool. He

75

recognized the contrast between pouch and couch, and when he was asked later why he had pointed to the pouch upon hearing that word, he answered, "Because I knew the other two weren't it." On the other hand, this same child did not recognize the stool, spool distinction and pointed to the stool for both stimulus words. When he was asked if he had ever heard the word spool before, he said, "No, but we have one at home." He was then asked what you do with it, and he replied, "You sit on it." In this case, it was as though he were treating the forms spool and stool as allophonic variants of the same word, similar to what the youngest children were doing, and yet he used a more mature strategy in dealing with the pair pouch, couch.

A further possible implication of the results concerns the nature of children's internal phonological representations of word forms. A phonological system in which two sounds, for example /p/ and /k/, are contrastive only in minimal pairs containing specifically known words is a less abstract phonological system than one in which /p/ and /k/ are not only contrastive in pairs with known words but in potentially any minimal pair. The less abstract, or more concrete, phonology seems characteristic of the 3-year-old children, who consistently recognized the /p, k/ contrast in the pair peas, keys, both of which were highly familiar, but who never recognized the same /p, k/ contrast in the pair pouch, couch, containing the unfamiliar word pouch. The older children, on the other hand, exhibited a more abstract, adultlike phonology, one in which the two sounds were not only distinctive in pairs with known words but in any potential word pair.

5. Summary

In summary, this study has shown age-related differences in the effect of word familiarity on preschool children's ability to recognize phoneme distinctions in minimal pairs. It was found that 3-year-olds rely heavily on their knowledge of the test items for recognizing a contrast whereas 5-year-olds are generally able to recognize a contrast irrespective of what the particular test words are. In his dissertation, Barton takes the position that children are able to perceive the majority of phonological contrasts of their native language by the time they begin to speak. While this might very well be true, this study has shown that there are still important differences between preschool children and adults, and that children's phoneme identification abilities may not become completely adultlike until several years after they have begun speaking.

Footnotes

[1] During pilot testing, the subject's mother was occasionally present and sitting behind the child. However, this was not part of the normal procedure for the main study.

[2] When the child did not know what the picture was, he or she was then asked what one could do with it, or what it looked like. This was to ensure that the child had some conceptual knowledge of the pictured item.

References

Barton, D. "The role of perception in the acquisition of phonology," doctoral dissertation, London, Indiana University Linguistics Club, 1976.

Clark, E. "Awareness of language: some evidence from what children say and do." In The Child's Conception of Language, Sinclair, A., Jarvella, R.J., & Levelt, W.J.M. (eds.), Springer-Verlag, 1978.

Edwards, M.L. "Perception and production in child phonology: the testing of four hypotheses." Journal of Child Language 1: 205-219, 1974.

Garnica, O. "The development of phonemic speech perception." In Cognitive Development and the Acquisition of Language, Moore, T. (ed.), Academic Press, 1973.

Shvachkin, N. Kh. "The development of phonemic speech perception in early childhood." In Studies of Child Language Development, Ferguson, C.A. & Slobin, D.I. (eds.), Holt, Rinehart, & Winston, 1973.

Acknowledgments. I wish to thank D. Rutherford, D. Kistler, and B. Litowitz for helpful comments and support. I am also grateful to the children and their families for their participation in this study.

TONE ACQUISITION: SOME GENERAL OBSERVATIONS

by Brian King

University of Ottawa

0. ABSTRACT
    In spite of the dearth of material on tone
acquisition some tentative generalizations do
emerge. A recent study made by the author on
Taiwanese tone acquisition indicated that tones
are acquired before segmentals, level tones are
acquired before contour tones, tones which are
maximally opposed are acquired first and that
there is a close relationship between the stages
of tone acquisition and syntactic development.
The present paper discusses these results in light
of previous research and suggests that they have
a general applicability to the tone acquisition
process. Some possible explanations are offered
to account for these phenomena by drawing on research on tone language typology.

1. INTRODUCTION.
    There have so far been few studies made of
children acquiring tonemic distinctions in tone
languages. When we consider how many of the
world's languages are tonal it is evident that
more research is necessary before any strong
claims can be proposed with confidence. Many
areas of the world, where tone languages are spok-
en, remain for which we have little or no data on
tone acquisition. To date, the bulk of our data
is from Asian tone languages, although a few fragmented studies exist for African tone languages.
With these limitations, however, some interesting
tentative generalizations do emerge.

    The results of a recent cross-sectional/
longitudinal case study on tone acquisition in
Taiwanese by King (1980) show a certain paralle-
lism with those of previous research. The present
paper discusses four general aspects of the tone
studies. Some reasons are suggested for these
phenomena.

2. DISCUSSION.

2.1 Tones vs. Segmentals

There is sufficient evidence to suggest that it is universally true that tones are acquired before segmentals. Not only has this been found to be the case for Taiwanese (King op.cit.), Mandarin (Li & Thompson 1977), Cantonese (Tse 1978), but is also true for non-Chinese languages such as Thai (Tuaycharoen 1979) and African languages such as Luo (Blount 1970), and Ga (Kirk 1973).

Crystal (1973) notes that prosodic features in general are acquired early in the child's development. Other studies such as Kaplan & Kaplan (1970) suggest that the rising and falling intonation patterns in English can be discriminated as early as 8 months. It would appear that non-segmental features such as pitch are perceptually more salient than segmental features and are, therefore, more easily acquired in the early stages. However, we would like to propose an additional reason to explain why tones are acquired before segmentals. This is related to tone language typology. Although Wang (1967), in his model of tone features, allows for a maximum of 13 different tones, no tone language has yet been found to distinguish this many tones. In fact, tone systems rarely contain more than 6 tones using only F_o to distinguish them (Hombert 1978).

Hombert estimates that 30% of tone languages have systems with 2 tones and another 30% have systems with 3 tones. Systems with 4, 5, and 6 tones are estimated to comprise 15%, 10% and 15% respectively of the number of tone languages. On the other hand, if data on phonemic systems are compared, it is apparent that the number of phonemes in a language will always be greater than the number of tones. For example, Sigurd (1963) has calculated that the smallest possible number of phonemes in a language is 10 and the upper limit 80, with 95% of the world's languages having between 14 and 43 phonemes.

The observation that tones are acquired before segmentals in the acquisition process is, therefore most likely related to two factors. Firstly, non-segmentals such as pitch are perceptually more salient than segmentals, and, secondly, tone systems are typologically more complex than phonemic systems. The number of distinctions to be made in a tone system is, therefore, a lot smaller than in a phonemic system. This thus contributes to the relative ease with which children appear to acquire tone systems.

2.2 Level Tones are Acquired before Contour Tones

Data from various studies indicate that level tones are acquired before contour tones. This was found to be true for Taiwanese, Cantonese, Mandarin, Thai, and Luo. In Taiwanese there were two level tones, a high level and a low level tone present in Stage 1 in the study made by King (op. cit.). The interesting point here is that these two tones were used as substitutions for other tones which were not yet present in the child's system. The high level tone was not only used for words carrying this tone, but also for words having the rising tone (⌄). Similarly, the low level tone appears to have been used for any tone that was non-high. It was used to replace the low falling, the high falling and the mid level tones in the speech of both of the Taiwanese subjects studied at this stage. The fact that contour tones were consistently replaced with level tones in our study suggests that the latter are more basic than the former. Results from other studies and from tone language typologies further strengthen this hypothesis. For example, Tse (op. cit.) found that his Cantonese subject acquired only the high and low level tones in Stage 1.

Similarly, one of Li and Thompson's Mandarin subjects is reported as only having level tones in the earliest stage of his/her speech. For Thai Tuaycharoen (op. cit.) found that only the mid level and low level tones were present in the speech of her subject in the early stage of tone acquisition. Also the same phenomenon of level tones being present at this stage is reported by Blount (op. cit.) for Luo. One of his subjects used high and low level tones with her first utterances and also used these tones as substitutes for others in the system, although we are given only limited data on this point.

In a study on tone language typology, Maddieson (1978), by drawing on data from a wide fariety of the world's tone languages, concludes that level tones are not only more common than contour tones, but that there exists an implicational universal, whereby, any tone language that has a contour tone in its system will automatically have at least one level tone as well. This means that we can expect to find tone languages with only level tones but no tone languages with only contour tones and no level tones. Given Jakobson's (1967) discovery that there is a correlation between the order in which children acqure sounds and implicational universals, it is not surprising that this also appears to be valid for the order in which tones are acquired.

It seems fair to point out here that there are problems involved with this viewpoint. Firstly, another typological study conducted on Chinese dialects by Cheng (1973) indicated that falling tones are more common than level tones. However, as Maddieson suggests, it is likely that Cheng's results are due to the inclusion of intonational factors in his data.

Some apparent exceptions to the generalization that all tone languages will have at least one level tone are found in the Chinese dialect of Chen Xian spoken in Hunan Province, as reported by Yang (1957). The tone system of this dialect is described as having 2 rising tones and 2 falling tones. In the same study the dialect of Gui Yang has 3 rising and 1 falling tone. However, since Yang's study reports on over 70 different dialects, of which only 2 violate the level tone generalization, it is questionable if these do in fact represent true counterexamples. The latter example is particularly open to close scrutiny. It is described as having 3 contrasting rising tones, a phenomenon which has not been reported elsewhere and clearly violates Wang's (op. cit.) system of universal tone features.

Nevertheless, the case for level tones as basic components of tone languages and consequently as being acquired before contour tones in languages acquisition is quite strong. Our studies from tone acquisition are by no means numerous but are taken from languages other than Chinese dialects and this suggests that the findings have some general application to the tone acquisition process as a whole. The data on tone acquisition, therefore, indicate that Jakobson's theory of the correlation between implicational universals and language acquisition is equally valid for non-segmentals as for segmentals. Of course, a lot more studies on both tone language acquisition and tone language typology are needed before we can decide how far this correlation is true.

2.3 Tones which are Maximally Opposed are Acquired First

A principle of maximal opposition may be one of the factors governing the order in which children acquire distinctions in tone languages. This was proposed by Jakobson (1967) to account for the order of appearance of phonemic contrasts, and was based on the successive differentiation of of distinctive features. For example, according to Jakobson, the development of a phonemic system is the result of filling in the space between two sounds. /p/ is a consonant and /a/ is a vowel and they differ from each other in every respect. The contrast between the two sounds is maximal and it is these sounds that appear first in the child's language.

If we examine the data on tone acquisition we find that level tones are always present in Stage 1 of the acquisition process. These are, in most cases, a high level and a low level tone. In Thai there was a mid level and a low level tone

(Tuaycharoen, 1979). In one of Li and Thompson's
(1977) Mandarin subjects a high level tone and a
falling tone were present. From the data it
appears that tonal development can be explained in
much the same way as segmental development. The
initial contrast is one between high and low,
which is the maximal possible contrast in the level category. The next contrast to appear is between level and contour and then the various finer
distinctions in the contour and level categories
are acquired. Table 1, below, illustrates how
this principle has been applied in the acquisition
process of the various tone languages for which
data are available.

TABLE 1
THE ORDER OF TONE ACQUISITION IN TAIWANESE
(KING 1980), MANDARIN (LI & THOMPSON 1977),
CANTONESE (TSE 1978), AND THAI (TUAYCHAROEN
1977).

	STAGE 1	STAGE 2	STAGE 3
TAIWANESE	˥ (˩)	˩˥ ˧ ˩˧ ˩˥	˥ ˩
MANDARIN	˥ ˩˥	˩˧ ˥˩	˥˩ + ˥˩ → ˧˥ + ˥˩ (sandhi rule)
CANTONESE	˥ ˩	˧ ˩˧ ˥ ˧ ˧	˨˩ ˨
THAI	˧ ˩	˩˥	˩˥˩ ˥

In general, tones perceptually close to other
tones in the system are acquired later. For example, the low falling tone in Taiwanese, the low
rising and low mid level tones in Cantonese and
the falling rising tone in Mandarin are all acquired later in their respective systems. In Thai,
although the same principle is applicable, there
are likely other factors which explain why the
high tone was acquired latest (see King op. cit.).
Furthermore, a multi-subject study of Thai tone
acquisition is obviously necessary when we consider Sarawit's (1976) passing remarks on her findings. She notes that her subject used rising
tones before falling and contour before level

tones.

An examination of tone system typologies reveals interesting parallels with the sub-systems of children in the process of acquiring tones. Hombert (op. cit.) calculated that 90% of two-tone systems are constituted by high and low tones, 65% of three-tone systems have high, mid and low tones and 20% have high, low and falling tones. The two most common types of four-tone systems are high, low, falling and rising (40%) and high, mid, low, and falling (30%). We can hypothesize that a child acquiring a tone system will not, at any stage of the acquisition process, have an unnatural tone system. The data in Table 1 seem to support this hypothesis. For example, if we take a point in the acquisition process where there are three tones present in the sub-systems of the Taiwanese and Cantonese subjects, we find that these are perfect examples of the two most common three-tone systems. Taiwanese has high, low and falling tones and Cantonese high, low and mid level tones.

It appears that the order in which tones are acquired is closely related to perceptual distinctiveness and typological naturalness. We can also expect articulatory difficulty to be an important factor here. Further study will help us to gain a fuller understanding of the role of each of these factors in the acquisition process.

2.4 Tone Acquisition and Syntactic Development
A close relationship may be noted between the stages of tone acquisition and syntactic development. In all the studies made so far, acquisition was completed by the end of Stage 3. By the time that children are ready to start using multi-word utterances, they, therefore, have mastered the tone system. The number of tones in the system or the absence or presence of tone sandhi does not seem to have been an important factor in influencing the actual time taken to master the tone system. In all cases the process was completed in 6-8 months.

84

The reason for the relationship between the acquisition of the tone system and syntactic development is perhaps more obvious in Taiwanese. Since the Taiwanese tone system has a complex set of sandhi rules which come into operation in syntactic environments such as boundaries of noun phrases, verb phrases, sentences, adverbs and embedded sentences (Liao 1972), it would not be surprising if these rules served as syntactic processing devices during the acquisition process. Although not all Asian tone languages have tone sandhi rules as complex as those in Taiwanese, it does seem to be a typological characteristic for tone sandhi to be potentially present. Even if a tone language is described as having no sandhi rules, such as Thai (Tuaycharoen op. cit.), we sometimes find that changes in the pitch contours related to stress and syntax are reported (Samang 1972). We, therefore, suggest that the function of intonation as a syntactic processing device, especially when it has the effect of producing tone sandhi, is largely responsible for relationship between the stages of tone acquisition and syntactic development observed in our data. Of course, more research is needed to find out the role intonation plays in supplying syntactic information to the listener, expecially in those tone languages commonly described as not having tone sandhi.

3. CONCLUSION.
Before the generalizaions presented in this paper can be thought to be conclusive, more data must be gathered on the tone acquisition process. However, the approach taken here has been shown to be potentially fruitful and our tentative generalizations are, in most cases, well-supported by tone language typology.

REFERENCES

Blount, Ben G. (1970). "The Prelinguistic System of Luo Children". <u>Anthropological Linguistics</u>. 12.9 pp.326-41.

Cheng, Chin Chuan. (1973). "Quantitative Study of Chinese Tones". <u>JCL</u>. Vol. 1, No. 1. pp.93-110.

Crystal, David. (1973). "Non-Segmental Phonology in Language Acquisition: A Review of the Issues. <u>Lingua</u>. 32. pp.1-45.

Fromkin, Victoria A. (ed.) (1978). <u>Tone: A Linguistic Survey</u>. Academic Press Ltd.

Gandour, Jackson T. (1978). "The Perception of Tone". in Fromkin (ed.).

Hombert, Jean-Marie. (1978). "A Model of Tone Systems". in <u>Elements of Tone, Stress and Intonation</u>. Ed. Donna Jo Napoli, Washington, D.C.: Georgetown U. Press.

Jakobson, Roman. (1967). <u>Child Language, Aphasia Phonological Universals</u>. The Hague: Mouton.

Kaplan, E. L. & Kaplan, G. A. (1970). "The Prelinguistic Child". in J. Eliot (ed.) <u>Human Development and Cognitive Processes</u>. New York: Holt, Rinehart & Winston.

King, Brian. (1980). <u>The Acquisition of Tone in Taiwanese</u>. Taibei: Fu Ren University, M.A. Thesis.

Kirk, Lorrain. (1973). "An Analysis of Speech Imitaions by Ga Children". <u>Anthropological Linguistics</u>. 15.6 pp.267-75.

Li, Charles N. & Thompson, Sandra A. (1977). "The Acquisition of Tone in Mandarin-Speaking Children". <u>J. Child Language</u>. 4. pp.185-200.

----------------(1978). "The Acquisition of Tone". in Fromkin, (ed.).

Liao, Chiu-Chung. (1971). The Syntactic Environment of Tone Sandhi in Taiwanese. Taibei: Taiwan Normal University, M.A. Thesis.

Maddieson, Ian. (1978). "Universals of Tone". in Universals of Human Language, Vol. 2: Phonology Ed. Greenberg, Stanford U. Press.

Samang, Hiranburana. (1972). "Changes in the Pitch Contours of Unaccented Syllables in Spoken Thai". in Tai Phonetics and Phonology. Ed. Jimmy G. Harris & Richard B. Noss. Central Institute of English Language.

Sarawit, Mary. (1976). "Assimilation in Child Language Acquisition". in Tai Linguistics in Honor of Fang-Kuei Li. Ed. Gething et all. Chulalongkorn U. Press.

Sigurd, Bengt. (1963). "A Note on the Number of Phonemes". Statistical Methods in Linguistics. No. 2.

Tse, John Kwock-Ping. (1978). "Tone Acquisition in Cantonese: A Longitudinal Case Study". J. Child Lang. 5. pp.191-204.

Tuaycharoen, p. (1979). "An Acount of Speech Development of a Thai Child: From Babbling to Speech". in Studies in Tai and Mon-Khmer Phonetics and Phonology. ed. Thongkum et all.

Wang, William S.Y. (1967). "The Phonological Features of Tone". International Journal of American Linguistics. 33. pp.93-105.

Yang, Shih-Feng. (1957). "Tonal Distribution of Dialects in Hunan". (in Chinese). BIHP. 29.1 pp.31-57.

The acquisition of Japanese pitch-accent

Chieko Kobayashi
Tezukayama Gakuin
Junior College

0. Introduction

This paper presents an analysis of the acquisition of Japanese pitch-accent.[1] As an initial attempt, the acquisitional processes of two characteristics of Tokyo-type accentuation, that is, (1) the basic unit of accent, and (2) accentual patterns of nouns, are discussed. The data for this study are based on recorded material taken at 1;6 and 1;11, part of longitudinally collected material of one child, a girl, born in Tokyo and raised by parents, who both speak with a Tokyo-type accentuation.

1. Adult accentual patterns

Japanese pitch-accent is basically a word accent characterized by marked accents in the underlying forms, which are realized as surface pitch contours by application of phonetic realization rules. In the accentual system of standard Japanese, a word may contain at most one marked accent which indicates the location of a pitch-fall in a word. Thus, in this type of accentuation, the location of the accented mora is phonologically significant. With this accent marked, the surface pitch contour of a word is realized by two phonetic rules: (1) Moras preceding and including the accented mora are high-pitched, whereas those following the accented mora are low-pitched. (2) The initial mora of a word is low-pitched, unless that initial mora itself is accented in the underlying form. Thus, a 4-mora word with the marked accent in the third mora is pronounced as $m/m\ m\backslash m$ (L-H-H-L), with pitch drop after the third mora. In this accentual system, there are n+1 possible accentual patterns for n-mora words, including unaccented words which contain no marked accent in the underlying forms. The word-final accent is not phonetically distinguishable from no accent unless followed by another word including a particle.

One characteristic of Tokyo-type accentuation is that it requires two units of accent, moras and syllables, to account for accentual behavior. In addition to the basic unit of mora which indicates the place of pitch-fall, syllables are required as accentual units on which accentual rules such as reduction or preaccentuation operate. Accentual rules affect basic word accents when words occur in a sequence, forming a phrase accentually, and produce one pitch pattern for the entire phrase.

2. Child accentual patterns

Table 1 and Table 2[2] present the pitch patterns of all the identified nouns the child produced in the recorded material of 60 minutes and 70 minutes each, consisting of natural dialogue between the child and her mother and enlisted child responses.

At the age 1;6, the child's vocabulary was still very limited and one-word utterances dominated her speech, though she began to use multiple-word constructions.[3] Words, including those for father, mother, grandmother, bath, etc., which remained fairly constant segmentally from the earliest months of development, were pronounced with characteristic Japanese pitch patterns and assumed at this stage relatively stable phonetic forms, though her speech contained unidentifiable utterances and repetitive sequences with sounds familiar from babbling stages.

At 1;11, after an interval of five months, the child's language showed dramatic changes in number of words used, phonetic stability, utterance length, and utterance variety. Multiple-word utterances were spoken very freely and in various constructions. Even three or four word sequences were not infrequent, along with the occurrence of noun-following particles such as ga or wa, illustrated in the following examples:

syntactic structures   examples

  N N Neg P   oʃi:ŋo koe na:i yo
                         'This is not an apple.'

```
N  N  N  N  P        papa ni:/kai ue o:/sinoto/yo
                     'Father is upstairs, working.'
N  P  V              temme na a:u⤴
                     'Is there television?'
N  N  Cop  P  P      ku:mpata' to𝄪u na no/yo
                     'There is only one Teddy bear.'
```

The data under consideration show the following results in the child's acquisition of accentuation at this stage:

The unit of accent

The most striking feature of the child noun accentuation at 1;6 is that she produced no change in pitch contours in long syllable types of (C)VV, (C)VN and (C)VC. The second mora in such syllables, whether it is a vowel length, a vowel [i] or [e], a nasal or a consonant,[4] is always pronounced on the same pitch level as the preceding mora; thus, the entire syllable is either high-pitched or low-pitched, without change in pitch levels within the syllable. See, for example, the following items in Table 1: high-pitched, ba:ča (37), čitta (8); low-pitched, pa:či (6), čiči (5). Since pitch fall in a word occurs at the end of a syllable, not after the first mora, a syllable, not a mora, constitutes the basic unit of accent for indicating the location of a pitch fall. The child has not acquired the mora-syllable division, accentually nor segmentally.

At the age 1;6, the unit of accent in the child system for bearing accent is assumed to have the following syllable structures:

syllable structures	examples
(C)V	bu (10), ya (28)
(C)VV	na: (16), nagnag (18)
(C)VN	wa~wa (4), bo~bo (21)
(C)VC	totto (30), čitta (8)
(C)VVN	u:mma (3), ne:~ne (7)

At the age 1;11, syllables are still considered
to constitute the basic unit of accent, since in the
overwhelming number of words long syllables are
pronounced on the same pitch level without change in
the middle. However, though not a single occurrence
was observed in noun accentuation presented in Table
2, the beginning of accentual mora-syllable division
was noted in a very limited occurrences in the
syllable type of (C)VV. In negative nai forms, verb
negatives and a few adjectives, a pitch-fall was
observed after the first vowel, as in na:i no, ina:i
yo 'not be', iya:nai no 'not need' and ita:i 'painful',
in variation with forms like na:i no, ina:i, iyanai no,
ita:i, akai 'red', etc., which occurred much frequently
without pitch-fall after the first vowel in the VV
sequence. In this type of syllable, segmentally too,
mora division began to appear, each mora recognized
as separate elements by the child, as seen in such
occurrence as ita: i, which was pronounced emphatically
with distinct mora division.

In other types of syllables, in the type (C)VN,
only two examples showing this division were found in
the analyzed data: the noun na:npa (28) and the form
papan for the sequence papa plus no 'father's'.
Segmentally, syllabic nasals became mostly distinct
nasal segments separable from the following consonant,
or clearly audible word-finally. No example was
found in the syllable type (C)VC, indicating pitch
fall after the first mora or marked pitch change
between the first and the second mora.

On the basis of these observations, at the initial
stage of accentual acquisition, syllables function as
the basic unit for producing pitch patterns without any
division indicating the unit of moras. It was observed
that mora-syllable division began to be acquired only
at the end of the second year of language development,
relatively late in phonological development.
Furthermore, the acquisition of this dichotomy is not
uniform, proceeding from (C)VV, to (C)VN and then to
(C)VC, of which no occurrence was observed at this
stage.

Accentual patterns of nouns

The child's accentual patterns at two stages, 1;6 and 1;11, are presented in Diagram 1, on the basis of surface pitch patterns of nouns described in Table 1 and Table 2.

Diagram 1. Accentual patterns of nouns

Nouns:	1-syl.		2-syl.		3-syl.		4-syl.	
	PP	UP	PP	UP	PP	UP	PP	UP

At 1;6:

   Accented: s̄s   s's   s̄ss ⎫ s'ss
                                       s̄ss ⎭

                                     sss ss's

   Unaccented: s̄ s   ss ⎱ ss   sss ⎱ sss
                             ss ⎰   sss*

At 1;11:

   Accented: s̄s s's   s̄ss ⎫ s'ss   s̄sss s'sss
                                   s̄ss ⎭

                                   sss ⎫ ss's   sss ss's ss
                                   ssss ⎭

                                           ssss ⎫ sss's
                                           ssss ⎬
                                           ssss ⎭

                        ss ⎫ ss'
                        ss ⎭

   Unaccented: s̄ s   ss ⎫ ss   sss ⎫ sss   ssss* ⎫ ssss
                            ss ⎭   sss ⎭   ssss ⎭

where, s stands for a syllable, PP for phonetic patterns and UP for underlying patterns. Accentual patterns marked by * indicate that these patterns were observed in other recordings though no example was found in the data treated here.

At the age 1;6, as seen in Table 1, di-syllabic
nouns occurred in three pitch patterns, H-L, L-H
and Level, whereas tri-syllabic nouns showed pitch
patterns H-L-L, H-L-H, L-H-L, L-H-H and Level. Since
the occurrence of level pitch contours is considered
as a phonetic variation of L-H pitch contour, di-
syllabic nouns are analyzed to have two basic accentual
patterns, initial accent and no accent.[5] Three
syllable nouns are assumed to have three accentual
patterns in the child's underlying system, initial,
medial and no accent, since level pitch contours are
a phonetic variation of the L-H-H pattern, as in di-
syllabic nouns, and the H-L-H pattern is considered
as inaccurate realization of the H-L-L pattern.[6]
Thus, at this stage, with the absence of the contrast
between final accent and no accent, the child accentual
system has only n-possible patterns for n-syllable
words, one minus from the adult accentual patterns;
di-syllabic words show two-way contrast, whereas
three syllable words exhibit three way contrast.
Mono-syllabic nouns, which occurred with level pitch,
were all analyzed as unaccented. There were no
examples of nouns consisting of more than three syllables.
    In the data taken at 1;11, in which the child
speech contained various sequences of a noun plus a
particle, though still rather infrequent compared to
those without noun particles, word-final pitch fall
began to appear, as illustrated by the following
examples: hana:\wa 'as for flower', a:ʃi:\yo 'my leg',
o:ʧi:\wa 'my house is', ŋa:u\no 'cat's', which occurred
in alternation with forms without pitch fall. On the
basis of these occurrences, though very limited and
inaccurate in some forms, we may assume that at this
stage the child began to acquire final accent in
contrast with no accent, which produced a three-way
contrast in di-syllabic nouns, approaching a step
toward the adult system with $n+1$ possible accentual
patterns for n-mora words. In three syllable nouns
no example was observed to indicate a clear contrast
between final accent and no accent, with less complete
paradigm in four syllable nouns. As in the age 1;6,
mono-syllabic nouns occurred in one pitch pattern,
analyzed as unaccented.

Both at 1;6 and 1;11, we note that surface
pitch patterns the child produced considerably
differed from those of adults, indicating insufficient
acquisition of phonetic realization rules.
Especially noted is the frequent occurrence of level
pitch contours without lowinitialness, such as H-H,
H-H-H, or H-H-L, which were[7]observed even when the
initial syllable was short,[7] and the occurrence of
high pitch after a low-pitched syllable following
a high pitch, as in H-L-H, which was analyzed as
a phonetic variation of initial accent H-L-L in this
study.[8]

The child data analyzed above show that the
acquisition of a phonological feature, that is,
marked accent, indicating a distinctive pitch fall,
precedes that of surface phonetic features such as
lowinitialness, giving support to the generally
claimed principle that phonological features are
acquired prior to phonetic features. It is
observed that among accentual patterns initial
accent[9] is the earliest acquired pattern, whereas
final accent, which has the same pitch contour as
no accent, indistinguishable by itself, is the last
to be acquired. Here we may add that the child data
contained no example indicating clearly the acquisition of accentual rules such as accent reduction
in a phrase. At this stage, each word was pronounced
with distinct word accent not affected by phrase
rules, as in the sequences kiyo toma 'yellow ball'
or o:kɪːno jiji 'big letter'.

Notes

[1]For the discussion of the difference between
'pitch' in a tone language like Mandarin Chinese
and 'pitch' in a pitch-accent language like standard
Japanese, see McCawley, 1968 and 1979. Hyman, 1978,
also discusses in detail the issue of tone and accent.

[2]The data for Table 1 are based on 60 minutes of
recording, taken in two sessions in one day, in which
the child was asked questions by her mother on things
and animals in books, on her father who was out and
her grandmother, with natural dialogue on the child
activities such as going to toilet, etc.

The data for Table 2 are based on two recordings, 30 minutes and 40 minutes. She was asked to name things in her books, to tell stories, and was questioned on her kin people. She was also engaged in activities like drawing, going to the toilet, eating oranges and drinking tea and milk.

[3]Though at earlier stages, utterances like papa bu: 'Daddy, car' (at 1;0) or mama:~ma 'Mommy, food' (at 1;1) were observed, multiple-word constructions began to occur around 1;4 with some regularity. At 1;6, they consisted mostly of the following types: noun + particle no, negative + no or yo, noun + particle with or without a particle, noun + noun, noun + verb. Miyahara, 1974, states that in her child two-word utterances appeared at 1;4 and that particles were first recorded at 1;6.

[4]The vowel [i] which varied with [e] in the same word is ana- lyzed as the high vowel in the underlying form as distinct from the mid vowel [e] which showed no variation. The second element of a long syllable is often very short and/or inseparable from the following element. Syllabic nasals were not fully developed as one nasal segment, sounding as a prenasalization of the fol- lowing consonant, or incomplete velar closure word-finally.

[5]Alternatively, this can be analyzed as final accent, with the result that the child system then lacks unaccented patterns.

[6]Alternatively, this can be analyzed as a distinct accentual pattern, but other facts including variation show that this analysis is preferable.

[7]Level pitch contours occurred in both long and short sylla- bles, though rather infrequent when the initial syllable was short.

[8]The same contour also occurred in multiple-word utterances, such as mama/no 'mother's', cuppo/wa 'as for the train', with considerable frequency.

[9]Here we may mention that a marked tendency to place initial accent (and also medial accent in tri-syllabic nouns) was ob- served in accentual variation. For example, in Table 2, in adult unaccented or final accented nouns, 21 out of 45 di-sylla- bic nouns showed variation with initial accented forms. This is an indication of the child's strategy to cope with the acquisi- tion of the accentual system in which the location of a pitch- fall constitutes the most prominent feature.

Table 1. Child accentual patterns at 1;6: Noun accent[1]

	Gloss	Child forms
1.	mother	ma͞ma, ma͞~ma, ma:͞ma, ma͞:, ma͞?(2)
2.	father	pa͞pa(4), pa:͞pa(2), pa͞po:, pu͞pa, pa͞pa?, pa͞pu:, pa͞ppa, pa͞:
3.	food	u͞mma(3), u:͞mma, u:͞mma?, u͞mma, ma͞?
4.	dog	wə͞wə, wɔ:͞wɔ, wa~͞wa~, wa͞~wa, wə͞wə, o:͞wə, wə͞
5.	urine	ʃi͞ʃʃi, či͞čči, ʃi͞ʃʃi, či:͞čči, či͞:, či͞(2)
6.	pants	pa͞či, pa:͞či, pa:͞č
7.	sleep	ne~ne, ne:~ne, ne:~ne
8.	train	či͞tta, či͞ta
9.	train	ʃu͞po, či͞bo
10.	car	bu͞bu(2), bu͞
11.	bee	ha:͞či
12.	stomach	po~po
13.	cat	ŋa:͞ŋa, na͞ŋə
14.	bus	bu͞ʃ
15.	yes	ha:͞i
16.	what	na͞(4), na:͞e, na:͞, na:͞⌄
17.	carrying	u~bu
18.	tidying	na:͞i̯nai̯, na:͞nai̯, naə͞haə̯, na͞na?, na͞inai̯(2)
19.	leaf	ha͞ppa(I)
20.	horse	o:͞ma
21.	dragonfly	bo~͞bo(I)
22.	tiger	to:͞ɟa(I)
23.	this	ko͞?, ku͞?(3), ku͞(3), ko͞:, ku͞~, ko͞e
24.	train	po͞po(2), po͞po:, pa͞pu:, po͞po:(2), po͞po, po͞papo
25.	cap	bo͞či:
26.	bath	bu:͞we, bu:͞we, bu͞:
27.	train	di~͞ča, ɟe~͞ta, ɟi͞ʃa

96

28. no   īya(3), īya:, ȳa, ȳa?
29. pig   būta:(2)
30. fish   tōto, tottto
31. mouse   tūtu
32. father   papaĉa
33. goldfish kĩtotto, kũtatta
34. fish   ototo(I), ototo
35. pain   taĝtaị
36. over   o?øuhaɛ, o?øuhaị, oçi:ha
37. grand-   oba:ta, ba:ĉa, batta
    mother
38. bath   bu:ĉa

Table 2. Child accentual patterns at 1;11: Noun accent

1. mother   mama(9), mama:(2), ma:ma(3), mamma
2. father   papa(8), papa:(3), pappa, pa:pa(3)
3. train   ŝuppo(3), ŝuppo:(2), ŝupo:, ŝupo(3),
              ŝippo, ŝuppoị, ŝi:ppo, ŝuba(2), ĉupo,
              ŝuppo(4), ĉippo, ĉipo
4. bus   baŝu, ba:ĉi, baĉĉi, ba:ĉu, baĉi, boĉi
5. urine   ŝikko, ĉikko, ĉi
6. bear   ku?ma
7. chopstick ha:ŝi
8. squirrel biĉĉu(I)
9. which   doĉĉi
10. dog   wa:ĉa
11. ship   øuhe(I), uhe, u:he
12. cake   keki
13. kitten   piĉĉi(2)
14. sleep   ɲe:ɲe, ne:he, ne:nhe
15. lemon   li:ma?(I)

97

16. peeling   mu̅ki(7), mu̅ke(3)
17. more   mo̅tto(4), mo̅:tto(3), mo̅to(2), mo̅ččo:
18. car   bu̅:bu, bu̅bu
19. name   ša:mbo, šambo, čambo
20. who   ta:e
21. rain   amme, amɲe, a:me, ame
22. not yet   maɲa(3), mada(2), ma:ɲa
23. all   jembo(2), je:mbo, je:mbo, je:mbo
24. dog   wanwan, wa~wa~(2), wa:nwan, wanwa, wəwə,
          wanwan, wa:nwan, wa?
25. letter   jiji(3), ji:ji(2), jiji?(2), ji:ja,
          jiji(2), ji:ji:
26. orange   mika:, mika?, mi?ka:n, mikkan, muika, muka
27. standing   tačči, tačči
28. cat   ŋa:u(2), ŋa:u, ŋu:, ɲa:ŋa
29. what   na?, na, ni:, nani, na:ni(2), naɲi, na:ɲi
30. pants   pa:nči, pa:nču
31. please   do̅:zo(I)
32. red   aka, a:ka
33. book   ho̅~
34. airplane   bu̅, bu̅:
35. monster   kaᴀju, ka:ju, ka:ʃi(2), koju(2), kaju(3),
          ko:ju(2)
36. ball   bo̅:u, bo̅:bu
37. leaf   happa, pa̅?, pa̅
38. upstairs   ni:kai(2)
39. truth   o~to, honto, onto:
40. balloon   øu:če, øu:še:(2), øu:šen(4), øu:še(2),
          øu:če(2), øu:šen, u:še, u:šen, ku:še:,
          øu:še, øu:če, øu:še:n, øu:ši:n

98

41. watch   to̩ke:

42. horse   o̩ma, om̩ma

43. there   mu:ko

44. thank you   ta~k̩u, tank̩u

45. drum   tae̩ko(4), taeko(3), tai̩ko(2), tai̩ko

46. give me   ču̩a:(2), ču:a̩, ču̩ai̩, ču̩a, šu̩a:, ča(3),
                ča:, čo:, či(3)

47. newspaper   šim̩bu, šim̩bo

48. other   hok̩ka:

49. shoes   k̩uk̩k̩u

50. that   soe

51. mask   me?(I)

52. up   ue, we, e

53. yellow   ki:yo(2), ki̩yo

54. round   ma:ŋu(4), ma:ŋ̩u(2), ba:ŋ̩u

55. train   de:nča, ji̩ša

56. leg   a:ši:, a̩či, a:ši, a̩ča

57. hand   te̩te, te:te(2)

58. mouth   ku:či, kuču

59. ear   mi̩mi(I), mi̩mi, mi:mi

60. eye   me:me, ŋe:ŋe. ŋe:ŋe

61. paper   ka:ni, k̩a:hi, ka̩mi, ka̩mi(2)

62. flower   ha̩na, ha̩na(2), ha̩na:ˈ

63. apple   riŋ̩go, i̩yo, ni:yo, jiŋgo(3), jiŋ̩ŋo(2),
                ji:ŋgo(3), ji:ŋŋo:, o̩ji:ŋgo

64. no   i̩ya(3), i̩ya:(2), ya(6), i̩ya(3), ya̩(2), ya:(2),
                ya:(2), ya?(5), i̩ya:(3), i̩ya (2)

65. this   ko̩ye(9), ko̩e(9), ko:e(3), ko:ya(2), ku̩e,
                koe(2), ko(3), ko:(4), ko:e, ku, ko̩ye(3),
                ko̩ya(4), ka̩ya, ko̩ai

66. that   a̯ye, a:ya, aye(2), a̅ye

67. here   ko̅ko(2), ko:ko(3), ko̅ko(2), ko̅ko(3),
              ko:ko(2), kokko(3)

68. house   o:či, o:uči(2), o:či:', očči, hočči

69. tea   oča(2), oža(2)

70. ball   yo̅yo, yo:yo(2), yo:yo, yo̅yo(8), yoiyo

71. fish   to̅to, totto, toto, totto, toto:

72. telephone de:nwa(I), de:~na(I), de:~ya, denya, denha

73. milk   hu:nu:(2), ŋu:ŋu:(3), ŋu:ŋu(3), ŋu:ŋu:, ŋu:ŋ

74. nose   ha̅na(2)

75. ball   čama(3), čama?, čuma, toma(2)

76. dirty   bačči, ba:te

77. mouse   čučču, ču

78. flag   patta(I)

79. next   čugi, teni

80. tail   šippo(2)

81. bear   kumpotta(2), kumbotta, ku?bača, ku~pačča?,
              kumbata~, kumpača, kumpata, čumbotta(2),
              kumpotan, čimbota, kumpota, bumbotta

82. monkey   čašša, šoššo, šiššа~, čačča, ço?ço, ča:iča(3
              čaiča~, šarša, ča:rča(3), ča:rčan(2), čačča:
              ča:ruča:(2), šarša, ša:rušama, šašama

83. wolf   okkani, okane, okane:, o:kani, oka:ne,
              hakka:ne

84. goldfish kintotto, ku~totto

85. train   šupoča, šubuta, šubutača

86. rabbit   u:šaša

87. father   papača

88. ball   čamača, čamaču

89. baby   akaka, akkača?

90. television temme, te:mne, temi

91. pillow   makkuwa

92. out   okoto

93. grandmother   ba:ča, ba:čan, bo:ta

94. airplane   ko:ki, koki, ko:ku

95. one   toču(2), çitoču(I)

96. mat   otto, otto~(2), hotton

97. work   ošinoto, ošu:noto, ošuma, o:ši:

98. socks   čitta

99. driver   u:ţe:~šu:(I)   u:~tenša

100. Express   ši:~ka:nče?(I)

101. monorail   ma:bukko:(I)

102. worm   memeku:ji(I)

103. red train   akačubo

104. one by one   točujuču(3)

105. head   atama(I), ata:ma(2), atama, atama(3), ata:ma, ta:ma, atama

106. ship   okune(I), okuna, okuna(3), okune(3)

107. two   tačiu

108. mouse   do?meni(I)

109. eye   omeme, one:me

110. over   o?øumai, o?øuma:i

111. horse   o:mača, omača

112. sun   oçišuma:

113. sparrpw   šu:meča, šumeta

114. red ball   akači:ma

---

[1] Phonetic forms are transcribed in broad phonetic transcription. [V] indicates the shortness of the vowel, [:] vowel length, [Ç] a palatalized consonant, [?] glottal closure, [ŋ] a velar nasal, and [~] a nasalization. The symbol [o] is used for phonetic [ɔ] for typing convenience. Numbers in parentheses indicate the frequency of multiple occurrences. Forms marked by (I) indicate that they are repetitions of the immediately preceding mother's words.

References

1. Hyman, L.M., "Tone and/or accent", in Elements of tone, stress and intonation, edited by D.J. Napoli, Georgetown University Press, 1978.

2. Kobayashi, C., "Dialectal variation in child language", in Child language - An international perspective, edited by P.S. Dale & D. Ingram, University Park Press, 1981.

3. McCawley, J.D., The phonological component of a grammar of Japanese, Mouton, 1968.

4. McCawley, J.D., "Some tonal systems that come close to being pitch-accent systems but don't quite make it", Chicago Linguistic Society, 6, 1970, reprinted in Adverbs, vowels, and other objects of wonder, The University of Chicago Press, 1979.

5. Miyahara, K., "The acquisition of Japanese particles", Journal of child language, 1, 1974.

THE RELATIONSHIP BETWEEN PHONOLOGY AND SYNTAX IN 30 CHILDREN AGED 2;0 TO 2;6

Anne Watson and Amy Swenson
Ontario Institute for Studies in Education
Toronto, Ontario, Canada

Within phonological theory the relation between phonetic development and phonological development remains unknown (Ingram, 1981). Also, there is little consistency between phonological theory and broader theories of language development (Ferguson & Garnica, 1975). Part of the problem in developing phonological theory stems from the lack of a large data base (Ferguson & Farwell, 1975; Ferguson & Garnica, 1975). Furthermore, a lack of "a consistent set of procedures and criteria" (Ingram, 1981, p.1) makes cross-study comparisons difficult to perform.

In this study a description of the relationship between phonetic and phonological levels of development is attempted on a relatively large sample (N=30), using the standards of phonetic/phonological analysis meticulously laid out by Ingram (1981). Furthermore, a description of the relationship between these features and syntax, another aspect of language development, is also performed. Finally, some implications of these findings for language development theory are addressed.

1. METHOD

1.1 Data Description

These data are a subset of those collected for a longitudinal study of child language (Watson, in preparation). Described here are some phonological and syntactic data for all 30 children in the larger study, collected at Time 1 when the children's ages ranged from 2;0 to 2;6.

1.2 Subject Selection

Fifteen male and fifteen female subjects were selected from two-parent families where the father worked outside of the home while the mother acted as the child's primary caretaker. The children were talking in at least single-word utterances, in English. Table 1 displays a breakdown of subjects by age and sex.

Table 1: Distribution of Subjects by Age and Sex

Age	Male	Female	Total
24 months	3	-	3
25 months	2	1	3
26 months	2	3	5
27 months	2	3	5
28 months	4	1	5
29 months	2	3	5
30 months	-	4	4
Totals	n=15	n=15	N=30

1.3 Procedure

The children were tape-recorded in their homes in free play with their mothers for 15 minutes. Written contextual notes were taken by the principal investigator who interacted minimally during taping. Depending on the mothers' subsequent judgments of representativeness of this "natural, everyday conversation" a further recording session was offered, to be held no later than one week after the first (n=3 were re-recorded based on the immediate tape play-back to mothers). Verbatim transcripts were made immediately following the taping session, and mothers were given the tape and transcript for amendments to these preliminary glosses within two or three days of the taping. A further n=2 children were retaped following their mother's amending of the transcript and expressing concern at that time about the representativeness of the speech sample. All "2-session" mothers were required to select the "better" of the two tapes.

The amended transcripts were then re-amended as they were entered into a DECsystem 10 computer. Then a phonetic transcription was made on the computer hard-copy by the co-author. All transcriptions made by either author were performed while listening to the original tapes on a TCT/200 transcribing machine.

Agreement between the two authors on the finalized versions was high (94%). Reliability of the phonetic transcriptions was established by having a third party (a University of Toronto, Linguistics Department graduate student) phonetically transcribe two tapes selected from the sample. Even though this independent third party tended to make narrower distinctions between some vowel sounds which resulted in a larger count of phonetic forms, the scores appearing in this paper did not differ significantly from those derived from his transcriptions.

1.4 Syntactic Measure

As a general indication of syntactic complexity, vis a vis utterance length, a mean length of utterance (MLU) was computed in morphemes. Essentially, Miller's (1981) version of Brown's rules were used, except that negated forms of auxiliary verbs, such as "doesn't" or "can't" were counted as 2 morphemes.

1.5 Phonetic and Phonological Measures

Based on Ingram's (1981) procedures the following scores were obtained:

1. <u>Articulation Score</u> --The number of sounds mastered by the child was expressed by

this weighted score. The total sounds "acquired" and "in transition" were calculated using an individually determined criterion of frequency. These totals were then weighted in favour of the most frequently used sounds. The grand total of these weighted scores equals the "articulation score".

2. <u>CV Syllables</u> --The proportion of all phonetic forms comprised solely of a simple combination of 1 consonant + 1 vowel (in that order) was computed.

3. <u>Closed Phonetic Forms</u> --The proportion of all phonetic forms ending with a consonant was calculated.

4. <u>Phonetic Match</u> --The proportion of all different phonetic forms which match the most common phonetic form(s) of the words they were intended to represent was computed. In cases where two common adult forms exist, such as [inʌf] and [ən ʌf] for "enough", credit was given for both or either form.

5. <u>Lexical Match</u> --The proportion of all lexical items for which the child produced at least one phonetic form matching the adult - form(s) was calculated.

6. <u>Homonymous Forms</u> --The number of phonetic forms representing two or more lexical types was computed and divided into the total number of phonetic forms. An example of an homonymous form is [dɔ] where it is used to represent both "dog" and "call".

7. Homonymous Types --Any lexical type having an homonymous form as one of its phonetic types was considered an "homonymous type". For example, "dog" may be correctly pronounced as [dɔ g] once, but because it is also pronounced elsewhere in the transcript as [dɔ], a form already determined as an homonymous form (above), it is considered an homonymous type. Total homonymous types were divided into total lexical types to calculate the proportion of homonymous types.

The Articulation score (see 1, above) reflects a child's ability to produce the sounds used in spoken English. It is a measure of the phonetic inventory whose development is known to be associated with increasing maturity of the human organism (Ingram, 1976, Chapter 2). Ingram's method of calculating this score avoids giving undue credit to sounds not yet frequently used by the child.

Scores 2 and 3 each address the development of phonetic combination patterns, that is, the ability to produce the sounds in various syllabic positions. The earliest syllables children produce are CV and CVCV-reduplications (Ingram, 1976). CVC, or "closed" syllables, tend to appear roughly six months later (Ingram, 1976), with high proportions of them usually associated with older children (see Ingram, 1981, Table 12, p.101). Therefore, in the application of the speech sounds to the syllabic structure of the language, low proportions of CV Syllables (score 2) and high proportions of Closed Phonetic Forms (score 3) should be associated with better development of phonetic combination patterns.

Scores 4 and 5, Phonetic and Lexical Matching scores, both measure the child's accuracy of pronunciation. Increasing accuracy in correct phonological application of the developing sound system seems to follow a developmental pattern related to Piagetian cognitive stages (Ingram, 1976, Table 1, p.13). High proportional scores in these two measures reflect phonological accuracy.

According to Priestly (1980) a reduction of homonymy is synonymous with an "increased ability to make phonological distinctions" (p.414). Therefore, low scores on measures 6 and 7, "homonymous forms" and "homonymous types" respectively, are associated with development of phonological refinements.

In summary, the measures reflect how well a child is (1) acquiring sounds and (2),(3) combining them -- the phonetic skills. Measures (4),(5) reflect how well a child is applying the sounds meaningfully, while (6) and (7) reflect refinements being made in their application -- the phonological skills.

1.6 Analysis
    A matrix of correlation coefficients was obtained for all variables in the study.

2. RESULTS

    Correlation coefficients representing the relationships between all measures are displayed in Table 2. The results are discussed according to the phonetic/phonological taxonomy described above.

Table 2: Correlation Coefficients -- All Measures

	ART	CVS	CLF	PHM	LXM	HOF	HOT
CVS	-.09						
CLF	-.03	-.80**					
PHM	.47**	-.49**	.56**				
LXM	.19	-.55**	.62**	.77**			
HOF	-.25	.41*	-.25	-.34	-.25		
HOT	-.36*	.36*	-.23	-.38	-.16	.95**	
MLU	-.26	-.45*	.49**	.30	.44*	-.13	-.04

```
                 *  significant at p<.05
                **  significant at p<.01

        Where:  ART = Articulation Score
                CVS = Consonant-Vowel Syllables
                CLF = Closed Phonetic Forms
                PHM = Phonetic Match
                LXM = Lexical Match
                HOF = Homonymous Forms
                HOT = Homonymous Types
                MLU = Mean Length of Utterance
```

2.1 Relationships Among the Phonetic Variables

The phonetic variables were Articulation Score (ART), Consonant-Vowel Syllables (CVS) and Closed Phonetic Forms (CLF). A large, negative correlation exists between CV Syllables and Closed Phonetic Forms. Since both sets of scores are derived proportions of the total amount of phonetic forms, this result is neither surprising nor revealing in language samples consisting mainly of monosyllabic forms (mean=75% of all phonetic forms were monosyllables). In this case a high proportion of CV forms is concomitant with a low proportion of any form ending with a consonant.

More revealing is the the absence of any significant relationship between Articulation and either of the other two phonetic scores. Children with more sounds mastered were expected to be those who would also evidence the higher proportions of closed phonetic forms, which are later-appearing in development. Contrary to expectations there was a lack of correlation, suggesting instead that the number of acquired sounds has little to do with the propensity towards combining them in either simple (i.e., early appearing) or more complex ways.

2.2 Relationships Among the Phonological Variables

The phonological variables were Phonetic Match (PHN), Lexical Match (LXM), Homonymous Forms (HOF) and Homonymous Types (HOT). Phonetic Match and Lexical Match obtained a significant level of correlation (r=.77, p<.01). This suggests that the children who frequently hit upon a correct adult-like pronounciation of a targetted lexical item (i.e., high proportion of Lexical Matches) were the same children whose phonetic forms most frequently matched an adult form of their words. In other words, those who applied sounds correctly to words were also those evidencing less varied phonetic forms.

The negative, but not quite significant, correlation between Phonetic Match and Homonymous Forms suggests that those children who pronounced more recognizable words were less likey to use one phonetic form to represent two (or more) lexical items. Similarly, those same children were significantly less likely to represent any lexical item with an homonymous form as one of its phonetic forms (i.e., to use Homonymous Types). In other words, those whose "utterings" most often resembled adult words tended to make more use of the finer phonemic distinctions between sounds within words.

2.3 Phonetic Versus Phonological Variables

Table 3 demonstrates this subset of correlation coefficients, extrapolated from Table 2. Only those relationships reaching a level of significance beyond p<.10 are reported here.

Table 3: Correlation Coefficients Between Phonetic and Phonological Variables

Phonological	Phonetic ART	CVS	CLF
PHM	.47**	-.49**	.56**
LXM	-	-.55**	.62**
HOF	-	.41*	-
HOT	-.36*	.36*	-

       * significant at p<.05
      ** significant at p<.01

The significant correlation obtained between Articulation and Phonetic Match indicates that larger phonetic inventories were associated with higher proportions of correctly applied phonetic forms. This is surprising as one might have expected many phonetic "misses" (i.e., lower proportions of correctly applied forms) to result in a wider range of sounds being articulated within these incorrect phonetic forms.

Phonetic inventory size, as represented by ART, had no systematic association with proportion of lexical items pronounced correctly.

ART correlated in a negative direction with both types of Homonymy, reaching significance (r=-.36, p<.05) in the case of Homonymous Types. This negative association is not surprising in that homonymy necessarily entails the use of the same sounds in phonetic forms intended to represent different words. In young children the same sounds are often used in error, producing erroneous homonymy (e.g., /do/ for "go", "no" and "dough"). Wherever these same sounds are used it is likely that the substitution sound is one already frequently found (and scored) in the phonetic inventory, while the missed sound would frequently by a less well-used one (i.e., not scored for ART) The more homonymy in chidlren, the lower the articulation score.

Of extreme interest are the strong, significant correlations between CV Syllables and all of the Phonological variables. The negative association between CV Syllables and phonological accuracy measures suggests that as children add variety to their phonetic combinations beyond simple CV constructs, so they become more facile in producing correct phonetic forms for targetted words. Increased complexity in sound combinations occurs at the same time as increased accuracy in application of sounds. The positive association between CV Syllables and measures of Homonymy indicate that children still producing more simple sound combinations were most likely to make fewer fine phonemic distinctions within words.

The strong positive correlations observed between Closed Phonetic Forms and the phonological accuracy measures (PHM and LXM) reflect the (predictable) association between pronouncing final consonants and applying sounds in words correctly.

2.4 Relationships Between Articulation and MLU
The bottom row in Table 2 displays these relationships.

In regards to relations between MLU and the Phonetic variables, small MLU's were associated with high proportions of CV Syllables, while large

MLU's were associated with high proportions of Closed Phonetic Forms. Hence, advanced syntactic development can be said to accompany more complex phonetic combinations, but is unrelated to number of sounds mastered (ART).

The results of correlating MLU with the Phonological variables demonstrated only one significant relationship. MLU correlated positively and significantly with Lexical Match (r=.44, p=<.05). Advanced syntactic development can be said to be strongly associated with number of lexical items having at least one accurate phonetic form. It did not seem to be associated with actual numbers of correct phonetic forms produced nor with the amount of homonymy found in those utterances.

3. DISCUSSION

The relationship between phonetic and phonological development appears to be complex, but can be simplified by specifying and describing the development of different aspects of each variable.

In the first place, within phonetics, the process whereby children acquire the sounds of their language appears to be substantially different from the process whereby they learn how to combine those sounds in increasingly complex ways. It is suggested here that mastery of sounds depends primarily on the physical development of the articulatory muscles and hasn't a great deal to do with the levels of development of "language". It seems that once some kind of a phonetic inventory is available, it is used in simple combinations which frequently do not match adult forms of words. However, larger phonetic inventories are associated with greater accuracy in producing adult-like phonetic forms and less homonymy. Therefore, the more sounds mastered, the greater the likelihood of making finer discriminations between sounds, thereby producing more "hits" with attempted phonetic forms. It follows that actually producing fine phonological distinctions awaits motoric control in 24-30 month old children, whereas, according to Schvachkin (1973), awareness and perception of these distinctions is complete by 24 months of age.

The development of complexity in combinations of sounds is correlated highly with increasing ability to use those combinations accurately in producing targetted words. The ability to use longer words and to correctly say these words when one intends to say them does not seem to hinge on the size of one's phonetic inventory (at least for 2 year-olds). The development of these word length and accuracy features appears to follow a separate acquisitional path, and one that is highly interrelated. In keeping with Ferguson and Farwell's model of phonology (1975), it is suggested here that these features comprise (as a total package) those susceptible to "individual variation in phonological development" while the ability to produce sounds and to produce fine distinctions between sounds is tied to those "'universal phonetic tendencies' which result from the physiology of the human vocal tract and central nervous system" (p.437).

The phonetic/phonological distinction applied in defining the variables to be measured in this study turns out to be inapplicable to Ferguson and Farwell's model. Some aspects of phonetic development, namely the combining of sounds into syllables, are associated with individual differences in general linguistic development, as are some aspects of phonological development, namely lexical matching accuracy. On the other hand, those aspects of phonetic and phonological mastery which concern the ability to form sounds and produce fine phonemic discriminations between these sounds, are likely tied to physiological development.*

This conclusion is supported by the lack of significant difference between this group of 30 children and an age-peer group of 8 linguistically stimulated children on number of sounds acquired (Swenson and Watson, 1981), despite large differences between these groups on Closed Syllables, Lexical and Phonetic Matches, and MLU.

Furthermore, because MLU is not associated with the children's age in this age-restricted sample (r=.08, n.s.), MLU can be described as operating under an individually determined rate of development. It is proposed here that the determinants of the individualized development of MLU in any child operate simultaneously on those interrelated phonetic and phonological features not associated with physiological maturation. The results support this proposal; MLU, CV Syllables, Closed Phonetic Forms and Lexical Match are highly interrelated, yet unrelated to Articulation Score.

In future, language development theory must account for the levels of development in any one feature (such as syntactic complexity) being associated with levels of development of other features, such as phonological accuracy. The child who is linguistically advanced compared to his/her peers seems to be similarly relatively advanced in many features which concern the application of sound to meaning. These might be

----

*Homonymy appears to be related to both types of development. However, results based on these scores are suspect because neither Homonymous Forms nor Homonymous Types take into account acceptable forms of homonymy, such as "two", "to" and "too".

described as the language variables, as distinct
from the speech variables (the phonetic
inventory). The development of the speech
variables appears quite unrelated to language
development, at least at age two. Perhaps the
growth curve for the sounds inventory has levelled
off by this age. Further research is implied.

REFERENCES

Dale, P.S. Language Development: Structure and
Function, 2nd. Edition Holt, Rinehart and
Winston, 1976.

Ferguson, C.A. and Farwell, C.B. Words and sounds
in early language acquisition. Language, 1975,
51 (2), 419-439.

Ferguson, C.A. and Garnica, O.K. Theories of
phonological development. In E. Lenneberg and E.
Lenneberg (Eds.) Foundations of Language
Development, v.1 Academic Press, 1975, 153-180.

Ingram, D. Phonological Disability in Children
London: Edward Arnold, 1976.

Ingram, D. Procedures for the Phonological
Analysis of Children's Language Baltimore:
University Park Press, 1981.

Lee, L. Developmental Sentence Analysis
Evanston, Ill.: Northwestern University Press,
1974.

Miller, J.F. Assessing Language Production in
Children Baltimore: University Park Press
1981.

Priestly, T.M.S. Homonymy in child phonology. J.of
Child Language 1980, 7, 413-427.

Schvachkin, N.K. The development of phonemic
speech perception in early childhood. English
translation (from Russian) in Ferguson and
Slobin (Eds.) Studies of Child Language
Development New York: Holt, 1973.

Swenson, A. and Watson, A. The effects of an
infant language stimulation program on phonology
and syntax two years of age Paper presented

at the Second International Congress for the
Study of Child Language. University of British
Columbia, August, 1981.
Watson, A. The Interrelationships Among Various
Aspects of Language Development in Two-Year-Olds
University of Toronto Doctoral Dissertation, in
preparation.

CHILDREN'S AWARENESS OF THEIR OWN PHONO-ARTICULATORY ACTIVITY

Branka ZEI
University of Geneva, Department of Psychology
24, rue du Général Dufour
1204 - GENEVE (Switzerland)

Highly sophisticated techniques of experimental phonetics have, no doubt, revealed many articulatory parameters of speech sounds. They have not however yielded results telling which of the parameters are potentially the elements that are controlled in speech production. In order to find out about the articulatory features that appear to the speaker as being of primary importance for his production of speech sounds, an experiment was done in which naive subjects were asked to describe how they made speech sounds. As the subject can only describe the features that he has become aware of, awareness as such came into the focus of attention.

The aim of this paper is, on the one hand, to shed some light on the articulatory parameters that appear to be of psychological importance to speech production, and on the other to describe the development of awareness of speech sound production in children aged 4 to 9.

Within the framework of Piaget's genetic theory of knowledge, awareness is defined as the conscious knowledge and understanding of the functioning and the structure of one's own cognitive unconscious. Awareness is therefore considered to be the result of a cognitive process which Piaget calls "la prise de conscience". As the becoming aware is a cognitive process in itself, it involves an assimilation of sensorimotor actions into the existing conceptual schemes. It also involves an interiorization of sensorimotor actions thus leading towards the elaboration of concepts. It therefore appears that the subject cannot become aware of an action unless he already possesses or constructs the appropriate representation schemes. The degree of awareness thus seems to be determined by the subject's conceptual framework. The conceptual framework in question must not be taken as a conglomerate of concepts but as a coherent system of coordinated notions.

Having defined awareness of sensorimotor actions as conceptual representations of these actions, a study of awareness
becomes the study of conceptual representations. Now, an
observer can have access to the subject's awareness only
through some of the subject's semiotic expressions e.g.
drawings, gestures, language. In our experiment language
played this role so that the subject of the study was children's conceptual representations of their own speech sound
production, as expressed by means of language.

In our experiment, the population consisted of 60 children aged 4 to 9 divided into 6 groups of 10 per age. Their
first language was English and they were attending the
International School of Geneva. Prior to the experiment,
age group 4 had not been taught how to read or write. The
children were interviewed separately and were asked to pro-
nounce one by one 14 different sounds and to describe how
they had produced them (e.g. Experimenter : Could you please
say /b/. Child : /b/. Experimenter : How did you make it ?).
The phonemes were presented in the following order : /ə,s,
g,i,b,æ,t,ɔ,u,ei,m,a,əu,z/.

Considering the fact that our questions broke to some
extent, or at least diminished the automaticity of action,
an element of active regulation was introduced. Many children spontaneously slowed down their phono-articulatory
activity in order to be able to observe it. This brought an
element of choice and comparison of one action with other
possible actions thus leading to an awareness of the most
actively controlled parameters. Now what are the articulatory features that the subject may become aware of ? It
is well known that articulatory parameters have little stability across different speakers. As far as vowels are
concerned experimental phonetic research has shown that
neither specific articulatory positions nor absolute formant values were universally invariable for a given vowel
(Fant G. 1973, Dunn 1950). It was shown that most of the
acoustic and articulatory features are relational in
character and thus imply comparisons rather than absolute
values (Fant G. 1973, Peterson G.E. 1951, Dunn 1950). As
far as consonants are concerned, their articulatory features
show a little more stability across different speakers.
Bilabial closure for example is not usually replaced by
another kind of closure that would yield the same acoustic

effect. Nasal resonance also seems to be achieved solely by the lowering of the soft palate.

Having in mind numerous articulatory variations one could expect different subjects to give different descriptions of pronunciations of the same phoneme. In addition to this, each articulatory movement can further be analysed into a number of phases :
- the starting (neutral/resting) position
- the displacement as such
- the target position
- the release movement (off target position)
- final (neutral/resting) position.

Faced with such a variety of observable sensorimotor parameters, we presumed that the subject would choose those that appear as being of primary importance.

Experimental Data

The children's answers were classified according to the types of descriptors they used. Two categories of descriptors were thus distinguished : those referring to various organs and those referring to various aspects of speech production. By organs were meant parts of the body having a specific function in the production and modification of the air-stream. The children mentioned the following organs : lips, tongue, teeth, throat, chest, abdomen and mouth (1). By aspects were meant the accompanying activities like breathing, blowing, pushing, as well as the vibratory effects like infra-sound (called "vibrations") and sound proper (called "acoustic aspect").

The answers concerning each of the organs and aspects were then subdivided into a number of "features" one of which (called "use of ...") designated the identification of the organ involved while the other features denoted particular movements, states, shapes and positions of eah organ.

The data, which included 1730 verbal answers and 64 answers given by gesture, were submitted to Benzecri's

(1) The term "mouth" was used by the children to denote the oral cavity as a composite organ stretching from the lips to the pharynx.

(1973) statistical technique of factor analysis of correspondances which enabled us to grasp the structural aspect of the data as well as their oppositional character.

Feature occurrences

All the features did not have the same frequency of occurrence throughout ages 4-9. Oral and abdominal features, which were considered to denote the more general aspects of phonetic activity have somewhat similar curves. They start with a relatively high frequency of occurrence and, after an initial rise from age 4 to 5, decrease reaching their lowest point at age 8.

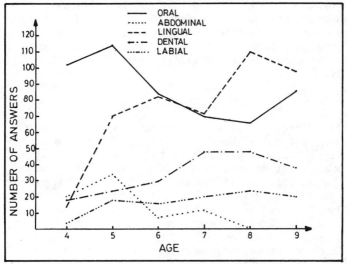

Figure 1 - Total number of occurrences of oral, abdominal, lingual, dental and labial features at each age.

The features denoting specifically articulatory aspects have the opposite tendency. They start with a relatively low frequency, increase up to age 8 and slightly decrease at age 9.

On the whole in the expression of awareness of phonetic activity we can distinguish four periods. The initial period (age 4) is marked by the predominance of general aspects of speech production concerning oral, laryngeal and abdominal activity. The second period (ages 5, 6, 7) is characterized by an ever increasing expression of specifically articulatory aspects (i.e. those concerning lingual, labial, dental, guttural and air-supply features) and a decreasing expression of global aspects of speech production.

The third period (age 8) is marked by a relative predominance of articulatory aspects (oral features have their lowest value while abdominal features do not appear at all).

The fourth period (age 9) is marked by a slight decrease of expression of specifically articulatory aspects. The observed increase in frequency of oral features does not however allow us to conclude that the global aspect of speech production has increased. This is because the mentioned increase concerns two features (i.e. "mouth rounding" and "location (of activity) inside mouth") that can not be taken as denoting typically general aspects of speech production.

Types of features

In order to compare some general aspects of various features, all the answers were regrouped into new categories. Each category was defined by one general trait. Thus for example all answers that denoted the identification(1) of an organ were considered to belong to the same category while those expressing various movements and activities(2) were put into another. New categories varied from one organ/ aspect to another but several were the same.

The two categories common to all organs were :
-     organ identification
-     movement/activity involved.

A comparison of the frequency curves (figure 2) shows that the two categories have opposing tendencies.

---

(1)   This included features like : "I used my lips", "I did it by my lips", "I talked with my lips".

(2)   This included features like : "lip opening", "lip closing", "lip rounding", "lips move up", "lips move down", etc..

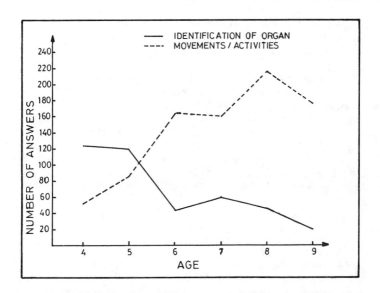

Figure 2 - Total number of occurrences of features denoting
organ identification and various movements and
activities.

We can see that at ages 4-5, in the majority of answers, the children simply identified the organ involved.
On further questions most of the four and the five year-
olds explained that they used the mentioned organs for talking, speaking or saying something. Thus it seems that in
this case the organ (part of the body), its motor activity
and its functional result (communication) conceptually
appear as a whole. Most of the four year olds did not
express any awareness of the intermediate activity of producing speech sounds. To the question "How did you make
it ?" they answered "By talking with my .... (name of
organ)" or "I used my ... (name of organ) for speaking".
At age 6 the conceptual dissociation of organs (parts of
the body) and their movements is more frequent and it continues throughout ages 6-9 (1). Originally unique (global)
conceptual schemes gradually become conceived of as composed of various substructures involving finer and finer
distinctions of actions and parts of organs. Organs taken

_____

(1) This statement is true only in the context of speech
     production.

globally are mentioned less and less because they are assigned less and less of an inherent (self evident or even necessary) power of speaking activity.

This phenomenon of gradual differentiation of the parts of a complex conceptual scheme, (which resembles the analogous phenomenon on the sensorimotor level) reflects first of all in the increasing number of phonetic features and dimensions on which they were manifested. By "dimension" we mean a common trait serving as a basis of comparison for opposing features, e.g. on the dimension "direction of movement" we find the features: upwards, downwards, sideways, forwards, inwards and outwards.

Dimensions and their corresponding features expressed at each age.

* = more than five occurrences
X = five or fewer occurrences

Dimension	Feature	Age					
		4	5	6	7	8	9
Type of air-passage used	Nasal		X			X	X
	Oral (mouth)	*	*	*	*	*	*
State of oral air-passage	Closed/obstructed		X	X	X	X	
	Open	*	X	*	X	*	X
State of guttural passage	Blocked			*	X	X	X
	Hollow					X	X
Organ identification	Lips	*	*	X	X	X	X
	Teeth	X	*	X	*	X	X
	Tongue	*	*	*	*	*	*
	Throat (velar + laryngo-pharyngeal area)	*	X	*	*	*	*
	Throat (velar specified by demonstration)		*		*	*	*
	Chest	X	X		X		
	Abdomen	*	*	*	*		X
Organ movement	Mouth	X	X	X			
	Lips	X	X	X	*	X	X
	Throat						X

Dimension	Feature	Age					
		4	5	6	7	8	9
Shape of oral (mouth) orifice	Rounded		X	X	X	X	*
	Straight (nonrounded)		X			X	*
Type of mouth movement	Closing	X	*	*	*	X	*
	Opening	*	*	*	*	*	*
	Rounding	X	X	*	X	X	*
Direction of mouth movement	Upwards		X	*		X	X
	Downwards		X	*		X	X
	Forwards (protrusion)					X	
	Inwards (protrusion, rounding)			X	X	X	X
	Outwards (spreading/protrusion)		X	X	X	*	X
	Sideways (spreading)						X
Part of mouth involved	Front					X	X
	Middle						X
	Back			X	X	X	*
	Top		X			X	X
State of lips	Closed/together	X	X	X	*	*	
	Open						X
Shape of lip opening	Rounded			X	X	X	X
	Spread stretched				X		
	Straight (neutral) (nonrounded)						X
Type of lip movement	Closing	X	X	*	*	*	*
	Opening	X	X	*	*	*	*
	Rounding					*	
Direction of lip movement	Outwards (Spread & protrusion)		X		X	X	
	Inwards (protrusion – tight closure)		X	X	X	X	*
Part of lips involved	Middle					X	X
	Corners						X

Dimension	Feature	Age 4	5	6	7	8	9
Tongue position/ contact	Against teeth		*	*	*	*	*
	At top of mouth/gums	X	*	X	X	*	*
	In "normal" place, floating (doesn't touch anything) off the bottom of mouth		X			*	X
	At bottom of mouth		X	X		*	*
	In the middle of mouth					X	X
Shape of tongue	Straight	X	X	X	X		X
	Curled			X	X	X	X
Direction of tongue movement	Upwards		X	*	*	*	*
	Downwards			*	*	*	*
	Forwards			X	*	*	*
	To the back				*	*	*
	To the front			*			
Tongue tension	Stiff tongue					X	
Part of tongue involved	Front (tip)		X	*	X	*	X
	Sides		X	X	X	X	
	Middle		X	X	X	*	X
	Back		X	X	X	X	*
Row of teeth	Top/upper teeth				X	X	
	Bottom/lower teeth			X	X	X	
Teeth position/ movement	Together/closure	X	*	*	*	*	*
	Apart/opening			X		X	*
Speed of action	Slow						X
	Fast					X	*
Auditory impression	Whisper (voiceless)	X					
	Buzzing, hissing, strident		X	X		X	X
	Low pitch						X
	High pitch						X
Vibratory sensations	Vibrations	X	X			X	X

126

Dimension	Feature	Age					
		4	5	6	7	8	9
Sound source	Voice		X	*	*	*	*
	Noise			X	X	X	X
	Sound			X	X	X	X
Air supply	Breath/breathing		X	*	*	*	*
	Blowing		X	*		*	*
Syllabic structure	CV/VC			CV	VC	VC	VC
Pushing effort	Pushing		X	*	X		*

As shown in these tables, some of the dimensions concern target states, shapes and positions (i.e. more static aspects) while other concern movements as such and their directions (kinetic aspects).

In order to find out whether there was any difference, in terms of awareness, between static and kinetic aspects of speech production, all the answers expressing an awareness of a state, position or shape of an articulatory organ were grouped together and quantitatively compared with those expressing movements and actions.

We notice that the awareness of static and kinetic aspects of articulation increases with age and that many more answers concern kinetic than static aspects. It appears that on the level of representation, movements override in importance the target states of articulation at all ages.

If articulation were a matter of succession of target states one would expect target positions to be conceptualized at least to the same extent as the movements themselves.

Obviously the functionally inherent purpose of articulatory movements is not to reach target positions but to produce sounds for communication. In this context target positions appear as end-states that are among the inevitable but unimportant results of articulatory actions. We see in figure 3 that the increase of awareness of static aspects is nearly parallel to that of the kinetic aspects.

127

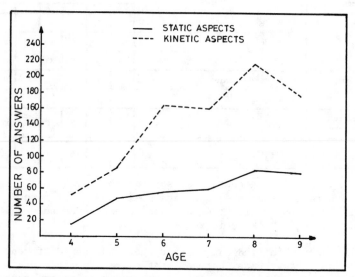

Figure 3 - Number of occurrences of answers denoting static and kinetic aspects of sound production.

A comparison of curves representing the number of features and dimensions with those representing kinetic and static aspects reveals that the increase in features and dimensions concerns the kinetic aspects more than the static ones.

Since articulation involves sequences of movements we can suppose that verbal expression of awareness of these movements implies concepts of succession in space and time which, in turn, involve operations of placement, displacement, relative displacement and co-displacements.

Indeed the awareness of sequences of movements (phases of articulation) was not expressed at all ages and its accuracy and frequency also varied. It concerned the closing/opening stages of plosives /b,m,t/ and the opening/closing stages of the diphthongal glides /eɪ/ and /ɘʊ/.

The number of answers in which the children spontaneously pointed out the sequences of movements varied with age in the following manner:

Number of answers	Age					
	4	5	6	7	8	9
	–	4	11	14	10	21

At age 5, in two answers the given order of phases was incorrect. The children noticed that there were two phases but could not reconstruct their exact sequence. As of age 6 all sequences of movements were correctly reconstructed. Most of the answers concerned the mouth/lip closing/opening for /b/ and /m/ and only a few referred to /t/ and the diphthongs. It is interesting to note that the two phases mentioned for /t/ were not always the same as those mentioned for the other stop consonants. They were given at ages 8 and 9, and they mainly concerned :

phase 1 : the displacement movement of the tongue from its neutral (starting) position

phase 2 : the pressure and the pushing forward of the tongue. The release stage of /t/ was less frequently mentioned. For /b/ and /m/ throughout ages 6 to 9 the first phase concerned the mouth/lip closure and the second the mouth/lip open state or opening movement. Sequences of movements were less often given for the plosive /g/.

At ages 8 and 9 the awareness of the speed of movements was mentioned for /b/m/t/ and /g/ and concerned the release stage (off the target position) describing it as a quick movement. These consonants were spontaneously compared with vowels (both diphthongs and monophthongs) which were described in terms of slow mouth movements.

The chronological order of appearance of answers (1) expressing various types of movements and their directions was found to be the following :

Age 4 : opening
Age 5 : opening, closing
Age 6 : opening, closing, upwards, downwards, rounding
Age 7 : opening, closing, upwards, downwards, forwards, "to the back"
Age 8 : opening, closing, upwards, downwards, forwards, "to the back", outwards
Age 9 : opening, closing, upwards, downwards, forwards, "to the back", inwards.

---

(1) Only answers with more than 5 occurrences were taken into consideration.

We can conclude that at age 4 articulatory movements are mainly assimilated to one representational scheme : mouth opening. At 5, they are mainly assimilated into a couple of opposing schemes : mouth opening/closing. At age 6, the movements are conceptualized also in terms of a couple of opposing directions : upwards/downwards. At this age mouth rounding movement is conceptualized. At age 7, another couple of directions are added i.e. forwards and "to the back".

As to the articulatory states and positions they were mainly expressed in the following chronological order :
Age 4 : open (mouth)
Age 5 : closed/together (teeth), tongue against teeth
Age 6 : open (mouth), closed/together (teeth), tongue against teeth, closed/blocked (throat), tongue against top gums.
Age 7 : closed/together (teeth and lips), tongue against teeth.
Age 8 : open (mouth), closed/together (teeth and lips), neutral position (tongue), at bottom of mouth (tongue).
Age 9 : closed/together (teeth), open/apart (teeth), at bottom of mouth (tongue).

To express tongue positions the children mainly used three points of reference : teeth, top gums, and mouth bottom. These observations concern only the features with more than 5 occurrences and they are by no means applicable to all answers.

Phonemes

In order to find out to what degree each phoneme contributed to the phonetic distinctions, we summed up the contribution values of each phoneme, found throughout ages 4 to 9, and obtained the following rank order :
highest contribution value → lowest contribution value
/ z / ɔ / s / g / b / m / u / t / a / əʊ / ə / i / æ / ei /

From the above we see that the six consonants involved in our experiment as well as two rounded vowels (/ɔ/u/) contribute more to the data variance than the other central or front vowels.

At each age the following phonemes were found to have rela-
tively high (1) contribution values. They are given here
in decreasing order of their contribution values :
Age 4 : /s/z/ ; /m/b/ ; /t/ ; /əʊ/u/ ; /æ/i/.
Age 5 : /z/ ; /əʊ/u/ ; /g/
Age 6 : /s/ ; /m/b/.
Age 7 : /u/ ; /m/ ; /g/.
Age 8 : /z/s/ ; /b/.
Age 9 : /z/ ; /m/ ; /g/.

We could conclude that bilabial articulation is a feature that contributes most to phonetic distinctions. It was
present at all ages (4-9) as strongly characterizing both
rounded vowels and bilabial consonants.

The second "most distinctive" feature complex appeared
to be coronal (alveolar/dental) articulation of fricatives.
It appeared at all ages except at age 7.

The third "most distinctive" feature complex was found
to be velar plosive articulation. It appeared with strong
contributions to data variance at ages 5, 7 and 9.

The three feature complexes thus point to three areas
that seem to be particularly liable to phonetic conceptualization : bilabial, coronal-alveolar-dental, velar.

The phonetic oppositions revealed by the factor analysis allow us to draw a few conclusions about children's
motor categorization of sounds :

I - In spite of the differences in descriptions given at
    different ages, some groups of phonemes were assigned
    common features throughout ages 5 to 9 thus constituting
    motor categories of their own.
    We could perhaps refer to them as motor "archephonemes"
    underlying phonological oppositions.
    Phonemes   Features
    Group 1 : /m/ /b/   mouth/lip closing/opening
    Group 2 : /ɔ/ /u/ /əʊ/   mouth/lip rounding
    Group 3 : /t/ /s/ /z/   lingual/dental articulation.
    Motor distinction between the first two groups is based
    on the opposition between closing/opening movements on
    the one hand and rounding movements on the other.

_____

(1) Only those values that were at least three times higher
     than the lowest one were taken into consideration.

131

Group 3 opposes groups 1 and 2 by its lingual and/or dental features. It also often shared some features with vowels /i/ and /ei/. A fourth, but less consistantly repeated group, consists of the consonant /g/ and vowels /ə/ɶ/ɔ/ their common feature being : "guttural". We have thus obtained three general categories: labial, lingual, guttural, which include all the sounds presented in the experiment with the exception of /a/ which was assigned features from all the three categories. The most uniform descriptions were given for /g/ and /ə/ i.e. guttural/velar articulation.

II.- The results also show that vowel /i/ and the coronal consonants were often assigned the same features. Note that as the point of articulation of /i/ is quite close to the area in buccal space, in which vowels cannot be specified in terms of the formant frequencies (Ladefoged, 1969, p. 102) its articulation might require more of articulatory feed-back.
Vowels /ɔ/ and /u/ are also situated in such an area and as our experimental results show, the expressed awareness of their articulation scored high contribution values to the total data variance.
Within the framework of the vowels presented in our experiment, the results lead us to believe that rounded and close front vowels involve more of tactile-kinesthetic control in the above larynx area, while central and open vowels involve less of such control.

On the whole our results give evidence of the existence of an internalized three-dimensional spatial representation of the vocal tract. They also show that the children's conceptualization of their vocal activity in speech production proceeds from the general to the particular characteristics of action. The choice of the latter centers first on the most salient features by which one motor category (archephoneme) is opposed to another.

REFERENCES

Benzécri, J.P., 1973, L'analyse des données (Dunod, Paris).

Fant G. 1973, Speech Sounds and Features,
    The MIT Press, Cambridge, Massachussetts, and
    London, England.

Ladefoged P. 1969, Three Areas of Experimental Phonetics,
    Oxford University Press, London.

Ladefoged Peter, 1979, Articulatory parameters, in Proce-
    edings of the Ninth International Congress of
    Phonetic Sciences, Copenhagen, Denmark.

Peterson, G.E. 1951, The phonetic value of vowels, Language,
    27.4, 541-553.

Key[(*)] to phonetic transcription used in the text

Vowels and diphthongs :		Consonants :	
i	as in see /si/	b	as in bad /bæd/
æ	as in hat /hæt/	t	as in tea /ti/
a	as in arm /am/	g	as in get /get/
ɔ	as in saw /sɔ/	s	as in so /səʋ/
u	as in too /tu/	z	as in zoo /zu/
ʌ	as in ago /əgəʋ/	m	as in man /mæn/
eɪ	as in page /peɪdʒ/	h	as in how /haʋ/
əʋ	as in home /həʋm/	k	as in cow /kaʋ/

(*) According to "A Concise Pronouncing Dictionary of
     British and American English" (OUP, 1972) by
     J. Windsor Lewis.

TOWARD AN EMPIRICAL DEFINITION OF "STAGE"
IN LANGUAGE DEVELOPMENT

Wm J. Baker & Bruce L. Derwing

The University of Alberta

Some years ago we collected a massive corpus
of data on the acquisition of five inflectional
morphemes in English; 500 responses were elicited
from each of 112 subjects, who ranged in age from
3 to 9 years. The basic stimuli consisted of a
fully representative set of 73 nonsense stems, as
well as single representatives of each of the irregular noun and verb stem classes. The hope was
to get as complete a picture as possible of the
course of development of all five of these constructions, as well as to resolve some theoretical questions about the kinds of rules that children learn and the explanations for them. Iron-
ically, although a few papers have appeared based
on small portions of this huge data set, the
great mass of these data have yet to be analyzed
and have languished in computer files now for the
better part of a decade.

The main reason these data have, until now,
proven intractable from the standpoint of a systematic analysis concerns the fundamental problem
faced (on a smaller scale) by all other cross-
sectional developmental studies: how are subjects
to be grouped or "blocked" into coherent strategy
groups or <u>stages</u>? The oldest and most familiar
procedure, of course, is simply to group subjects
on the basis of age, since most developmental
studies show significant age effects. The correlation of age with developmental data is often
depressingly low, however; in the study by Innes
(1974) to be discussed shortly, for example, age
and performance correlated at .414, a significant
correlation but one that indicates only 17%
common variance between the two measures. Rather

better results have sometimes been reported using
"mean length of utterance" (MLU's) to form performance groups, but this has proven to be too
gross and arbitrary a metric, as well. A third
approach, employed by Innes when her age-based
analysis failed to yield any clear developmental
trends, was to block subjects in terms of total
achievement (or "total percent correct" scores),
an approach which at least had the advantage of
revealing a reasonably interesting developmental
picture. However, even apart from the question
of the imposition of an arbitrary standard of
"correctness" in this work, the question of the
number of distinct groups or stages could not be
seriously approached in this way. (Innes merely
set her number of achievement groups at the same
value as she had age groups in her original, un-
successful analysis.) Even in longitudinal studies, incidentally, where the question of chronological sequence is at least clear, the question
of stage boundaries (or transitions) remains, and
with it the question of the precise number of
stages involved.

In sum, the essential problems with previous
approaches to the "blocking" of data in cross-
sectional research are the following: (1) stage
analyses are imposed on the data in a most arbitrary manner, rather than allowed to emerge from
the data themselves; (2) hence the rules, strategies, or cognitive reorganizations associated
with such arbitrarily defined stages lack a re-
quisite measure of empirical support. Clearly,
the basic assumption of the "stage" hypothesis in
developmental work is that a transition from one
stage to another carries with it the implication
that the child has become capable of mastering
new (or at least different) classes of problems.
On this logic, analytical techniques are required
which will identify data patterns, and hence provide support for conjectures about new rules or
strategies. In other words, data analytical
methods are required which are sensitive not
merely to individual responses or incidences, but
to response patterns or coincidences. We believe

135

that the procedures to be outlined briefly here
represent a significant breakthrough in the direction desired. Our purpose throughout the remainder of the paper will be to illustrate the
application of this technique to one particular
set of developmental data, so that some of its
most important advantages may become apparent.
For this purpose we will not use the large corpus
of data about which we spoke earlier, but rather
the more manageable data set of Sue Innes'
(1974). She presented 24 nonsense stems to a
sample of 120 children, ranging in age from 2 to
7 years, eliciting novel plural forms in much the
same manner as Berko (1958). Fortunately, though
her own analysis was based on an implied standard
of "correctness," Innes recorded her full data in
terms of the child's own responses, regardless of
whether they corresponded to the adult "norm."
Almost 97% of responses involved either one of
the three "regular" allomorphs (/z/, /s/, or
/Iz/) or a "null" allomorph in which the uninflected stem was simply repeated as a response.

As noted earlier, Innes immediately focused
her attention on group responses, with groups determined by age or overall "correct" performance,
but we will begin by focusing on the individual
response profiles in order to identify patterns
among items within each child. If we set aside
any a priori notion of "correct" vs. "incorrect," we can consider the response vector from
each child as portraying how that child would
partition or categorize the 24 stems in Innes'
test. This information can be converted into a
"coincidence" matrix which will provide us with
information about the pairwise treatment of sets
of objects for each individual child. An example
of such a matrix is shown in Figure 1. The matrix contains the common symbol (i.e., one of the
response codes) at the intersection of a given
row and column wherever the child treated both
objects in the same way; otherwise, the entry is
a zero. It has been proven that such a matrix of
pairwise comparisons contains within it all
information with respect to all possible

136

triplets, quadruplets, etc., so that full pat-
terning information is represented.

A matrix of this type was constructed for
each subject for the 24 item responses. This
generated 276 entries in the lower triangular
section of a 24 x 24 matrix for each subject and
provides us with a basis for comparing pairs of
subjects in terms of differences in patternings
among responses. If we make an element-by-ele-
ment comparison between subject pairs, count the
number of mismatches, and divide the result by
276, we can define a distance metric for all possible pairs of subjects. This metric will be
zero when two subjects provide identical patternings (i.e., the two subjects will be zero distance apart) and will equal 1.0 if the pair are
completely dissimilar. This functions as a Eu-
clidean distance metric which, when computed for
all subject pairs, yields a distance matrix which
can then be submitted to a cluster analysis to
determine if subject or strategy groups can be
empirically distinguished in the data.

Following the identification of subject
groups, if any, we can next determine the dis-
tances between objects (items) within each of the
subject groups. Here distance can be defined as
the proportion of subjects who did not treat a
given pair of objects in the same way (as indicated by a failure to provide a common response
to both). Again, we have a distance metric which
ranges between zero and 1.0 and which is amenable
to subsequent cluster analysis.

Among Innes' subjects were a few who provided nothing but null responses and another, larger set who consistently provided data according
to the "regular" or adult pattern. Both groups
produce distributional problems from the standpoint of statistical analyses, since the subjects
are constants with respect to each other within
these groups (zero distance apart) and they also
bear a fixed relationship to the remaining
subjects. In order to allow for useful forms of

statistical analyses, therefore, an inclusion
criterion specifying that a subject had to have
at least 3 items and no more than 21 items in
conformity with the adult pattern was adopted.
This eliminated 8 subjects from the lower end and
18 on the higher end, leaving 94 subjects for
further analysis. The 94 x 94 distance matrix
for the subjects was subjected to a hierarchical
cluster analysis. The results of this analysis
are presented in Figure 2.

In general, statistical criteria do not exist for deciding the issue of how many groups are
indicated by such a display, but extensive randomization tests were conducted with these data
to establish the distributional properties of
this particular data set. From this it was concluded that linkages or pairings which have a
value in excess of about 1.5 are more heterogene-
ous than one would expect from chance pairings
(at a decision level of .05). Notice that a
horizontal line drawn at a level of 1.5 indicates
four groups, which consist of the subjects included under the four branches of the tree diagram that would be cut by such a line. Thus the
first 13 subjects constitute one group (Group I),
the next 7 another (Group II), and the last two
groups (III and IV) consist of 49 and 25 subjects, respectively. The full analysis suggests
that, all things considered, we have four distinguishable strategy groups and we would expect
Groups III and IV to provide clearer results than
I or II.

A specific distance matrix was next computed
among the 24 stimuli for each of the four subject
groups, and each of these was then subjected to a
similar cluster analysis. The results for Group
I are presented in Figure 3, which indicates
three somewhat weakly defined sets of stem-types.
The stems ending in /u,d,i,m,r,g/ may be distinguished, as a set, and those in /f,p,t/ as well,
and then the remainder of the items as a block.
We should keep in mind, however, that the
response profiles for the individual items were

<u>not</u> the basis for the clusterings, but rather the proportion of subjects who, individually, did the <u>same thing</u> to a given item pair. (The response profiles for /ð/ and /v/, for example, were almost identical to those for /u/ or /g/, in terms of the proportion of subjects in this group who gave /z/ rather than null responses, but the former pair are not in the same cluster. An item-by-item analysis, ignoring patterns among items, would have pooled these and missed the fact that the same "rule" does not cover these items within subjects. That is to say, even though the /z/ allomorph is occasionally attached to /ð/ or /v/, its use there is not consistent with its use with /u/ or /g/.)

The group of stem-types on the right, from /u/ to /g/ (Cluster 3), are being pulled together because of their consistent treatment by the members of this subject group. These subjects <u>either</u> give them null responses <u>or</u> they attach the /z/ allomorph but, whichever they do, they do it quite consistently to the entire set. It is this <u>common</u> <u>treatment</u> of the item sets that leads them to be detected as a cluster distinct from the other items. Ignoring details which cannot be included here (for full details, see Baker & Derwing (1982)), the Group I data suggests that the acquisition of the system for pluralization begins equally with /s/ and /z/ allomorphs, but with no evidence for the use of /Iz/. Subjects, however, do not immediately apply these allomorphs to all of the members of the stem-classes to which they might apply. Two subsets were systematically inflected by about half the subjects, while the remainder were uninflected or unsystematically tagged. From the perspective of the adult norm, these subjects did not show strong control of any item.

Group II subjects, of whom there are only seven, also provide three stem-type clusters as shown in Figure 4. They turned out to be distinguished from Group I subjects primarily by their almost complete mastery of the /z/ allomorph with

respect to their Cluster 3. This set has five
members in common with Cluster 3 for Group I.
This suggests that there is some common property
for the set which elicits an early common treatment under the /z/ allomorph. Since the average
age of both groups was almost identical, these
might constitute two somewhat different kinds of
beginnings: for Group II only the /z/ allomorph
was used systematically, whereas Group I subjects
showed some systematicity in the use of both /s/
and /z/. Neither group exibited more than a mere
trace of the /Iz/ allomorph

The cluster statistics for the objects as
processed by the 49 members of Group III indicate
three clearly distinct clusters (Figure 5). The
first cluster was formed as a consequence of mastery of the role of the /z/ allomorph for all appropriate stems except /ð/. In a similar vein,
the third cluster is produced by mastery of the
role of the /s/ allomorph for all appropriate
stems except /θ/. Stems ending in /θ/ and /ð/
fall into Cluster 2 with the sibilants, for which
the majority response was still null throughout.
Interestingly, this group also showed the first
clear emergence of the /Iz/ allomorph and, with
its emergence, the first appearance of duplication errors (e.g. croinzes) and overgeneraliza-
tions (e.g., to stems ending in /f/ or /v/).
Unlike the /z/ and /s/ allomorphs, whose distributions now clearly suggest the mastery of a
quite general voicing assimilation rule, the /Iz/
allomorph gives every appearance of a "completely
new" suffix: its channeling toward the sibilant
sounds would seem to account naturally for the
duplication errors after the /s/ and /z/ endings,
and its overgeneralization to the remaining fricatives would seem to be a natural consequence of
the fricatives' inclusion, prior to this phase,
in the same class as the sibilants. (Chronologi-
cally, Group III was not much older than Groups I
and II, but there was, nevertheless, a minor
trend for age relative to increased skill in performance.)

Group IV, with its 25 members, shows, in Figure 6, another clearly distinct set of clusters and, in fact, the precise partitioning of the objects into the three classes anticipated by the adult system. Cluster 1 is based on almost complete mastery of the /z/ allomorph and it now includes both /ð/ and /v/. Cluster 2 is based on almost full mastery of the /s/ allomorph, now including /θ/ and /f/. Cluster 3 showed only a very slight improvement in the control of /Iz/ relative to the sibilants, so the main feature of this subject group was the sorting out of the sibilants from the other fricatives, with the consequent elimination of duplication and over-generalization errors.

Finally, for the sake of completeness, we can briefly discuss the 18 subjects who were set aside because they showed fewer than three items different from the adult norm. Naturally, these subjects showed almost complete control of all items from the standpoint of the adult pattern, and a cluster analysis of their data would surely support this. What is interesting to note is that, insofar as any significant number of errors remained, they were all in the sibilant category. This clearly suggests that the last component of the adult system to be mastered is the /Iz/ allomorph, and the last stem-types to be sorted out are those which already end in /s/ and /z/, the pair that ought to be the most confusing for the learner. The mean age of this group was also considerably higher (5.78) than those of the preceding samples, but it still included one 3-year-old and three 4-year-olds. The age distribution for all of the subject groups is shown in Table 1, which provides its own eloquent argument against the blocking of developmental data by age prior to analysis for strategies and trends (cf. especially Group III).

This paper has demonstrated, with a degree of clarity that we believe is rather remarkable for developmental data, the manner in which the system for pluralization in children is acquired.

Logically, a longitudinal study on a large sample
of children would be required to demonstrate con-
clusively that the sequence suggested here by our
Groups I/II to IV and our last group is, in fact,
a series of stages through which each individual
child passes, but the data presented strongly
suggest that this is the case.

The data on how the process begins are the
weakest, but this is probably a natural consequence of how we must test for this kind of production skill. The children must, of necessity,
be able to comprehend the task before we can include them in the study. Given this, our data
indicate that the child moves rapidly into a
Group III type of performance, so that we managed
to observe only a small number of cases in the
earlier phase(s). Group III shows a well-established rule structure in that the Group III subjects have mastered both the /z/ allomorph and a
general rule for voicing assimilation. (That
this is true for adults has been established independently in a series of miniature artificial
language studies.) These children are now in a
position to detect exceptions to this analysis in
the form of a separate /Iz/ marker, with which
they now begin to experiment. It appears, with
rather low frequency, as a duplicate marker, and
is also occasionally overgeneralized to the
non-sibilant fricative stems, but with no great
consistency. Group IV children, where they use
/Iz/ at all, have correctly restricted its use to
the sibilant class, but it is not until the final
stage that it is consistently used with this
class in preference to the null response. (We
might add here that the MAL studies mentioned
previously show no evidence of a general vowel
insertion rule, which supports our analysis of
/Iz/ as a distinct lexical variant.)

In sum, Groups I and II have begun to acquire the most general and most widely distributed part of the adult rule, as reflected in the
"elsewhere" condition; Group III is beginning to
discover exceptions to this general /z/ usage;

142

and Group IV has correctly sorted out the target set for those exceptions which require /Iz/. Our final group showed mastery of the full system.

In conclusion, we believe that the analytical methods outlined in this paper, which focus on the within-child response patterns, have clarified the acquisition process and provided an empirical basis for expressing the rule system learned and used by the child. More importantly, however, we believe that the methodology outlined is quite general in its application and should prove effective in many other areas of investigation as well. In particular, we are now looking forward to applying it to the very large corpus of data previously mentioned which has lain dormant for so long but from which we now fully expect to find evidence for new intermediate stages, particularly in the treatment of the large number of stems that involve final consonant clusters.

REFERENCES

Baker, W. J. & Derwing, B. L. Response coincidence analysis as evidence for language acquisition strategies. Applied Psycholinguistics, 1982, 3, No. 3.

Berko, J. The child's learning of English morphology. Word, 1958, 14, 150-177.

Innes, S. J. Developmental aspects of plural formation in English. Unpublished Master's thesis, University of Alberta, 1974.

Stim. Resp.	/c/ Nul	/ŋ/ /z/	/b/ /z/	/ʒ/ /z/	/l/ /z/	/v/ /z/	/n/ /z/	/u/ /z/	/d/ /z/	/i/ /z/	/m/ /z/	/r/ /z/	/g/ /z/	/f/ /s/	/p/ Irr	/k/ Nul	/θ/ /s/	/t/ /s/	/s/ Nul	/ʃ/ /Iz/	/ǯ/ /Iz/	/č/ /Iz/	/ž/ Nul	/z/ Nul
/c/ Nul	-																							
/ŋ/ /z/	0	-																						
/b/ /z/	0	N	-																					
/ʒ/ /z/	0	N	N	-																				
/l/ /z/	0	N	N	N	-																			
/v/ /z/	0	N	N	N	N	-																		
/n/ /z/	0	N	N	N	N	N	-																	
/u/ /z/	0	N	N	N	N	N	N	-																
/d/ /z/	0	N	N	N	N	N	N	N	-															
/i/ /z/	0	N	N	N	N	N	N	N	N	-														
/m/ /z/	0	N	N	N	N	N	N	N	N	N	-													
/r/ /z/	0	N	N	N	N	N	N	N	N	N	N	-												
/g/ /z/	0	N	N	N	N	N	N	N	N	N	N	N	-											
/f/ /s/	0	0	0	0	0	0	0	0	0	0	0	0	0	-										
/p/ Irr	0	0	0	0	0	0	0	0	0	0	0	0	0	0	-									
/k/ Nul	Nul	0	0	0	0	0	0	0	0	0	0	0	0	0	0	Nul								
/θ/ /s/	0	0	0	0	0	0	0	0	0	0	0	0	0	s	0	0	-							
/t/ /s/	0	0	0	0	0	0	0	0	0	0	0	0	0	s	0	0	s	-						
/s/ Nul	Nul	0	0	0	0	0	0	0	0	0	0	0	0	0	0	Nul	0	0	Nul					
/ʃ/ /Iz/	0	0	0	0	0	0	0	0	0	0	0	0	0	0	0	0	0	0	0	-				
/ž/ /Iz/	0	0	0	0	0	0	0	0	0	0	0	0	0	0	0	0	0	0	0	Iz	-			
/č/ /Iz/	0	0	0	0	0	0	0	0	0	0	0	0	0	0	0	0	0	0	0	Iz	Iz	-		
/ž/ Nul	Nul	0	0	0	0	0	0	0	0	0	0	0	0	0	0	Nul	0	0	Nul	0	0	0	Nul	
/z/ Nul	Nul	0	0	0	0	0	0	0	0	0	0	0	0	0	0	Nul	0	0	Nul	0	0	0	0	-

Figure 1. The "coincidence" matrix for Subject 46.

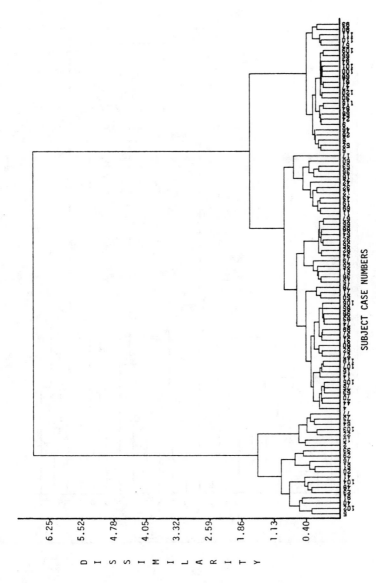

Figure 2. Subject groups for Innes data (N = 94).

145

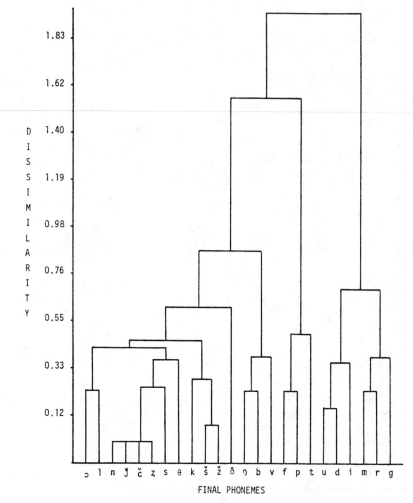

Figure 3. Phoneme clusters for Group I (N = 13).

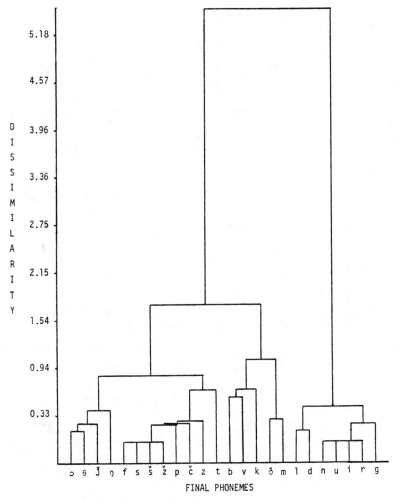

Figure 4. Final phomeme clusters for Group II (N = 7).

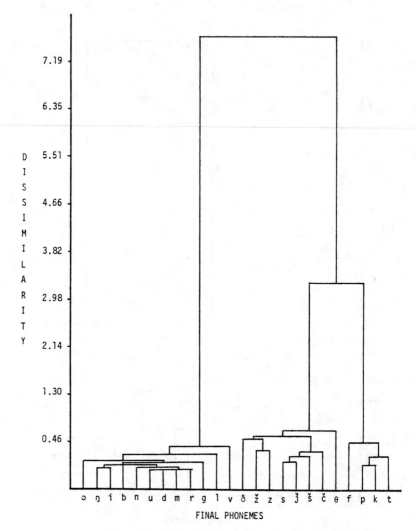

Figure 5. Final phoneme clusters for Group III (N = 49).

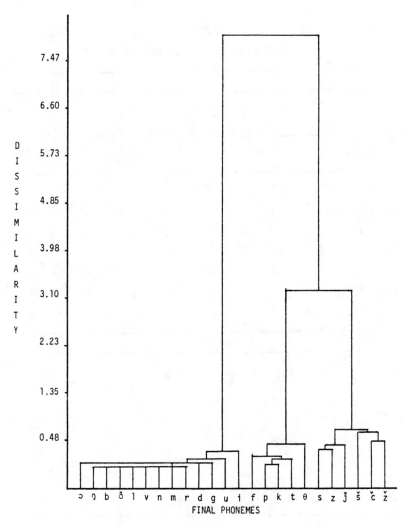

Figure 6. Final phoneme clusters for Group IV (N = 25).

TABLE 1

FREQUENCY DISTRIBUTION OF AGES BY GROUPS

	Age						
Group	2	3	4	5	6	7	Total
< 3	4	2	1	0	1	0	8
I	2	4	3	1	1	2	13
II	2	1	0	3	0	1	7
III	9	9	8	12	7	4	49
IV	3	3	5	2	6	6	25
> 21	0	1	3	2	5	7	18

WORD-ORDER INVARIANCE AND VARIABILITY IN FIVE
CHILDREN'S THREE-WORD UTTERANCES: A LIMITED-SCOPE FORMULA
ANALYSIS

by Guy Ewing,
University of Toronto

ABSTRACT

This paper presents diachronic evidence to support the kind
of limited-scope formula analysis of children's first word
combinations advanced in Braine (1976). It is shown that
this kind of analysis entails developmental processes in syntax. An explicit formulation of these processes is provided,
and it is demonstrated that, given a limited-scope formula
analysis of two-word utterances, the processes correctly
predict word-order invariance and variability in subsequent
three-word utterances. The data base for this analysis is
periodic transcripts for four children from 1;8 to 2;1, and
diary entries for a fifth child from 1;9 to 2;1. The paper
ends with an appeal for more evidence for the developmental
processes posited, and, in general, for the limited-scope
formula approach to the analysis of early word combinations.

In his 1976 monograph, "Children's First Word Combinations,"
Martin Braine presents what he calls a "limited-scope formula analysis" of children's two-word utterances. According to
this analysis, children find word-order patterns for semantic
relations at various levels of generality. A limited-scope
formula analysis contrasts with some other semantic analyses
of word order in early child speech, for example, a case grammar analysis, in that it does not try to match word-order
patterns to some highly general set of semantic relations,
for example, Fillmore's case relations. As can be seen from
the list of examples of Braine's limited-scope formulae in
(1), the generality of the patterns, or, to use Braine's
terminology, the scope of the formulae, can be quite limited.

(1)   Main types of limited-scope formulae
      Braine (1976), pp. 56-57

      (a)   Patterns that draw attention to something, for

151

example, <u>see + X</u> or <u>here/there + X</u>; or identify
something, for example, <u>it/that + X</u>; or assign
class membership, for example, <u>X + Y</u> 'X is (a)
Y' . . .

(b) Patterns that remark on specific properties of
objects, for example, <u>big/little + X</u>, <u>hot + X</u>,
<u>old + X</u>.

(c) A pattern expressing possession: <u>X + Y</u> 'X's Y'
or 'X has a Y'.

(d) Patterns that note plurality or iteration, <u>two</u>
<u>+ X</u> . . .

(e) Patterns concerned with recurrence, or alternate
exemplars of a type, for example, <u>more + X</u>,
<u>other + X</u>.

(f) Patterns concerned with disappearance of objects,
for example, <u>allgone + X</u>.

(g) Patterns expressing negation, for example <u>no + X</u>.

(h) A pattern expressing actor-action relations.

(i) Patterns concerned with location, for example,
<u>X + (Prep) here/there</u>, <u>X + Y</u> 'X is in, on, has
moved to Y'.

(j) Patterns that request, for example, want + X
. . . <u>have-it + X</u>.

Like all accounts of the development of word order in child
speech, a limited-scope formula is hard to prove, but we can
provide supporting evidence for it. In this paper, I show
that a limited-scope formula analysis of two-word utterances
can be used to make predictions about word-order invariance
and variability in subsequent three-word utterances, and that
these predictions are supported by data for five children for
1;6 to 2;0, approximately, including periodic transcripts
from two-hour sessions at six-week intervals for four of the
children, and diary entries for the fifth child. I also

describe one instance in which a limited-scope formula analysis clearly makes different predictions than a case grammar
analysis and in which the predictions made by the limited-
scope formula analysis are supported by my data.

If, in learning to speak, a child starts out with word-order
patterns for semantic relations at various levels of generality, like those in (1), he/she must, during development, integrate these patterns to create the more inclusive patterns
of adult speech. Two main kinds of integration, which I call
vertical integration and horizontal integration, will be necessary. These processes are illustrated in (2).

(2)   The integration of limited-scope formulas

    (a)   Vertical integration

        big/little + X
              hot + X   property + X

    (b)   Horizontal integration

        Type A big/little + X
                see + X   see + bit/little + X

        Type B   actor+action actr+actn+ent
           action+entity acted on   acted on

    (c)   Vertical integration before horizontal integration

        big/little + X
              hot + X property + X
                         see + X see + property + X

    (d)   Horizontal integration before vertical integration

        big/little + X
             see + X see+big/little+X
             hot + X see+hot+X see+property+X

In the first place, patterns like <u>big/little + X</u> will have

153

to be integrated with patterns like hot + X to create more
inclusive patterns like property + X, and, eventually,
Adj + N. This is what I call vertical integration, since
one pattern is being superimposed on another to create a
more general pattern. Second, patterns like big/little + X
will have to be integrated with patterns like see + X
to create more inclusive patterns like see + big/little + X.
This is what I call horizontal integration, since one pattern
is being added to another to create a longer pattern.

As can be seen in (2b), two kinds of horizontal integration
are possible. In the case of see + big/little + X, one
limited-scope formula, big/little + X takes the place of an
element in another limited-scope formula, X in see + X, and
takes on the same semantic role as this element. I have
labelled this type of horizontal integration type A horizontal integration. The other type of horizontal integration,
which I have labelled type B horizontal integration, combines
limited-scope formulas like actor + action and action + entity acted on by linking them together at the common element,
in this case, action.

Usually, both vertical and horizontal integration will apply
to a formula, in one order or the other. For example, vertical integration will apply to big/little + X either before
or after horizontal integration to create see + property + X.
If, as in (2c), vertical integration applies first, horizontal integration will combine see + X and property + X to
create see + property + X. If, as in (2d), horizontal integration applies first, vertical integration will combine see
+ big/little + X and see + hot + X to create see + property
+ X.

It can be seen that a limited-scope formula analysis can predict the development of invariant word order for three-word
utterances along a number of paths. For example, in (3) we
can see three paths to SVO word order which show up in the
periodic data.

(3)   Vertical and horizontal integration leading to SVO word
       order in three-word utterances. Roman numerals indicate
       the recording sessions at which the utterances occurred,
       or at which formulae were posited. Ages and MLU values
       for the recording sessions are listed in the appendix.

                               154

CHILD: A

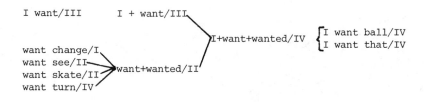

```
I want/III        I + want/III
                              ╲
                               ╲I+want+wanted/IV  ⎰I want ball/IV
want change/I╲                                     ⎱I want that/IV
want see/II──╲
want skate/II─►want+wanted/II
want turn/IV╱
```

VERTICAL   HORIZONTAL
INTEGRATION   INTEGRATION
                 (TYPE B)

CHILD: C

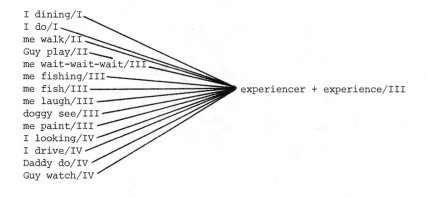

```
I dining/I╲
I do/I╲
me walk/II╲
Guy play/II╲
me wait-wait-wait/III╲
me fishing/III──╲
me fish/III──────────experiencer + experience/III
me laugh/III──╱
doggy see/III╱
me paint/III╱
I looking/IV╱
I drive/IV╱
Daddy do/IV╱
Guy watch/IV╱
```

VERTICAL INTEGRATION

(continued on next page)

155

CHILD: C (cont.)

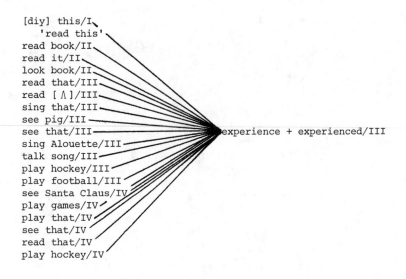

```
[diy] this/I
   'read this'
read book/II
read it/II
look book/II
read that/III
read [ Λ ]/III
sing that/III                    experience + experienced/III
see pig/III
see that/III
sing Alouette/III
talk song/III
play hockey/III
play football/III
see Santa Claus/IV
play games/IV
play that/IV
see that/IV
read that/IV
play hockey/IV
```

VERTICAL INTEGRATION

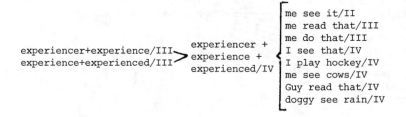

```
                                                  ┌ me see it/II
                                                  │ me read that/III
experiencer+experience/III    experiencer +       │ me do that/III
                              experience +        │ I see that/IV
experience+experienced/III    experienced/IV      │ I play hockey/IV
                                                  │ me see cows/IV
                                                  │ Guy read that/IV
                                                  └ doggy see rain/IV
```

HORIZONTAL
INTEGRATION
(TYPE B)

156

CHILD: J

Guy catch/I ⟶ human actor + action/I
Mama sitting/I ⟶

eat it/I ⟶ action + it/I
read it/I ⟶

> VERTICAL
> INTEGRATION

human actor+action/I ⟶ human actor+action+it/I
action + it/I

Mama read it/I
Mama get it/I
you zip it/I
you mash it/I

> HORIZONTAL
> INTEGRATION
> (TYPE B)

A's path is made with the formulae <u>I + want</u> and <u>want + wanted</u>,
C's path with the formulae <u>experiencer + experience</u> and <u>ex-
perience + experienced</u>, and J's path with the formulae <u>human
actor + action</u> and <u>action + it</u>. In each case, a pattern for
invariant word order is established by the child's use of horizontal integration (type B) interacting with his/her use
of vertical integration. Developmental paths of this kind
were found in the data for all five children.

As well as predicting word-order invariance along a number of
paths, a limited scope formula analysis, in conjunction with
the processes in (2), predicts the occasional snag in word-
order development. Suppose a child wanted to order three
words, a, b, and c, from two limited scope formulae which ordered them as follows in two-word utterances: a + b, a + c.
Suppose, further, that neither a + b nor a + c could perform
the same semantic role as one of the elements in the other
formula. In this case, unless the child has additional

157

information from adult input, she/he would not know whether to produce a + b + c or a + c + b. She/he would order a before either b or c, but she/he would have to order b and c randomly, perhaps choosing different orders at different times. That is, given the situation that I have described, a limited-scope formula analysis, in conjunction with the processes in (2), predicts that word-order variation may occur, and it predicts exactly what variation may occur. Of course, it does not predict that word-order variation will occur, since the child can always make use of additional information from adult input to solve the puzzle created for her/him by her/his limited/scope formulae.

A parallel situation arises when a child tries to order a, b, and c from the limited-scope formulae a + c and b + c. In this case, the word orders a + b + c and b + a + c are both possible.

Of course, word-order variability will occur in a three-word utterance if it contains elements that have variable word order in prior two-word utterances. In some cases, a child will have only one ordered pair to work with, and in some cases, he/she will have no ordering to work with at all.

These predicted snags show up in the diary area for G, which is, of course, more detailed data than the periodic data for the other children. In (4) we see that, combining up + entity wanted up and up + bed, G got both up bed Daddy and up Daddy bed. Combining big + entity and two + entity, he got big two truck, big two stone, and big two bah-bah, and also two big book and two big boy. Combining no + negated with a variable pattern, phenomenon + more/more + phenomenon, he got no playbath more, no hot more, no baby more, and no cereal more, and also no more camera and no more hot.

(4) Vertical and horizontal integration leading to variable word order in G's three-word utterances. Times indicate first occurrences of word combinations, unless they are starred, in which case they indicate unique occurrences. Times for formulae indicate the times at which the formulae were posited.

158

```
up dirty/1;9(3)*
up door/1;9(28)*
up Daddy/1;10(5)        up + entity wanted up/1;9(28)
up baby/1;11(14)*
```

VERTICAL
INTEGRATION

```
up bed/1;10(10)          up + bed/1;10(11)


up + entity wanted up/1;9(28)        up bed Daddy/1;10(19)*
        up + bed/1;10(11)            up Daddy bed/1;11(28)*
```

HORIZONTAL
INTEGRATION

```
PROBLEM TYPE:    a + b              a + c + b
                 a + c              a + b + c
```

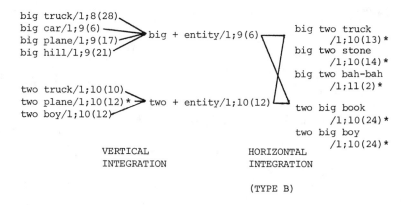

```
big truck/1;8(28)
big car/1;9(6)                             big two truck
big plane/1;9(17)    big + entity/1;9(6)        /1;10(13)*
big hill/1;9(21)                           big two stone
                                                /1;10(14)*
                                           big two bah-bah
                                                /1;11(2)*
two truck/1;10(10)
two plane/1;10(12)*  two + entity/1;10(12)
two boy/1;10(12)                           two big book
                                                /1;10(24)*
                                           two big boy
                                                /1;10(24)*
```

VERTICAL   HORIZONTAL
INTEGRATION   INTEGRATION

(TYPE B)

```
PROBLEM TYPE:    a + c              a + b + c
                 b + c              b + a + c
```

159

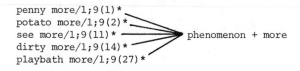

```
no bean/1;9(1)
no Daddy/1;9(9)
no outside/1;9(10)          no + negated/1;9(5)
no up/1;9(11)
no bed/1;9(17)
```

(partial list)

VERTICAL
INTEGRATION

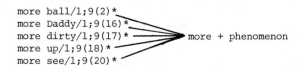

```
penny more/1;9(1)*
potato more/1;9(2)*
see more/1;9(11)*           phenomenon + more
dirty more/1;9(14)*
playbath more/1;9(27)*
```

VERTICAL
INTEGRATION

```
more ball/1;9(2)*
more Daddy/1;9(16)*
more dirty/1;9(17)*         more + phenomenon
more up/1;9(18)*
more see/1;9(20)*
```

VERTICAL
INTEGRATION

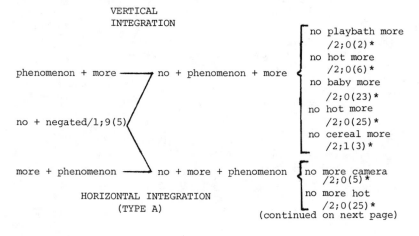

```
                                                    ┌ no playbath more
                                                    │    /2;0(2)*
                                                    │ no hot more
phenomenon + more ─────→ no + phenomenon + more  {  │    /2;0(6)*
                                                    │ no baby more
                                                    │    /2;0(23)*
                                                    │ no hot more
no + negated/1;9(5)                                 │    /2;0(25)*
                                                    └ no cereal more
                                                         /2;1(3)*

more + phenomenon ─────→ no + more + phenomenon  { no more camera
                                                        /2;0(5)*
     HORIZONTAL INTEGRATION                        no more hot
          (TYPE A)                                      /2;0(25)*
                                        (continued on next page)
```

(continued on next page)

160

PROBLEM TYPE: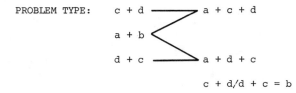

$$c + d/d + c = b$$

Up bed Daddy/up Daddy bed is a particularly valuable example
because it can be used to compare predictions about word
order variability made by a limited-scope formula analysis
with predictions made by a case grammar analysis.

Consider the data for G in (5).

(5) UTTERANCE   CONCOMITANT BEHAVIOUR

Daddy there/1;9(17)   Getting me to go there.
Daddy 'side/1;9(20)   Getting me to go outside.
Daddy stair/1;9(22)   Getting me to carry him down the stairs.
Daddy down/1;9(23)*   Getting me to sit down on the floor with him.
up Daddy/1;10(4)   Getting me out of bed in the morning.
up bed/1;10(10)   Getting me out of bed in the morning.
up dirty/1;9(3)*   Getting me to wipe sand off of his hands.
up door/1;9(28)*   Getting me to open a door.
up baby/1;11(14)*   Getting me to unfold and clip fast the
                            the baby stroller.

From this data, we can formulate three limited-scope formulae,
Daddy + place wanted, up + entity wanted up, and up + bed.
Under a case grammar analysis, we would have to say that Agent
and Goal are not ordered with respect to each other. On the basis
of up bed, we could say that Goal and Source are ordered with
respect to each other, but this conclusion would have to remain
tentative, since up bed is the only evidence for this ordering
in the diary data.

Now consider what will happen when Adam wants to combine up,
Daddy, and bed. Given the limited-scope formula analysis,
Adam will order up first, before both Daddy and bed, but he

may not consistently order Daddy before bed or bed before Daddy. As can be seen in (4), both orders do in fact occur.

Given the case grammar analysis, up and Daddy will not be ordered. Up and bed may be ordered. Daddy and bed may also be ordered, as the data in (6) indicates.

(6) UTTERANCE   CONCOMITANT BEHAVIOUR

    car lane/1;10(24)*   Watching a car go out of a lane.
    truck lane/1;11(0)   Watching a truck come out of a lane.

This data suggests that Agent is ordered before Source, but, as in the case of up and bed, the paucity of the evidence requires that such an analysis be tentative.

Considering all of the possibilities under a case grammar analysis, the word orders shown in (7) will be possible for a three-word utterance combining up, Daddy, and bed.

(7) Possible orderings for up, Daddy, and bed under a case analysis

    (a) If all of the cases involved are unordered:

          up Daddy bed
          up bed Daddy
          Daddy up bed
          bed up Daddy
          Daddy bed up
          bed Daddy up

    (b) If Goal and Agent, and Goal and Source are unordered, but if Agent is ordered before Source:

          up Daddy bed
          Daddy up bed
          Daddy bed up

    (c) If Goal and Agent, and Agent and Source are unordered, but if Goal is ordered before Source:

162

```
            up Daddy bed
            Daddy up bed
            up bed Daddy
```

(d)   If Goal and Agent are unordered, but if Goal is
      ordered before Source, and if Agent is ordered
      before Source:

```
            up Daddy bed
            Daddy up bed
```

It can be seen that the limited-scope formula analysis makes
different predictions than a case grammar analysis, and that
the case grammar analysis fails by predicting too much variation in three-word utterances, in (7a)-(7c), or the wrong
variation, in (7d). The limited-scope formula analysis makes
exactly the right predictions.

Moreover, the limited-scope formula analysis predicts that,
in three-word utterances including the elements Daddy and
place wanted, Daddy will occur before place wanted. This
prediction is not made by the case grammar analysis, which,
if anything, predicts that Daddy and place wanted will occur
in both orders, since Agent and Goal are not ordered. As can
be seen in (8), the prediction made by the limited-scope formula analysis is borne out.

(8)   G's three-word utterances with the elements Daddy and
      place wanted

```
            Daddy turtle on/2;0(25)
            no Daddy bed/2;1(7)
            Daddy hole go/2;1(8)
            Daddy down go/2;1(11)
```

In this paper, I have provided diachronic evidence supporting
a limited-scope formula analysis of two-word utterances, and,
in one case, evidence which favours a limited-scope formula
analysis over a case grammar analysis. On the basis of the
small amount of diachronic evidence which I have presented,
I cannot make a strong case for a limited-scope formula analysis, but I have presented this evidence because I think that
it is a valuable and interesting kind of evidence which needs

to be pursued. Also, my argument has brought out a number of questions which need to be pursued, among them, exactly how does vertical integration proceed, how does horizontal integration proceed beyond three-word utterances, and what evidence beside word-order variability can be found for vertical and horizontal integration. These are subjects for further diachronic research.

REFERENCES

Bowerman, Melissa (1976). Semantic factors in the acquisition of rules for word use and sentence construction. In Morehead, D.M., and A.E. Morehead, eds., <u>Normal and deficient child language</u>. Baltimore: University Park Press, 1976.

Braine, Martin D.S. (1976). Children's first word combinations. Monographs of the Society for Research in Child Development: 41;1 (serial 164).

Clark, Ruth (1974). Performing without competence. <u>J. Child Lang</u>: 1, 1-10.

Ingram, David (1979). Early patterns of grammatical development. Paper prepared for the conference "Language Behavior in Infancy and Early Childhood," Santa Barbara, 1979.

Maratsos, Michael P., and Mary Anne Chalkley (1980). The internal language of children's syntax; the ontogenesis and representation of syntactic categories. In Nelson, Keith, ed., <u>Children's language</u>, v. 2. New York: Gardner Press, 1980.

APPENDIX   Age/MLU for the children in the periodic study

child (sex)
                                session

4	I	II	III	IV
F (f)	1;7(17)/1.06	1;8(17)/1.42	1;10(3)/1.46	1;11(26)/1.50
A (f)	1;8(21)/1.53	1;10(11)/1.13	2;0(2)/1.53	2;1(16)/1.87
C (m)	1;9(17)/1.16	1;10(26)/1.36	2;0(17)/2.10	2;1(18)/1.91
J (m)	1;8(26)/1.64	1;10(7)/2.01	1;11(25)/2.48	2;1(12)/2.76

THE FUNCTION OF NOUN PHRASES IN PRODUCTION AND COMPREHENSION: SOME FURTHER EVIDENCE ON THE CONTRIBUTION OF SEMANTICS TO EARLY GRAMMAR

Christine J. Howe
Department of Psychology, University of Strathclyde

Towards the end of their second year, children start producing strings of words which have the pause structure and intonation contour of sentences. A large number of these sentence-like strings will contain what adults would regard as nouns. Sometimes, they will contain two 'nouns'; at other times, they will contain one noun plus what seems to be a 'verb' or an 'adjective'. In the first case, the two nouns will almost always refer to inter-related entities as with Tea teddy produced while teddy was being given a cup of tea. In the second, the single noun will refer to an entity which was involved in the action or state identified by the verb or adjective. An example would be Mummy wash produced while Mummy was doing the laundry. Since 1970, many researchers have been interested in what children are trying to express when they use nouns in such strings. Are they trying to express the roles which entities play, or merely the associations which entities hold? To interested researchers, it has seemed that resolving the issue would contribute to the grammatical representation, and hence explanation, of early sentences.

Until the mid 1970s, the issue was regarded as fairly non-controversial. There seemed a wealth of evidence showing that the structure of children's speech varies with referent role. This was considered proof that early sentences express roles. Unfortunately, both the evidence and its interpretation can be questioned. With respect to the evidence, claiming correlations between linguistic structure and referent role requires independent evidence of referent role. The extralinguistic context was believed to provide such evidence but this was frequently not the case. For instance, Bowerman (1973), Braine (1976) and Kernan (1970) were convinced that the context proved that object-nouns are preceded by possessor-nouns and followed by location-nouns. On closer analysis, it turns out that both kinds of noun were generally used to refer to the broader of two spatio-temporally contiguous entities. Hence, the context could not have been used as independent evidence for referent role. As I have pointed out in Howe (1976), perceptions of context were themselves influenced by word order, making any claim that order co-varies with referent role irretrievably circular.

Another distinction which cannot be made by simply observing the extra-linguistic context is the difference between dynamic and static events. Afterall, the same events can be viewed as 'sleeping' which is dynamic or 'being asleep' which is static, as 'holding' which is dynamic or 'having' which is static. However if speakers demonstrate, through linguistic means or otherwise, how they are construing given events, it will generally be clear how they would interpret integral parts of those events. This means that if children describe events with action-verbs revealing their dynamic analysis, it will usually be clear what they would regard as the agents and objects of those actions. Consequently, it seems likely that when Bloom (1970), Braine (1976) and Brown (1973) concluded that children place agent-nouns before action-verbs and object-nouns after, they were making claims which the wider context could substantiate. The same can be said of Wieman's (1976) claim that agent-nouns receive lighter stress than object-nouns. Thus, here are two instances of structure co-varying with referent role. Unfortunately, neither need indicate the expression of referent role. Placing words in the order agent-noun plus action-verb plus object-noun could, as Schlesinger (1976) has also pointed out, equally reflect the child's image of reality. Stressing object- rather than agent-noun could, as Wieman more or less admits, result from a tendency to emphasize 'new' rather than 'given' information.

In a sense, these comments about agent- and object-nouns are more worrying than the previous comments about possessor- and location-nouns. They demonstrate the great difficulty in showing that roles are being expressed even when structure does co-vary with referent role. They begin to suggest looking for a completely different approach to the issue. One alternative which once appealed to me (Howe, 1976), is observing children's reactions to the interpretations other people place on their speech. Now I realize that this approach could not differentiate accurate/inaccurate interpretations of what the child was trying to

167

communicate from accurate/inaccurate interpretations of what she was trying to express. To give an example, showing that hitting something with a ball is rejected as a response to Hit ball does not necessarily mean that the child was expressing the object role. It would certainly mean that the child wanted someone to put the ball in the object role. Hence, it would demonstrate communicative awareness of roles, an unremarkable discovery in view of work by Bates, Camaioni and Volterra (1975), Bruner (1975), Dore (1975), Greenfield and Smith (1976) and Halliday (1975). However, wanting does not necessarily imply saying and the child's remark might still be expressing a simple action-entity association.

If neither the physical nor the social context provides the key, the problem of whether early sentences express roles begins to look intractable. However, asking whether early sentences express roles may be too restricting given the theoretical issue which underpins the research, namely grammatical representation. From the theoretical point of view, the real question is whether children have semantic knowledge of roles and such knowledge may be reflected in ways other than their spontaneous speech. One alternative way might be their responses to the speech of other people and there are numerous seemingly relevant studies of this issue. Some of them involve children acting out reversible sentences like The cow kisses the horse. Taking research reviewed by Bever (1970) together with the study reported by de Villiers and de Villiers (1972), it appears that children fail on such tasks until sometime after the onset of word combination. However, it might be argued that very young children have difficulty making agents other than themselves perform actions, implying specific task problems rather than general misunderstanding.

The remaining studies involved children acting as agents and found high levels of success at, or even before, the beginnings of word combination. These studies include work by Huttenlocher (1974) and Shipley, Smith and Gleitman (1969) where children were asked to comply with such commands as Give me the ball and Show the cookie to Julie. They also include work by Sachs and Truswell (1978) using more exotic commands like <u>Smell lorry</u> and <u>Tickle ball</u>. Unfortunately, compliance with all these commands is open to interpretations other than semantic knowledge or roles. In every case, children were putting entities into the only roles they could realistically play in the specified actions. Hence, they could have succeeded by interpreting the remarks as requests to associate entities and actions and making the most plausible associations in context. To overcome this problem, it would be necessary to use entities which could play several equally probable roles. This would, of course, be very difficult to achieve with real entities.

Some headway might be made with pictures which showed entities in two roles. In this situation, the task would involve discriminating pictures in response to instructions which specified one role. One study which used this approach to investigate semantic knowledge of possession was reported by Golinkoff and Markessini (1980). However, for reasons given in Howe (1981a), this study fails to demonstrate semantic knowledge of roles until sometime after the onset of word combination. Recently, I have also used the approach in a study concerned with semantic knowledge of benefaction and location. The study has also been summarized in Howe (1981a) but it will be elaborated here because of its relevance to the present discussion. The study was designed to differentiate what are probably the two plausible views on semantic knowledge of benefaction and location. The first is the widely-held view that it has emerged by the time children produce their first sentences. The second is that it is acquired around the time it is expressed in speech. From Brown's (1973) analysis of such 'role markers' as prepositional phrases and possessive inflections, this would be towards the beginning of the third year.

Subjects

The study involved two groups of children. Each group contained six boys and six girls who lived in a predominantly lower middle-class suburb of Glasgow. The children in one group were within 20 days of 22 months (mean age = 22 months, 6 days) and were expected to be at the beginning of

169

word combination. The children in the other group were within 20 days of 28 months (mean age = 28 months, 7 days) and were expected to be acquiring 'role markers'.

Procedure

The children were presented in their homes with three tasks. The first was to play tea party with me for an unspecified time period, in practice 20 to 35 minutes. As the children's speech was tape-recorded, this task provided information about their expressive language. It also allowed me to introduce benefactive expressions like There's the tea for Mummy and locative expressions like Put the cup on the saucer while remaining fairly informal. Hence, it acted as a warm-up for the second task which was the tests of semantic knowledge.

The second task involved two tests, one concerned with semantic knowledge of benefaction and the other with semantic knowledge of location. Part I of each test checked relevant vocabulary. Pictures of the four entities to be used during later parts were presented singly and the child asked What is it? Appropriate labels were accepted and used subsequently. Alternatives were suggested to inappropriate labels. Mastery of labels was re-checked by presenting the pictures in two pairs and asking the child to 'show me' each entity in turn.

Part II was included to ensure that semantic knowledge of roles was being tested, and not grammatical knowledge of how roles are expressed. The four pictures to be presented in the third and fourth parts were shown one at a time. For benefaction, they were a man giving tea/cake to a lady and vice versa. For location, they were a girl putting a hat/shoe on a boy and vice versa. As each picture appeared, the child was given an appropriate benefactive or locative expression and encouraged to use it. For example, at the very least the child might be told: Look, here's the man. And here's the cake. The man's giving the cake to the lady. The cake's for the lady. The cake's for the lady. Can you say that? Sometimes, the 'training' took much longer. It was assumed that if some children had semantic knowledge of

170

roles but did not know how to express it, they would pick up the relevant constructions at least for the duration of the tests. Hence, they would not be handicapped on subsequent parts by grammatical limitations.

In Part III the child was shown the pictures in pairs. Each pair kept agent and beneficiary/location constant while varying object. For example, one pair consisted of a man giving tea/cake to a lady and another of a girl putting a hat/shoe on a boy. With these pairs, the child might be asked <u>Where's the cake for the lady</u>? and <u>Where's the hat on the boy</u>? Four pairs of pictures were presented during Part III of each test. Part III was not in itself a test of semantic knowledge of roles. Children could get the correct answer by simply locating labelled objects. Rather, Part III checked mastery of the test procedure by presenting the pictures and the instructions to be used in Part IV.

Part IV contained the tests of semantic knowledge. Here again, the child was shown the pictures in four pairs, one pair at a time. This time, however, each pair kept object constant while alternating agent and beneficiary/location. For instance, one pair consisted of a man giving cake to a lady and a lady giving cake to a man. Another consisted of a girl putting a hat on a boy and a boy putting a hat on a girl. The child would again be presented with questions like <u>Where's the cake for the lady</u>? and <u>Where's the hat on the boy</u>? Half the children received the benefactive test first and half the locative. The order of pictures in each part was varied across children. Once this task was over, the children were presented with the third task which was a modified version of the Uzgiris & Hunt (1975) object permanency scale. This was to ensure that they had reached the cognitive level at which they could comprehend roles. Hence failure on the semantic tests would be more likely to reflect linguistic deficiencies than cognitive ones.

Results

The first 100 utterances of each tape recording were transcribed and mean lengths of utterances (MLU) calculated using Brown's (1973) rules. Ten of the 22-month-olds were within his 'Stage I' (mean MLU = 1.56). Hence they could be said to be at the start of word combination. Eleven of the 28-month-olds were within Brown's 'Stages II or III' (mean MLU = 2.69). This is the period when devices which clearly mark roles are acquired. Then performance on the object permanency scale was analyzed. All children could cope with visible, and indeed invisible, displacements, showing they had reached the cognitive level required to understand roles. Finally, the children's scores on Part I, III and IV of each semantic test were computed. They were given one point if they touched the correct picture, making a maximum score of four points for each part. The mean scores are given in Table 1.

Insert Table 1 about here

Taking one age group and one part at a time, the scores obtained on each test were compared. The randomization test (Siegel, 1956) showed no difference between tests, so subsequent analysis took the combined scores only. All children obtained maximum scores on Part I. When asked to decide between eight pairs of pictures, the children should make four correct choices by chance. All children scored more than four on Part III. Analysis by randomization test showed that the scores on Parts I and III were highly unlikely to have arisen by chance in either age group ($p = 0.0005$ in all cases). In other words, the children understood the vocabulary and the test procedure. In Part IV, the 28-month-olds obtained a mean score of 5.16 and the 22-month-olds a mean score of 3.58. Analysis by randomization test showed that the scores of the 28-month-olds were unlikely to have arisen by chance ($p = 0.05$). The scores of the 22-month-olds were very likely to have arisen by chance ($p = 0.43$).

Discussion

The first three parts of the semantic tests tried to ensure that failure on the fourth could not result from

172

TABLE 1: Mean Scores on Semantic Tests

Test	22-month-olds		
	Part I	Part III	Part IV
Benefactive	4.00	3.50	1.83
Locative	4.00	3.58	1.75
Combined	8.00	7.08	3.58

Test	28-month-olds		
	Part I	Part III	Part IV
Benefactive	4.00	3.67	2.33
Locative	4.00	3.75	2.83
Combined	8.00	7.42	5.16

lexical, grammatical or procedural confusions. If they
succeeded, chance performance on Part IV must surely be
interpreted as not knowing that language encodes benefaction
and location. Since it is hard to imagine semantic knowledge of roles emerging in a non-systematic fashion, chance
performance on Part IV probably also indicates not knowing
that language encodes other roles. As a more or less direct
corollary, it must also signify the belief that language
encodes associations of entities, actions and states-of-
affairs. Thus, if the first three parts did preclude other
interpretations, the chance performance of the 22-month-olds
on Part IV must indicate a semantic system based on association rather than roles. Looking at the 22-month-olds
alone, it is obviously impossible to guarantee that other
interpretations were precluded. However, once the data from
the 28-month-olds are considered, a guarantee seems more
reasonable. The 28-month-olds performed significantly
above chance but far below perfection. Since it is hard to
explain their performance except in terms of emerging knowledge, it becomes difficult to interpret the 22-month-olds'
performance as anything but the lack of knowledge.

As mentioned earlier, the theoretical motivation for
studying early semantics is grammatical representation.
Therefore, it would be inappropriate to end without discussing the grammatical implications of denying semantic knowledge of roles. The first point is that it implies reject-
ing 'case grammar' representations of early sentences.
Various writers including Bowerman (1973), Brown (1973),
Edwards (1973), Kernan (1970) and Wells (1974) have tried to
represent 'Stage I' speech using case categories akin to
those developed by Chafe (1970) and Fillmore (1968). The
present research suggests that these categories might be
more appropriate after Stage II, with simpler categories
like 'entity' and 'action' being applied at Stage I. However, rather than pursue this possibility further, a second
point should be noted. The data from the 28-month-olds must
raise doubts about whether semantic knowledge of roles
really does precede its linguistic encoding. It could be
that semantic knowledge follows lexico-grammatical knowledge,
perhaps because children reflect on the real-world corre-

lates of expressions they have learned. If so, no semantically-based grammar could provide an adequate representation
of children's speech, irrespective of whether that grammar
presupposed roles or something simpler. On the contrary,
adequate representation would demand a grammar in which
semantic categories were secondary or, as linguists would
say, 'interpretive'.

To many psychologists, the possibility of interpretive
semantics should be resisted at all costs. Thanks to its
espousal by Chomsky (1965) and Katz and Fodor (1963), interpretive semantics is closely associated with transformational generative grammar and, as McNeill (1966) first demonstrated, this grammar necessitates innate capacities for
language. However, despite their close association, interpretive semantics and transformational generative grammar
could, in theory, be separated. For instance, it could be
argued that children develop a conceptual awareness of
reality which is independent of language but reflected in
their communicative intentions. Their desire to realize
these intentions leads them to increasingly conventional
communicative expressions. However, as they discover more
adequate expressions, they reflect on what else can be
achieved using those expressions, for example what else can
be referred to and what else can be predicated. Given this
sequence, children will be moving from communicative intentions through linguistic and, perhaps, nonlinguistic
expressions to semantic categories. Although this is
essentially an interpretive position, it is a far cry from
transformational generative grammar. It implies a grammar
based on communicative rather than syntactic categories.
Since communicative categories will be independent of, and
prior to, their linguistic expression, it also implies
continuity between prelinguistic and linguistic communication.

Although it would be premature to become too enthusiastic about these ideas, they can be given some support. As
mentioned earlier, there is considerable evidence that
communicative intentions predate their linguistic expression.
Recently, there have also been signs that failure to realize

communicative intentions precipitates linguistic growth. The fact that children often fail to realize their own intentions was highlighted by Ryan (1974). In a recently-published study of mother-child interaction (Howe, 1980, 1981b), I found many instances of such failures and, in Howe (1981b) suggested why they might contribute to linguistic growth. More importantly, I also considered whether children could be motivated by failure to realize other people's intentions, and found some potentially supportive evidence. The mothers in my study varied greatly in the conversational demands they made of their children. Moreover, the more compelling the demands, the faster the children progressed on several measures of semantic and grammatical development, indicating a possible causal connection. Going beyond the question of communicative pressures, there is another, more theoretical, reason for being sympathetic to the ideas outlined here. As I shall explain elsewhere (Howe, 1982), a communicatively-based grammar with interpretive semantics is highly compatible with Piaget's (1978) new equilibration model. Since this model provides a completely general account of development, accepting the proposed grammar would obviate any need for specifically-linguistic capacities.

It may come as a surprise to find that Piaget's equilibration model commits him to a grammar in which semantics are interpretive. It has often been thought that Piaget's (1952, 1955, 1962) work on sensori-motor development implied quite the opposite, a semantically-based grammar. However, all this work claims is that conceptual awareness of reality develops through direct interaction with the environment. Subsequently, it is reconstructed on the symbolic level, thereby permitting language. In other words, nothing was said about the relation between grammar and semantics on the symbolic level. It was not until his book on equilibration that Piaget implicitly commits himself one way or the other, and here it is unmistakably in the interpretive direction. This makes for a rather ironic conclusion. Because Piaget's work has often been taken to mean a semantically-based grammar, the view that semantic knowledge of roles emerges by the beginnings of word combination has generally been regarded as a Piagetian position on language. In this paper, I have argued that semantic knowledge of roles may be a much later development. However, I am now suggesting that this might also be inherently Piagetian.

References

E. BATES, L. CAMAIONI & V. VOLTERRA. The acquisition of performatives prior to speech. Merrill-Palmer Quarterly, 1975, 21, 205-226.

T.G. BEVER. The cognitive basis for linguistic structure. In J.R. Hayes (ed.), Cognition and the development of language. New York: Wiley, 1970.

L. BLOOM. Language development: form and function in emerging grammars. Cambridge: M.I.T. Press, 1970.

M. BOWERMAN. Early syntactic development: a cross-linguistic survey with special reference to Finnish. Cambridge: C.U.P., 1973.

M.D.S. BRAINE. Children's first word combinations. Monographs of Society for Research in Child Development, 1976, 41, No.1.

R. BROWN. A first language: the early stages. London: George Allen & Unwin, 1973.

J.S. BRUNER. The ontogenesis of speech acts. Journal of Child Language, 1975, 2, 1-19.

W.L. CHAFE. Meaning and the structure of language. Chicago: University of Chicago Press, 1970.

N. CHOMSKY. Aspects of the theory of syntax. Cambridge: M.I.T. Press, 1965.

P.A. de VILLIERS & J.G. de VILLIERS. Early judgements of semantic and syntactic acceptability by children. Journal of Psycholinguistic Research, 1972, 1, 299-310.

J. DORE. Holophrases, speech acts and language universals. Journal of Child Language, 1975, 2, 21-40.

D. EDWARDS. Sensory-motor intelligence and semantic relations in early child grammar. Cognition, 1973, 2, 395-434.

C.J. FILLMORE. The case for case. In E. Bach & R.T. Harms, (eds.), Universals in linguistic theory. New York: Holt, Rinehart & Winston, 1968.

R.M. GOLINKOFF & J. MARKESSINI. 'Mommy sock': the child's understanding of possession as expressed in two—noun phrases. Journal of Child Language, 1980, 7, 119-135.

P.M. GREENFIELD & J.H. SMITH. The structure of communication in early language development. New York: Academic Press, 1976.

M.A.K. HALLIDAY. Learning how to mean: explorations in the development of language. London: Edward Arnold, 1975.

C.J. HOWE. The meanings of two-word utterances in the speech of young children. Journal of Child Language, 1976, 3, 29-47.

C.J. HOWE. Mother-child conversation and semantic development. In H. Giles, W. Robinson and P. Smith (eds.), Language: Social psychological perspectives. Oxford: Pergamon, 1980.

C.J. HOWE. Interpretive analysis and role semantics: a ten-year mésalliance? Journal of Child Language, 1981a, 8, 439-456.

C.J. HOWE. Acquiring language in a conversational context. London: Academic Press, 1981b.

C.J. HOWE. The equilibration of language. Paper to be presented at B.P.S. Workshop on 'Cognitive bases of early language'. University of York, April 1982.

J. HUTTENLOCHER. The origins of language comprehension. In R.L. Solso (ed.), Theories in cognitive psychology: the Loyola Symposium. Potomac: Erlbaum, 1974.

J.J. KATZ & J.A. FODOR. The structure of semantic theory. Language, 1963, 39, 170-210.

K. KERNAN. Semantic relations and the child's acquisition of language. Anthropological Linguistics, 1970, 12, 171-187.

D. McNEILL. Developmental psycholinguistics. In F. Smith and G. Miller (eds.), The genesis of language: a psycholinguistic approach. Cambridge: M.I.T. Press, 1966.

J. PIAGET. The origins of intelligence in children. London: Routledge & Kegan Paul, 1952.

J. PIAGET. The child's construction of reality. London: Routledge & Kegan Paul, 1955.

J. PIAGET. Play, dreams and imitation in childhood. New York: Norton, 1962.

J. PIAGET. The development of thought: equilibration and cognitive structures. Oxford: Blackwell, 1978.

J. RYAN. Early language development: towards a communicational analysis. In M.P.M. Richards (ed.), The integration of a child into a social world. Cambridge: C.U.P., 1974.

J. SACHS & L. TRUSWELL. Comprehension of two-word instructions by children in the one-word stage. Journal of Child Language, 1978, 5, 17-24.

I. SCHLESINGER. Is there a natural word order? In W. Von Raffler-Engel and I. Lebrun (eds.), Baby talk and infant speech. Amsterdam: Swets & Zeitlinger, 1976.

E.F. SHIPLEY, C.S. SMITH & L.R. GLEITMAN. A study in the acquisition of language: free responses to commands. Language, 1969, 45, 322-342.

S. SIEGEL. Non-parametric statistics for the behavioural sciences. New York: McGraw Hill, 1956.

I. UZGIRIS & J. HUNT. Assessment in infancy: ordinal scales of psychological development. Illinois: University of Illinois press, 1975.

G. WELLS. Learning to code experience through language. Journal of Child Language, 1974, 1, 243-269.

L.A. WIEMAN. Stress patterns of early child language. Journal of Child Language, 1976, 3, 283-286.

Learning New Word Order: The Role of Animate Referents

Henrietta Lempert
Psychology Department
University of Toronto

Studies on passive sentence comprehension abound in literature on language development. The lesson of these investigations is that competence cannot be directly read off from performance. A child who does not "know" a form may still interpret it correctly under one set of conditions, and consistently misinterpret it under a different set of circumstances. Even when a child understands the form, a compelling visual experience can sometimes override that knowledge.

The same applies to production. In spontaneous speech, children sometimes use a syntactic form at an age when researchers claim they are unable to do so. Also, while they may use the form in conversation with another child, they may not do so when speaking to an adult (French and Nelson, 1981; McCabe, 1981). Even when external conditions are otherwise constant, a child may restrict his use of a syntactic form to particular visual contexts, producing it in one context, but not in another.

What aspects of a visual display are able to control children's production of passive sentences? When children aged six to nine years are asked, "What is happening in this picture?", they usually reply in active sentence form. However, the chances of the child's using a passive sentence are higher for animate than for inanimate acted-upons. They increase even more for pictures showing animates being affected by inanimate rather than animate actors (Baldie, 1976; Hayhurst, 1967; Harris, 1978).

Is there any continuity between the circumstances under which children are most likely to produce a passive sentence description and those under which they are best able to learn to produce the form? If animacy differences play a role with respect to production of passives, they might also do so with respect to the initial appearance of the form in speech. However, how can this possibility be verified? If the child does not as yet have a form at his disposal, how can we induce him to produce it?

Our solution was to use imitation for the purpose of teaching passive sentence frames ("The ___ is ___ed by the ___"). We then asked children to use these frames to describe events in which animacy of the actor and of the patient were systematically varied. We expected that children would find it easier to use the subject noun slot for animate than for inanimate patients.

The 27 children in Experiment 1 ranged from 3;0 to 4;10 years (mean, 3;11 years) and came from two university day care centers. When tested for comprehension of passives, their accuracy ranged from 0% to 75% (mean, 42%). They were randomly assigned to one of three training conditions, comparable in mean age and in mean pretest comprehension.

Twenty passive sentences were constructed for each condition, using ten different verbs. These sentences were designated training items. A second set of 12 sentences were formed with the same verbs as for training, but using different nouns. These sentences were designated "probes".

The experimenter enacted the meaning of each sentence with toys. For imitation items, the experimenter described the event in passive sentence form. The child repeated the sentence. For probes, the experimenter enacted the event, and asked the child to describe it in the "new way". Probes were randomly interspersed among the imitation items.

For one group of children, dynamic inanimate patients were acted on by animates, for example, 'bear pushes car', 'tiger chases airplane'. These children were supposed to imitate and to produce passives which had inanimate-animate order, for example, "The car is pushed by the bear". We will refer to this group as the "DI-patient" training group.

For a second group, animates were affected by dynamic

181

inanimates, for example, 'car pulls tiger', 'truck hits girl'. Passive sentences for this group had animate-inanimate order, for example, "The tiger is pulled by the truck". This group will be termed the "A-patient" training group.

For a third group, static inanimates were acted on by animates in some events, for example, 'girl washes kettle', 'tiger carries chair'. In the remaining items, static inanimates were acted on by dynamic inanimates, for example, 'truck bumps house', 'tiger pushes piano'. This group is termed the "SI-patient" training group.

Training and probe elicitation required two sessions for most children, but some needed three or four sessions. These were one or two days apart. After training, children were tested for generalization and for posttraining comprehension.

Results of Production Training

To clarify presentation of the data for probes, we will call responses which name the acted-upon before the actor "correct-order passives". "Reversed passives" have actor-first order. The term "passive" refers to overall correct and reversed order passives and is used in the sense of passive sentence frame.

Probe responses were classified by sentence type as follows: (1) Correct-order Passive; (2) Reversed Passive, (3) Reversed Active, and (4) Active. Reversed actives and actives include responses with a passive marker or with an incorrect preposition (e.g. "Tiger chased to the bear" and "Bear chase by tiger" given the event 'bear chases tiger').

Table 1 shows the mean number of responses in each sentence category. Visual inspection of reversed and correct-order passives indicates clear differences according to condition. This impression was confirmed by statistical analysis. Correct-order passives differed significantly according to condition ($F(2,34)=5.64$, $p<.01$). They occurred more often in the A-patient group than in the SI-patient group ($p<.01$), and more frequently in the SI-patient group

182

than in the DI-patient group (p < .05).

Table 1

Mean Number Sentence Types to Probes (MAX=12)

	Condition			
Sentence Type	A-patient	DI-patient	SI-patient	Mean
Passive				
Correct-Order	5.0	1.2	3.0	3.1
Reversed	2.1	3.8	3.3	3.1
Active				
Correct Order	2.9	5.4	5.0	4.1
Reversed	0.0	0.1	0.1	0.1
Omissions or				
Unscorable	2.0	1.5	0.6	0.6

Production patterns differed within each condition. The A-patient group showed mainly correct order ($F(1,24)=7.14$, $p < .01$), the DI-patient group showed mainly reversed order ($F(1,24)=4.70$, $p < .05$), while the SI-patient group showed no asymmetry ($F(1,24) < 1$). A separate analysis of (correct order) active sentences revealed that these did not differ significantly in the three conditions ($F(2,24)=2.46$, $p > .05$).

To this point, the data coincide with expectations in that the A-patient group shows mainly correct order for passives, and the DI-patient group shows mainly reversed order. However, since the acted-upons are inanimate for the SI-patient group, they should also show reversed order. Analysis of individual response patterns in this condition revealed that only four of the eight children who produced passives show the expected pattern.

As it turned out, one of the four children who produced more correct than reversed passives had learned a "rule" for

183

the structure. There is no evidence that the other three children did so. Perhaps, the "nonreversibility" of events in the SI-patient condition helped them use word order correctly.

Since we have raised the issue of nonreversibility, we need to consider whether outcomes for the A-patient training group actually involve confusion about the actor and the patient. Since events were potentially reversible in this condition, perhaps children assumed that the animate was the "more probable" actor. Their correct order passives would then have "actor-first" order. Clearly, this possibility must be ruled out since they should have showed the same confusion in their active sentences. However, there were no "reversed actives" at all.

The A-patient group is the only one to show a clear preference for patient-first order. However, it is premature to attribute this outcome to the use of animate patients. Preschool children favor actor-first order, but may do so less strongly for inanimate than for animate actors. Actor animacy may be as important as patient animacy.

We had not included a condition in which animates acted on other animates. Would actor-first order predominate for animate actors (as in the DI-patient condition)? Or would animate patients be able to override children's propensity for actor-first order, even with animate actors. In putting these questions to test, we decided to entice children in the latter direction by including items in which a (dynamic) inanimate affected an animate. While we could not predict word order for animate actors, we expected mainly correct order for inanimate actors.

For this purpose, we took ten imitation and six probe items from the A-patient training condition. A second set of ten imitation and six probe items was formed by combining two animates, for example, 'horse chases bear', 'tiger pulls horse'.

As we had exhausted the subject pool in the first two schools, children in a third day care center were studied. They were not comparable to the first group, as they were mostly children of recent immigrants from the West Indies. This difference, however, provided an opportunity to test the generality of the "animate-first" pattern in the A-patient condition. Thus, we repeated A-patient training with a new group of nine children aged 2;11 to 5;0 years (mean, 4;1). Their mean comprehension was 58%. In the other condition were ten children aged 3;3 to 5;0 years (mean, 4;1) with mean comprehension of 47%. The training procedure was the same as before.

Results of Production Training: Experiment 2

Since the acted-upon was animate in both conditions, we will change our terminology. The A-patient condition will be termed "D-actor". The condition which had animate (A) and also inanimate (D) actors will be called "A,D-actor".

Table 2

Mean Number Sentence Types to Probes (MAX=12)

	Condition		
Sentence Type	D-actor	A,D-actor	Mean
Passive			
Correct-Order	5.9	2.0	3.9
Reversed	2.9	3.5	3.2
Active			
Correct Order	2.1	5.4	3.8
Reversed	0.1	0.4	0.3
Omissions or			
Unscorable	1.0	0.7	0.9

Production data, classified by sentence type, are in Table 2. The analysis of variance revealed that noun order in passives varied according to condition ($F(1,17)=11.46$, $p<.01$). D-actor training again led to significantly more correct than reversed passives ($F(1,17)=9.91$, $p<.01$). This group also produced more correct order passives than the A,D-actor group ($F(1,17)=17.25$, $p<.01$), who showed a trend towards more reversed than correct passives.

Since we had expected different noun order patterns in the A,D-actor group according to actor, reversed and correct passives were examined separately for animate and inanimate actors. Clear differences emerged. For animate actors, 73% of passives were reversed and 27% had correct order ($F(1,9)=37.56$, $p<.01$). For inanimate actors, 55% were reversed and 45% had correct order ($F(1,9)<1$).

We had expected to find more correct than reversed passives for inanimate actors, but instead found no asymmetry. These outcomes stress the importance of the type of actor. Animate actors propel children towards standard word order; their influence spreads to inanimate actors. However, even when word order approaches conflict, children still evidence an independent preference for animate/inanimate order.

Even this conclusion depends on the specifics of the event. Analysis of correct and reversed passives in the D-actor groups across Experiments 1 and 2 revealed that noun order varied according to verb (actually, according to how the verb was enacted). The relevant data, based on 18 children, are shown in Table 3.

Table 3

Number Correct and Reversed Passives to Each Verb
(A patient/D-actor Groups, Experiments 1 and 2

Verb	Correct	Reversed	Verb	Correct	Reversed
Lift*	18	6	Hit*	15	12
Pull	14	0	Bump	9	5
Turn	9	2	Touch	7	5
Push	10	5	Chase	6	4
Carry	6		Follow	4	4

*Verb occurred twice in probes

Actions which produced the most asymmetry (lift, pull, push, turn (around in a circle) involved prolonged contact during which the patient's position changed. Contact of brief duration (hit, bump, touch) was less effective, but these actions resulted in minimal or else no movement to the patient. Since 'carry' (prolonged contact without movement) shows the same pattern, a clear change in position appears to be an important determinant of noun order. However, contact also plays a role. Mutual action, in the absence of contact (chase, follow) led to minimal asymmetry.

To summarize, even three-year-olds can use noun order correctly in passives when describing events in which animates are affected by inanimates. However, change to the patient helps them to do so. Perhaps, when animates move or otherwise change, they become relatively more "salient" than inanimate actors. But are these children subsequently able to use noun order correctly under different circumstances?

Generalization and Comprehension

One to two days after production training ended, children were tested for their ability to generalize passive sentences by 12 pictures which showed animate actors and three types of acted-upons (animate, dynamic inanimate, and static inanimate). The pictures, drawn in black ink, showed events such as 'lion wash window', 'lion wash horse', and 'lion push wheel'. The children were asked to describe the pictures in the "new way". Following generalization, their comprehension of passive sentences was tested.

Results for Generalization

The mean number of correct and reversed order passives for each type of patient are shown in Table 4. We summarize noun order propensities for each training condition:

(1) The static inanimate group showed no difference between correct and reversed passives $(F(1,24) < 1)$.
(2) The dynamic inanimate patient group (Experiment 1) produced significantly more reversed than correct passives $(F(1,24) = 4.83, p < .05)$.

187

(3) The animate patient + inanimate actor group in
Experiment 1 produced few passives, but tended towards
reversed order (F(1,24)=1.74, p>.05). The corresponding
group in Experiment 2 produced significantly more reversed
than correct passives (F(1,17)=6.87, p<.05).
(4) The animate patient + animate/inanimate actor group
(Experiment 2) showed a nonreliable trend towards more
correct than reversed passives.

Table 4

Mean Correct and Reversed Passives to Generalization (MAX=4)

Condition	Noun Order	Type of Patient		
		Animate	Dynamic	Static
Experiment 1				
SI-patient	Correct	0.8	1.0	0.4
	Reversed	0.6	0.3	0.3
DI-patient	Correct	0.2	0.1	0.0
	Reversed	0.8	1.1	0.1
A-patient	Correct	0.3	0.4	0.0
	Reversed	0.3	0.7	0.1
Experiment 2				
A-patient/	Correct	0.4	0.1	0.0
D-actor	Reversed	1.6	1.8	0.7
A-patient/	Correct	1.3	0.7	0.5
A,D-actor	Reversed	0.1	0.5	0.2

To summarize, although children in the A-patient + D-
actor condition had quite consistently produced correct
order in their passives to probes, they did not do so on
generalization, even for animate patients. However, analysis

of generalization data across conditions revealed that children who had experienced animate patients during training show some transfer to the same referent category. In Experiment 1, this was obscured by a floor effect, but in Experiment 2, animate patients elicited most of the correct-order passives ($F(2,34)=4.64$, $p<.05$). Conversely, DI-patients elicited most of the reversed passives ($F(2,34)= 5.03$, $p<.05$). Thus, there is some evidence, admittedly restricted, for situation-specific transfer.

Results for Comprehension

Comprehension was tested by asking children to enact their interpretation of the meaning of 12 passive sentences. Before production training, comprehension ranged from 39% to 58% for the five groups across Experiments 1 and 2. Although mean comprehension changed after production training, the range was still the same (39% to 58%). All differences were unreliable in Experiment 1 and also in Experiment 2.

It would be premature to conclude that production training had no effect at all on comprehension. It does, but whether this is manifest varies with age as well as with pretraining performance. In Table 5, children are ranked in four categories according to their scores for posttraining comprehension. Mean age and mean pre- and posttraining comprehension are shown for each category.

Table 5

Relation Between Age, Pre- and Posttraining Comprehension

	Comprehension		Age
Posttraining Score	Pretest	Posttest	Mean
0 - 3 (n=10)	31%	20%	3;9
4 - 6 (n=15)	38%	39%	3;8
7 - 9 (n=13)	51%	62%	4;1
10-12 (n= 8)	55%	89%	4;4

Children whose posttraining accuracy ranged from 0 to 6 are somewhat younger overall than those whose posttraining scores ranged from 7 to 12. On pretest, the former tend to assign the role of actor to the first-named referent. Most of them maintained the same approach after training. Perhaps they saw no need to change their approach since they already had a "solution".

Among those children who mainly showed inconsistency before production training are eight children who subsequently used structural information to interpret passive sentences. Perhaps it is coincidental that these children tend to be somewhat older than those children who did not benefit positively from production training. However, it may also be the case that as age increases, children are better able to transfer information across different situations.

Summary and Conclusions

We have completed our exposition of the data and are now able to return to the question with which we began. We have found that animacy differences clearly matter when children are trained to produce passives. Also, they matter in the same ways as for children who already are able to say passives. Perhaps the underlying substrate is the same.

Even in pictures, animates "appear" more active than inanimates, regardless of their semantic role. Animates do things and react to action. Their actions and reactions are attention catching. The propensity for animate/inanimate order may actually involve a propensity to take the more active ("salient") entity in the scene as a frame of reference for utterance.

Our second question concerns the relevance of the results for learning word order relations. On what basis did the animate patient + inanimate actor group produce correct order in passives? At some level, they must have recognized the correspondence between noun order in their passive sentences and the referent's semantic role in the event. However, they may have been able to use patient-first order only when this order was supported by the visual context.

Whether or not a child can be induced to try new word order depends on whether the nonlinguistic context corresponds or conflicts with using a more established form. When the context supports established syntactical patterns, the child will not even attempt a new form (as in the animate actor + dynamic inanimate patient condition). If the context is not conducive to a customary form, but is congruent with a new form, then the child can be induced to try the new form.

In its initial appearance, knowledge of new word order is not at the child's conscious disposal. A new form is susceptible to response competition from an "older" or more established way of speaking, and thereby, is applicable only under circumstances that facilitate its use. The nonlinguistic context is critical not only with respect to the emergence of a form in speech, but also with respect to maintaining it while it becomes established in the child's linguistic repertoire.

The younger the child is, the less able he is to reflect on the base for his knowledge, and therefore, the more vulnerable is he to the impact of the immediate stimulus field. Our impression of what young children know depends on the specifics of the stimulus field. Under one set of circumstances, children behave as if they know the structure of passives. Under a different set of conditions, the same children behave as if they do not do so. However, if our estimate of competence depends on the stimulus environment, we are unable to make any claims about the extent of young children's linguistic knowledge until we have scrutinized that knowledge under all possible circumstances.

References

Baldie, B.J. The acquisition of the passive voice. Journal of Child Language, 1976, 2, 331-348.

Harris, M. Noun animacy and the passive: a developmental approach. Journal of Experimental Psychology, 1978, 20, 69-73.

Hayhurst, H. Some errors of young children in producing passive sentences. Journal of Verbal Learning and Verbal Behavior, 1967, 6, 634-639

Notes

French, L.A. and Nelson, K. Temporal knowledge expressed in preschoolers' descriptions of familiar activities. Paper presented at Child Language Research Forum, Stanford University, 1981.

McCabe, A. The incidence of conditional statements in the natural speech of young children. Paper presented at Society for Research in Child Development, 1981, Boston.

THE NON-INTERACTION OF LINGUISTIC AND COGNITIVE NOTIONS OF GENDER IN THE LANGUAGE OF YOUNG ISRAELIS

Yonatha Levy
Psychology Department, The Hebrew University, Jerusalem

Gender systems in languages are typically areas in which syntactic and morphophonological distinctions interact with a partially relevant semantic distinction. Because of this partial overlap, the acquisition of gender systems is a potentially promising area in which to investigate the interaction between cognitive development and language development. By comparing children's linguistic performance in places in the system in which gender notions are imperative for making the correct linguistic choices or in places where the semantic gender distinction could be used as a partial strategy for handling animate nouns; by comparing those to the children's knowledge of the linguistic system of gender in general, one can infer the presence or absence of an interaction between the two levels.

In this paper I shall look at acquisitional data which concern two such places in the Hebrew gender system in an attempt to address the issue of the interaction between cognitive and linguistic notions of gender in the speech of young children.

Let me start with some facts concerning Hebrew gender: In Hebrew all nouns are either masculine or feminine and are typically characterized as such by their final syllable. Adjectives agree in number and gender with their head nouns. Verbs, pronouns and even some prepositions agree in number, person and gender with the noun as illustrated in examples 1 - 4 below.

Examples:
1. ha-yéled   ha-katán   holéx.   (mas.sg.)
   'the boy'   'the little'   'goes'.

2. ha-yaldá   ha-kataná   holéxet. (fem.sg.)
   'the girl'   'the little'   'goes'.

3. ha-yeladím   ha-ktaním   holixím. (mas.pl.)
   'the children' 'the little' 'go'.

4. ha-yeladót   ha-ktanót   holxót.
   'the girls'   'the little'   'go' (fem.pl.)

The sex of the referents of animate nouns fully determine the linguistic gender of these nouns. The natural
sex of the referents of the nouns overrides all linguistic
considerations. For example, it is perfectly natural to
hear sentences such as:

rosh   ha-xúg   amrá
the chairman of   the department   said
when the chairman is a woman.

The first study concerns the acquisition of referential
pronouns and verb forms. The data come from a longitudinal
study of the linguistic development of my son Arnon in his
third year of life. The sample that this data is drawn
from was collected when Arnon was 2;2-2;10. Before age 2;2,
there were only masculine forms of verbs and pronouns in his
speech. Following that stage feminine forms became frequent.

Tables 1, 2 of Data

Table 1. Frequency distribution of singular pronouns plus
          verbs in Arnon (age 2;3 - 2;10)

	Pronoun + Verb Forms				
	fem.+fem. sg. sg.	fem.+masc. sg. sg.	masc.+masc. sg. sg.	masc.+fem. sg. sg.	N
Addressing Second Person Females Singular	40.8% (202)	29.9% (148)	20.3%	–	494
Referring to Third Person Males Singular	18.4% (29)	14.6% (23)	67.0% (106)	–	158
Referring to Third Person Females Singular	79.3% (134)	–	20.7% (35)	–	169

Table 2. Frequency distribution of singular verb forms in Arnon (age 2;2 - 2;10).

Inflected Verb Forms				
Addressing	fem.sg.	mas.sg.	mixed forms	N
Second Person Females Singular	48% (72)	39.4% (59)	12.6% (19)	150
Referring to Third Person Male Singular	4.8% (4)	95.2% (80)	–	84
Referring to Third Person Female Singular	82.4% (84)	17.6% (18)	–	102

These data refer to the <u>singular</u> pronouns and verb forms only, for reasons that are irrelevant for us here. Let me say just this: there was absolutely no confusion between singulars and plurals or among persons. The only confusion in Arnon's use of the pronouns and verb forms was in gender.

Note that these tables present no data for second person masculine singular, since these forms were correct all the time. In addressing second person masculine, which in this sample was exclusively his father, Arnon used the form that was most frequent in our home at that time and, more importantly, the form which was used to address him, namely, the masculine singular. In this he followed the common practice of children learning inflected languages (Slama-Cazacu, 1973; Berman-Aronson, 1978).

In addressing feminine singular which was mostly, though not exclusively, his mother, Arnon performed close to chance level, while in addressing third persons he performed way above chance, but still not perfectly.

What can explain the marked difference between Arnon's performance in addressing second person feminines versus his performance in referring to third persons? Let us look

195

briefly at the task of selecting referential pronouns
and inflected verb forms. In general, at the heart
of this task is a recognition of the gender of the referent
noun, be it natural gender for animates, or linguistic
gender for inanimates. In addition, one must learn the
formal properties of the particular pronoun system and
verb inflections.

Consider the pronoun system in Hebrew: First person
singular pronoun ani 'I' in Hebrew is not inflected for
gender. Thus, Arnon, his father and his mother refer to
themselves with the same pronoun. However, second person
pronouns are inflected for gender. So, while Arnon and
his father can be referred to with the use of the same
pronoun, ata 'you', masculine, his mother requires a
different form, at 'you', feminine. A further difficulty
may arise from the fact that ata 'you' masculine, ends
in the typically feminine /a/ suffix.

The situation in third person pronoun assignment is
much more favorable: the forms for 'he' and 'she' have
endings which are neither the typical feminine stressed
/a/ or /t/, nor the typically masculine consonantal ending.
Furthermore, third persons can be referred to either by
the use of a pronoun or by mentioning their names. For
example: one can use interchangeably, in the same utterance,
'the teacher', 'the neighbor', 'the baby' or simply 'he'.
In Hebrew these nouns have typical masculine endings --
moré, šaxén, tinók, while their feminine counterparts have
typical feminine endings -- morá, šxená, tinóket. Proper
names in Hebrew often, though not always, also share the
typical masculine and feminine endings.

Thus the child will often have formal linguistic
information concerning nouns that are used to refer to
third persons. He may be familiar with their plural forms
and the forms of the adjectives that they take, and resort
to that information when a choice of a pronoun is called
for; whereas second persons as subjects of inflected verbs
in a conversation are always an unnamed 'you'.

An additional factor concerns the contextual situation
which is often ambiguous with regard to the referents of
a speech act when third persons are involved; whereas it

196

rarely is so for second persons. The child has good reason to draw upon all the information available to him in order to use third person forms appropriately. So, it seems that the two year old Hebrew learner has a lot to go on formally and functionally when he needs to distinguish in his speech between 'he' and 'she' but has relatively few formal clues to help him decide between 'you-masculine' and 'you-feminine'.

It seems that, for the distinction between second persons, the cognitive notion becomes imperative. If a child has a relatively well defined cognitive notion of gender that he acknowledges as relevant to his language system, he should have little difficulty in using referential pronouns and inflected verbs. If he lacks that semantic knowledge, there should be a marked difference between his ability to correctly assign referential pronouns to third persons, where a lot of formal clues exist, and his choice of second person pronouns when there is so little to go on formally.

Arnon's inability to draw upon a relevant cognitive distinction and use it linguistically seems to be the reason for the differences in his performance with regard to second and third persons (Tables 1, 2). The lack of an appropriate semantic distinction made the formal clues the sole determinants of his acquisitional pattern.

It is reasonable to expect considerable individual differences in the acquisitional patterns of these forms. The sex of the child, the structure of individual families and the people that the young child is closely involved with may affect the nature of the input language and with it the particular forms with which the child will have difficulties. Still, some diary studies and anecdotal data that have been reported (Berman, to appear) on the acquisition of Hebrew pronouns suggest that among the referential pronouns the second person pronouns indeed emerge last.

The second study was concerned with the availability of a semantic approach to the acquisition of gender forms. Such an approach can only handle one portion of the acquisitional task, namely, that which involves animate nouns. The hypothesis was that, at a time when the children were not yet in control of the morphophonological details of gender distinctions in nouns and adjectives, if they possessed the relevant semantic distinction, they would do better on linguistic tasks which involve animate nouns than on tasks which involve inanimate nouns. One of the tasks that was used to test this hypothesis was a comprehension test of adjective-noun agreement.*

Twenty-eight nursery school children whose mean age was 2;7 were tested. The children were all native monolingual Israelis. They were first borns and came from educated middle class families. The procedure was as follows: A set of toys was arranged in front of the child. The objects were all extremely familiar and the child knew their names. Among the toys were animate and inanimate objects designated by either masculine or feminine nouns. The questions were of the following form: who or what--which in Hebrew are undifferentiated--so: who is cute? big? little? etc., with the adjective inflected for gender and number. For every adjective that appeared in the questions there were masculine and feminine animate and inanimate objects that fit the semantics of the adjective but only two objects that fit also with its form. For example: on the table were a few green objects, but only one green feminine animate toy and one green feminine inanimate toy. Either one of these two objects could be the answer to the question: 'who is green?' with the adjective marked for feminine singular. Now, since in Hebrew there is no distinction of animacy as in 'who' versus 'what', the child could choose whether to refer in his answer to an animate or an inanimate noun.

Altogether there were sixteen questions asked. The test lasted 10-15 minutes and was repeated twice: once with toys and once with drawings, for reasons which do not concern us here.

---

*A methodological problem arises with regard to this study which concerns the interpretation of data from tests of comprehension. I believe it can be overcome but the discussion will far exceed the limitations of this paper.

Results from both tests show that the children made absolutely no errors in the singular-plural distinction, while they erred considerably in the gender forms.

Table 3. Distribution of replies in comprehension test of adjective agreement. (N = 28; mean age 2;7)

	Animate			Inanimate			N
	correct	incorrect	n	correct	incorrect	n	
Toy Test	80	72	152	19	20	39	191
Picture Test	56	51	107	17	18	35	142

Toy-test: Of the 191 answers obtained from the children, 152 referred to animates and 39 to inanimates (Binomial test Z = 8:10 p .05). Of those answers referring to animates, 80 reflected a correct gender choice and of the answers referring to inanimates, 19 reflected a correct gender choice.

Drawing-test: Of the 142 answers obtained, 107 referred to animates while 35 referred to inanimates (Binomial test Z = 5.96 p .05). Of the answers referring to animates, 56 reflected a correct gender choice. Of the answers referring to inanimates, 17 reflected a correct gender choice.

These data then show that the children were extremely biased towards the animate toys but this bias was not reflected in a better knowledge of the inflectional system for the animate nouns. The proportion of correct versus incorrect answers shows that there was not a marked difference in the children's linguistic performance with these two classes of nouns; overall, they were 50% correct in all noun classes.

Whatever the status of the children's semantic-cognitive notion of gender at that time, there seemed to be no indication that they were using it to improve upon their knowledge of the linguistic gender distinction. Besides being in poor control of the morphophonological clues that can be used to determine agreement, these two-and-a-half year olds also lacked a relevant semantic notion of gender which could have been used to predict agreement for animate nouns.

These results accord well with a previous study of the acquisition of plural forms of nouns in Hebrew (Levy, in press) where longitudinal and cross-sectional data supported a model of acquisition in which no use was made of a semantic notion of gender. The children seemed to work out a system of pluralization solely on the basis of the morphophonological properties of the noun endings.

In sum, the data from these two studies attest to the non-interaction of cognitive and linguistic gender in the language of two-year old Hebrew speakers. Considering the cognitive literature on the development of gender notions, this acquisitional pattern is not at all surprising. Since most studies point to the fact that children under three do not have an established gender concept, in particular they lack gender distinctions for others, it is perhaps to be expected that these children will not be sensitive to the role that this concept is playing in the linguistic system that they are striving to master.

References
1. Berman, R. (1978) Early verbs: comments on how and why a child uses his first words. International Journal of Psycholinguistic Research, 5, 21-39.

2. Berman, R. (to appear) The acquisition of Hebrew. In: Slobin,D.I.(ed) Cross-linguistic Studies of Language Acquisition, Hillsdale,N.J. Lawrence Erlbaum.

3. Levy,Y. (in press) The acquisition of Hebrew plurals-the case of the missing gender category. Journal of Child Language.

4. Slama-Cazacu,T. (1973) The learning and use of oblique cases by children. In: Introduction to Psycholinguistics. The Hague: Mouton, 239-250.

Mayan telegraphese:
Stage I speech in Quiché Mayan[1]

Clifton Pye

One of the most striking characteristics of
children's early speech is its 'telegraphic' quality. The first sentences children produce re-
semble adult telegrams in that they contain mainly
nouns and verbs, and few, if any, inflections,
prepositions, or articles. At least this is the
way children learn English. Acquisition data from
Quiché, a Mayan language spoken in the western
highland region of Guatemala, shows that not all
children proceed in this way. Instead, Quiché
children learned to use certain, perceptually
salient verb suffixes quite early, suggesting the
primacy of intonation in morphological development. I collected longitudinal records from four
Quiché children, aged 2;0 to 3;0. I visited the
children in their homes over a nine-month period,
approximately once every two weeks for a one-hour
play session during which I recorded their speech.
Quiché was the predominant language in all the
households although some of the parents could
speak Spanish. The children spoke only Quiché
during the play sessions, this being the language
that my assistants and I used with them (see Pye
1980 for details of the study).

For reasons of space, I must confine the
present discussion to the final syllables of the
Quiché verb. Quiché is an agglutinative language
with a complex verb structure:

(1) aspect + (object) + (movement) + subject +
verb root +

$$\left(\begin{Bmatrix} \text{transitivizing} \\ \text{intransitivizing} \end{Bmatrix} \text{suffix}\right) + \text{(termination)}$$

Quiché children must learn to use the complete
verb in talking about everyday events. In the
beginning, though, their first verbs are incomplete, as shown in (2) and (3):[2]

201

(2) (Talking about Al Tiya:n's doll)
    A: La: utz kawiloh (k+Ø+aw+il+oh, asp.+3s+
2s+see+term.)
    Al Tiya:n (2;2): jah? loh. (=k+Ø+inw+il+oh,
asp.+3s+1s+see+term.)

    .....

    A: kawarik. (ka+Ø+war+ik, asp.+3s+sleep+
term., 'He's sleeping')
    Al Tiya:n: lik. (=kawarik)

(3) (Talking about a plastic duck)
    Al Cha:y (2'9): loq' ech wa?. (=kaqaloq',
asp.+3s+1p+buy)
    Mother: kaqaloq' qe:ch wa?e (ka+Ø+qa+loq',
'We will buy it') 'We'll have to buy one of our
own'
chata: chare le: mu?s, a kasipaj chuweh, cho?qa
chareh. (k+Ø+a+sip+aj, asp.+3s+2s+give+trans.,
'you give it') Ask the white man, 'Will you give
it to me?', say to him.
    Al Cha:y: paj weh. (=a kasipaj chuweh 'Will
you give it to me?')

The children always observed the syllable divi-
sions in their words, not the morpheme boundaries.
The Quiché verb often undergoes resyllabification
so that the syllable boundaries do not match the
boundaries between morphemes. In (2), for
example, A (an assistant) asked Al Tiya:n whether
she liked her doll, using the Quiché idiom a: utz
kawiloh 'Is it good to see?' The morphemes of
the verb, /k+Ø+aw+il+oh/ (lit. 'you see it'),
resyllabify as ka-wi-'loh, with primary stress on
the final syllable. Al Tiya:n used only the
final syllable, which contains the final consonant of the verb root plus the termination marker.
In her next utterance (again talking about her
doll), Al Tiya:n reduced the verb kawarik to its
final syllable. (At this stage in her phonological development, Al Tiya:n regularly substituted /l/ for /r/ in all environments.) This
syllable is again composed of the final consonant
of the verb root and the termination marker. In

202

(3), Al Cha:y tells her mother that they will
have to buy a plastic duck like the one that I
had brought. Her first utterance uses the final
syllable of the verb kaqaloq', which in this
instance, happens to be the verb root. Al Cha:y
then imitated her mother and asked me to give the
duck to her, using the final syllable of the verb
kasipaj. This syllable contains the final consonant of the verb root plus the transitivizing
suffix of derived transitive verbs.

The children's use of syllables is interesting in light of recent studies indicating the
syllable's importance in language perception.[3]
The processing of speech in syllabic units has
special implications for morphological development. Inflectional morphemes which consist of
segments, not syllables, could be expected to
pose difficulties for children in the early
stages of phonological development. Languages
like Quiché, in which the morphemes frequently
do not correspond to the syllables due to extensive resyllabification, would pose additional
problems for language learners. At the time in
which examples (2) and (3) were recorded, the
children were still in the early stages of
syllable development (see Table 1). Ninety-one
percent of the verbs in Al Cha:y's first five
samples contain only one syllable while seventy
percent of Al Tiya:n's verbs in her first eight
samples contain only one syllable. Their verbs
had a CVC form or, in exceptional cases, a CV-CVC
form. As their language developed, the children's
verbs gradually increased in the number of syllables that they contained, until, in the final
samples, only a third of their verbs were monosyllabic. The Quiché children added new syllables
to the front of those they were already producing,
in effect, working from the back of the verb to
the front.

The one-syllable-per-word production limit
forces Quiché children in the early stages of
language acquisition to make a choice of which
part of the verb they will produce. If children

AL TIYA:N

Age	2;1.7	2;1.17	2;1.22	2;1.30	2;3.10	2;7.8	2;7.28	2;10.13
No. of verbs	17	2	16	24	41	40	86	152
% Monosyllabic	88	100	56	79	93	60	48	33
% Disyllabic	12		44	21	7	30	40	53
% 2 syllables						10	12	14

AL CHA:Y

Age	2;9.3	2;9.8	2;9.16	2;9.28	2;10.21	3;0.8	3;1.5	3;3.28
No. of verbs	19	27	55	64	86	97	120	74
% Monosyllabic	90	93	95	86	73	56	60	32
% Disyllabic	5	7	4	11	22	37	29	51
% 2 syllables	5		1	3	4	5	6	14

TABLE 1. Syllable structure development of two Quiché children

operated according to a semantically-based strategy, one would expect them to pick out that part of the verb which encodes the major meaning (Brown 1973) or that remains unchanged in different environments (Slobin 1973). Such a hypothesis predicts that Quiché children would first produce the verb root, since it is the part of the verb that encodes the central meaning and remains unchanged. In fact, 62 percent of the monosyllabic verbal utterances in Al Tiya:n's first eight samples contained the verb root, while Al Cha:y used the verb root in 72 percent of her monosyllabic verbs in her first six samples. Although this may seem like a reasonable amount of the data, I would claim that the instances where the semantic hypothesis fails are severe enough to call it into question.

Examples (2) and (3) show that the children sometimes used only part of the verb root in their verbal utterances. There are many instances in the data in which the children did not use any part of the verb root at all. This happened either because the verb was in phrase-final position and had a termination marker attached to it or because the verb stem was polysyllabic, as was usually the case when it contained a transitivizing or intransitivizing suffix. Al Tiya:n's utterances in (2) are examples of termination marker use, while Al Cha:y's utterances in (3) show first, the use of the verb root, and second, the use of the transitivizing suffix. The children also used passive, anti-passive, perfective, and causative suffixes on their early verbs, although not very frequently. An hypothesis based on perceptual saliency is a possible alternative to semantically-based explanations of children's early speech. In particular, stress and utterance-final position seem to make some syllables stand out in relation to others. The salience of utterance-final position is probably due to the latency effect, people will remember best what they hear last. In addition, utterance-final syllables participate in the terminal intonation contours

which Bolinger (1978) has found consist of a set
of basic patterns imposed on sentence intonation
in almost all languages. Slobin (1973) and Kuczaj
(1979) have noticed that children pay most attention to the ends of words, and learn suffixes
before prefixes. The role of stress in language
acquisition is rather more problematic. Bolinger
notes that stress is subservient to the requirements of sentence intonation and that what is
usually taken as the characteristic stress on
words is the result of using words by themselves
in 'citation form' where they form one-word sentences and bear a sentence accent. Bolinger
reserves the term 'stress' for the assignment of
intonational accent to a typical syllable in
words. The requirements of intonation are free
to override stress assignments, resulting in a
variable stress placement. Compare, for example,
the variable stress on the word thirteen as:
1) the answer to the question,'How many people are
in this room?', and 2) its use in the chant,
'Thirteen men on a deadman's chest...' This is
one reason investigators have minimized the role
of stress in language acquisition. Those who try
to make child language conform with generative
theories assume that the syntactic or semantic
structures are basic and that children learn to
use stress only after they have mastered these
basics. Bloom (1973:61-3) reported that her
daughter did not use the prosodic features of
stress and intonation linguistically until she
had learned two-word constructions (but see
Branigan 1979). However, if we ignore the syntactic role of stress for the moment and concentrate
instead on the form of children's first words,
there is clear evidence that children do pay
attention to stress. Many investigators have
noted children's tendency to drop unstressed
syllables, especially those in pretonic position
(cf. Miller and Ervin 1964:13, Waterson 1971 for
English; Vogel 1975 for Rumanian; Berman 1981 for
Hebrew; Feurer 1980 for Mohawk; MacWhinney forthcoming for Hungarian; Nokony 1977 for Dakota-
Sioux; and Bowerman 1973 for Finnish). There are
also a number of experimental studies which

confirm children's tendency to preserve stressed syllables.[4]

One could hypothesize that children would be more likely to notice an utterance-final, stressed syllable. In the speech of adult Quiché speakers, primary stress is assigned to the rightmost vowel of a word if that vowel is long or is followed by a consonant; otherwise, stress falls on the penultimate vowel (Norman 1976). In most Quiché verbs, the final vowel is the one that receives primary stress. In utterances where the verb is final, the verb's stressed syllable would also be utterance-final. (Although Quiché is a VOS language, the subject and object are not overtly expressed when sufficient information is encoded by the person markers on the verb.) One could test the perceptual hypothesis against the semantic hypothesis by examining the child's use of verbs in which the verb root was not the final syllable of the verb. If the children were following a semantic strategy, they should use the root syllable of the verb whereas, if they were following a perceptual strategy, they should use the final, stressed syllable. I counted the number of cases, accordingly, in which the verb root was not the final syllable of the verb for four subjects from whom I had obtained early acquisition data. Besides Al Tiya:n and Al Cha:y, they included two boys, A Carlos (3;0) and A Li:n (2;0). I used only the samples which contain over seventy percent one-syllable verb forms: the first eight samples of Al Tiya:n, the first six samples of Al Cha:y, the first three samples of A Carlos, and two samples of A Li:n. The results are shown in Table 2. Using the binomial test, the results from each subject are significant at $p=.005$ (two-tailed). The results consistently favor the perceptual hypothesis over the semantic.[5]

The children did not simplify their acquisition task by using the final syllable of the verb rather than the verb root. The final syllable poses unique difficulties for a child's Dialect

Monosyllabic Verbs Whose
Root Morpheme ≠ Final Syllable

Subject	Total number of monosyllabic verbs[a]	Semantic Hypothesis[a,b]	Perceptual Hypothesis[a,c]
Al Tiya:n	108	8	40
Al Cha:y	410	23	119
A Carlos	65	3	16
A Li:n	56	3	22

TABLE 2. Test of semantic and perceptual hypotheses on verbs

[a] Tokens

[b] Use of the root rather than the final syllable

[c] Use of the final syllable rather than the root

Acquisition Heuristic, or DAH (the Quiché word meaning 'lad'). Grammatically, the form of the final syllable depends not only on the lexical class of the verb, but also on whether the verb is in phrase-medial or phrase-final position. Semantically, the syllable distinguishes several quite subtle meanings, including the perfective. It is, thus, extremely surprising that the children should use the final syllable rather than the verb root. Al Tiya:n and Al Cha:y made errors in their use of the final syllable on only 14 percent of the verbs in their first tapes. Al Tiya:n had acquired the final syllable, in terms of Brown's (1973) and Cazden's (1968) criterion, by her eighth sample (2;3.19), while Al Cha:y had acquired the final syllable by her tenth sample (3;0). This was long before they had learned the aspect and person markers on the verb, and even before they had acquired the Quiché prepositions and articles (Pye 1980). Moreover, the children systematically distinguished between the phrase-medial and phrase-final forms of the verbs even before they learned to mark the distinction appropriately. They only omitted verbs in phrase-medial position while tending to use the phrase-final form only in phrase-final contexts.

This is a typical example of the variation to be found in children's morphological development (cf. Brown 1973 and Cazden 1968). As Slobin (1973) points out, children do not generalize across morpheme or sentence boundaries. While there can be large variations in the percentage presence of a particular morpheme in its obligatory contexts, the variation is limited to the obligatory contexts only. Children do not supply new morphemes at random. While children may possess a more adult-like knowledge of word and sentence forms, unpracticed articulatory routines limit their productions to one syllable of the words or two words of the sentence (Menn 1978). The variability in child language is precisely what should occur if physical routines are being built up slowly to accomplish the demands of language. Children do not follow strict two-syllable-per-word or

two-word-per-sentence limits because the limits
are not a part of their linguistic competence.
Children gradually develop more adult-like speech
by practicing the articulatory routines necessary
to realize the patterns that are already a part
of their linguistic knowledge.

I have already shown how the Quiché children
were largely limited in their initial samples to
producing only a single syllable of their verbs.
Operating under this constraint, they chose the
syllable that received primary stress. They could
not apply this strategy to the SAME syllable each
time, however, since the stress on the verb shifts
with the linguistic context. In phrase-final position, the termination marker is stressed while in
phrase-medial position, the verb stem receives the
primary stress. The children were therefore
forced to learn two syllables for some verbs, even
though they could produce only one of the syllables in each utterance. This suggests that the
children used the stressed syllables as a means
of simplifying their linguistic productions.
Stressed syllables may provide children with the
means of organizing a serial behavior (Lashley
1951) by giving them a framework on which they
can build the phonological segments. Stressed
sentence accents play the central role in keeping
the beat and defining the overall rhythmic pattern.
Unaccented syllables may then be positioned relative to the accents, similar to the metrical
account of stress proposed in Liberman (1978) and
Liberman and Prince (1977). Under such an hypothesis, children would first define the major
sentence constituents in terms of intonation and
stress, and then go on to supply the words.
Before children can talk, they must learn to sing.

The Quiché data shows that a great deal of
morphological complexity is possible from the
start of language development. A Stage I that
concentrates solely on the acquisition of major
meanings and that lacks grammatical morphemes is
not true of all languages. Nor does syntactic
development necessarily precede morphological

210

development as Leopold (1939) suggested. Rather, the structural characteristics of the language that children are attempting to learn have profound effects on the forms of their first words. If the language is of the isolating type, such as English, the children will first acquire isolated words and with them build syntactic constructions. If the language is of the synthetic type, of which Quiché is only a partial example, the children may acquire one or more suffixes along with the first word roots. In extremely synthetic languages, such as Eskimo, in which a single highly inflected word may form a sentence, children have no choice but to start morphological development before learning syntax. Whatever the structure of the language may be, children must work within the limits of their phonological development.

In the space that remains, I shall try to place the preceding remarks within a larger prosodic theory of language development, specifically the observations Bolinger (1978) has made on the importance of intonation in language development. Syllabicity, stress, and utterance-final position are intimately connected with intonation in language. Utterance-final position takes part in the pausal phenomena of a language, including the terminal intonation contours. The syllable is the primary unit of intonation. A rising, falling, high, or low pitch affects an entire syllable, not just individual segments. Stress is correlated with the high or low points of the intonational contour. Hyman (1978) reports that historically, word stress is actually derived from intonation. Recent language acquisition theories have dismissed intonation (when they mention it at all) as a peripheral characteristic of language which serves an emotional rather than a communicative function. This view is due in large part to the generative theories of language which generate intonational contours from a syntactic or semantic base. The viewpoint that I would espouse here is that intonation is primary (at least in the acquisition of language), and that children discover other aspects of language

211

by analyzing intonational contours.

An innate capacity for distinguishing and controlling intonation would enable infants to differentiate speech from non-speech, and maternal speech from non-maternal. A built-in tie between intonation and affective state would provide infants with their first clue to the connection between sound and meaning. Infants could then analyze both intonation and meaning to discover their constituents. The relative prominences of pitch and pause, in conjunction with the clustering effect of processing speech in syllabic units, would provide children with their first clues for slicing up the intonational patterns, revealing first syllables, then words and phonological segments. Morphology and syntax would result from the concatenation of syllables and words. And as Bolinger points out 'once the repertory of words and syntactic patterns has been mastered, intonation is free to embrace larger stretches of speech, up to paragraphs, carrying on both an organizing and an illocutionary role' (1978:514). Natalie Waterson (1971) has shown how children use prosodic features in developing a phonological system. I hope I have demonstrated how Quiché children use intonational clues to acquire the forms of their first verbs. It remains to document children's attention to intonation in other stages of language acquisition and in other languages.

Footnotes

1. The Wenner-Gren Foundation and the Organization of American States supported the field
research on which this paper is based.

2. The phonemic inventory of Quiché consists
of the following sounds:

Consonants							Vowels			
p	t	tz	ch	k	q		i	i:	u	u:
b'	t'	tz'	ch'	k'	q'	?	e	e:	o	o:
		s	x		j	h		a	a:	
m	n									
	l	r								
w			y							

The apostrophe (') indicates glottalization, vowel
length is phonemic, ? represents the glottal stop,
and the sound /h/ only occurs in word-final position. For other references to the structure of
Quiché, see Mondloch (1978), Kaufman (1977), or
Norman (1976).

3. Ingram (1978:151) points out that some
phonological processes, such as unstressed syllable deletion and reduplication, operate on
entire syllables, while others, such as consonant
cluster reduction and the deletion of final consonants, function primarily to simplify syllables.
Menyuk (1976:93) notes that, 'The child appears to
organize his production in terms of the features
of syllables rather than the features of the segments in the syllable. Co-articulation effects
can be observed in that both forward (pop for pot)
and backward tot for pot) assimilation occurs.'
Indeed, there are several experiments which show
that the syllable is a more natural unit of linguistic perception than the phonological segment.
Savin and Bever (1970) found the subjects responded to whole syllable targets more quickly
than to single segment targets. When asked to
press a switch as soon as they heard the word bat
or sit, or when they heard the sound /s/ or /b/,

213

the subjects responded more quickly to the syllables. Savin and Beyer concluded that speech is analyzed directly into syllables and that phonemes can then be extracted from the syllables when necessary. More recently, Mehler, Dommergues, Frauenfelder, and Segui (1981) found that subjects responded more quickly to a target when it was not divided by a syllable boundary. They uses pairs of words sharing the first three phenemes but having different syllable structures (eg. pa-lace and pal-mier). They found that subjects reacted more quickly to targets which correspond to the first syllable of the word than to those which did not, independently of the target size. Mehler et al conclude that the syllable constitutes a unit of speech processing.

4. Viktor (1917, cited in MacWhinney forthcoming) had children imitate three syllable words in Hungarian. He found that they preserved the first syllable for its stress and the third for its recency. However, if they preserved only one syllable, it tended to be the first. Klein (1978) investigated the factors determining which of the consonants children produced in polysyllabic words in English and which they distort or omit. She worked with five children aged 20-24 months. The relative markedness of a segment was not a significant factor in the children's production; they did not attempt unmarked consonants more often than marked ones. While the children varied in the extent to which they reduced or preserved syllables in polysyllabic words, in all cases it was stress, or stress interacting with serial position, which determined whether a consonant was maintained or was the dominant consonant in consonant simplification processes. Blasdell and Jensen (1970) used strings of four nonsense syllables to test which string children aged 28-39 months were most likely to imitate. They found that primary stress (though not secondary stress) and utterance-final position favored the children's imitation of a syllable. Dupreez (1974) found a similar result in his study of imitations of adult

utterances by three 18-month olds. These children almost always imitated a stressed, utterance-final word, and tended to imitate a pre-final, stressed word, sometimes followed by the final non-stressed word.

5. The Quiché mothers' speech to their children is neutral in regard to this question, since the full verb stem and termination marker system are preserved in it. The mothers simplify their verbs by dropping the aspect and person markers. For example, the verb chatsepeloq, ch-at-sep-el-oq, asp.-2s-kneel-pos.-term., 'You kneel!' may be shortened to sepeloq or even peloq. The mothers most often used the full form of the verb, including aspect and person markers, when addressing their children.

References

Berman, Ruth A. 1981. Regularity vs anomaly: the acquistion of Hebrew inflectional morphology. Journal of Child Language 8.265-82.

Blasdell, Richard, and Paul Jensen. 1970. Stress and word position as determinants of imitation in first-language learners. Journal of Speech and Hearing Research 13.193-202.

Bloom, Lois. 1973. One word at a time: the use of single word utterances before syntax. The Hague: Mouton.

Bolinger, Dwight. 1978. Intonation across languages. Universals of human language, Vol. 2: Phonology, ed. by Joseph H. Greenberg, 471-524. Stanford: Stanford University Press.

Bowerman, Melissa. 1973. Early syntactic development: a cross-linguistic study with special reference to Finnish. Cambridge: Cambridge University Press.

Branigan, George. 1979. Some reasons why successive single word utterances are not. Journal of Child Language 6.411-21.

Brown, Roger. 1973. A first language: the early stages. Cambridge, MA: Harvard University Press.

Cazden, Courtney, B. 1968. The acquisition of noun and verb inflections. Child Development 39.433-48.

Dupreez, Peter. 1974. Units of information in the acquisition of language. Language and Speech 17.369-76.

Feurer, Hanny. 1980. Morphological development in Mohawk. Papers and reports on child language development (Stanford) 18.25-42.

216

Hyman, Larry M. 1978. Word demarcation. Universals of human language, Vol. 2: Phonology, ed. by Joseph H. Greenberg, 443-70. Stanford: Stanford University Press.

Ingram, David. 1978. The role of the syllable in phonological development. Syllables and segments, ed. by Alan Bell and Joan Bybee Hooper, 143-55. Amsterdam: North-Holland.

Kaufman, Terrence. 1977. Some structural characteristics of the Mayan languages with special reference to Quiché. Ms. University of Pittsburgh.

Klein, Harriet. 1978. The relationship between perceptual strategies and productive strategies in learning the phonology of early lexical items. Indiana: Indiana University Linguistics Club.

Kuczaj, Stan A., II. 1979. Evidence for a language learning strategy: on the relative ease of acquisition of prefixes and suffixes. Child Development 50.1-13.

Lashley, Karl S. 1951. The problem of serial order in behavior. Cerebral mechanisms in behavior: the Hixon symposium, ed. by Lloyd A. Jeffress, 112-36. New York: Wiley.

Leopold, Werner. 1939. Speech development of a bilingual child, 4 vols. Evanston, Ill.: Northwestern University Press.

Liberman, Mark Yoffe. 1978. The intonational system of English. Indiana: Indiana University Linguistics Club.

-----, and Alan Prince. 1977. On stress and linguistic rhythm. Linguistic Inquiry 8.249-336.

MacWhinney, Brian. Forthcoming. The acquisition
    of Hungarian. The cross-cultural study of
    language acquisition, ed. by Dan I. Slobin.
    Hillsdale, NJ: Erlbaum.

Mehler, Jacques; Jean Yves Dommergues; Uli
    Frauenfelder; and Juan Segui. 1981. The
    syllable's role in speech segmentation.
    Journal of Verbal Learning and Verbal
    Behavior 20.298-305.

Menn, Lise. 1978. Phonological units in beginning
    speech. Syllables and segments, ed. by Alan
    Bell and Joan Bybee Hooper, 157-71.
    Amsterdam: North-Holland.

Menyuk, Paula. 1976. Relations between acquisi-
    tion of phonology and reading. Aspects of
    reading acquisition, ed. by John T. Guthrie,
    89-110. Blatimore, MD: The Johns Hopkins
    University Press.

Miller, Wick, and Susan Ervin. 1964. The develop-
    ment of grammar in child language. Mono-
    graphs of the Society for Research in Child
    Development 29 (Serial no. 92).9-34.

Mondloch, James L. 1978. Basic Quiché Grammar.
    Institute for Mesoamerican Studies, publica-
    tion no. 2. Albany, NY: State University of
    New York.

Nokony, Alicia. 1977. Meaning development in one
    child acquiring Dakota-Sioux as a first lan-
    guage. Vancouver: University of British
    Columbia thesis.

Norman, William. 1976. Quiché text. Mayan texts
    Vol. 1, ed. by Louanna Furbee-Losee, 40-60.
    Chicago: University of Chicago Press.

Pye, Clifton. 1980. The acquisition of grammatical
    morphemes in Quiché Mayan. Pittsburgh:
    University of Pittsburgh dissertation.

Savin, H. B., and Thomas G. Bever. 1970. The non-perceptual reality of the phoneme. Journal of Verbal Learning and Verbal Behavior 9.295-302.

Slobin, Dan I. 1973. Cognitive prerequisites for the development of grammar. Studies of child language development, ed. by Charles A. Ferguson and Dan I. Slobin, 175-208. New York: Holt, Rinehart, and Winston.

Vogel, Irene. 1975. One system or two: an analysis of a two-year-old Romanian-English bilingual's phonology. Papers and Reports on Child Language Development (Stanford) 9.43-62.

Viktor, Gabriella. 1917. A gyermek nyelve: a gyermeknyelv irodalmanak ismertetese fokent nyelveszeti szempontbol. Nagyvarad: Beres es Held.

Waterson, Natalie. 1971. Child phonology: a prosodic view. Journal of Linguistics 7.179-211.

Grammatical Comprehension: A Question of Style?

David N. Shorr   and   Philip S. Dale
Central Washington   University of
    University   Washington

Many fine papers have been presented at this
Congress dealing with the content, sequence, and
processes of language acquisition. We hope that
what we have to report this afternoon is as stimulating to you as the previous papers have been
to us. We say this because we will be addressing
a topic often selectively ignored, or at least
ignored until those occasions when data, pains-
takingly collected, fail to confirm our otherwise
brilliant insights into language acquisition. We
will be discussing the validity of one popular
method of assessing a grammatical comprehension
facility in young children: that employed in the
picture-pointing grammatical comprehension test
It will be argued that young children's performance on such a test is dependent not only on a
"true" grammatical comprehension facility, but
also on a particular cognitive style, or response
disposition, commonly referred to as reflectivity.
We will further argue that the relationship between picture-pointing grammatical comprehension
test performance and reflectivity is, to a large
extent, an artifact of measurement. That is,
this relationship is substantially stronger than
the "true" relationship between grammatical comprehension and this cognitive style in children.
Lastly, we will discuss some theoretical and practical implications of these contentions. The potential for substantive implications is high since
picture-pointing grammatical comprehension assessment is widely used in both research and diagnostic screening.

To begin, since reference has been made to a
"true" grammatical comprehension facility, it
ought to be defined. This is no simple task, but
it is worth the effort if for no other reason than
to remind us how diverse and elusive our workaday

constructs are. Terms such as syntactic comprehension, language structure comprehension, or simply language comprehension have all been used to refer to the same concept (Bellugi-Klima, 1971; Carrow, 1974; Fraser, Bellugi, and Brown, 1963; Lee, 1970; Miller and Yoder, 1973; and Parisi, 1971). Grammatical comprehension refers to the generation or reconstruction of the semantic content encoded in well-formed, multi-morpheme utterances. For example, in the utterance, the girl chases the boy, one componet of the semantic content is the Agent status of the first noun phrasé (the girl). A listener's reconstruction of this meaning is a product of grammatical comprehension processes. Grammatical comprehension has also come to refer to a listener's assignment of meanings encoded in what are commonly referred to as function morphemes. These morphemes include various meaning-bearing inflections, prepositions, demonstratives, determiners, negatives, modal verbs, as well as others. Such morphemes often do not have easily discernible meanings when in isolation, but rather display their full meanings in the context of other morphemes. For example, the modal verb, will, in the utterance, they will build a snowman, marks the encoded event as taking place at some future time. Again, the reconstruction of this aspect of meaning is considered a product of grammatical comprehension processes. It may be evident in the above two examples that the grammatical comprehension construct is very broad and in need of additional formalization. We add, however, that for those of us who have had reason to make use of a robust grammatical comprehension construct, it presents a fair amount of intuitive sense. Needless to say, the central role of intuition with regards to linguistic phenomena is well-established.

Reflectivity is a more homogeneous construct. It is defined as the degree to which an individual evaluates an explicit set of alternative solutions to a problem before opting for a particular solution (Messer, 1976). Highly reflective individuals evaluate more solutions than do low reflective individuals, who are often referred to as impulsives.

Figure 1 illustrates a straightforward method of

Figure 1

Example MFT Item

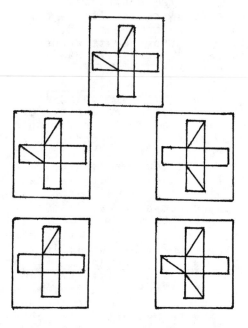

assessing reflectivity. A child is shown a set of
five drawings of a geometric pattern, and her attention is directed to the top one, called the standard. The child's task is simply to identify
which drawing below the standard is exactly like
it. Now, as in all things we choose to measure,
there is variability in the accuracy with which
children perform on such tasks. Why? First let
us rule out three weak explanations. The first is
that this is a complex problem solving task for
which children with more "general intelligence" are
better equipped to solve than other children. In
fact, this is not a very complex task at all. It
is a simple matching-to-standard task which does
not even include a cross-modal transformation

component: i.e., the task takes place entirely in the visual modality. Second, individual differences in performance on such tasks cannot be explained by differences in children's "memory" skills. The task demands virtually no memory activity whatsoever: the problem and its potential solution being simultaneously and continuously available to the child. And third, differences in "visual acuity," except in the most extreme cases, cannot account for differences in performances on such tasks.

What we are suggesting is that differences in children's performances on tasks like that of Figure 1 do, in fact, result from differences in reflectivity style. When confronted with such tasks, the more reflective child is more likely to consider the various alternative drawings (solutions) as viable matches for the standard (problem) before opting for a particular drawing. Performance on a set of tasks similar to that in Figure 1, which is referred to as a matching figures test item, was our operational definition of reflectivity in the two experiments to be described shortly. Before doing this, however, a description of the picture-pointing grammatical comprehension task is also necessary. Figure 2 contains a typical picture-pointing grammatical comprehension task. In a standardly administered version of such a task, a child is shown a set of drawings and simultaneously read a stimulus utterance. This utterance appropriately describes the events depicted in a single drawing. The task is to identify which drawing depicts the meaning of the utterance. Now in order that such a task assess some aspect of grammatical comprehension, the events depicted in at least one of the alternative drawings must be encodable by an utterance which differs from the stimulus utterance only in aspects of its grammatical content. That, we are sure, is an earful. The following example should clarify things however. The stimulus utterance read to the child when presented with the drawings in Figure 2 is, <u>the girl chases the boy</u>. It des-

223

Figure 2

Example PPGCT Item for Sentence,
The Girl Chases the Boy

cribes the upper-left drawing. The task of selecting the appropriate drawing for the utterance has
the potential for assessing grammatical comprehension because the upper-right drawing can be reasonable described by an utterance differing from the
stimulus utterance in grammatical content only:
this being, the boy chases the girl. The sample
picture-pointing task, or item, of Figure 2 is
typical of items on such tests as the Northwestern
Syntax Screening Test, the Miller-Yoder Test of
Grammatical Comprehension, and the Test for Auditory Comprehension of Language, to name a few.

As you may have noticed, there is a great similarity between the method by which reflectivity
is assessed and the picture-pointing grammatical
comprehension test. Again, we have few qualms
about the method as employed in a measure of reflectivity. In fact, the method as employed in a
standardly administered picture-pointing grammati-

cal comprehension test in large part measures reflectivity also. This, at least, was the primary hypothesis of the first of our two studies.

Our first study consisted of administering a battery of tests to 24 four- and five-year-olds. These included a matching figures test, a standardly administered picture-pointing grammatical comprehension test, and an object-manipulation grammatical comprehension test. This latter test requires children to act out the meaning of utterances with small toys and other manipulable objects. For example, a toy tiger and lion are placed before the child and the child is instructed to act out the sentence, the tiger chases the lion. We reasoned that such a procedure would not be substantially influenced by reflectivity style, if for no other reason than that it does not provide the child with explicit alternative solutions. The child must generate her own solutions if, in fact, more than one is generated. This is an activity much closer to one we have in mind when we refer to "true" grammatical comprehension activities. Note that we are not suggesting that an object-manipulation procedure is, overall, a more appropriate technique for assessing grammatical comprehension, only that it is less likely to be influenced by reflectivity style.

Two aspects of the results of our first study will be discussed. Table 1 lists the intercorre-

Table 1

Correlations among Tests

	STAN PPGCT	OMGCT
MFT	.51	.10
STAN PPGCT		.52

MFT X STAN PPGCT > MFT X OMGCT

225

lations among the three tests. The measure of reflectivity, labelled "MFT," is substantially correlated with picture-pointing grammatical comprehension performance (r = .51), which is labelled "STAN PPGCT." Furthermore, this correlation is substantially and significantly greater than the correlation between the reflectivity measure and object-manipulation grammatical comprehension test performance (r = .10), which is labelled "OMGCT."

Table 2 presents the correlations between aver-

Table 2

Within Test Response Latency X Score Correlations

MFT	+.38
STAN PPGCT	+.23
OMGCT	-.02

age response latency and number of items correct for each test. It is characteristic of matching figures tests that response latency is correlated with the number of items correct.* This is predictable, since children who more carefully evaluate alternative solutions should be taking more time to respond. As indicated in Table 2, the correlation between latency and accuracy for the STAN PPGCT is similar to that for the MFT. This provides additional, test-internal, evidence that a picture-pointing grammatical comprehension test measures reflectivity to some large degree.

---

*The correlation between latency and accuracy on a matching figures test is generally reported as negative. This is because the accuracy measure typically used is an error score. The measure in the present study was the number of items correct. The expected correlation between latency and accuracy was, therefore, positive.

One might argue that these findings do not show that the strong relationship between the reflectivity measure and the <u>standardly</u> administered picture-pointing grammatical comprehension test is at all artificial. That is, reflective children may in fact be better at grammatical comprehension, and the correlation obtained followed directly from this fact. This argument ignores the low correlation between the reflectivey measure and object-manipulation grammatical comprehension test performance. There are certainly reasons, however, for being skeptical of object-manipulation assessment.

We, however, reject the above interpretation on both conceptual and empirical grounds. First, both our casual and formal accounts of grammatical comprehension stress that it is a relatively automatic activity. Something is said to us and we immediately generate a single meaning for it, be this meaning correct or incorrect. This may even be more true of young children, who do not recognize the ambiguity, or psuedo-ambiguity, of events as readily as do adults. Grammatical comprehension does not typically involve generating a set of potential meanings for an utterance and then consciously evaluating the merits of each. In other words, the activity or process of grammatical comprehension is about as different from the activity of reflectiviy as one could imagine. On this ground alone we would be skeptical of a hypothesis for a strong relationship between grammatical comprehension and reflectivity.

Armchair speculation aside, our second study addressed this issue directly. In this study, 32 four- and five-year-old children were administered four tests: the three tests of the previous experiment and a <u>modified</u> picture-pointing grammatical comprehension test. The modification employed simply insured that all children looked at each picture alternative before responding to the spoken utterance. This was accomplished by a very sophisticated procedure: tapping each picture and saying, "look here" until the child had at least momentarily examined the picture.

The results of our second experiment are presented in Table 3. The _modified_ picture-pointing

Table 3

Correlations among Tests

	STAN PPGCT	MOD PPGCT	OMGCT
MFT	.69	.41	.23
STAN PPGCT		.65	.35
MOD PPGCT			.43

MFT X STAN PPGCT > MFT X OMGCT

MFT X STAN PPGCT > MFT X MOD PPGCT

grammatical comprehension test is labelled "MOD PPGCT." The major finding of our first experiment was replicated. Of particular interest, however, is the significant difference between the correlation for the MFT and STAN PPGCT (r = .69) and that for the MFT and MOD PPGCT (r = .41). As expected, the simple and _grammatically irrelevant_ modification of the picture-pointing procedure has led to a substantially weaker relationship between the reflectivity index and picture-pointing grammatical comprehension test performance. Also note that there is an increase, albeit non-significant, in the correlation between picture-pointing and object-manipulation test performances when the picture-pointing grammatical comprehension test is our modified version. This suggests greater convergent validity for the modified picture-pointing test.

At this time we will end this necessarily brief account of our research. We assure you that more experimental rigor was adhered to than described here. We would rather address some implications of our findings however,

First, what differential effect, if any, would reflectivity style have on the relative difficulty of picture-pointing test items? Keep in mind that such a difficulty is the primary evidence used in "order of acquisition" comprehension studies. Does responding with low reflectivity have consequences for the difficulty of some items more than others? The answer is a tentative yes. It is tentative because we can't identify a logical class of grammatical content which is differentially effected by reflectivity. The evidence suggesting that reflectivity does differentially effect item difficulty is as follows. The correlation between picture-pointing test item difficulty across the two experiments under standard administration procedures is a respectable .81. The correlation between STAN PPGCT item difficulty and MOD PPGCT item difficulty in experiment 2 is only .68. It appears that our modification of the picture-pointing procedure has had some effect on relative item difficulty.

Certainly the area in which our findings have, or should have, their greatest implication is in the diagnosis of "delayed" or "disordered" language development. As mentioned previously, picture-pointing grammatical comprehension tests are currently being used for diagnostic purposes. Our data suggest that a standardly administered picture-pointing test may lead to the classification of a child as low in comprehension skills when, in fact, she is only low in reflectivity, and possibly then only at the time of testing. We venture to say that this is an undesirable outcome, for both the clinician and the child.

In spite of all that's been said, and some which has not, we feel that the picture-pointing technique of assessing grammatical comprehension is useful. No method of assessment is entirely satisfactory, and yet we are well aware of the need for objective measurement. Also, assessment instruments are not only evaluated in terms of their

validity. Their ease of administration and reliability are also important considerations. Picture-pointing tests fare relatively well with respect to these considerations. We strongly suggest, however, that picture-pointing grammatical
comprehension tests be developed and normed with
the addition of procedures which reduce an otherwise reflectivity bias.

References

Bellugi-Klima, U. Some language comprehension
tests. In C.S. Labatelli (Ed.) Language
Training in Early Child Education. Chicago:
University of Illinois Press, 1971.

Carrow, E. Test for Auditory Language Comprehension. Austin, Texas: Learning Concepts, 1974.

Fraser, C., Bellugi, U., and Brown, R. Control
of grammar in imitation, comprehension, and
production. Journal of Verbal Learning and
Verbal Behavior, 1963, 2, 121-135.

Lee, L.L. A screening test for syntax development. Journal of Speech and Hearing Disorders,
1970, 35, 103-112.

Messer, S.B. Reflection-impulsivity: A review.
Psychological Bulletin, 1976, 83, 1026-1052.

Miller, J.F., and Yoder, D.E. Assessing the Comprehension of Grammatical Form in Mentally Retarded Children. Paper presented at the Third
Congress of the International Association for
the Scientific Study of Mental Deficiency, The
Hague, The Netherlands, September, 1973.

Parisi, D. Development of syntactic comprehension
in preschool children as a function of socio-
economic level. Developmental Psychology,
1971, 5, 186-189.

THE LAST SHALL BE FIRST: ON THE ACQUISITION

OF THE AFRIKAANS DOUBLE NEGATIVE

JAN VORSTER*

ABSTRACT

The schema *No + Nucleus*, proposed by Wode (1977)
as a universal step in the acquisition of nega=
tion, failed to appear in longitudinal data from
two Afrikaans children between the ages of 18 and
30 months. The transition from single *nee* (no)
to *Nucleus + nie* (not) in the data is explained
in terms of the relative salience of the sentence
adverbial *nee* (no) and the obligatory sentence-
final *nie* (not) in the speech addressed to the
children. From the children's deletions it ap=
pears that of the postverbal Neg element, charac=
teristic not only of Afrikaans but also of cognate
languages such as Dutch and German, and the reite=
rative sentence-final *nie*, peculiar to Afrikaans,
it is the latter that is acquired first.

* Human Sciences Research Council, Private Bag
  X41, Pretoria, 0001, South Africa.

231

INTRODUCTION

The purpose of this paper is

- to explain how a peculiarity in the Afrikaans negation system apparently precludes what has been suggested as a universal step in the acqui= sition of negation;
- to show that the second of the two Neg elements, characteristic of the most common type of Afri= kaans negative sentence, is acquired before the first.

Wode (1977) criticizes existing studies of the acquisition of negation systems for failing to make overt predictions with a cross-linguistic validity. While McNeill (1970) is the only one to aim at a theory with predictive capacity, Wode questions his opinion that *Neg* + *S* ∾ *S* + *Neg* is really the beginning of negation, and that such utterances are semantically and developmentally the same. McNeill fails to distinguish between anaphoric and non-anaphoric negation, the distinc= tion being that in the former the negative rela= tionship does not hold between the Neg element (no) and the rest of the utterance, whereas in the latter it does. Thus (1) is non-anaphoric, where= as (2) is anaphoric:

(1) No funny (It is not funny)

(2) No sugar (Q: Do you want salt? A: No, I want sugar)

Wode argues that if *Neg* + *S* ∾ *S* + *Neg* mark the beginning of negation, the options should be in free variation, implying that the word order for negated 2-word utterances is free. This, however, is not the case: in the 20-odd sources available to him, Wode found predominantly *Neg* + *S* struc= tures. This is explained as follows: children use anaphoric negation before they use non-anapho=

ric negation, deriving their model for word order from the anaphoric negations in the speech of adults. When they move on to non-anaphoric 2-word negations, they overgeneralize the established anaphoric pattern.

AFRIKAANS NEGATION

The negation system in Afrikaans is unique in a sense important to the present argument. Although there is a strong paradigmatic correspondence be= tween the formal negating devices employed by Afrikaans, Dutch, German and English (see Table 1) and although the syntagmatic placing of the Neg particle in Afrikaans is virtually identical to the placing of its Dutch and German counterparts, there is an obligatory sentence-final *nie* in all Afrikaans sentences in which position 4 in the following structural description is filled:

(3)   1   2   3   4   5
     verb   ...   Neg   ...   *nie*

It follows that all Afrikaans negations have a sentence-final negative element, and since the most common negating device occupying position 3 is *nie* (not) it also follows that *most* Afrikaans negations end in *nie*. For the simplified register addressed to small children this holds virtually without exception.

METHOD

Subjects

Over a period of one year fortnightly samples were taken of the verbal interaction between four young children and their mothers. Each sample, lasting 30 minutes, was tape-recorded and transcribed. When sampling commenced the children were all 18 months old, with an MLU marginally above 1. Two of the children show an interesting and comparable

development of the negation system, while the
other two show no development at all, merely pro=
ducing isolated instances of *nee* (no). The pre=
sent description is therefore confined to two
children's data, a girl 'Freda' and a boy 'Deon'.

Scoring procedure

Since every sentence is embedded in a context - a
body of known information - and since much infor=
mation is either transferred referringly or non-
verbally, or is tacitly assumed to have been
transferred, deletions and substitutions are com=
mon in the use of language. This is particularly
so in small children's language. For these rea=
sons Bloom (1970) advocates cognisance being
taken of context, situation and non-verbal beha=
viour in trying to penetrate the child's knowledge
of his language. According to Van der Geest et
al., this is best done by distinguishing systema=
tically "between the semantic intent or message -
the information the child intends to give, as
determined from context, situation, and non-verbal
behaviour - and the realization or code which is
realized on the verbal level" (1973 : 41).

The procedure followed here is to establish what
the child's semantic intent is with each utterance
by considering the linguistic and non-linguistic
context, and to compare this semantic intent, in
the form of a well-formed paraphrase, with the
child's realization of it. A similar technique
has been used by Snow et al. (1976) to compare the
speech of mothers from three social classes, and
by Van der Geest et al. (1973) to compare the
speech of children from three social classes.
Here it is used to compare the developing speech
of children with the adult norm.

RESULTS AND DISCUSSION

The first occurrences and frequencies of the main
negation types for Freda (F) and Deon (D) are
shown in Table 2. These data contradict Wode's
predictions.

In the first place, anaphoric negations do not
precede non-anaphoric negations. In Deon's data
the first anaphoric negation appears after a ne=
gated copula construction and a negative impera=
tive. By the time Deon produced 7 anaphoric nega=
tions, he had also produced 10 other negations.
Freda's first anaphoric negation only appears in
sample 20, by which time she had already produced
a mixed bag of 50 other negations. These data
support Park, who found that "In Early stage I
nein was indeed used in the non-anaphoric function,
but, contrary to Wode's theory, ALL of the 13 *nein*
constructions referred to non-anaphoric negation"
(Park, 1979 : 148).

In the second place, the non-anaphoric type *no-
funny*, common not only in Bellugi's (1967) data
but apparently also in the cross-linguistic data
available to Wode, is virtually non-existent in
the present data. The only instance is the utter=
ance

(4)   NEE ek is nie KWAAD nie[1]
      NO   i   am not CROSS not

occurring twice in Freda's sample 11 (age 1.11.15).
In all other (non-anaphoric) cases the negating
device *nie* (not) is used.

The non-occurrence of the *no* + *Nucleus* type of ne=
gation in the present data can hardly be ascribed

---

[1] Words actually spoken by the child appear in upper case,
     paraphrased words in lower case, and a morpheme-accurate
     translation in italics.

235

to a sampling error. Of the nine types of struc=
tured negations identified in the data, the least
frequent, anaphoric negation, occurs 15 times and
the most frequent, copula constructions, 55 times.
It is therefore far more likely that the one in=
stance of *nee* + *Nucleus* should be an unproductive
'deviant' utterance than that similar cases
actually feature in the children's speech but were
missed in sampling.

A more profitable avenue to explore would be the
differences between, on the one hand, Afrikaans
negation and, on the other, the systems on which
the generalizations of McNeill and Wode have been
based. It will be argued here that the Afrikaans
negation system, introduced to the child as part
of his[2] primary linguistic data, precludes the
step *no* + *Nucleus* (Wode's step II B). The argu=
ment hinges on the relative salience of *nee* (no
and *nie* (not) in the primary linguistic data (PLD).

It seems to have been established that *no* (and its
correlates in other languages: *nee*, *nein*, etc.)
is the universal starting point for negation.
This is not surprising if one considers the extent
to which *no* features in the child's first intro=
duction to the notion of negation. In the speech
addressed to both Freda and Deon it appears in the
following contexts:

- alone, as a blanket negative imperative, with
  emphatic intonation
- before a non-negated sentence, again with nega=
  tive imperative force
- before a negative imperative
- before a negative declarative

The sentence adverbial negative *no*, strengthening
or reinforcing the negative aspect of a sentence,
is also conspicuous in Bellugi's data:

---
[2] The masculine form of pronouns refers to both sexes.

"In Period A we find many sentences in the
mothers' speech of this sort: 'No, don't
sit on that.' 'No, you can't go out.' 'Oh
no, that isn't yours.' 'No, you don't drink
grape juice with a spoon.', and so forth."
(Bellugi, 1967 : 27).

Crucial features of this sentence adverbial nega=
tive are its discreteness, immutability and sen=
tence position. Unlike *not*, it is in no way in=
volved in the complexity of English grammar, com=
bines with no other element, and retains its privi=
leged sentence-initial position. In contrast, the
not in Bellugi's four examples is reduced to the
status of an enclitic particle even lacking sylla=
bic salience, and is attached to three different
elements from two different grammatical categories
occupying two different sentence positions. A
contrast, therefore, of salience and constancy
with non-salience and variability.

In languages like German, Dutch and Afrikaans the
equivalent of *not* is not dependent on auxiliary
support, nor does it tend to be reduced to the
status of a non-syllabic enclitic. Yet in these
languages too the child's introduction to the no=
tion of negation comes via *no*, as can be seen from
the primacy of holophrastic denials in children's
speech. In Afrikaans, however, after a period
characterized by holophrastic *nee*, the child moves
on to *Nucleus* + *nie* while in other languages there
is a period characterized by *no* + *Nucleus* before
not (*nicht*, *niet*, etc.) appears.

While the Afrikaans-learning child undergoes his
initiation into the world of negation, and produces
his holophrastic *nee*'s under the influence of the
highly salient sentence adverbial negative in his
PLD, he is at the same time exposed to an equally
salient feature of Afrikaans negation: the second,
highly constant, sentence-final *nie* (see Table 3).
Since *nee* is by no means an indispensible feature

237

of a structured negation, and since it does not occur in the PLD with nearly the same frequency as the sentence-final *nie*, it seems logical for the Afrikaans child, when embarking on structured negations, to produce *Nucleus + nie* in preference to *nee + Nucleus*.

It could now be argued, in the light of the fi= gures in Table 3, that *nie* would be a more likely holophrastic negation for the Afrikaans-learning child than *nee*. Against this notion three argu= ments present themselves.

In the first place, isolated (emphatic) *nee* is common in the child's PLD, whereas isolated *nie* does not occur. In the second place, although the overall relative frequencies of sentence-initial *nee* and sentence-final *nie* in the PLD, shown in Table 3, may suggest a constant ratio through time, the fact of the matter is that there is a clear tendency for the latter category to increase in frequency relative to the former (see Figure 1 for Freda's mother and Figure 2 for Deon's mother).

The third argument refers to the experiments re= ported by Shipley et al. (1969) and Smith (1970), suggesting that a distinction be made between primary linguistic *data* (the ambient language en= vironment) and primary linguistic *input* (that which the child *'allows in'*). In these experiments it was found that children are more inclined to listen to utterances of which they recognize the initial words than to utterances with strange (or nonsense) initial words. It seems reasonable to assume that the very young child, exposed to a high frequency of sentence adverbial negatives, would pay attention to these without necessarily remaining 'tuned in' right to the end of the ut= terance - which of course is where the sentence-final *nie* occurs. In consequence, his holophrastic negations are modelled on the sentence adverbial

238

negative. Only when his increasing attention span allows the child to stay with an utterance all the way, does he become aware of the most conspicuous feature of an Afrikaans negative sentence, i.e. that it invariably ends with *nie*. This awareness presumably precedes or coincides with, the time when the child starts producing structured nega= tions, with the result that he progresses from ho= lophrastic *nee* to structured *Nucleus* + *nie* without the intermediate step *no* + *Nucleus* found in e.g. English.

CONCLUSION

In the present data the tendency to treat the sen= tence-final *nie* as dominant, is pervasive and fairly persistent. It occurs in all the sentence types negated by both children, and as Figure 3 shows the *Neg* particle (the first *nie*) is one of the last categories to be realized regularly. Al= though Deon's language is more advanced than Fre= da's, the conspicuous correlation between the chil= dren's deletions shows that these are not random. Both children tend to delete elements containing what might be regarded as 'given' information, while realizing elements containing 'new' infor= mation. However, this argument can not apply to the two semantically identical negating particles. The only explanation for the low realization fre= quency of the postverbal Neg element (the first *nie*) compared with the reiterative sentence-final *nie*, is that the latter is acquired first.

REFERENCES

BELLUGI, Ursula. *The acquisition of the system of negation in children's speech.* Doctoral thesis, Harvard University, 1967.

BLOOM, Lois. *Language development: form and function in emerging grammars.* Cambridge, Mass., MIT Press, 1970.

McNEILL, David. *The acquisition of language.* New York, Wiley, 1970.

PARK, Tschang-Zin. Some facts on negation. *Journal of Child Language* 6, 147-151, 1979.

SHIPLEY, Elizabeth F., SMITH, Carlota S., & GLEITMAN, Lila R. A study in the acquisition of language: free responses to commands. *Language* 45, 322 - 342, 1969.

SMITH, Carlota S. An experimental approach to children's linguistic competence. In: Hayes, J.R. (ed.). *Cognition and the development of language.* New York, Wiley, 1970.

SNOW, Catherine E., ARLMAN-RUPP, A., HASSING, Y., JOBSE, J., JOOSTEN, J. & VORSTER, J. Mothers' speech in three social classes. *Journal of Psycholinguistic Research* 5, 1, 1-20, 1976.

VAN DER GEEST, Ton, GERSTEL, R., APPEL, R., & TERVOORT, B. *The child's communicative competence.* Mouton, The Hague, 1973.

WODE, Henning. Four stages in the development of L_I negation. *Journal of Child Language* 4, 87- 102, 1977.

TABLE 1:   SOME NEGATING DEVICES EMPLOYED BY AFRI=
           KAANS AND THREE COGNATE LANGUAGES

Afrikaans	Dutch	German	English
nie	niet	nicht	not
nee	nee	nein	no
geen	geen	kein	no
niemand	niemand	niemand	no-one
nêrens	nergens	nirgends	nowhere
niks	niets	nichts	nothing
nooit	nooit	niemals	never
...	...	...	...

(Table 2 on next page.)

TABLE 3:   RELATIVE FREQUENCY OF SENTENCE-INITIAL
           NEE AND SENTENCE-FINAL *NIE* IN THE DATA
           OF FREDA'S AND DEON'S MOTHERS

	Freda's mother	Deon's mother
Total negations:		
Number in data	390	582
$\overline{X}$ per sample	16,96	25,30
Sentence-initial *nee*:		
Number in data	112	212
$\overline{X}$ per sample	4,87	9,22
% of total negations	28,72	36,43
Sentence-final *nie*:		
Number in data	298	443
$\overline{X}$ per sample	12,96	19,26
% of total negations	76,41	76,12

TABLE 2: NEGATED SENTENCE TYPES

Type	First Occurrence*		Totals**		
	F	D	F	D	F+D
Holophrastic Nee	3	1	54	40	94
Copula Construction	13	8	21	34	55
+ Intransitive Verb	13	14	19	12	31
- Auxiliary	12	14	8	20	28
+ Transitive Verb	13	14	13	8	21
Imperative	12	5	10	9	19
Anaphoric negation	20	12	4	11	15

* Sample number. Initial age = 18 months;
sampling interval = 2 weeks.

** In total of 24 samples each.

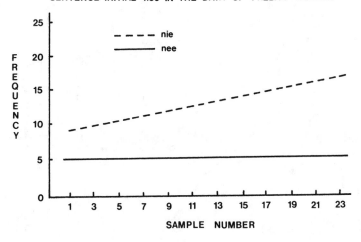

FIGURE 1: INCREASE OF SENTENCE-FINAL nie RELATIVE TO SENTENCE-INITIAL nee IN THE DATA OF FREDA'S MOTHER

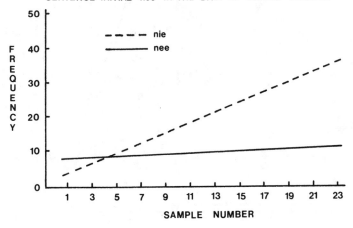

FIGURE 2: INCREASE OF SENTENCE-FINAL nie RELATIVE TO SENTENCE-INITIAL nee IN THE DATA OF DEON'S MOTHER

FIGURE 3: PERCENTAGE REALIZATION OF KEY CATEGORIES

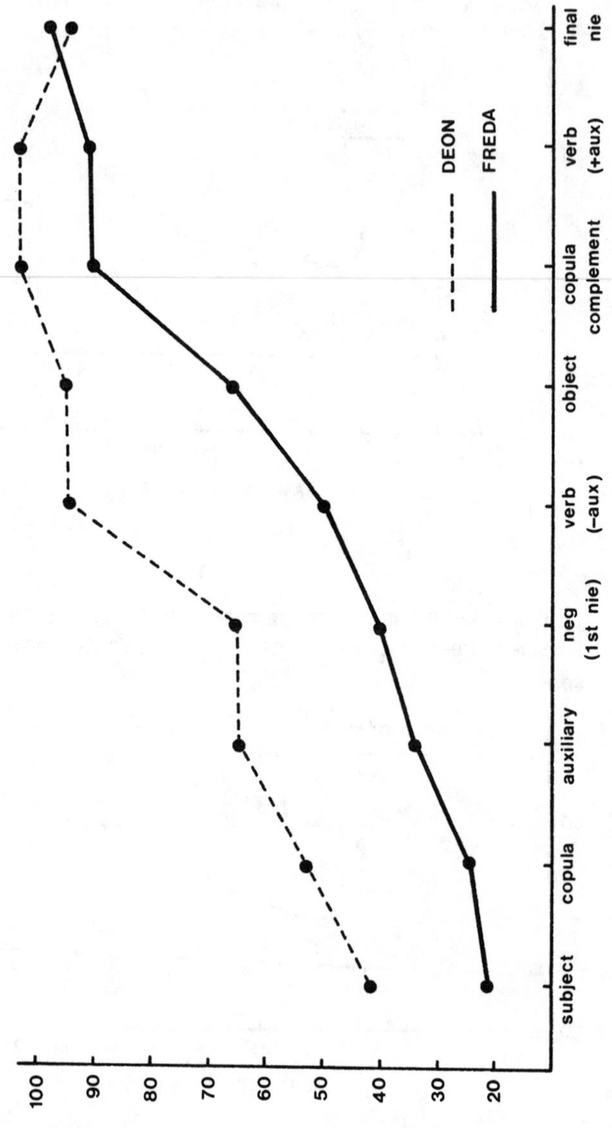

244

Frequency of Usage, Semantic Complexity, and the
Acquisition of Set-Relational
Quantifiers in Early Childhood

Camille Hanlon

Department of Child Development
Connecticut College

Acknowledgements

This research was supported by U.S. National Institute
of Mental Health Small Grant MH-27638. The author wishes to
express her appreciation to Dr. Roger Brown for the generous
sharing of his data; to the children, teachers, and adminis-
trators of the Connecticut College Children's School and Pine
Point School of Stonington, Connecticut for their cheerful
help; and to her undergraduate research assistants, Ms.
Theresa Carpino, Ms. Kathryn Tweedie Erslev, Mr. Harold Flagg,
Ms. Nathalie Lowe, and Ms. Beverly Sweny for their competent
and dedicated work on the project.

245

Today, I want to describe some empirical research on children's acquisition of English set-relational quantifiers. These are words like <u>all</u>, <u>some</u>, <u>no</u>, <u>none</u>, <u>each</u>, <u>every</u>, <u>any</u>, <u>another</u>, <u>other</u>, <u>both</u>, <u>either</u>, and <u>neither</u> as they are used to quantify nominals. At the First Congress I described a model of the semantic structure for this domain and showed that children learning English as a first language understand and produce the simpler forms first in accordance with the law of cumulative structural complexity (Hanlon, 1981). In this talk I want to report that those quantifiers that are most frequently used in conversation are learned earliest, so that frequency of conversational usage is also an excellent predictor of order of emergence for these quantifiers. These new findings raise the question of whether we need the structural model to understand the processes of acquisition, or whether more or less accidental variations in conversational frequency are sufficient to account for the order in which the terms are mastered. After a brief summary of the latest results, then, I would like to address these alternatives in the context of what we already know about language learning and language use. Then I will consider the import of these results as a part of an emerging pattern of empirical findings in the study of the processes of first language acquisition.

Here is a brief analysis of the adult semantic structure. This model is based on contrasts of four different types. The first contrast consists of three levels of generality in reference—generic, specific, and non-specific. The generic level refers to members of the general class named, as in the sentence, "Some trees are deciduous." The specific level refers to a specific set as in "Some of these trees are deciduous." And at the non-specific level the potential reference set is left unspecified, as in "We planted some trees." Not every quantifier may be used at every level; lexical gaps appear within the general pattern, and morphological and syntactic variations occur across levels. Table 1 lists the forms to be found at each level of generality of reference, with examples of each type of use. The meaning of each quantifier word may also be described in terms of a characteristic transformation of a supposed reference set to an actual one. For example, the meaning of the word <u>some</u> can be described as "an indefinite portion of the suppositional set." Transformational descriptions for the terms studied can be found in Table 2. Furthermore, one subset of these terms is appropriately used only when the suppositional set size is two (both, either, neither). Another subset of terms (each, every) is restricted to the case of distributive predication. That is, the relevant predicates outside the quantified nominal must be interpreted as describing the members of the set individually, taken one at a time. It is the difference in meaning between the sentence, "All of the children in the class sang a song," and the sentence, "Each of the children in the class sang a song."

In my earlier report I described two studies, one of longitudinal production and another of cross-sectional comprehension, which yielded a consistent order of acquisition for these terms. This order was strongly related to cumulative semantic complexity in terms of the model. In the present analysis I have correlated adult conversational frequency measures with two indices of children's comprehension. The motive for the analysis was one of simple curiosity. It seemed unreasonable to assume that frequency would not be related to the phenomenon under study because it played no role in the theory.

For several methodological reasons, this analysis focuses on variation across quantifiers within the specific level of reference, only. First, this is the level at which the greatest number of different lexical forms are used. Second, the objective testing of comprehension is least problematic at this level. Third, the frequencies of forms at this level are generally intermediate to frequencies at the generic and non-specific levels, making it relatively unlikely that threshold or ceiling effects would mask the relationships of interest. Fourth, comparisons within levels of generality of reference hold relatively constant syntactic variations in form so that the effects of other variables can be isolated.

The adult conversational frequency measures of primary interest to us are those derived from parent speech with their children. The measures used were the total frequencies of parental usage in the longitudinal corpora for three children (Roger Brown's transcripts for Adam, Eve, and Sarah). The rank orders of frequency for the set of specific quantifiers are highly consistent in the parental (mainly

247

maternal) speech of these three children. The Spearman rank-order correlation co-efficients can be seen in Table 3. Their magnitude made an average rank order across parents seem useful, and the correlations of this average ranking with the rank order for each family are also given in Table 3. Furthermore, the extent to which the parents of Adam, Eve, and Sarah used these quantifiers in specific reference did not vary significantly with the developmental levels of their children, so total frequencies seemed the most valid and reliable index of parental usage. It is worth noting that several simpler measures of spoken word frequency for adults (Howes, 1966) and for school-age children (Wepman & Hass, 1969) also yield the same range of high positive correlations, both with each other and with the parental frequency measures reported here. This consistent variation in frequency of spoken use is observed even though these words all fall within the most frequent category of the Thorndike-Lorge word count (1944).

A cross-sectional sample of 75 children ranging in age from three to seven years provided data for the two quantifier comprehension tasks. For 61 of these children we had complete data for both tasks (four through seven years old; the three-year-olds received a shorter form of the test) and these are the basis for the correlational analyses that I am going to describe. Details of the method of this part of the study, including relevant characteristics of the sample, the testing procedures, the scoring reliability, and the validation of the scoring against adult norms are too lengthy to provide here, but are given in the First Congress report. Briefly, the subjects were given sets of identical objects and then they responded to requests using each of the quantifier words in a consistent sentence context across a series of trials. So for the task called Cookies the child on a particular trial might be given a set of two pretend cookies and requested to "Give him (the Cookie Monster) either of the cookies." For Letters, instead of feeding the Cookie Monster, the children learned to be postpersons by putting letters into a set of postboxes in response to similar quantified requests. The sentence contexts for each task are given in Table 4. Each quantifier was tested on three different trials per task, each quantifier appearing once in random order within each third of the series of trials.

The original hypotheses about order of comprehension of these terms were tested with an index of individual deviation from the predicted order (Loevinger's Hii). Since no subject deviated from that order, the group percent passing each quantifier (two out of three trials) on each task might reasonably be tested as an index of a general sequence of acquisition in the comprehension of those terms. Table 5 shows the respective percentages for each quantifier for each task. The correlation between the acquisition orders based on these results for the two tasks taken separately is high enough to justify averaging the task results to derive an average order of comprehension difficulty for the set of quantifiers (a Spearman rho, of .92), significant at the .001 level of probability).

Now all that remains is to report the relationships between the parental frequency measures and the comprehension test results. These are shown in Table 6. The best summary measure is the correlation between the mean parental frequency order and the mean comprehension order. The Spearman coefficient for this relationship is .77, which is significant at the .005 level of probability. The consistently high, positive correlations in this matrix must make it clear that the relationship we are assessing is a general, reliable one. Thus, it seems worthwhile trying to understand the nature of the connection. The truth is, very few indices of parent behavior show any significant relationship to children's development, short of the most obvious effects of total neglect or abuse. A relationship of such magnitude and stability, then, seems worth investigating.

One obvious and relatively uninteresting possibility is that of threshold effects. These could operate on the exposure side, so that the children might just learn a word when they hear it the first time, with the most frequent words on the average heard earliest. This possibility we cannot rule out absolutely on the basis of the present data, but it seems unlikely given the general frequency range for the set of quantifiers and their cross-topic and cross-listener generality.

Indeed, an associative frequency effect seems a more plausible explanation for these findings than does a simple exposure threshold effect. Few people think that a single experience of a word in use is sufficient for a child to

249

learn its meaning, but it seems possible that more adequate understanding would grow relative to the number of such experiences. Perhaps differences in the level of comprehension of a set of related terms during acquisition can be accounted for in terms of relative frequency of exposure. Few versions of learning theory or information theory of which I am aware would fail to predict this outcome.

But how does this account fit with the larger pattern of developmental findings on the acquisition of linguistic forms? The recent trend has been to stress children's tendency to assimilate their experience with a language to their current level of understanding of that language. The expectation has been that, for high-frequency forms at least, differences in linguistic or cognitive complexity rather than frequency of usage would determine their order of mastery. And the findings have been consistent, in the main, with this view. For example, Brown's report on children's production of a high-frequency set of English grammatical morphemes (1973) showed clearly that it was the semantic and grammatical complexity and not the parental frequency of the forms that predicted their order of acquisition. Gentner's cross-sectional acquisition study of some English verbs of possession (1975) also argues the semantic complexity interpretation. Many other studies of lexical acquisition supporting this view could be cited. Often the relative frequency of the forms is not reported, since it is not a variable of interest to the investigator. Furthermore, experimental studies are often designed to show that variables other than frequency (good form, perceptual salience, etc.) are more powerful determinants of lexical semantic acquisition (e.g., Mervis, 1976). This latter type of study is useful in showing that when the variables of frequency and cognitive structure are separated, it is cognitive structure that determines ease of acquisition. The language learning model upon which they are based, however, gives us no clue as to why we should find a strong negative relationship between frequency of usage and semantic complexity in the case of natural language acquisition itself.

For enlightenment on this point, we must turn to descriptive linguistics. I would like to suggest that an important design feature of natural language involves assigning more structurally complex forms to rarer occasions of usage. The best-documented case of this characteristic is the inverse relationship between word length and frequency reported by George Kingsley Zipf (1935, 1949), who argued that it was a function of the Principle of Least Effort. However, a case more relevant to our present finding is that of linguistic marking. Marking is a pervasive phenomenon at every level of the structure of natural languages (Greenberg, 1966). In lexical marking, sets of related semantic contrasts are assigned distinctive forms in a way that matches the usual case with the structurally simpler form. Both formally and semantically marked words tend to be more restricted in their distribution than are the corresponding unmarked terms (cf. Lyons, 1977). Since semantic marking can be described as the presence of an extra component of meaning in the semantic structure for a word, one would on these grounds expect an inverse relationship between frequency and semantic complexity. Indeed, the relationship between semantic marking and distributional restriction can be seen very clearly in the set of quantifiers under study. For example, both is marked with respect to all in that it bears the component of meaning "two", and it is correspondingly restricted in its appropriate reference to such sets.

Suppose, then, that there is a tendency for natural languages to provide the simplest forms for those things that are likely to be said more frequently. What are the implications of such a possibility for the study of first language acquisition processes? It would certainly make the correlation of frequency and structural complexity the usual case in natural language studies (cf. Brown & Hanlon, 1970). However, the over-all pattern of evidence would lead one to hypothesize that frequency of usage of linguistic forms might not work directly through the building of associative strengths as it applies to the learning of each individual child. Instead it might be one of the variables which shape the language of the community as a whole. What might be the communicative advantage of the language design feature that we suggest? Apart from minimizing the effort required in everyday language use for the fluent, it would place the novice in an early position of strength as an active conversant. Just the role that would explain best the remarkable progress that the young child normally demonstrates in acquiring a first language.

251

References

Brown, R. A first language: The early stages. Cambridge, Mass.: Harvard University Press, 1973.

Brown, R. & Hanlon, C. Derivational complexity and order of emergence in child speech. In H. Hayes (Ed.), Cognition and the development of language. New York: Wiley, 1970.

Gentner, D. Evidence for the psychological reality of semantic components: The verbs of possession. In D. Norman & D. Rumelhart (Eds.), Explorations in cognition. San Francisco: Freeman, 1975.

Greenberg, J. Language universals. The Hague: Mouton, 1966.

Hanlon, C. The emergence of set-relational quantifiers in early childhood. In P. Dale & D. Ingram (Eds.), Child language: An international perspective. Baltimore: University Park Press, 1981.

Howes, D. A word count of spoken English. Journal of Verbal Learning and Verbal Behavior, 1966, 5, 572-604.

Lyons, J. Semantics (Vol. 1). Cambridge: Cambridge University Press, 1977.

Mervis, C. Acquisition of object categories. Doctoral dissertation, Cornell University, 1976.

Thorndike, E. & Lorge, I. The teacher's word book of 30,000 words. New York: Teachers College, Columbia University, 1944.

Wepman, J. & Hass, W. A spoken word count (children - ages 5, 6, and 7). Chicago: Language Research Associates, 1969.

Zipf, G. The psychobiology of language. Cambridge, Mass.: Houghton-Mifflin, 1935.

Zipf, G. Human behavior and the Principle of Least Effort. Cambridge, Mass.: Addison-Wesley, 1949.

Table 1

English Set-Relational Quantifiers as They Occur
at Three Levels of Generality in Reference

Quantifier	Example of use
	Generic Level
all	Mommy, why do all animals have tails?
no	No wolves talk like that.
some	Some animals wake up in the morning time.
any	They don't want any cranky little girls that are tired.
each	Each person is a world apart.
every	What every little girl plays with-- wet, soggy tea bags.
	Specific Level
all	Drinking all my grape juice.
none	I don't want to share none of my books.
some	You can't have some of my candles.
any	Do you know any of the kids?
(the) other	You marry de other cat, Miss Cat.
another	Have another of these.

253

Quantifier	Example of use
each	Dey not go...each one is gonna have a flat tire.
every	Every people...every man's gonna drive de car.
both	Hold it all the way like that, with both fingers.
either	Some are on either side, see?
neither	Neither pen is mine.

Non-specific Level

no	No children are in it.
some	I going make some groceries.
any	I don't have any toys in here.
another	Hey, let's do another page.

254

Table 2

Definitions for English Set-Relational Quantifiers
Expressed as Transformations of Suppositional
into Actual Reference Sets

Quantifier	Definition
all	The actual reference set is identical to the potential reference set.
no, none	The actual reference set is null or empty.
some	The actual reference set is an indefinite portion of the potential reference set.
any	The actual reference set is an indefinite portion of the potential reference set, with an equal chance or selection across all members or portions of the potential reference set.
another	The actual reference set is an indefinite new member of the potential reference set.
(the) other	The actual reference set is that portion of the potential reference set remaining after a specific subset has been subtracted.
each	The actual reference set is identical to the potential reference set. Also, the relevant predicates outside the nominal must be applied distributively. That is, the predicates must be interpreted as describing the members individually, or taken one at a time.

Quantifier	Definition
every	The actual reference set is identical to the potential reference set. Also, the predicates outside the nominal are applied to set members distributively, with stress on the exhaustiveness of the process.
both	The actual reference set is identical to the potential reference set. Further, the potential reference set is a previously specified set of two.
either	The actual reference set is one member of the potential reference set, with an equal chance of selection across set members. Further, the potential reference set is a previously-specified set of two.
neither	The actual reference set is null or empty. Further, the potential reference set is a previously-specified set of two.

Table 3

Intercorrelations Among the Rank Orders of Specific Quantifier Frequencies for the Parents of Adam, Eve, and Sarah

Parental Frequency	Parental Frequency			
	Adam	Eve	Sarah	Mean
Adam		.81	.80	.98
Eve			.77	.81
Sarah				.88
Mean				

Note: The entries in this table are Spearman rank order correlation co-efficients. N = 10 (the number of specific quantifiers). The range of probability values for the significance of these co-efficients is .001 to .005.

Table 4

Sentence Contexts for the Quantifiers Used
in the Comprehension Tasks

Task   Instruction

Letters

                        all
                        none
                        some
            "Put   any   of the letters in a box."
                        both
                        either
                        neither
                        each

            "This is a special letter. Now

                        (the) other
            put   another of the   letters in a box."
                        all of the

Cookies

                        all
                        none
                        some
            "Give him any   of the cookies
                        both
                        either
                        neither
                        each

            "This is a special cookie. Now

                        (the) other
            give him   another of the   cookies."
                        all of the

See Note on next page.

258

Table 5

Percent of Four- through Seven-year-old Subjects
Passing Each Quantifier Comprehension Test in Each Task
(Pass = 2 out of 3 trials correct, N = 61)

| | Task | |
Quantifier	Letters	Cookies
all	100	100
none	87	89
some	89	92
any	93	92
other	80	93
another	49	51
both	100	100
either	46	46
neither	31	43
each	31	3

Note for Table 4

For all trials except those with both, either, and neither,
sets of four identical objects are presented. For trials
with these quantifiers, two objects are used. For the trials
with the other, another, and an additional control set with
all, the "special" object instructions are used. On these
trials the "special" object is one of the four identical
objects presented. It is placed slightly apart from the
others, and so designated.

Table 6

Correlations Between Parental Frequency Measures
and Comprehension Measures for English Set-Relational
Quantifiers Used in Specific References

Parental Frequency	Comprehension Task		
	Letters	Cookies	Mean
Adam	.61	.73	.65
Eve	.47 (NS)	.72	.56
Sarah	.82	.95	.88
Mean	.74	.83	.77

Note: The entries in this table are Spearman rank order co-
efficients, with N = 10. All of the correlations in
the table are significant at the .05 level of probability or better, with the exception of the entry
marked NS. The probability for this co-efficient is
.08. The others range from .001 to .045. The data
for parental frequencies are longitudinal (3 $\underline{Ss}$);
those for comprehension are cross-sectional (61 $\underline{Ss}$).

Willem Kaper

The use of some complementary or antonymous
verbs by children and adults

It is a well-known phenomenon that children
often replace a lexical item (a word or an
expression) by its antonym, so that from the
viewpoint of adult language the child says
the opposite of what he intends to express,
e.g., hot instead of cold. The child mostly
uses the item in the normal meaning as well.
So in my opinion Leopold (1949a:143) is right
when speaking of "a striking special case of
extension of meaning". I cannot give any example providing evidence that a child uses a
word or an expression exclusively in the opposite meaning. Probably this is never the
case. I intend to discuss the use of some antonyms in the course of this paper, but first
I will try to analyse a couple of verbs which
"are in complementary rather than contrasting
relation" (Leopold 1949a:145). They are the
very interesting verbs zoeken 'look for' and
vinden 'find'. Consider the examples (1)-(8).

(1) 'k Ga in de andere doos kijken - of ik
    daar wat zoek 'I will have a look into
    the other box - (to see) if I look for
    something there'. E 4;1.16.
(2) Gaan we haar zoeken? 'are we going to
    look for her?' (meaning: are we going
    to meet auntie at the railway station?).
    E 4;1.25.
(3) Wat moet je vinden? 'what do you want to
    find?' E 4;5.28.
(4) Zal ik hem vinden? 'shall I find it?'
    (speaking of a file card). E 4;9.21.
(5) Soll ich's mal finden? 'shall I find it?'
    Hdg 5;3.15 (Leopold 1949b:107).
(6) Find mir den Ball! 'find the ball for me!'
    (after being corrected for using find in-
    stead of such:) Nein, finden, vom bloßen

Suchen habe ich nichts 'no, find, only looking for is of no use to me'. Child cited by Kainz (1943:62); no age.
(7) Geh, find mal mein Bilderbuch, ich kann's nich garnich suchen! 'go and find my picture-book, I cannot look for it not at all!' Bubi Scupin at about 2;7 (Scupin 1907:148).
(8) Even kijken, of ik het kan opvinden '(I will) just look if I can find it up' (viz. a place in a book of maps, by means of the index). E 8;2.21.

In Dutch adult language both of the verbs under discussion presuppose "not-having" something. When we focus our attention on the attempt to have we say zoeken, when on the result we say vinden. In the speech of my eldest son Erik (E) the use of these verbs was inadequate - i.e. deviant from adult use - up to his ninth year. In (1), one month and a half after his fourth birthday, he uses zoeken meaning vinden. In this period of his life, however, he repeatedly said vinden in similar contexts; in other words, he used both zoeken and vinden to express the notion 'find'. At about the same age, in (2), we hear zoeken in the sense of 'meeting a person at the railway station'. In adult speech we never use the verb in this meaning, but we can understand the deviation only when assuming that the usual meaning of zoeken, viz. 'try to find', lies at the root of it. The child avails himself of a possibility of extending the meaning of a word, neglected in his mother tongue, but realized in another language, for in French we can say chercher quelqu'un à la gare 'to meet somebody at the railway station'. Such "international correspondences" between child language and foreign languages are already repeatedly observed in child language research (Bowerman 1978:284 and 1980:296; Kaper 1977: 303). They are not restricted to extensions of meaning and there are many individual differences. The special quality of each individual correspondence may be due to the merest chance, but it seems inherent to language use that they do occur. It may be worth while to pay more attention to this phenomenon.

Easily accounted for is (3), spoken by the boy at about four years and a half. He asks what his father wants to find. Although the usual question in such a situation is Wat zoek je? 'what are you looking for?' we cannot say that E substitutes vinden for zoeken here. Both Wat zoek je? and Wat moet je vinden? could be paraphrased as 'what do you try to find?' The child's formulation of the question is unusual, but in the construction as it is the verb vinden is adequate. Less acceptable is (4), because one can at most offer to 'look for' something; whether the attempt to find it will be successful remains to be seen. However, what the boy wants to attain is the 'finding' of the file card, and that explains the use of vinden instead of zoeken. Leopold's daughter Hildegard (Hdg) asks the same question in German at a somewhat later age in (5). Leopold (1949b:107) classifies this utterance under "loan translations", which apparently is a plausible explanation, because in English we can ask Shall I find your hat? But since E never heard English, with him this explanation cannot obtain; we can only speak of an accidental international correspondence. The correspondence is not complete, to be sure, for when we ask Shall I find your hat? we know where to find it, which is not the case in E's and Hdg's situation.

The above-mentioned use of find in English is also possible in a request such as Please, find Mary's hat for her. In Dutch and in German this imperative, as in (6) and (7), is ungrammatical. But we can understand the pro-

test of the child cited by Kainz in (6). Unfortunately Kainz does not give the age, but
the critical remark speaks well for a certain
mental maturity. Keeping this protest in mind
we cannot say that in (7) Bubi Scupin simply
mixes up _finden_ and _suchen_. He wants to see a
result, viz. the appearance of the book;
'looking for it' is what he already does himself without any result. This lack of result
is expressed in a rather awkward way, but we
cannot expect a 2½-year-old to say something
like 'I am vainly looking for it'. Consequently we may suppose that the child has a
notion of the current meanings of the verbs
in question.

Even at a later age knowledge of the meaning
of a word does not exclude deviant use. In
the first half of his ninth year E spoke (8).
Of course he wanted to 'look up' (Dutch _op-_
zoeken) the place by means of the index,
hoping to 'find' it (Dutch _vinden_). The compound _opvinden_ 'find up' may be considered a
contamination of these verbs. But what I want
to emphasize is that neither .... _of ik het_
kan opzoeken nor .... _of ik het kan vinden_
would have expressed exactly what the boy
wanted to communicate. Evidently he knew very
well that he 'could' - was able to - look it
up, so that _opzoeken_ would have been inadequate in this context. True, he wanted to
try to 'find' it, but _vinden_ does not express
the opening of the book of maps and the consulting of the index. Consequently this child
has constructed a new compound which is just
the thing for his purpose.

It is interesting to find that also adults
now and then erroneously use _zoeken_ instead
of _vinden_, not only as a slip of the tongue,
but also in written texts. See (9)-(11).

(9) Proberen parallellen in de taal der vol-

wassenen te zoeken 'try to look for parallels in adult language'. Note of father.
(10) (quotation from the explanatory memoran-
dum to a bill dated August 15, 1962, published in the newspapers:) Het volstrekt
ontbreken van enig Nederlands eigenbelang
naast het opkomen voor de rechten van de
bevolking deden de regering besluiten te
trachten een krachtiger steun voor de bevolking te zoeken in de volkerengemeen-
schap 'the complete lack of any Dutch
self-interest, along with standing up for
the population's rights decided the government to attempt to look for a more
vigorous support of the population in the
community of nations'.
(11) Waar kan 'k 'em zoeken? 'where can I look
for it?' (viz. for the spectacles, Dutch
bril, which is singular). Question asked
by father.

As a directive for my study of child language
I made the note cited in (9). Immediately
after having written it down I cancelled the
word zoeken and replaced it by vinden, but
the error - probably a contamination of zoeken and its synonym proberen te vinden 'try
to find' - is essentially the same as the one
of opzoeken and vinden in (8). Also the error
of the same kind in (10) - in an official
document! - is instructive in this respect,
the more so as I did not notice the antonymous use of zoeken when for the first time
reading the text myself. But zoeken in (11),
although at first hearing striking us as
strange, expresses broadly what I meant: I
wanted to ask where my attempts to find my
glasses could be successful. 'Waar kan ik
hem vinden' would have suggested that the
addressee knew where to find them. Retro-
spectively I think that the formulation Waar
zou ik hem kunnen vinden? 'where could I
possibly find them?' would have been prefer-

able. Nevertheless the actually spoken sentence expressed exactly what I meant. Like in (3) and (8) the utterance may at first hearing strike us as strange, but on close inspection the seemingly deviant formulation is not unreasonable.

Now I will turn to the use of some antonyms.

(12) Nel stoel halen - gang 'Nel fetch chair - corridor'. (meaning: Nel - the servant-girl - is taking the chair to the corridor). H 1;11.6.

(13) Hij is veel te lief om een pak slaag te geven 'he is much too sweet to give a thrashing'. Vivie, about 10. Nee, om een pak slaag te krijgen 'no, to get a thrashing'. Bartke, about 10; correcting. (Personal communication).

In (12) my younger son Hans (H) wants to communicate the fact that the servant-girl is taking a chair to the corridor. However, by making use of the verb <u>halen</u> 'fetch', in fact he says the opposite. The right word would have been the antonym <u>brengen</u>, the equivalent of the English 'bring'. Different from English, Dutch <u>brengen</u> is used not only to indicate that something is brought towards the speaker, but also that it is taken away from him to some point on which he focuses his attention. So <u>halen</u> implies the notion <u>brengen</u>: we cannot 'fetch' something without 'bringing' or 'taking' it somewhere. The misuse of the more comprehensive word by H may be due to misunderstanding its meaning when used in a situation. For when the servant-girl performs what she is speaking of as <u>de stoel halen</u> 'fetching the chair', part of her performance is taking up the chair and carrying it somewhere.

In (13) we can observe that a child by age ten

may be more or less conscious of the antonymous use of a verb, without noticing, however, that it is caused by a difference in point of view. The girl Vivie intends to say that her little brother is too sweet to get a thrashing, but taking the point of view of the castigator she uses the verb <u>geven</u> 'give' instead of <u>krijgen</u> 'get', forgetting that normally the subject of the infinitive in the construction <u>om te + inf</u> is identical with the subject of the main clause. Her friend Bartke, intuitively placing herself in the position of the little boy, duly corrects her, although we may safely assume that the syntactic rule mentioned before was not known to her.

Also the Dutch verbs <u>komen</u> 'come' and <u>gaan</u> 'go' express contrary notions: a movement towards and away from the speaker (or his focuspoint), respectively. I have not noted any example indicating that my sons confused these words, except in compounds. See (14)-(20).

(14) O, wantje is uitgekomen! 'oh, little mitten has come off!' H 2;4.28.
(15) Pappa, hoe laat was je opgegaan? 'Daddy, at what time did you rise (literally: had you gone up)?' E 6;2.29.
(16) Wat ben jij laat opgegaan! 'how late you got up (literally: you have gone up)!' H 4;1.0.
(17) Had je'm horen opgaan, Piet? 'had you heard him going up, Piet?' (meaning: had you heard Piet getting up?). H 4;1.7.
(18) Ik kwam laat op! 'I got (lit.: came) up late!' H 4;1.21.
(19) Wat komt die Erik laat op! 'how late that E is getting (lit.: coming) up!' H 5;1.4.
(20) Pappa, nu komt de zon nèt op 'Daddy, just now the sun is rising' (spoken at midday, when the sun broke through; at about the same time:) Mamma, voor is de

> zon al ònder en achter nog niet 'Mammy,
> in front (of the house) the sun is al-
> ready down, and at the back not yet'.
> H 4;3.1.

In (14) the English translation does not show
the deviation from normal language use, but in
Dutch we prefer uitgegaan in this context; in
fact the mitten has moved away from the hand
of the child. In Dutch this use of uitkomen is
antonymous, whereas in English expressions
such as a button has come off are common.
Again an international correspondence between
Dutch child language and English adult speech.

At much later ages H interchanges opkomen and
opgaan to express the notion 'get up from
bed', which meaning neither of them have in
standard Dutch; the usual term is opstaan
'rise'. The examples (16)-(19) show his
deviant use. Also from E - as late as at 6;2.
29 - I noted opgaan in this sense (15), but
since this example falls on exactly the same
calendar day as (16) from H, E is likely to
have taken over the expression from his
younger brother. The use of opgaan instead of
opstaan may be due to the fact that these
words are phonetically similar, and that the
opposite of opstaan 'get up' is: naar bed
gaan 'go to bed'. The equalization of opgaan
and opkomen is not unknown in adult language
when referring to the rising of the sun: 'de
zon komt op' and 'de zon gaat op' are synonymous. Both expressions were familiar to
the boys, although, as (20) shows, the exact
meaning was not yet clear to H in his fifth
year. This familiarity may explain the use
of these verbs as synonyms in other contexts.

Curiously enough I noted afterwards several
examples from the parents using both opgaan
and opkomen in the sense of opstaan 'get up
from bed'. Most instructive are those from

the father, quoted in (21)-(23), because of
his hesitations and self-corrections:

(21) (in reply to mother's question whether he
had knocked up H:) Ja, maar of dat wil
zeggen dat hij opgekomen is ..... (correcting himself:) opgegaan is ..... 'yes,
but if that is to say that he has come up
..... gone up .....'. Father.
(22) Dan moet je wachten tot de jòngens opkomen ..... (correcting himself:) .....
de jòngens opgaan 'then you must wait
till the bòys come up ..... the bòys go
up'. Father.
(23) Is Erik nou al op- ..... gegaan? 'has E
already ..... gone up now?' Father, hesitating because he could not find the
right word immediately; speaking -gegaan
he was conscious of his being wrong.

I will not exclude the possibility that the
father was willy-nilly influenced by his
younger son.

A special case of antonymous use of words is
the substitution of a negative local adverb
for the positive one by E in (24) and (25):

(24) Ik wil nergens zitten 'I want to sit no-
where' (meaning: I want to sit somewhere).
E 3;4.22.
(25) Ik wil nergens opzitten 'I want to sit
down on nothing' (meaning: I want to sit
down on something). E 3;5.24.

Phonetically there is only a slight difference
between these antonymous adverbs: the positive
ergens 'somewhere' is made negative by pre-
posing n-. E spoke the negative form instead
of the positive one at least during a month.
In both examples the adverb is combined with
the verb zitten 'sit', from which one gets the
impression that this linguistic form is more or

less stereotyped.

In (26) H proceeds the other way round, speaking the positive temporal adverb ooit 'ever' meaning nooit 'never':

(26) 't Wordt o zo'n leuke auto, die je nog
     ooit van je leven gezien had 'it's going
     to be oh so nice a car that you had ever
     seen in your life' (speaking of a drawing
     he was about to make; meaning: ..... that
     you never saw in your life). H 3;10.17.

This occurred repeatedly with him at about age 3;10, exclusively in the relative clause ..... die je nog ooit van je leven gezien had 'that you had ever seen in your life'. Here it is hardly doubtful that the child thoughtlessly reproduced the stereotyped phrase ooit van je leven, usual in exclamations such as Heb je zo iets ooit van je leven gezien? 'did you ever see something like that?', a rhetorical question the tenor of which is negative. This explains the antonymous use of ooit by H.

Of course I will not presume to draw convincing conclusions from a small number of rather random examples. But I hope to have shown the necessity of studying child language in continuous comparison with colloquial adult speech. It is very likely that in that way we shall find that child language, although in many respects undeniably deviant from adult speech, essentially does not differ from it, because in both of them potential linguistic forms inherent to the language the child is acquiring are actualized. And it is useful in doing so to realize how complicated human language is, especially concerning meaning.

References

Bowerman, M. (1978). The acquisition of word meaning: an investigation into some current conflicts. In N. Waterson & C. Snow (eds.), The development of communication. Chichester -New York-Brisbane-Toronto: Wiley, pp. 263-87.

Bowerman, M. (1980). The structure and origin of semantic categories in the language-learning child. In M.L. Foster & S. Brandes (eds.), Symbol as sense. Academic Press, chapter 18, pp. 277-99.

Kainz, F. (1943). Psychologie der Sprache: Vol. 2. Stuttgart: Enke.

Kaper, W. (1977). Observations on the use of some auxiliaries by Dutch children and adults: meaning and grammaticality. Kwartalnik Neofilologiczny 24, pp. 303-09.

Leopold, W.F. (1949a). Speech development of a bilingual child: Vol. 3. Evanston, Ill.: Northwestern University Press.

Leopold, W.F. (1949b). Speech development of a bilingual child: Vol. 4. Evanston, Ill.: Northwestern University Press.

Scupin, E. & Scupin, G. (1907). Bubis erste Kindheit: ein Tagebuch über die geistige Entwicklung eines Knaben während der ersten drei Lebensjahre. Leipzig: Grieben.

The Acquisition of the Meaning of Mood Terms

Stan A. Kuczaj II   Denise R. Clark

Southern Methodist University

Children learning their first language must learn that words are symbols which may be used to refer to a variety of entities. Much of the research on children's acquisition of word meaning has focused on words which refer to objects (e.g., dog) or on antonyms such as before-after and less-more (see Clark, in press, for a review of this literature). The tendency to concentrate on these sorts of words has left the study of lexical meaning acquisition in an unbalanced state of affairs. On the one hand, we have learned a fair amount about the acquisition of the meaning of object words such as dog and that the theory which motivated the work on antonyms is most likely not correct (see, for example, Kuczaj, 1975; Kuczaj and Maratsos, 1975; Kuczaj, 1981). On the other hand, we have largely ignored the development of other sorts of words and the development of semantic relations necessary for the creation of semantic fields and the semantic system (Kuczaj, 1982). In the present study, we have chosen to investigate the acquisition of the meanings of words which do not refer to objects but rather to internal emotional states. More-over, the words comprise a semantic field which allows some consideration of the influence of the development of semantic relations on the acqui-sition of the words of concern.

The acquisition of the meaning of mood terms would seem to be of considerable importance to children, for the acquisition of such words and their meanings [and the correct linking of a word to its meaning(s)] allows children to comment on their own emotional states as well as those of others. There is evidence that preverbal children (i.e., children who have not yet begun to use words) can both communicate and comprehend certain

272

emotional states (Bretherton, McNew & Beeghly-Smith, 1981; Blount, in press). It seems certain that by the age of 2½ years, children are "not only aware that other people have feelings but also actively try to understand the feelings they observe" (Borke, 1971, p. 263).

Investigators have also found that children begin to produce mood terms during the second year of life (Bretherton and Beeghly, in press; Bretherton, et al, 1981; Kagan, 1981). Although young children seem capable of referring to non-present emotional states as well as present ones, they were more likely to use such terms to refer to their own emotional states than to other's emotional states (Bretherton and Beeghly, in press; Bretherton et al., 1981).

The present study extends the work of previous investigators by systematically assessing children's knowledge of particular mood terms. It also attempts to discern the semantic relations which children use to structure their emotional term semantic field. More specifically, we were concerned with the question of whether the mood terms used by young children constitute a loose-knit collection of meanings or a set of related meanings.

Russell and Mehrabian (1977) suggested that three independent and bipolar dimensions are necessary and sufficient to adequately define emotional states. The dimensions they suggested were (1) pleasure-displeasure, (2) degree of arousal (active/passive), and (3) dominance-submissiveness. In more recent work, however, Russell (1978, 1979) found that only two dimensions (pleasure) displeasure and degree of arousal) seemed to be involved in mood term meaning.

In the present study, we attempted to ascertain if and when these dimensions entered into the mood term meaning system during the course of development.

Method

Subjects. Subjects were 40 preschool children ranging in age from 3,0 (years, months) to 6,11, grouped according to chronological age. There were five male and five female children in each age group. The mean ages for each group were 3,7; 4,7; 5,4; and 6,6.

Target words. The mood terms investigated in the present study were selected with regard to (a) their correspondence to mood terms produced in spontaneous speech by children in a similar age group and (b) Russell and Mehrabian's (1977) three factor theory of emotions. Initially, transcripts of 16 children's spontaneous speech were analyzed (none of these children participated in the present investigation). The 16 children's ages ranged from 1,11 (years, months) to 5,8. Included in these analyses were longitudinal samples for two children from age 1,11 through 3,2 and from age 2,5 through 5,6. On the basis of these analyses, a list of representative mood terms for the age range of concern was generated.

Two words were selected from the list of mood terms obtained from the analysis of the spontaneous speech transcripts to represent each of five categories of emotional states as described by Russell and Mehrabian (1977). Their theory suggests that emotional states may be described by three independent and bipolar dimensions: (a) pleasure-displeasure, (b) high arousal-low arousal, and (c) dominance-submissiveness. The five categories of word types were selected to represent pleasure, high arousal, and dominance (word type one: happy, friendly); displeasure, low arousal, and submissiveness (word type two: lonely, sad); displeasure, high arousal, and dominance (word type three: hate, mad); displeasure, high arousal, and submissiveness (word type four: scared, upset); and pleasure, high arousal, and submissiveness (word type five: love, surprised).

274

Procedure. In order to assess the children's
understanding of emotional terms, each subject
was given two tasks. The first task consisted of
ten short stories, presented one at a time, with
each story immediately followed by three questions
regarding a character in the story. Each word was
represented with the questions reflecting one
correct "yes" response and two correct "no"
responses. For example, after hearing the story
"Johnny just got a bunch of new toys. He is
playing with the toys with his best friend," the
subject was asked "Does Johnny feel happy? Does
Johnny feel sad? Does Johnny feel upset?" The
ten stories were presented in a random order to
each child. Similarly, the order of presentation
for the questions for each story was randomized
for each child.

    The second task consisted of a pair of
questions regarding the ten emotional words (happy,
friendly, lonely, sad, hate, mad, scared, upset,
love, and surprised). For each word the child was
asked "How do you feel when you're (emotional
word)?" and "What do you do when you're (emotional
word)?", with the exception of love ("How do you
feel/What do you do when you love somebody?") and
hate ("How do you feel/What do you do when you
hate something?"). The "how do you feel" question
was always asked prior to the "what do you do"
question. However, the presentation of the ten
emotional words was random for each child.

Results and Discussion. Total correct responses
for the story task will be considered first. The
responses for the story task were divided according to the type of response that the child should
have made with questions with "yes" responses being
called "main questions" and questions with "no"
responses being called "auxiliary questions."
As might be expected, the children's overall performance on the tasks tended to improve with age.
The analysis of variance for the responses to the
story questions indicated a significant age effect,
$F(1,32) = 7.64$, $p > .01$. A significant effect of the

child's sex was also evident, $F(1,32) = 7.64$, p<.01, with females performing better than males. The children correctly answered significantly more main questions ($\bar{X} = 79\%$ correct) than auxiliary questions ($\bar{X} = 68\%$ correct), $F(1,20) = 13.54$, p<.01.

Correct responses for the main questions were also analyzed. The analysis of variance for the main questions indicated a significant effect of sex, with females performing better than males, F, $(1,32) = 13.23$, p<.01, and age, with children's performance improving with age, $F(3,32) = 20.63$, p<.001. An analysis of variance also indicated a significant age effect, $F(3,20) = 21.90$, p<.001, for correct responses to the auxiliary questions.

Word type also proved to be significant for the auxiliary questions, $F(4,20) = 21.16$, p<.001. There was a significant difference between word types three and five and between word types two and three, with children performing better on word type three than on word types two or five. No other word type differences were significant.

There is evidence (Russell, 1978; 1979) that the third dimension (dominance-submissiveness) in Russell and Mehrabian's (1977) three factor theory of emotions is not as important as the authors originally suggested. As a result, an additional analysis was done looking at only the first two dimensions of affect. The following three groups of words were compared on total correct responses on both main and auxiliary questions: (a) pleasure, high arousal; (b) displeasure, low arousal; and (c) displeasure, high arousal. The only significant difference in performance with respect to these categories was on main questions and showed performance on word type "a" to be significantly better than on word type "c", $t(30) = 2.19$, p<.05.

The overall picture presented by the above data is one of some confusion. For example, words such as <u>hate</u> and <u>mad</u> appeared to be the easiest words for the auxiliary questions, but were among the most difficult for the main questions. The following analyses involve individual words rather than groups of words in an attempt to lessen the confusion. Table 1 shows the rank order (from most to least easy) of the ten words for the main task and each term's characteristics.

Table 1

	Word	Characteristics
1.	love	pleasure/high arousal/submissive
2.	happy	pleasure/high arousal/dominance
3.	friendly	pleasure/high arousal/dominance
4.	lonely	displeasure/low arousal/submissive
	upset	displeasure/high arousal/submissive
5.	hate	displeasure/high arousal/dominance
	surprised	pleasure/high arousal/submissive
6.	sad	displeasure/low arousal/submissive
7.	scared	displeasure/high arousal/submissive
8.	mad	displeasure/high arousal/dominance

The rank order (from least to most difficult) for each word for the auxiliary question was as follows: (1) mad, (2) upset, (3) happy, (4) hate, (5) sad, (6) love, (7) friendly, scared, (8) lonely, (9) surprised.

It appears, then, that in regard to identifying the presence of a mood, children focus on pleasure and high arousal. But in regard to identifying the absence of a mood, children seem to pay most attention to high arousal and a bit less attention to displeasure (which seems to be a significant factor).

In the present task, children must compare the emotion they've identified in the story with each target word. A correct "no match" decision was most likely when the target term reflected high arousal and displeasure. A correct "match" decision was most likely when the target term reflected high arousal and pleasure.

These patterns support Russell's (1978, 1979) contention for a two-dimensional account of the mood term semantic field. High arousal seems to be the most general significant factor for young children, with the influence of the pleasure/ displeasure dimension depending on whether a "match" or "no match" decision is involved. This suggests that children find it easier to distinguish pleasure from displeasure than to distinguish high arousal from low arousal (see also Borke, 1971). Thus, the pleasure/displeasure dimension should be acquired before the high/low arousal dimension.

The above results and speculations are based on the data obtained in the comprehension task. Children's responses to the "how do you feel" and "what do you do" questions provide further support for these speculations. Young children's answers contain more reference to high arousal than to any other variable. With increasing age, reference to pleasure and displeasure appears, as does reference to low arousal. The following are examples of children's responses to "how do you feel" questions when the target word was mad: "I throw things (3;4); "I tear up something" (4;6); "horrible" (5;4); "I don't feel very good" (6;8). Of course, these examples reflect age trends rather than a perfect relation between age and type of answer. There were activity-based answers from six-year-olds (e.g., "I kick sand", 6;9) and one reference to displeasure from a three-year-old ("I just don't like nobody", 3;7).

Summary

The findings of the present study suggest that the rudiments of a mood term semantic field is present in three-to-six-year-old children.

There appears to be continual development of the mood term semantic system during the preschool years, such that an initial loose-knit collection of meanings become integrated with a semantic field.

The type of emotional term with which the child must deal appears to be another important factor in the acquisition of mood terms. Regarding the word types that were derived from Russell and Mehrabian's (1977) three factor theory of emotions, it appears that some types of words are "easier" than others for different conditions. The children's significantly better performance on the auxiliary questions on word type three than on word type two or five, as well as the overall significance of word type for auxiliary questions, indicates that the inferences they must make regarding the <u>absence</u> of an emotional state in an individual may be easier for some words than for others. Similarly, the significantly better performance on main questions with words representing the dimensions of pleasure and high arousal as compared to the dimensions of displeasure and high arousal, indicates that it is easier to make inferences about the presence of some emotional states than others. Also, the significant interaction between question type and word type indicates that it is easier for a child to make decisions of different types for different words.

There are still many questions to be considered. (1) What is the relation of comprehension and productive use of mood terms by children?, (2) What are the basic (i.e., first acquired) mood terms? (Bretherton and her colleagues have begun to unravel the answer), (3) What is the precise relation of word meaning acquisition and the acquisition of the semantic dimensions?

References

Blount, B.G. The ontogeny of emotions and their

vocal expression in infants. In S. Kuczaj
(Ed.), Language development: language, thought
and culture. Hillsdale, N.J.: Lawrence
Erlbaum Associates, in press.

Borke, H. Interpersonal perceptions of young
children: Egocentrism or empathy? Developmental Psychology, 1971, 5, 263-269.

Bretherton, I., & Beeghly, M. Talking about
internal states: The acquisition of an implicit
theory of mind. Developmental Psychology, in
press.

Bretherton, I., McNew, S., & Beeghly-Smith, M.
Early person knowledge as expressed in
gestural and verbal communication: When do
infants acquire a "theory of mind?" In
M. Lamb & L. Sherrod (Eds.), Infant social
cognition. Hillsdale, N.J.: Lawrence Erlbaum
Associates, 1981.

Clark, E.V. Meaning and concepts. In P. Mussen
(Ed.), Carmichael's manual of child psychology,
Vol. 3, New York: Wiley, in press.

Kagan, J. The second year: The emergence of
self-awareness. Cambridge, MA: Harvard
University Press, 1981.

Kuczaj, S.A. II. On the acquisition of a semantic
system. Journal of Verbal Learning and Verbal
Behavior, 1975, 14, 340-358.

Kuczaj, S.A. II. Review of E. Clark, The ontogenesis of meaning. Journal of Child Language,
1981, 8, 505-509.

Kuczaj, S.A. II. The acquisition of word meaning
in the context of the development of the
semantic system. In C. Brainerd & M. Pressley
(Eds.), Progress in cognitive development
reserve, Vol. 2, Verbal processes in children.
New York: Springer-Verlag, 1982, 95-124.

Kuczaj, S.A. II, & Maratsos, M.P. On the acqui-
    sition of front, back, and side. Child
    Development, 1975, 46, 202-210.

Russell, J.A. Evidence of convergent validity on
    the dimensions of affect. Journal of Person-
    ality and Social Psychology, 1978, 36, 1152-
    1168.

Russell, J.A. Affective space is bipolar.
    Journal of Personality and Social Psychology,
    1979, 37, 345-356.

Russell, J.A., & Mehrabian, A. Evidence for a
    three-factor theory of emotions. Journal of
    Research in Personality, 1977, 11, 273-294.

Appendix

Stories

pleasure/arousal/dominance

1. $\overset{+}{h}\overset{+}{a}\overset{+}{p}py$:

    Johnny just got a bunch of new toys. He is
    playing with the toys with his best friend.

            Does Johnny feel happy?
            Does Johnny feel sad?
            Does Johnny feel upset?

    friendly:

    Jane is playing in the yard. A dog comes up
    to her and lets Jane pet him and play with him.

            Is the dog friendly?
            Is the dog mad?
            Is the dog surprised?

2. l̄ōnēl̄y:

Mike was going to the park to play. It
started raining and Mike had to stay home and
play inside all by himself.

      Did Mike feel lonely?
      Did Mike feel friendly?
      Did Mike feel surprised?

s̄ād

Susie's mommy has to go out of town. Her
mommy will fly on an airplane and go far away.

      Does Susie feel sad?
      Does Susie feel happy?
      Does Susie feel friendly?

3. h̄āt̄e:

Tommy does not like to eat spinach so his mom
does not cook spinach for him to eat.

      Does Tommy hate spinach?
      Does Tommy love spinach?
      Is Tommy sad about spinach?

mad:

Cindy's friend just broke her favorite toy.

      Is Cincy mad?
      Is Cindy lonely?
      Is Cindy scared?

4. s̄c̄ār̄ed:

Ben is looking at a Halloween book with pictures of ghosts and witches.

      Is Ben scared?
      Is Ben mad?
      Does Ben hate the book?

<u>upset</u>:

Debbie is at the grocery store with her mom.
Debbie wants some candy but her mom said "no"
and Debbie didn't get any candy.

     Is Debbie upset?
     Is Debbie scared?
     Is Debbie happy?

5.   love:

Paul really likes his dog.

     Does Paul love his dog?
     Does Paul hate his dog?
     Is Paul upset?

<u>surprised</u>:

Mary was playing hide and seek with a friend.
Mary was looking for her friend when her
friend jumped out from behind a bush and said
"boo".

     Was Mary surprised?
     Was Mary lonely?
     Did Mary love the bush?

Children's Comprehension of Relational Terms:
Two Developmental Levels

Judith A. McLaughlin, Elizabethtown College
and
Roy Pea, Clark University

This study was designed to investigate the relationship between language and cognitive development; specifically, the relationship between children's comprehension of relational terms and their operational development, as measured by the ability to conserve. The ability to conserve is one of many abilities that Piaget took as evidence of concrete operational thought. For example, in the conservation of substance task, a child who believes that two balls of clay have the same amount of clay, despite changes in the height and diameter of the balls, is said to conserve substance and therefore demonstrates concrete operational thought.

Using conservation of substance as a further example, in the traditional conservation task, children are asked to ignore certain dimensions of the stimuli, such as height and diameter, and to decide whether the two balls of clay are equal solely on the basis of the relevant dimension, the amount of clay. Tasks that measure children's comprehension of relational terms often measure similar abilities. For example, when asked which of two balls of clay has more clay, a child must respond solely on the basis of the amount of clay, and not be misled by differences in the height and diameter of the balls. Thus, the two tasks, conservation and comprehension of relational terms, in part measure the same abilities.

Several researchers have offered this point as a criticism of the traditional conservation test: that the traditional test not only assesses the ability to conserve, but is also a test of children's understanding of relational terms. Griffiths, Shantz and Sigel (1967) suggested that children might fail the traditional conservation test only because they do not understand relational terms. While many studies (Donaldson & Wales, 1970; Holland & Palermo, 1975; Palermo, 1973; Townsend, 1974) have shown that young children do not perfectly comprehend relational terms, there has yet been no study that has demonstrated that there are children who can conserve, but who fail the traditional test of conservation solely because they do not understand relational terms.

One of the principal purposes of this study was to determine whether there are children who can conserve but who do not understand relational terms. In order to test that hypothesis, two tasks were used: a conservation test and a test assessing comprehension of relational terms. In this study, the relationship between conservation and relational term comprehension was tested in six different content areas: continuous quantity, discontinuous quantity, number, length, area, and substance.

In testing for comprehension of relational terms, two types of stimuli were presented to the children for comparison. The first type involved sets of stimuli in which the relevant dimension covaried with another dimension of the stimuli (Covarying condition). For example, in testing for comprehension of the relational terms referring to area, rectangular shapes were shown to the children. For half the sets of rectangles, the width of the rectangles was equal, so the relevant dimension, area, covaried directly with the length of the rectangles. The longer rectangle was always greater in area. For the remaining sets, the length of the rectangles was equal, so that the area covaried directly with the width of the rectangles.

In testing for comprehension of the terms referring to continuous and discontinuous quantity, the relevant dimension, quantity, covaried with either the height or the diameter of the containers, in the Covarying condition. The covarying dimensions for the other content areas were as follows: number covaried with either the length or the density of rows of objects; length covaried with extension at either end of the stimuli; and substance covaried with either the height or the diameter of the stimuli.

In this Covarying condition, the relevant dimension in each content area had a functional relationship with another dimension of the stimuli. According to Piagetian theory (Piaget, Grize, Szeminska & Vinh-Bang, 1968), children who are pre-operational are able to establish functional relationships

285

between two dimensions, to understand that as one dimension increases, the second increases also. Thus, in the present study, it was expected that pre-operational children would be able to comprehend relational terms when shown sets of stimuli in which the relevant dimension covaried with another dimension of the stimuli.

The second type of stimuli used to test for comprehension of relational terms involved sets in which the relevant dimension did not covary with the other dimensions of the stimuli (Non-Covarying condition). In these sets of stimuli, one of the dimensions was not held equal between all stimuli in a set. For example, in testing for comprehension of the relational terms referring to area, the longest rectangle did not always have the greatest area, nor did the widest rectangle. In the sets of stimuli used in the Non-Covarying condition, there was no consistent relationship between the relevant dimension and the other dimensions of the stimuli. According to Piagetian theory (Piaget, Grize, Szeminska, & Vinh-Bang, 1968), children who are pre-operational are not able to coordinate variation in three dimensions simultaneously, and thus would not be expected to comprehend relational terms when comparing non-covarying stimuli. This ability to coordinate three dimensions simultaneously in part enables concrete operational children to conserve and should also enable them to comprehend relational terms when comparing non-covarying stimuli.

In the comprehension test, each child was shown 12 sets of covarying stimuli and 12 sets of non-covarying stimuli for each of the six content areas. Each set consisted of four stimuli, a standard and three alternatives. Each set was shown to the child and the child was asked to point to the alternative that was more than the standard, less than the standard, and the same as the standard along the relevant dimension. In the comprehension test, each child was scored as "passing" for each term if the child responded correctly on 9 or more of the 12 questions in each condition, Covarying and Non-Covarying, for each content area. The probability of a child guessing correctly on 9 or more of 12 questions is less than .05. Thus, each child was scored as "passing" or "failing" for each of the three relational terms in each condition for each of the six content areas.

286

Each child was also given a conservation test in the six content areas. In the conservation test given for each content area, relational terms were not used in questioning. This task was used to provide a measure of the children's ability to conserve, unconfounded by their understanding of relational terms. The conservation test used in this study followed the traditional methodology, except that, rather than asking the children whether the two stimuli were the same along the relevant dimension, the children were asked whether two dolls, each given one of the stimuli, were both happy. Before being given the conservation trials, the children were trained on this task to respond solely on the basis of the relevant dimension. Five conservation trials were used in scoring.

On the basis of performance on this conservation test, each child was assigned to one of three stages, for each content area. Children who gave no correct responses were assigned to Stage 1 as non-conservers or pre-operational; children who gave from one to four correct responses were assigned to Stage 2 as transitional; and children who gave five correct responses were assigned to Stage 3 as conservers or concrete operational.

For each content area, the stimuli for the conservation and comprehension tasks were constructed of identical materials. For continuous quantity, the stimuli were clear plastic tubes filled with colored sugar. The stimuli for discontinuous quantity were clear plastic tubes filled with small, beadlike candies. The stimuli for number were Smarties, a candy similar in shape to M&M's. The stimuli for length were pieces of licorice; for area, rectangular cookies; and for substance, marshmallows.

A total of 48 children served as subjects. The children were selected from six age groups, from 4 years old through 9 years old, with eight children in each age group. To summarize the design of the study, each child was tested for comprehension of three relational terms (e.g., "more," "same," and "less") in both the Covarying and Non-Covarying condition of the comprehension test and for conservation, in all six content areas. The order of presentation of the conservation and comprehension tasks was counter-balanced within each age group. Additionally, the order of presentation of the co-varying and non-covarying conditions of the comprehension

287

test was counter-balanced. The order of presentation of the three relational terms within each condition and the order of tasks across the six content areas was randomized.

Table 1 shows the results of the conservation testing. None of the 4- and 5-year-old children were able to conserve in any of the content areas, while a majority of the 8- and 9-year-old children conserved in most content areas. These results correspond to predictions based on Piagetian theory and to results obtained on the traditional test of conservation.

Table 2 shows the results of the comprehension test. The majority of the non-conservers passed the covarying condition for each term. On the other hand, all of the transitional children and conservers passed the covarying condition, for every term. These results indicate that comprehension of relational terms when comparing covarying stimuli is attained at some point in the pre-operational period, before children are able to conserve.

Table 1

Percentage of Children in Each Age Group
in Stage 3 on Conservation Test

| Content Area | Age in Years | | |
	4-5	6-7	8-9
Discontinuous Quantity	0.00%	6.25%	43.75%
Continuous Quantity	0.00	6.25	43.75
Substance	0.00	12.50	46.25
Length	0.00	31.25	62.50
Number	0.00	25.00	67.50
Area	0.00	18.75	81.25

Table 2

Percentage of Children in Each Stage
Passing the Comprehension Test, by Condition

	Covarying		Non-Covarying	
	Stage 1	Stage 2&3	Stage 1	Stage 2&3
Discontinuous Quantity				
"less"	73%	100%	3%	69%
"same"	70	100	0	25
"more"	73	100	0	56
Continuous Quantity				
"less"	74	100	6	59
"same"	68	100	0	25
"more"	74	100	3	47
Number				
"less"	70	100	10	71
"same"	65	100	10	61
"more"	75	100	40	89
Length				
"shorter"	85	100	60	100
"as long as"	75	100	60	100
"longer"	80	100	27	86
Area				
"less"	81	100	54	91
"same"	73	100	35	86
"more"	77	100	27	86
Substance				
"less"	78	100	26	76
"same"	70	100	19	52
"more"	74	100	15	62

In the Non-Covarying condition, a majority of the non-conservers failed to comprehend every term, except those terms referring to length. In contrast, a majority of the transitional children and conservers passed each term in the Non-Covarying condition, except the relational term, "same," referring to discontinuous and continuous quantity. These results suggest that comprehension of relational terms when comparing non-covarying stimuli is attained at some point during the concrete operational period.

One of the principal purposes of this study was to determine whether there are children who fail traditional conservation tests because they do not understand relational terms. Table 2 presents results relevant to this question. Every transitional child and every conserver was able to comprehend all of the terms of the comprehension test in the Covarying condition. In fact, the only children who did not succeed for all terms in the Covarying condition were the very youngest children tested. Thus any child who answered correctly on one or more trials of the conservation test (as well as a majority of the children who answered no questions correctly) was also able to comprehend all of the relational terms used in the traditional conservation test. These results suggest that children acquire the ability to comprehend relational terms when comparing covarying stimuli before they are able to conserve, for all content areas. Therefore, an inability to comprehend relational terms does not prevent children from succeeding on the traditional tests of conservation.

According to Piagetian theory (Piaget, Grize, Szeminska, & Vinh-Bang, 1968), the ability to coordinate two covarying dimensions is attained by children before they acquire the ability to coordinate three dimensions varying independently. Therefore, in this study, it was expected that children would be able to comprehend relational terms when comparing covarying stimuli before they were able to comprehend relational terms when comparing non-covarying stimuli.

The results of this study pertaining to this hypothesis are shown in Table 3. The first column shows that there were children who failed both conditions, for every term. These children demonstrated no comprehension of relational terms in either condition. The second column shows that, for every

Table 3

Percentage of Children Passing and Failing
Each Condition of the Comprehension Test

Covarying: Non-Covarying:	Fail Fail	Pass Fail	Fail Pass	Pass Pass
Discontinuous Quantity				
"less"	17%	58%	0%	25%
"same"	19	75	0	6
"more"	17	69	0	14
Continuous Quantity				
"less"	17	60	0	23
"same"	17	75	0	8
"more"	17	63	0	20
Number				
"less"	12	40	0	48
"same"	12	46	0	42
"more"	10	29	0	61
Length				
"shorter"	6	17	0	77
"as long as"	10	17	0	73
"longer"	8	17	0	75
Area				
"less"	10	46	0	44
"same"	19	48	0	33
"more"	15	50	0	35
Substance				
"less"	12	46	0	42
"same"	17	50	0	33
"more"	15	52	0	33

term, there were children who passed the Covarying condition but failed the Non-Covarying condition. These children were able to comprehend relational terms when comparing covarying stimuli, but not when comparing non-covarying stimuli. The fourth column shows that, for every term, there were children who passed both conditions, children who comprehended relational terms both when comparing covarying stimuli and when comparing non-covarying stimuli. These results are in accord with the hypothesis that a functional understanding is acquired by children before an operational understanding of relational terms.

The third column of Table 3 shows that there were no children who passed the Non-Covarying condition, but failed the Covarying condition, for any of the relational terms tested. Thus, there were no children who comprehended relational terms when comparing non-covarying stimuli, but not when comparing covarying stimuli. These results support the hypothesis that there is a developmental progression in the attainment of the ability to comprehend relational terms. Children first achieve a level of comprehension in which they are able to comprehend the terms when comparing covarying stimuli, and only later achieve a second level in which they are able to comprehend the terms when comparing non-covarying stimuli.

Both the ability to conserve and comprehension of relational terms appear to be dependent upon operational development. Because pre-operational children coordinate dimensions functionally, they are able to understand relational terms when comparing covarying stimuli and they are also led to a belief that a given dimension must change when other dimensions are transformed. Similarly, because concrete operational children coordinate dimensions operationally, they comprehend relational terms when comparing non-covarying stimuli and they demonstrate a concept of conservation. Neither of these abilities, conservation or an operational comprehension of relational terms, necessarily precedes the other. There were children who could conserve but who did not operationally comprehend relational terms, just as there were children who operationally comprehended relational terms, but could not conserve. Rather than one ability being the necessary precursor to the other, both abilities are dependent upon and can be taken as evidence of the development of operational thought.

292

References

Donaldson, M., & Wales, R.J.   On the acquisition of some
relational terms.   In J.R. Hayes (Ed.), <u>Cognition and
the development of language</u>.   New York: Wiley, 1970.

Griffiths, J.A., Shantz, C.A., & Sigel, I.E.   A methodological problem in conservation studies: The use of
relational terms.   <u>Child Development</u>, 1967, <u>38</u>, 841-
848.

Holland, V.M., & Palermo, D.S.   On learning "less":   Language and cognitive development.   <u>Child Development</u>,
1975, <u>46</u>, 437-443.

Palermo, D. S.   More about less: A study of comprehension.   <u>Journal of Verbal Learning and Verbal Behavior</u>,
1973, <u>12</u>, 211-221.

Piaget, J., Grize, J.B., Szeminska, A., & Vinh-Bang.
<u>Epistemologie et psychologie de la fonction</u>.   Paris:
Presses Universitaires de France, 1968.

Townsend, D.J.   Children's comprehension of comparative
forms.   <u>Journal of Experimental Child Psychology</u>, 1974,
<u>18</u>, 293-303.

LEXICAL DEVELOPMENT
FROM THE PERSPECTIVE OF GENETIC-DRAMATISM

Roy D. Pea
Bank Street College and
Clark University
Heinz Werner Institute
for Developmental Psychology

&

Bernard Kaplan
Clark University
Heinz Werner Institute
for Developmental
Psychology

I

Our current information regarding the acquisition of language in children is recognizably extensive. At the same time it is admittedly fragmented and isolated. We view this as unwholesome, and our paper is intended to promote four aims instrumental to the goal of dissolving this state of affairs.

One aim is to make manifest a widespread, if unarticulated, sentiment that understanding any isolated aspect of linguistic activity cannot be achieved without a concurrent appreciation of many other aspects of language functioning: thus, an understanding of "lexical development" is unattainable without the consideration of syntax, morphology, and phonology, on the one hand, and pragmatics and even politics (Kress & Hodge, 1979) on the other.

A second aim, really an extension of the first, is to emphasize that the study of the child's linguistic activity may only be adequately formulated, undertaken, and interpreted in the context of conceptualizations of linguistic functioning in later life. One cannot comprehend child language in isolation from an understanding of adult linguistic functioning, both at its highest levels, and at its most primitive levels (e.g. in pathology).

A third goal is to argue for the need for an overarching perspective, not only for lexical and for language development, as considered in isolation, but for human development, of which linguistic functioning is, although a large part, only a part. A perspective is required that will integrate lexical and language development with the struggle of human beings to perfect

294

themselves; in Whitehead's (1929) phrase, "to live, live well, and live better".

The fourth purpose is to outline and exemplify such an overarching perspective.

II

Even as the Zeitgeist has vacillated from a preoccupation - now, with syntax; now, with semantics and cognition; now, with pragmatics and communication; and now, perhaps again, with syntax (Kessel, 1981), there is a pervasive sentiment that the study of isolated aspects of language behavior is inadequate not only to the understanding of language development as a whole, but even for a grasp of those abstracted aspects themselves.

Yet we all operate in our research as if we can, with impunity, violate "the Humpty Dumpty principle"; we break down the human child into the language-acquiring child, the word-acquiring child, and so on, and assume that someday, somehow, someone will come along and put all the pieces back together again. Not that we are unaware of the possible impact of these segregated aspects on one another. To take but a few examples, we know that newly-acquired verbs tend to be used in structurally less-complex sentences than are earlier-acquired verbs (Bloom, Miller & Hood, 1975); that "bursts" of higher than usual syntactic complexity may occur in settings (such as arguments) where the child is persistent in purpose (Ervin-Tripp, 1977); that scenes of utterances (e.g. absent versus present objects; peer-peer role-play versus adult-child dialogue) may affect the words, sentence structures, and types of speech acts that are used; and that ease of articulation and auditory salience may contribute to the avoidance or exploitation of specific words by young children (Barton, 1976; Ferguson & Farwell, 1975; Menyuk & Menn, 1979).[1]

But being aware of the inappropriateness of assuming isolability of aspects of language has not directed us to the adoption of holistic approaches; to the contrary, we continue to breed "experts" on elements and minutiae.

In contrast, workers in cognitive science studying learning, memory, and problem-solving have recognized that

295

performances in any one of these domains are subject to complex interactions among the agent's goals, the tasks imposed by the experimenter, the nature of the materials (content) to be dealt with, the contexts of performance, and the like. They have begun to drop the search for "general laws" of isolated psychological functions (cf. Bransford, 1979; Brown, 1980; Jenkins, 1979). To comprehend lexical development, we may need to embrace the paradox of dependencies of such development upon a multitude of factors seemingly external to words.

III

Yet another type of segregation has been promoted by an exclusive focus on child language. To take the case of "lexical development", do we not find that the study of child language (in general) and the child's dealings with words (in particular) is typically divorced, not only in practice but in theory, from the diverse ways of employing words among adults? More striking yet, do we see students of child language prepared to deal with the most advanced manifestations of linguistic functioning? We act as if the understanding of linguistic development in the child were possible, even likely, without any clarity as to the telos of linguistic development as realized in the poet, the rhetorician, the master "lexicographer". More rarely yet do students of child language and "lexical development" in children relate their studies of changes in word-meaning in children to collective phenomena in the history of languages, as, for example, Heinz Werner (1954) has done. Thus, our focus on a circumscribed population rather than on universal processes has blinded us to a full appreciation and extension of the comparative nature of our (presumably) developmental discipline.

But even if the "walls of Jericho" insulating language studies of child from those of adult, and individual from collective representations, were to tumble and fall, a neutral and putatively value-free account of linguistic or lexical change over time, whether concerning the old and the young, poets as well as plebians, cultural phenomena in addition to individual ones, would not constitute a developmental account. This is because "development" for us, as contrasted with "ontogenesis" or "history", belongs in the domain of ideals, norms, and standards; in a word, it is a VALUE concept (Werner, 1948, p. 46; Kaplan, 1966a; 1966b; 1967/1974; 1981a; 1981b; 1982a; 1982b).

What does this mean? First, that "development" must be distinguished from "change". Second, that "development", as a desideratum, something we seek to achieve for ourselves and to assist others to achieve, cannot be derived from facts, nor based on empirical findings (Kaplan, 1982a). Rather, it is a standard by which we assess or evaluate the innumerable changes during life. "Development" is a concept of stipulation, not a concept derived through induction.

Although this truism is often masked in psychological discussions of development, as in the name-game of personality development, cognitive development, metamemory development..., reflection will reveal its necessity. Piaget did not arrive at his notion of "development of intelligence" by drawing inductive generalizations from changes in the behaviors of his three children. Nor did Freud arrive at his conceptions of "psychosexual development" from inductive reasoning based on representative samples of children at different ages. We shall never find out what the "development" of language or any of its selected aspects "is", merely through empirical observations or experimental analyses. Before determining the "stages" of lexical or language development, we must already have some implicit conception of what we mean by "development" in the domain we study. What do we take as criteria that allow the judgement that someone is highly developed, linguistically or lexically, relative to someone else? Surely, not that they are older. And no doubt not that they so happen to do the same things that older persons do. We would not infer a leap in moral development if children who had never cheated began to cheat like many of their elders.

The point here is that development is a movement toward perfection; that one must know what the general lineaments of perfection would be in any performance domain in order to ascertain whether developmental advances have or have not occurred. Moreover, one must have such lineaments in mind to determine whether certain conditions in the lives of individuals facilitate, or are inimical to development.

297

For us, therefore, the study of lexical development is not a value-free inquiry, but an axiological as well as empirical enterprise, linked to intervention. We are concerned with lexical acquisition, whether that of individuals, cultural thesauri, or other "agents", because words are instrumentalities of great power; the full mastery of words is a desideratum. One will recognize that such mastery is not revealed simply by the use and understanding of words as conveying conventional meanings in customary contexts, such as are represented in the dictionaries of our time. Lexical development, in its more advanced reaches, entails the ability to exploit words in metaphor, metonymy, synechdoche, irony, and all the other figures of speech which are also figures of thought (Burke, 1945; Kaplan, 1961/1981). It entails the extension of words beyond their usual denotata to novel configurations and situations, a process some may stigmatize as "overgeneralization" among the young and illiterate, and glorify as "creativity" in themselves and their friends.[2] It entails the ability not only to decontextualize words, and to define them in isolation, but to recontextualize words, morphologically modifying their external forms so that they can take on different grammatical functions (Brown, 1973; Werner & E. Kaplan, 1950; Werner & B. Kaplan, 1963). It entails the ability, or "communicative competence" (Habermas; Hymes), to select the right words and locate them in the right places at the right time for the optimal realization of all speech acts or functions, and even to know when silence is the right "word". Thus lexical development can only advance <u>pari passu</u> with syntactic and pragmatic (or rhetorical) development. The "master lexicalist" is at once also a master syntactician and a master rhetorician (Cirillo & Kaplan, 1981).[3]

From this perspective, lexical developmentalists would not only, or even largely, confine their efforts to describing the actualities of human functioning during the first few years of childhood.[4] They would deal with human beings throughout the span of life, as they immerse themselves in the lexicons of different professions--jurisprudence, mechanics, theology, or linguistics--; as they write poetry and drama; as they function under transient stress or the enduring stress occasioned by brain-damage or schizophrenia (Kaplan, 1966b). Each of these inquiries into lexical functioning

298

would need to integrate syntactic, pragmatic, phonological, and morphological considerations. And such studies would have to be guided by the standard or _telos_ of lexical development - a perfect mastery, never even remotely achieved, which one might call "competence" in the fullest sense.

A sharp theoretical distinction between "development" and "ontogenesis" enables us to see that ontogenesis, the actualities of existence over the life span, does not _entail_ development. It is, indeed, because "development" is at least tacitly distinguished from ontogenesis --the ideal from the actual-- that it makes any sense to talk about "dips" in performance (Bever, 1981), or to refer to "systematic errors" (Bowerman, 1981) occurring in the history of children's uses of words. "Dips", "errors", "regressions", and "arrests" imply norms or standards, imply some ideal for assessing the actual.[5]

IV

We have already suggested that lexical change and lexical development interpenetrate with change and development of phonology, morphology, syntax, and pragmatics. It should come as no surprise if we go further and emphasize the "interfunctional relations" (Vygotsky, 1978)[6] of linguistic activity with other aspects of human behavior and experience. For certain purposes, one may prescind linguistic functioning and development from their natural embeddedness in the multifarious goal-directed actions of persons in society. But the evidence is overwhelming that the manner in which one uses language, the way in which one handles words, is affected by and affects a human being's cognitive, moral, and interpersonal functioning, and so on.

Yet such influences and interconnections are by and large neglected by students of child language or child lexicality, relegated to yet other experts, or taken to be of marginal interest to the enterprise of understanding linguistic development. Such insulation is testimony to the need for a general developmental perspective , an overarching developmental orientation that would encompass, in one system, comparative studies of a diversity of phenomena: ontogenetic, cultural, psychopathological,

299

neuropathological. A developmental point of view that would encompass phenomena taking place with respect to different time-scales: historical, biographical, diurnal, and microgenetic. A developmental perspective that would allow for, and encourage, a diversity of methods: phenomenological[8], naturalistic, hermeneutic, and experimental, and which would seek to integrate the findings from all of these different procedures[9]. Such an approach was advanced by Heinz Werner and his students (Kaplan, 1966b; Kaplan, 1961/1981; Werner, 1948, 1978; Werner, 1956/1978; Werner, 1954; Werner & E. Kaplan, 1950, 1952; Werner & B. Kaplan, 1956; 1963).

It is this organismic-developmental approach of Werner & Kaplan (see Werner, 1948, 1957; Werner & Kaplan, 1956, 1963; Kaplan, 1966a, 1966b, 1967; Wapner, Kaplan & Cohen, 1973; Wapner, Kaplan, & Ciottone, 1981; Pea & Russell, 1980; Russell & Pea, 1980) integrated with the dramatistic orientation of the renowned student of symbolic action in life and literature, Kenneth Burke (1945; 1950; 1966; 1972), that we refer to as Genetic-Dramatism (see Cirillo & Kaplan, 1981; Kaplan, 1981a, 1981b; Kaplan & Pea, 1981; Russell, 1982).

Genetic-Dramatism seeks to provide an explicit account of the perennial perspective, one which virtually all of us adopt in our everyday lives, and use in our transactions with others (Kaplan, 1981a). Leaving out, in this cursory presentation necessary qualifications and refinements, is it not the case that we all construe ourselves and others as agents operating in contexts or scenes to achieve certain ends or realize certain purposes? And that, in so doing, we use instrumentalities or means in the execution of our actions? Do we not in everyday life, and even in a laboratory, or a classroom, or a conference, evaluate our performances and those of others, as "primitive" or "advanced", by using tacit norms of perfection in order to make such assessments? Do we not both characterize and assess an agent's action, linguistic or otherwise, with respect to context and explicit (or imputed) goals? And do we not also construe the scene in which an agent is operating as well as the goals, conscious or otherwise, of the agent on the basis of our understanding of the action she or he performs?

300

In raising these kinds of questions, we have already introduced the famous pentad of Burke's Grammar of Motives and Rhetoric of Motives -- agent, act, scene, instrumentality, and purpose -- and have indicated their reticulate or organic relationships (see Figure 1). It should be obvious that acts or performances, linguistic,

----
(Insert Figure 1 here)
----

lexical, or otherwise, are easily susceptible to variation, given variations in any of the other components of human transactions in situations. Correspondingly, any "assessment" of an individual's level of functioning or developmental status with regard to a domain of action, such as lexical behavior, is "wild developmentalism" (on analogy to Freud's "wild psychoanalysis") if it is based on one or a few performances in circumscribed experimental or observational contexts (see Kaplan, Pea & Franklin, 1981).

In posing our questions, we also alluded to the normative status of the concept of development, a norm that enters into developmental assessments. In their formulation of a concept of development, distinct from ontogenesis, Werner & Kaplan (1956; 1963) introduce the orthogenetic principle (i.e., a principle pertaining to the genesis of perfection): "Wherever development occurs, it involves an increasing differentiation and hierarchic integration". Development in any domain, therefore, is defined as entailing the differentiation of conflated or fused parts, factors, or elements, and correlatively, the integration of these differentiated components into a functional unity.

We have applied this conception of development to lexical development when we earlier pointed out that developed lexicality interpenetrates with syntactic, pragmatic-rhetorical, morphological, and phonological development. Let us elaborate this point. A lexical master, one who shows a high level of lexical development, will be able to differentiate verbal concepts from each other (recognizing, in Goodman's phrase, that there is no "likeness of meaning"); she or he will have established the various modes of interrelationships among verbal concepts, e.g. hyponymy, synonymy, homonymy, antonymy; she or he will

301

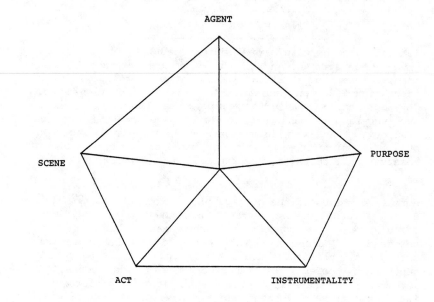

Figure 1. Burke's pentad of categories

know how to organize and reorganize words into well-formed utterances, and even ill-formed utterances for special communicational contexts; she or he will know how to select words and modulate them morphologically and phonologically with respect to different utterance contexts, and so on (e.g. Fillmore, 1971; Halliday, 1975; Lyons, 1977; Menn & Kaselkorn, 1977; Miller, 1978; Miller & Johnson-Laird, 1976; Werner & E. Kaplan, 1950). Of course, the fully competent, perfected lexicalist would be the master of all lexicons, past, present, and potential; capable of taking on any agent-status, of utilizing all lexical instrumentalities, in any scenes, with the full range of purposes, etc.

Now, no individual agent or social agent has ever remotely approached such perfection because, as embodied beings, we are limited, at best, to relative perfection with regard to very limited parts of very few lexicons. And even where we have attained a relatively high level of performance, the level of performances may drop, when we have no opportunity to plan (Ochs, 1979), or when we are fatigued, injured, frightened, depressed, or under the influence of other subversive contingencies (e.g. Werner & Kaplan, 1963; Kaplan, 1966b). How and when to intervene in order to overcome such "regressions" or "arrests" is of course one of the tasks of developmental psychology as a practico-theoretical discipline (Kaplan, 1982a).

As with critical theorists (Habermas; Horkheimer; Jay), those who espouse the perspective of Genetic-Dramatism take the perspective to be "reflexive". Its presuppositions, categories, and modes of analysis and intervention, insofar as they are taken to be applicable to other human beings, must also be applicable to those who theorize about and investigate human beings. We must assess our symbolic actions as we do those of others. Thus if we take lexical development, in one of its aspects, as entailing clarity and precision in the use of verbal concepts in scientific discourse, we must assess ourselves, and welcome assessment by others, as to where we are with respect to the tacit standards. We ask you to do the same. Only through such cooperative critical reflection on our own lexical activity in the study of lexical functioning, can we hope to advance the study of lexical development,

303

language development, and, most importantly, human development.

[1] We speak in terms of possibility rather than certainty because many such manifestations of "functional dependence" may not occur with other agents, other scenes, other purposes, and other instrumentalities than those involved in the different studies.

[2] Such seemingly neutral characterizations are clearly valuative in nature, and presuppose norms and standards of the investigators. They are also likely to be political in nature - suggesting that some state of affairs be altered, another promoted. We do not reject the use of such terms; only the pretense that they are neutral descriptions.

[3] That one is a master lexicalist, or highly advanced in lexical development, no more entails that one is highly advanced as a person than does being a master-carpenter or master-killer. Development -- "movement toward perfection" -- in one domain does not necessarily entail development in other domains, although some developments, as suggested here, may presuppose others. One scarcely needs the theoretical apparatus of "stages" or "decalages" to make this obvious point. For discussion, see Kaplan, Pea & Franklin (1981).

[4] It will be understood, from this developmental perspective, that current debates and experimentation in studies of "lexical" or "semantic development", focussing on whether "functions" or "features" are the predominant, first, or central aspect of early word-meaning acquisition (e.g. Clark, 1979; Nelson et al., 1978), are confined to a narrowly designated theoretical corridor.

[5] The political significance of using "actuarial" or "statistical" norms as standards -- "whatever most individuals of an age do is right for that age" -- is discussed in Kaplan (1982a) and White (1978, 1982).

[6] Although Vygotsky openly acknowledged the pioneering role of Werner's work in integrating developmental analysis

and experimental techniques, this role is rarely mentioned in psychological writings today (but see Wertsch & Stone, 1978).

[7] Some indication of the impact of Werner's work outside the presently circumscribed discipline of psychology may be found in: W. Shumaker, Literature and the Irrational; J. Love, Worlds in Consciousness: A Study of Virginia Woolf's Novels; R.D. Sack, Conceptions of Space in Social Thought: A Geographical Perspective; S. Arieti, Interpretation of Schizophrenia; H. Searles, Collected Papers in Schizophrenia.

[8] The relation of our perspective to that of the phenomenologist of social reality, Alfred Shutz, should be apparent from these comments. See Shutz, Collected Papers (3 vols.).

[9] We recognize that the future prospects of developmental research from such a developmental perspective depend upon its empirical viability. Such viability is contingent on concerted efforts, by ourselves and many others, at collaborative research which is truly integrative in nature, and directed toward the holistic nature (Werner & Kaplan, 1963) of human psychological functioning. Such large-scale attempts at addressing these issues have received scant attention to date. This paper may be viewed as a invitation to dialogue, about methods and effective ways of promoting the integration of the diverse "disciplines" called upon by the perspective. As one aspect of such a reorientation to psychology, we aim in an expanded paper to reanalyze results from a diversity of studies, from a wide range of "fields", which bear on lexical development from this developmental perspective. Kaplan & Pea (1981) provide a related analysis of reasoning activities, and Kaplan & Cirillo are currently engaged in a project on metaphor.

REFERENCES

Barton, D.P. The role of perception in the acquisition of
    speech. Ph.D. thesis, University of London, 1976.

Bever, T.G. (Ed.), Regressions in Mental Development: Basic
    Phenomena and Theories. Hillsdale, N.J.: Erlbaum, 1981.

Bloom, L., Miller, P. & Hood, L. Variation and reduction as
    aspects of competence in language development. In A.D.
    Pick (Ed.), Minnesota Symposium on Child Psychology,
    Vol. 9. Minneapolis: University of Minnesota Press,
    1975.

Bowerman, M. Starting to talk worse: Clues to language
    acquisition from children's late speech errors. In S.
    Strauss (Ed.), U-Shaped Behavioral Growth. New York:
    Academic Press, 1981.

Bransford, J.D. Human Cognition: Learning, Understanding,
    and Remembering. Belmont, Ca.: Wadsworth, 1979.

Brown, A.L. Learning and development: The problems of
    compatibility, access, and induction. Human
    Development, 1980.

Brown, R. A First Language: The Early Stages. Cambridge,
    Mass.: Harvard University Press, 1973.

Burke, K. A Grammar of Motives. Berkeley: University of
    California Press, 1945.

Burke, K. A Rhetoric of Motives. Berkeley: University of
    California Press, 1950.

Burke, K. Definition of man. Hudson Review, 1963-1964, 56
    (Reprinted in Burke, 1966.)

Burke, K. Language as Symbolic Action: Essays on Life,
    Literature, and Method. Berkeley: University of
    California Press, 1966.

Burke, K. Dramatism and Development. Worcester, Ma.: Clark
    University Press, 1972.

Cirillo, L. & Kaplan, B. Figurative action from the perspective of genetic-dramatism. In S. Wapner & B. Kaplan (Eds.), Towards a Holistic Developmental Psychology. Hillsdale, N.J.: Erlbaum, 1981.

Clark, E.V. Building a vocabulary: Words for objects, actions, and relations. In P. Fletcher & M. Garman (Eds.), Language Acquisition. Cambridge: Cambridge University Press, 1979.

Ervin-Tripp, S. From conversation to syntax. Papers and Reports in Child Language Development, 1977, 13.

Ferguson, C.A. & Farwell, C.B. Words and sounds in early language acquisition. Language, 1975, 51, 419-439.

Fillmore, C.J. Types of lexical information. In D.D. Steinberg & L.A. Jakobovits (Eds.), Semantics: An Interdisciplinary Reader in Philosophy, Linguistics, and Psychology. Cambridge: Cambridge University Press, 1971.

Halliday, M.A.K. Learning How to Mean: Explorations in the Development of Language. London: Edward Arnold, 1975.

Jenkins, J.J. Four points to remember: A tetrahedral model and memory experiments. In L.S. Cermak & F.I.M. Craik (Eds.), Levels of Processing in Human Memory. Hillsdale, N.J.: Erlbaum, 1979.

Kaplan, B. Radical metaphor, aesthetic and the origin of language. To appear in B. Kaplan, Collected Papers, in preparation, 1981. (Originally presented as a paper at a meeting of the American Psychological Association in 1961 in a symposium on Metaphor.)

Kaplan, B. The latent content of Heinz Werner's developmental psychology. In S. Wapner & B. Kaplan (Eds.), Heinz Werner: Papers in memoriam. Worcester, Mass.: Clark University Press, 1966(a).

Kaplan, B. The study of language in psychiatry: The comparative approach and its application to symbolization and language in psychopathology. In S. Arieti (Ed.), American Handbook of Psychiatry, Vol. 3.

New York: Basic Books, 1966b.

Kaplan, B. Meditations on genesis. Human Development, 1967, 10, 65-87.

Kaplan, B. Strife of systems: Tension between organismic and developmental points of view. (1967/1974). In Kaplan, B. Rationality and Irrationality in Development. Worcester, Mass.: Clark University Press, 1982(b).

Kaplan, B. Genetic-dramatism. In S. Wapner & B. Kaplan (Eds.), Towards a Holistic Developmental Psychology. Hillsdale, N.J.: Erlbaum, 1981.

Kaplan, B. Reflections on culture and personality from the perspective of genetic-dramatism. In S. Wapner & B. Kaplan (Eds.), Towards a Holistic Developmental Psychology. Hillsdale, N.J.: Erlbaum, 1981.

Kaplan, B. A trio of trials. To appear in R. Lerner (Ed.), Developmental Psychology: Historical and Philosophical Perspectives. Cambridge, Mass.: Harvard University Press, 1982(a).

Kaplan, B. & Pea, R.D. Reasoning from the perspective of genetic-dramatism. Heinz Werner Institute for Developmental Psychology, Working Paper, 1981.

Kaplan, B., Pea, R.D. & Franklin, M.B. Multiplying entities. Heinz Werner Institute for Developmental Psychology, Working Paper, 1981.

Kessel, F. (Chair) Symposium: The development of language and language researchers: Whatever happened to linguistic theory? (Contributions by Bowerman, Cazden, Maratsos, Pinker, Slobin). Presented at the Biennial Meeting of the Society for Research in Child Development, April 2-5, 1981, Boston, Massachusetts.

Kress, G. & Hodge, R. Language as Ideology. London: Routledge & Kegan Paul, 1979.

Lyons, J. Semantics (2 vols.). Cambridge: Cambridge University Press, 1977.

Menn, L. & Haselkorn, S. Now you see it, now you don't: Tracing the development of communicative competence. In J. Kegl (Ed.), Proceedings of the Seventh Annual Meeting of the Northeast Linguistic Society, 1977.

Menyuk, P. & Menn, L. Early strategies for the perception and production of words and sounds. In P. Fletcher & M. Garman (Eds.), Language Acquisition. Cambridge: Cambridge University Press, 1979.

Miller, G.A. Semantic relations among words. In M. Halle, J. Bresnan & G.A. Miller (Eds.), Linguistic Theory and Psychological Reality. Cambridge, Mass.: M.I.T. Press, 1978.

Miller, G.A. & Johnson-Laird, P.N. Language and Perception. Cambridge, Mass.: Harvard University Press, 1976.

Nelson, K., Rescorla, L., Gruendel, J. & Benedict, H. Early lexicons: What do they mean? Child Development, 1978, 49, 960-968.

Ochs, E. Planned and unplanned discourse. In T. Givon (Ed.), Syntax and Semantics. Vol. 12, Discourse and Syntax. New York: Academic Press, 1979.

Pea, R.D. & Russell, R.L. Foundations for a scientific theory of communicative development. Paper presented at the Fifth Annual Boston University Conference on Language Development, October, 1980.

Russell, R.L. Psychotherapeutic discourse: Notes on a framework for its future investigation. In R.L. Russell (Ed.), Language in Psychotherapy: Strategies of Discovery. New York: Irvington, 1982.

Russell, R.L. & Pea, R.D. Communicative interaction and its development: An organismic-developmental approach to 'doctor-patient' interaction. In H. Lasnik (Ed.), Proceedings of the International Congress on Applied Systems Research and Cybernetics. London: Pergamon Press, 1981.

Vygotsky, L.S. Mind in Society: The Development of Higher Psychological Processes. M. Cole, V. John-Steiner, S.

Scribner & E. Souberman (Eds.).   Cambridge, Mass.:
Harvard University Press, 1978.

Wapner, S., Kaplan, B. & Cohen, S.   An organismic-
developmental perspective for understanding
transactions of men in environments.
Environment and Behavior, 1973, 5, 255-289.

Wapner, S., Kaplan, B. & Ciottone, R.   Self-world
relationships in critical environment transitions:
Childhood and beyond.   In L. Liben, A. Patterson & N.
Newcombe (Eds.), Spatial Representation and Behavior
across the Life Span.   New York: Academic Press, 1981.

Werner, H.   The Comparative Psychology of Mental
Development. 2nd ed. New York: Harper, 1948.

Werner, H.   Change of meaning: A study of semantic processes
through the experimental method. J. General Psychology,
1954, 50, 181-208.

Werner, H.   The concept of development from a comparative
and organismic point of view.   In D.B. Harris (Ed.),
The Concept of Development: An Issue in the Study of
Human Behavior.   Minneapolis: University of Minnesota
Press, 1957.

Werner, H.   Developmental Processes: Heinz Werner's Selected
Writings. 2 vols.   S.S. Barten & M.B. Franklin (Eds.).
New York: International Universities Press, 1978.

Werner, H. & Kaplan, B.   The developmental approach to
cognition: Its relevance to the psychological
interpretation of anthropological and ethnolinguistic
data.   American Anthropologist, 1956, 58, 866-880.

Werner, H. & Kaplan, B.   Symbol Formation: An
Organismic-Developmental Approach to Language and the
Expression of Thought.   New York: Wiley, 1963.

Werner, H. & Kaplan, E.   Development of word meaning through
verbal context. J. of Psychol., 1950, 29, 251-257.

Werner, H. & Kaplan, E.   The acquisition of word meaning: A
developmental study.   Mono. Soc. Res. Child Devel.,

310

1952, No. 51.

Wertsch, J.V. & Stone, C.A. Microgenesis as a tool for developmental analysis. <u>Quarterly Newsletter of the Laboratory of Comparative Human Cognition</u>, 1978, <u>1</u>, 8-10.

White, S.H. Psychology in all sorts of places. In R. Kasschau & F.S. Kessel (Eds.) <u>Psychology and Society: In Search of Symbiosis</u>. New York: Holt, Rinehart & Winston, 1978.

White, S.H. The idea of development in developmental psychology. In R. Lerner (Ed.), <u>Developmental Psychology: Historical and Philosophical Perspectives</u>. Cambridge, Mass.: Harvard University Press, 1982.

Whitehead, A.N. <u>The Function of Reason</u>. Princeton, N.J.: Princeton University Press, 1929.

Semantic Categories in the Language of Working-Class Black Children[1]

Ida J. Stockman
Center for Applied Linguistics
Howard University

Fay Boyd Vaughn-Cooke
University of the District
of Columbia
Center for Applied
Linguistics

Introduction

In spite of the relatively long history of child
language research in the United States, investigations of
the acquisition of language by working-class Black children
in this country were not initiated until the mid-seventies
(Steffensen 1974; Stokes 1976; Reveron 1978; Cole 1979;
Kovac 1980). A feature, however, more noteworthy than the
relative recency of research on this population is the
theoretical framework that guided the initial investigations.
All of the researchers except Steffensen, employed narrow,
unidimensional frameworks which focused only on linguistic
form, though the limitations of this approach were pointed
over a decade ago (Bloom 1971).[2] Even within the domain of
form, research has been narrower still in that it has
focused just on those structures that differentiate Black
English (hereafter BE), the variety spoken by working-class
Black children, from Standard English (hereafter SE), the
mainstream variety. Research has shown that the two dialects
differ with respect to the frequency of occurrence of a
subset of phonological, syntactic, and semantic features.
These include copula and auxiliary verbs, plural, possessive,
third person singular, and past tense inflections (for a
comprehensive list of structures that differentiate BE from
SE, see Williams and Wolfram 1976). Descriptions of BE have
revealed the variable presence, and for some speakers
categorical absence of the differentiating forms (Labov 1972).
For example, constructions without copulas (e.g. she sleeping) and inflections (e.g. two hat, John hat, she go, he walk
home yesterday) are grammatical in BE, but not in SE. So
far, child language research on Black children has focused
solely on the subset of forms that differ in the two dialects.
To illustrate this point, it will be instructive to examine
the specific foci of the studies cited above.

Cole focused on the largest set of forms; she investigated 19 syntactic features that are characteristic of BE. These included copula and auxiliary verbs, multiple negation, plural, possessive, past tense, and third person singular inflections. The remaining researchers investigated a small subset or just one of the features examined by Cole. Stokes, for example, focused on negation, Kovac focused on copula and auxiliary verbs, Reveron examined inflections and Steffensen examined inflections, copula and auxiliary verbs and pronominal case.

The research reported in this paper represents a major shift with respect to the focus of language acquisition research on Black children. Specifically, the focus is shifted from a description of dialect specific features to the more general and universal features that BE speakers share with all speakers of English and with speakers of other languages as well. The new focus required a new framework; thus the narrow, unidimensional approach was abandoned, and following Bloom, Lightbown and Hood 1975, Bloom and Lahey 1978, Bloom, et al. 1980, a multidimensional approach which allows the investigator to view the child's emerging linguistic knowledge in terms of content, form and/or use interactions was employed. The motivation for the focus shift is to move language acquisition studies on Black children into the mainstream of the general child language research. This will require investigators to begin addressing some of the semantic and pragmatic issues that have been explored in more than a decade of research on children acquiring SE. The purpose of this paper is to present the results from the first stage of the semantic category analysis of a large scale study that exhibits the new focus in child language research on Black children.

Method

Description of Subjects

A cross-sectional/longitudinal data collection strategy is being used to track the language development of 12 Afro-American children across an 18-month-time period. Two girls and two boys are represented at each of three ages, which, at the beginning of data collection, were 18 months, 3, and 4 1/2 years. Eight of the children were first-born and/or only children and five were not.[3] None presented physical, sensory-motor, psychosocial or learning problems insofar as this could be determined from medical and school records, parents' case history reports, and our own informal observations of their behavior. At the beginning of language sampling, the four children at 18 months used primarily single words, which constituted 69% to 100% of the language responses. At older ages, the predominant productive language responses consisted of multiword constructions with no equivalency criteria of length and complexity imposed.[4] The children live in neighborhoods of Washington, D.C., where residents are predominantly working-class and monolingual. In these communities, BE is the principal spoken language.

Data Collection Procedures

Audio-visual recordings are made of the children's spoken language during monthly visits to their homes while they interact in routine conversation and low structured play activities with the investigators, family members and friends of the family. Relatively portable equipment (Beta-Max Sony Video Recorder, SLO-323 and JVC Color Camera, Model G-71US) is used to track the child's movements in a small area of the home. The Sony ECM-31 tie tack microphone is inconspicuously placed on the child's clothing; the extension cable allows free movement within a ten-foot radius, approximately. We obtained one to two hour language samples from each child at monthly intervals. The complete 18-month data base is expected to yield at least 144 hours of videotaped samples for the 18-month-olds and a total of 57,600 utterances for the analysis of the 3- and 4 1/2-year old-children.

Semantic Category Assignment Procedures

Following the general methodological orientation outlined in Bloom and Lahey, the transcripts of children's utterances were more or less randomly assigned in equal number to the two investigators who independently placed utterances in one or more of 17 semantic categories after carefully examining the utterances and the contexts in which they occurred. These included the following categories which have been described by Bloom and Lahey: action, existence, state, coordination, causality, antithesis, epistemic, location, negation, time, quantity, specifier possession, attribute, recurrence, dative and mood. Table 1 presents operational definitions and examples of each content

Table 1. Working Definitions and Illustrations of Semantic Categories[a]

Semantic Category	Working Definition (adapted from Bloom and Lahey, 1978)	Examples of Child's Utterance	Excerpts from Contexts
Action	refers to voluntary or involuntary movement that affects only the person or object engaged in the movement or both the object engaged in movement and another person or object.	He eating you wiping my nose	(C. pointing to a picture which depicts a boy eating) I. wipes child's nose
Existence	refers to an object's identity with or without specifying its properties or attributes.	a monster	I. who is that Shirrell? (C. pointing to picture in book)
State	refers to an external or internal condition or quality of objects, events, or actions.	mines big	(C. playing with toy car)
Location	refers to the site or place of objects states, actions, or events in a spatial field; the movement resulting in the positional state may or may not be specified.	one down here now put them in here	(C. picks up car from bottom of tracks) (C. placing beans in pot)
Dative	refers to the recipient of an object acted upon, where the recipient is animate and has the possibility of responding to the act by performing the act of receiving.	give me the car	(C's sister is trying to prevent him from playing with the race car.
Mood	refers to the attitude or disposition of a person toward an object, action, or state as one of obligation, desire, or intent	they can cook	(C. playing with dried beans and pretending to cook them)
Negation	refers to the nullification of an existing event, state, or action by denying or rejecting its presence.	No, they not good. They bad.	I. you think wolves are good.
Causality	refers to a dependent relationship between two or more states, objects, and/or actions as one of cause/effect.	we don't spose to have no bread tonight 'cause you see we going to a party	(C. pretends to cook some beans) I. What about bread?
Epistemic	refers to the dependent relationship between two or more object states, and/or actions as one of certainty or uncertainty.	I know how to do it	(C. blowing bubbles)

Table 1. Working Definitions and Illustrations of Semantic Categories (continued)

Category	Definition	Utterance	Context
Antithesis	refers to the dependent relationship between two or more objects, states and/or actions as one of opposition, qualification, or nullification.	She don't have no shoes on, but she do, and she do.	(C. looking at picture in book)
Coordination	refers to the temporal and/or spatial relationship between two or more independent objects, events, actions, or states.	one for you, and one for me	(C. gives one car to I. and keeps one car for himself)
Time	refers to when an action or state occurs including past, present and future temporal reference relative to the speaking event as well as aspectual features of temporal reference.	he cooking soup.	(C. and I looking at picture in book) I. Is he cooking? It sure looks like it.
Attribute	refers to properties or qualities of an object, action, or event which distinguish the object, action, or event from others of the same class.	big car	(C. pointing and looking at a car located near a door)
Specifier	refers to a single object, action, or state or designates a specific object, action, or state among a series of objects, actions, or states of the same or different class.	put the plate down	(C. picks up two plates and places them on the floor)
Quantity	refers to the number or portion of objects, actions, events, states.	I want some ice cream	(I. and C. are looking at a picture which depicts a wedding party) I. Why do you want to be there?
Possession	refers to the ownership of objects, states, actions, and events.	yours go right there	(C. points to place on track for another car)
Recurrence	refers to the reappearance of a previously present object, state, or action.	I want to get me another bag	(C's playmate is holding the toy bag used by the investigators to transport toys)

[a] To preserve space, the context excerpts are not presented in sequential relationship to the child's utterances as is typically done.

category. The 17 categories represented are smaller than the number described in Bloom and Lahey. In our effort to represent the most general categories of knowledge, we merged some categories, treated separately in the Bloom and Lahey description, e.g. Locative State, Locative Action, and Place are considered subcategories of location and are represented as one instead of three. The mean agreement between the investigators in making semantic category assignments averaged 96.2 (SD = 16.8) based on repeated judgments of a reliability sample that included 995 utterances distributed across 17 categories and 12 children.

Utterances that represented each semantic or content category at a given sampling period were inspected for every child to reveal which categories were productively used, i.e., occurred systematically in a child's system based on a criterion of productive use. Following Bloom and Lahey, productive use was defined as the occurrence of a semantic category in five or more different utterances and contexts. For each semantic category that met the productive use criterion, the relative frequency of occurrence in a given sampling period was computed by taking the total number of analyzed utterances as the N value.

The results that follow reveal the number and types of semantic categories that were productively used by the children at the three ages (18 months, 3- and 4 1/2-years) in the first sampling period only. These data, which form the baseline against which subsequent longitudinal comparisons are made, consist of 23 hours of spoken language and 5,597 utterances. Comparisons were made among the four children in each age group to determine group trends and among children at different ages to make inferences about developmental differences in performance.

Results and Discussion

The proportion of utterances representing each of the content categories that met the criterion of productive use in the first sampling period is shown for the 4 1/2, 3 and 18-month-old groups in Figures 1, 2, and 3, respectively. They reveal evidence for three predicted findings, each of which is stated and elaborated upon in the succeeding discussion.

317

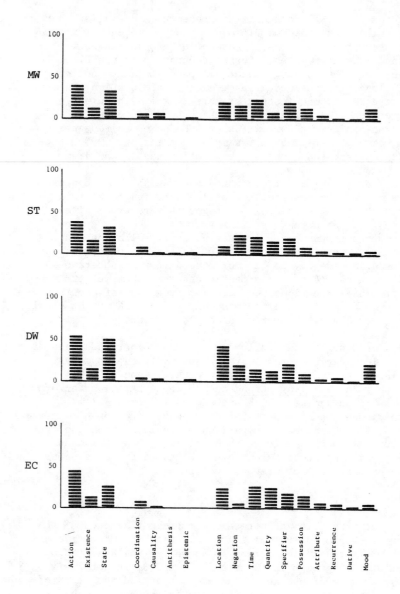

Figure 1.   Semantic Categories For The 4;6-Year-Old Children

318

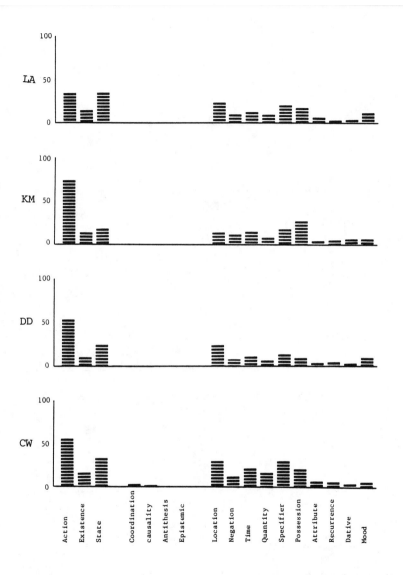

Figure 2.   Semantic Categories For The 3-Year-Old Children

319

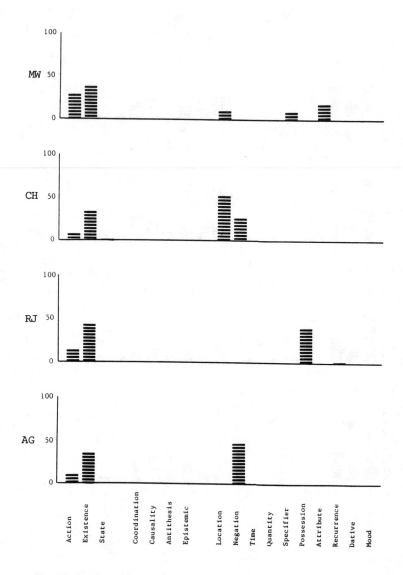

Figure 3.   Semantic Categories For The 18-Month-Old Children

320

1.   Working-Class Black children linguistically code the
      same general types of content categories that have
      been described for children acquiring other language
      systems.

      Inspecting the data for 4 1/2-year-old children in
Figure 1, remarkable similarity can be observed among the
four children in the types of semantic categories represented
in their first language samples. The data reveal that the
language of every child was sufficiently complex to represent a wide range of semantic categories that included action,
existence, state, possession, dative, locative, and temporal
relations, in addition to the more complex relations of
causality, epistemics, etc. Though their relative frequency
in any given child's language sample varied, all seventeen
categories were coded by one or more of the children studied.
In fact, to represent fully the semantic knowledge at 4 1/2-
years, the number and types of content categories included
in this analysis would require expansion to include, for
example, the child's linguistic coding of conceptual knowledge governing comparative and conditional relationships.
The data of Figures 2 and 3 suggest that the types of content categories represented in the children's language at
3 years and 18 months were emerging in the same direction
as that observed for the 4 1/2 year old children, though
given the younger ages, a smaller set of categories was
understandably used. The types of content categories represented by the nonmainstream English spoken by working-class
Black children have also been described for children
acquiring other language systems, including Standard English
(Bloom et al. 1975), Finnish (Bowerman, 1973), Samoan (Kernan,
1970), Italian, Serbo-Croatian and Turkish (Johnston and
Slobin).[5]

      This finding is not surprising given the expectation
that children universally acquire linguistic structures
for coding fundamental aspects of human experience that
relate to objects, time, location, action, etc. But the
findings are especially significant because they represent
the first major documentation of the development of semantic
knowledge in Black children. We predict these findings will
be particularly relevant within practical domains where
Black children's knowledge of language concepts has been
historically questioned.

321

2. The number and types of content categories represented
    in the language of working-class Black children in-
    creased as age increased.

Comparisons of data trends in Figures 1, 2, and 3 revealed that 4 1/2-year-old children linguistically coded a
larger number of the content categories than did 3-year-olds,
and of the three age groups the smallest set of content
categories coded was represented in the language of 18-month-
old children. Note that at least 15 (88%) of the 17
categories were coded by every 4 1/2-year-old child compared
to 13 (76%) for every 3-year-old child. Among the 18 month-
old children, just seven (41%) of the 17 categories were
represented in the language samples, viewed collectively.
For any one child, however, the number of content categories
represented varied from three to five (12 to 29%).

The four content categories that code complex semantic
relations (causality, coordination, epistemic, antithesis)
constituted the principal differences between the 3 and 4 1/2-
year-old children in the types of content categories coded
(see Figures 2 and 3). Whereas one or more of these categories was productively used by every 4 1/2-year-old, none
was productively used by 3-year-old children with one
exception (C.W.).

Like 3-year-old children, those at 18 months (see Figure
3), did not linguistically code the four content categories
of complex relations (causality, coordination, epistemic,
and antithesis). But, children in the 3-year-old and 18-
month-old groups differed in that the latter group also did
not code the content categories of state, time, quantity,
recurrence, dative, and mood in the first language sample.

It comes as no surprise that age is a critical factor
in accounting for the number and type of conceptual categories that are linguistically coded by working-class
youngsters since their linguistic knowledge, like that of
other children, would be expected to evolve over time as
a result of experience and maturation. Further, given
that children acquire their language systems over time,
knowledge of some language features would be expected to
emerge earlier than knowledge of others. One cannot,
therefore, study the working-class child's or any child's

language knowledge at one or two ages and expect to validly generalize the findings to children of all ages.

3. There were individual differences among children at the same age in the types and the relative frequency of content categories represented in the language samples.

Further inspection of Figures 1, 2, and 3 revealed individual differences in every age group with respect to the types of categories represented. Note for example that among the 4 1/2-year-old children, all 17 categories met the criterion of productive use in the first language sample of one child, S.T. Two children, N.W. and D.W., had productive use of all categories except one (antithesis) and the fourth child, E.C., lacked two of the categories (antithesis and epistemic).

Among 3-year-old children, C.W.'s coding of causality and coordination categories distinguishes his performances from the other three children. Two year old children, however, showed the greatest variability. As noted earlier, the number of categories represented in any one child's language sample ranged from three to five. The five categories coded by M.W. included action, existence, location, specifier and attribute; the four coded by C.H. included action, existence, location and negation; the three coded by A.G. included action, existence, and negation, whereas the three categories coded by R.J. included action, existence, and possession. Except for action and existence, none of the categories was represented in the language samples of all four children.

It is also clear from the data displays that the children differed within and across age groups in the relative frequency with which any given content category was represented in the language sample. Consider for example the action category: We note that among 4 1/2-year-old children the relative frequencies ranged from 39% for S.T. and M.W. to 53% for D.W. Among three-year old children, the range was even wider, varying from 35% for L.M. to 74% for K.M. Among 18-month-old children, the relative frequency of action utterances varied from 10 to 28%. Individual variability in relative frequency can be also observed for all the remaining categories.

It is likely that some of the individual differences can be accounted for by the specific types of activities and communicative interactions that would obviously vary across sampling events for different children given a naturalistic approach to data collection. The variability in the types of early content categories coded, suggests that content categories are probably not learned in the same order for all children. It is speculated that language use in the home environment may influence the particular types of categories that are coded earliest, as well as the specific linguistic forms used to represent them. For the very young child in particular, sources of language input are likely to be more restricted and tailored to the language patterns and conceptual distinctions that are most salient in a small group or family network compared to older ages when children are exposed to the larger speech community.

Irrespective of how one attempts to account for it, the fact of performance variability among individual working-class Black children means that their language competencies cannot be represented in a wholly stereotypic fashion.

Summary and Concluding Remarks

The results of this study revealed that Black children's language codes the same kinds of semantic categories that have been described for children acquiring other languages and that such knowledge evolves in an orderly sequence over time. While these findings were expected, they are significant because (1) they represent the first major documentation of the general kind of semantic content underlying the language of this group of speakers, and (2) they provide additional cross-linguistic and cross-cultural evidence that the semantic categories under study may be universally relevant to a description of any language system.

Our goal for the first stage of the semantic category analysis is to reveal the breadth of the children's knowledge of content, and this is why such a broad set of categories are being examined. Longitudinal analyses are being conducted to reveal further details regarding the order of emergence of particular categories (Stockman & Vaughn-Cooke, in prep). Subsequent goals will involve revealing depth of knowledge in specific categories. For example preliminary analysis has revealed the enormous complexity and range of semantic distinctions within a global category. To illustrate, our observations on location revealed that working-class Black children exhibit knowledge of dynamic locatives (e.g. go up, go down, throw over), which code movement orientation and direction, and static locatives (e.g. in there, on the ground, behind me) which code positional states (this distinction has been reported for SE speaking children by Bloom et al. 1975). In both the dynamic and static subcategories, locative knowledge appears to be further differentiated in terms of whether children can talk about location of actions, events, and objects (Stockman and Vaughn-Cooke, in prep.). A detailed description and an explanation of this differentiation will expand the knowledge base on location in general and on Black children's language in particular.

Footnotes

[1] Financial support for this research, which represents a subcomponent of a large scale investigation was provided by the National Institute of Education, Grant G-80-0135. Walt Wolfram and Cherie Bridgeforth are also members of the research team.

[2] It should be noted that Steffensen's employment of a multidimensional framework was not consistent. For example, she classified utterances exhibiting variable occurrence of copula forms according to three semantic categories, but this was not done for utterances exhibiting auxiliary and other forms that differentiate BE from SE.

[3] Birth order, though often controlled in studies of language development, may provide an unnecessarily restrictive condition for investigations of working-class Black children. The common practice of observing first-born children has been based on the assumption that the mother is the primary source of input to the first child. This, however, does not hold for the subjects in our study, who, irrespective of birth order, often live in an extended family environment that includes more than one caretaker.

[4] Although the mean length of utterance (MLU) has typically been used as an index for equating children's language development, it was not utilized in the subject selection process of this study for two reasons. First, MLU does not

appear to be an adequate index of grammatical development
after utterances exceed three or four words (Bloom and Lahey,
1978), which was the case for the 3 and 4 year old children
in this study. Its inadequacy in capturing the complexity
of Black children's language is further underscored by the
fact that conventional computation is biased toward language
specific features of mainstream varieties of English. See
also Brown's 1973 discussion (p. 71) of problems encountered
by Park when he attempted to calculate MLUs for German
speaking children.

[5]All of the studies except Bloom et al. focused on just a
small subset of the seventeen semantic categories evidenced
in the systems of working-class Black children.

References

Bloom, L. 1971. Why Not Pivot Grammar. Journal of Speech
and Hearing Disorders. 36, 40-50.

Bloom, L. and Lahey, M. 1978. Language Development and
Language Disorders. New York: John Wiley and Sons.

Bloom, L., Lahey, M., Hood, L., Lifter, K., and Fiess, K.
1980. Complex Sentences: Acquisition of Syntactic
Corrections and the Semantic Relations They Encode.
Journal of Child Language. 7, 235-362.

Bloom, L., Lightbown, P., and Hood, L. 1975. Structure
and Variation in Child Language. Monographs of the
Society for Research in Child Development, 40 (Serial
No. 60).

Bowerman, M.F. 1973. Early Syntactic Development: A
Cross-Linguistic Study With Special Reference to Finnish.
Cambridge University Press.

Brown, R. 1973. A First Language, the Early Stages.
Cambridge, Mass.: Harvard University Press.

Cole, L. 1979. Developmental Analysis of Social Dialect
Features in the Spontaneous Language of Preschool Black
Children. Unpublished Ph.D. Dissertation, Northwestern
University.

Johnston, J.R., and Slobin, D. 1979. The Development of
Locative Expressions in English, Italian, Serbo-Crotian,
and Turkish. Journal of Child Language 3, 529-546.

Kernan, K.T. 1970. "Semantic Relationships and the Child's
Acquisition of Language." Anthropological Linguistics,
12, 171-187.

Kovac, C. 1980. Children's Acquisition of Variable Features.
Ph.D. Dissertation, Georgetown University.

Labov, W. 1972. <u>Language in the Inner City: Studies in the Black English Vernacular</u>. Philadelphia: University of Pennsylvania Press.

Reveron, W.W. 1978. <u>The Acquisition of Four Black English Morphological Rules by Black Preschool Children</u>. Ph.D. Dissertation, Ohio State University.

Steffensen, M. 1974. <u>The Acquisition of Black English</u>. Unpublished Ph.D. Dissertation, University of Illinois. Champaign.

Stockman, I. and Vaughn-Cooke, F. In Preparation. An Investigation of Locative Knowledge in the Language of Working-Class Black Children.

Stockman, I. and Vaughn-Cooke, F. In Preparation. Order of Emergence of Semantic Categories: Evidence From Black English.

Stokes, N.H. 1976. <u>A Cross-Sectional Study of the Acquisition of Negative Structures in Black Children</u>. Unpublished Ph.D. Dissertation, Georgetown University.

Williams R. and Wolfram, W. 1976. <u>Social Dialect: Differences Versus Disorders</u>. Rockville, Md.: American Speech and Hearing Association.

Repairs: Learning to do it yourself

Michael F. McTear

School of Communication Studies

Ulster Polytechnic

Introduction

There are often points in the course of a
conversation when talk breaks down and repair is
necessary. Repairs can be initiated and carried
out either by the current speaker or by the
listener/next speaker (Schegloff, Jefferson and
Sacks 1977). This paper examines repairs by
current speaker (self-initiated self-repairs),
using as data transcripts of the spontaneous conversations of two children video-recorded over a
period of two years (ages 3;8 and 4;0 to 5;5 and
5;9 respectively). The paper focusses on syntactic aspects of the children's self-repairs. For
example:

> (1) Heather: so your na- so your name
>   (4;0)   hasn't got . um
>   so your . so . so you aren't a
>   girl . you're a boy

Here Heather initiates the repair by cutting off
name after na- and restarting the clause. After
got there is a brief pause followed by um, then
another restart, broken off after your. The solution to the repair in this case is a complete
restructuring of the originally projected
sentence.

Self-initiated self-repairs: types

Although the notion of self-initiated self-repair is clear enough, we find, on inspection of the data, a bewildering set of different types. Schegloff et al. (1977) cite examples which include word searches, attempts to be more explicit, structuring problems and corrections to propositional content.   There are also a variety of repair initiators, including cut-offs, sound stretches, filled and unfilled pauses.   Finally, repair solution can be realized by various means, such as word replacements, clause restructuring and paraphrased content.

It seems, then, that self-repairs are not a uniform phenomenon.   In some cases, they would seem to relate to speech planning processes, while in other cases they can be explained more in terms of self-monitoring by the speaker, where the repair can have the aim of being more explicit, accurate, polite or tentative.   In the developmental context there is also the important aspect of repair to some aspect of the linguistic system.   Similarly, repair initiators such as pauses and hesitations perform a variety of functions.   Pauses can be related to planning units in speech, that is, they indicate the nature of the cognitive processing of speech (Butterworth 1980).   They can also be related systematically to interactional factors such as the demands of the turn-taking system (Schegloff 1979).   Self-repairs may also be attributable to degeneracies of performance such as memory lapses and inattention (Chomsky 1965).   Yet others may be purely externally occasioned, as when a speaker is cut off in mid utterance by some outside noise or in response to some situational event such as another person entering the room.   It does not seem possible to determine the source of trouble unequivocably.   What we can do, however, is examine how the repair is executed.   Some repair solutions can be described in linguistic terms, for example, when a speaker makes a phonological, syntactic or lexical correction.   Syntactic repairs will be the focus of the present paper.

Self-repairs in the developmental literature

Self-initiated self-repairs have received little attention in the developmental literature. One possible reason for this is that they are unconsciously edited out at the transcription stage and simply not noticed (Clark and Andersen 1979:2). Indeed, repeated listening is necessary with particular focussing on the repair phenomena in order to avoid this natural, spontaneous editing out.

Clark (1978) reviews the literature on self-repairs in relation to children's developing awareness of language. Children seem to begin to make self-repairs from about one-and-a-half to two years of age. Their earliest repairs are pronunciations of single words, where the child changes pronunciation over several repeats until the listener shows signs of comprehension (see Scollon, 1979, for several examples). Slightly older children repair word endings, word order and word choices (Zakharova 1973:294; Leopold 1949, Vol. 4:114).

Clark and Andersen (1979) distinguish between repairs to the linguistic system, which are not motivated by attempts to be more intelligible, and repairs for the listener, which are motivated by the need to be understood. Repairs to the system seem to concern those items which the children are in the process of acquiring, where repairs go hand-in-hand with a growing awareness of and mastery of the system. So, for example, when children are mastering past tense forms, we would expect a closer monitoring of these forms. This does not imply that repairs lead to correction. Indeed, sometimes the repair replaces a correct item (in the adult system) with an incorrect item. For example,

> (2) Child: and she ate. she eated daddy
> bear porridge.

This is, however, evidence of the variable nature of the child's system at this stage. To take this point further, as Iwamura (1980) points out, errors provide evidence of the linguistic system and corrections substantiate this evidence by indicating what the child sees as violating the system. Similar findings are discussed by Rogers (1978), Karmiloff-Smith (1979a) and Savic (1980). Rogers examined the spontaneous repairs of five and six year olds. He found that the younger children's grammatical self-corrections mainly involved morphological rules, while those of the older children involved more complex syntactic structures. This suggests a relationship between type of self-correction and the state of the child's development of syntactic rules. Further support is provided by Savic (1980) and Ramge (1976). Savic found that the grammatical self-corrections of children aged 1;6 to 2;6 learning Serbo-Croatian mainly involved word-order rules. Ramge studied a three year old learning German and found that syntactic self-corrections reflected the child's current grammatical competence. Ramge also noted that many of his subject's self-corrections were motivated communicatively as attempts to take account of the listener by for-mulating the information more clearly or making the illocutionary force of the utterance more explicit. Finally, Karmiloff-Smith (1979) found a high frequency in children's self-corrections of determiners around age eight when they were beginning to develop an awareness of the pluri-functional status of determiners in French. For example: that the form les (the, plural) is used to express both plurality and totality. Karmiloff-Smith found that young children used les at first only to express plurality and that when they came to learn the function of totality, they expressed it at first with a different form, tous les (all the). Only at a later stage did they learn to express both functions simultaneously using les. Before this point many of their self-corrections indicated that they were at a transitional stage of development.

Frequency and types of self-initiated self-repairs in the data

All self-initiated self-repairs in the data were noted. They were then classified according to whether they are repairs to pronunciation, grammar or the lexicon. As can be seen from Table 1, the percentage occurrence of repairs in relation to all utterances of each child ranged from about 4% to almost 10%. Siobhan produced more self-repairs than Heather in each session. There was no general increase in the occurrence of self-repair in the later transcripts:

Table 1: Percentage occurrence of self-initiated self-repairs in relation to child's total utterances

Siobhan

	Age					
	3;8	4;3	4;6	4;9	5;1	5;5
% repairs	4.4	9.7	7.9	7.2	5.3	5.6

Heather

	Age					
	4;0	4;4	4;10	5;1	5;5	5;9
% repairs	4.1	8.0	3.1	4.3	4.5	4.3

Table 2 shows the percentage occurrence of each type of linguistic self-repair in relation to the total number of self-repairs. As we can see, repairs to pronunciation were infrequent. Repairs to grammar ranged from 0% to 15% of all self-repairs, while repairs to lexis ranged from 0% to about 15% of all self-repairs:

Table 2:   Percentage occurrence of "linguistic"
           self-repairs in relation to child's
           total self-repairs

Siobhan			Age			
	3;8	4;3	4;6	4;9	5;1	5;5
pronunciation	0	0	5	0	0	0
syntax	0	3	15	12	5	8
lexis	0	3	0	10	5	0

Heather			Age			
	4;0	4;7	4;10	5;1	5;5	5;9
pronunciation	2	0	0	5	2	0
syntax	7	13	11	13	8	5
lexis	15	14	11	8	11	0

As we can see, repairs to the linguistic system
were relatively infrequent in relation to the
total number of self-repairs. Scores for Heather
ranged from 21% to 26%, indicating that in general more of her self-repairs concerned the
linguistic system than Siobhan's.

Self-initiated self-repairs to grammar

     Repairs to grammar were evenly distributed
between the two children. They fell into different types, although no clear overall pattern
emerged. In some cases the repairs seemed to be
purely concerned with the grammatical system as
such while in other cases they seemed to be pragmatically motivated, having syntactic
consequences.

     The following are examples of grammatical
self-repairs which seemed to be concerned solely
with the grammatical system as such:

     (3) Heather: wha- who does that say?
         (4;0)

(4) Heather: she's just taking her lunch
    (4;0)   box in but h-do-aren't you?

(5) Siobhan: do you want more some books
    (4;0)   now . some more books?

(6) Heather: where's the old witch in this
    (4;7)   . . . on this book?
                 where's the old witch in this
                 book?

(7) Heather: well I hurt me
    (4;10)   I hurt myself

(8) Siobhan: I got nothing chopped off
    Heather: so . neither did I
    (4;10)

(9) Siobhan: and there's a the the biggest
                 garden

(10) Heather: I thought the bin go . went
     (5;5)   outside

In each case the child produces a grammatical item
and then follows it with an immediate self-
correction. For example (3), the non-personal
interrogative pronoun <u>what</u>, cut off at <u>wha-</u>, is
replaced by the personal pronoun <u>who</u>, the reason
being apparently because the question was attempting to elicit the name <u>Heather</u>, printed on a
lunch box which Heather was pointing to as she
asked the question. This is an interesting rep-
lacement as the usual form for this type of
question requires the non-personal form. Heather
might, however, be aware that the distinction is
important in other syntactic environments and,
realizing that the answer she wants to elicit is
a proper noun, feels that the personal form is
more appropriate.

(4) is an example of problems with tag forms,
attenuated by the fact that the tag is read-
dressed, that is, the main clause reference is
third person (<u>she</u>) while the tag is second person
(<u>you</u>). Here Heather is having trouble with

334

auxiliary agreement, alternating between what would seem to be attempts at using have and do before settling on be (aren't in agreement with be in she's).

(5) involves the ordering of premodifying items in the noun phrase. The correct structure for premodification in the noun phrase in English is

predeterminer-determiner-ordinal-
cardinal/quantifier-open class
premodifier-head

For example:

(11) both these last two rainy days
(Quirk, Greenbaum, Leech and Svartvik 1972:
146).

In (5) Siobhan first produces the ordering :
quantifier - (more) - determiner (some) -, then
corrects to some more.

(6) is a case of the choice of appropriate preposition. Here three attempts are made. In the first case, in is replaced by on, but this is subsequently replaced by in. Note that the cut-off point comes before book, the prepositional object, indicating that Heather has self-monitored items before she has actually produced them. Unlike many other cases the repair in the first line of (6) does not involve a recycling of a full clause structure but only of the prepositional phrase in which the repair is located. The repair in the second line does consist of a full clause, but this is probably occasioned by the fact that Heather is reinitiating her question, not just repairing her choice of preposition.

In (7) Heather corrects the pronoun me, replacing it with the reflexive myself which is required in the syntactic environment of I hurt X/X=I. As in many other cases, we might hypo-thesize that the repair was occasioned

335

sequentially. In this instance, the preceding
utterance was

(12) Siobhan: you hurt me

The immediate response incorporates items from
(12) but this is repaired to accommodate the rule
for reflexive pronoun usage.

(8) is probably also sequentially occasioned.
One means of expressing cohesive relations between
utterances is to use a substitution device
(Halliday and Hasan 1976), for example:

(13) A: I like that

B: so do I

Heather seems to be applying this rule in (8) but
then realises that the rule also involves polar-
ity agreement, that is, a prior negative requires
a negative, and so she replaces <u>so</u> by <u>neither</u>.

(9) is a case of syntactic relations, where
the choice of a superlative form (<u>biggest</u>)
requires the prior use of the definitive article.
Siobhan begins the noun phrase with the indefinite article <u>a</u>, which is usually required after
<u>there</u>, but replaces with <u>the</u> in anticipation of
the superlative form. The repetition of <u>the</u> is a
further indication of "trouble" at this precise
spot.

Finally, example (10) involves the choice of
tense in indirect speech. The use of the reporting verb (<u>I thought</u>) in the past tense occasions
back-shift of the verb in the reported clause
(<u>the bin goes outside</u>) to the past tense (see
Quirk et al. 1972:785ff. for discussion).
Heather shows awareness of this rule by replacing
the present tense form <u>go</u> with the past tense
form <u>went</u>.

What these examples suggest is that children
display in their self-repairs an awareness of

336

various grammatical rules. In each of the cases
presented here, (except for examples 3 and 6) the
repairs   contained a grammatical error which
was replaced by the correct grammatical form.
The examples discussed indicate the variety of
grammatical rules which have been acquired by the
children. It would be interesting to make comparisons in a larger sample between the grammatical rules involved in such self-repairs and the
acquisition of these rules by the children, showing whether the occurrence of grammatical self-
repairs is, as suggested by Clark and Andersen
(1979), related to those grammatical rules which
the children are in the process of acquiring.

The second set of examples does not involve
corrections of grammatical "errors" but rather
pragmatically occasioned repairs with grammatical
consequences. So, for example, a repair
occasioned by an attempt to be more explicit
might involve substituting a noun phrase for a
pronoun as in (14) - (16):

(14) Heather: and she's (1.1) this little
     (4;0)   girl's two year old

(15) Siobhan: she . my friend Heather knows
     (4;9)   how to take it off herself

(16) Siobhan: just put them up . up there
     (4;9)   alright the crayons?

(17) Siobhan: I could . could I cut them
     (4;3)   out?

(18) Heather: no you . do you want to put
     (5;5)   that in there?

(19) Siobhan: and this is just the table
               that you . like that table
               over there

(17) and (18) involve a change of sentence type,
declarative to interrogative and (probably)
imperative with surface subject <u>you</u> to

interrogative. These repairs are probably pragmatically motivated, as the interrogative forms fulfil the function of making the utterance more tentative and polite, by offering the addressee the choice between yes and no as a response.

The change in (19) from a projected relative clause structure the table that you- to a comparative structure the table like that table over there can be explained in various ways. It might have been occasioned by a concern for content, if Siobhan realised that the table she was talking about was not related to a table that had some connection with a table of her addressee but was like one in the room to which she could point. Another possible explanation could be that Siobhan ran into trouble with the projected relative clause structure, perhaps at the point of finding a suitable verb (the table that you Verb) and changed to a more manageable structure. Clearer cases of this phenomenon, referred to as "repair conversion" (Schegloff 1979), will be discussed below.

The discussion in this section has been concerned with those repairs which were classified as grammatical. It is also appropriate, however, to discuss some other phenomena related to repairs which are not necessarily grammatical, where the repair reveals interesting evidence about the children's grammatical competence. One point is that the majority of repairs involving a cut-off in mid-sentence, that is, after Subject-Auxiliary/ verb, resulted in a recycling or restructuring which involved a full clause structure:

(20) Heather: I was going to r-
    (4;7)   I was going to go down to your
                 house

In cases where the trouble occurred in a subordinate clause, then usually only the subordinate clause was recycled:

338

```
(21) Siobhan:    you can't do it in the car
     (4;3)       because my house isn't very em
                 my house isn't very far

(22) Heather:    has that got sharp wings that
     (4;0)       can (1.0) uh
                 that makes a noise on the
                 bottom
```

In other cases, such as (6), the recycling involved only the appropriate constituent, for example, a prepositional phrase. These examples are further indications of the children's grammatical system, as the ways in which they recycle show how they orient towards clause structure as well as showing an awareness of subordinate clause and constituent structure.

A second point concerns the location of repairs. Although a repair can be initiated anywhere within a turn (Schegloff 1979), an inspection of the child data revealed certain regularities. For example, repairs appeared to be concentrated either at turn beginnings or in post verbal positions within the clause. The following are examples of post verbal repairs:

```
(23) Heather:    you have the blue chairs and I
     (4;0)       have that . I have that wee
                 chairs don't we?

(24) Siobhan:    and I'm going to put mine in
     (3;8)       my . my basket so I nam

(25) Siobhan:    that's the same table as . as
     (4;6)       our one isn't it Daddy?

(26) Heather:    pretend that's a . pottie for
     (5;5)       the . bathroom
```

This distribution of repairs towards clause final position would seem to lend tentative support to the claim that in verbal planning the speaker plans the overall semantic content of his utterance but sometimes has trouble in retrieving particular items (Butterworth and Beattie 1978).

A third point concerns the phenomenon of repair conversion (Schegloff 1979:273). This occurs when, for example, a word search is initiated, usually with a filled pause (um, uh) but the repair solution is not a lexical item but a reconstruction of the sentence-so-far, thus avoiding the need for the missing element. In other words, a lexical repair is resolved by a syntactic solution. Example (1) illustrates repair conversion:

> (1) Heather: so your na- so your name hasn't
>   (4;0)   got . um so your
>   so . so you aren't a girl .
>   you're a boy
>   you're called Michael

Focussing on the second repair initiated at the end of the first line, we can see that Heather is having trouble finding a suitable object noun phrase to express the idea that the addressee's name is masculine (this example also illustrates the location of repairs at post verbal position discussed above). Instead of supplying this missing lexical item, Heather's solution is to restructure the idea with different syntax (lines 3 and 4). Example (27) also illustrates repair conversion:

> (27) Heather: did you bring . the um
>   (4;0)   did you bring some of this .
>   to playschool
>   uh things that's got wee
>   things on . wee streety things

Here trouble arises again at the post verbal position when Heather is unable to find an appropriate noun to follow the determiner the in the object noun phrase. Her first solution is lexical in that she substitutes the noun phrase some of this, but then she further specifies with the syntactic structure of noun + relative clause (things that's got wee things on) and further specifies wee things by introducing a second premodifier in the appositive noun phrase <u>wee streety things</u>. These examples are interesting in that they illustrate the child's ability to resolve what was essentially a lexical problem with a syntactic solution.

Concluding remarks

There are several implications which can be drawn from the present study. Developmentally, we have seen how repairs are an indication of the development of linguistic awareness, the ability to monitor one's speech and to take account of the listener's requirements. Repairs to syntax are a possible indication of the state of the child's linguistic system. Much more extensive data would, however, be required to show the relationship between a child's syntactic repairs and his/her stage of syntactic development. Methodologically, we have seen that repairs are a systematic, though by no means uniformly occasioned phenomenon. There has been a tendency in the analysis of syntactic development to idealise away from "performance" phenomena in the interest of underlying linguistic competence. For example, in the LARSP system for the analysis of grammatical disability, self-repairs of the type that have been discussed here are disregarded (Crystal, Fletcher and Garman 1976). However, repairs are a rich sort of data, which may be crucial to the analysis of a child's linguistic competence, as it is possible that it is precisely at the point of repair that a child reaches the limits of his/her current ability. For this reason, repairs should not be ignored but should be incorporated explicitly into the analysis.

References

Butterworth, B. (ed.) (1980): Language Production. New York: Academic Press.

Butterworth, B. and Beattie, G. (1978). Gesture and silence as indicators of planning in speech. In R. Campbell and P. Smith (eds.), Recent Advances in the Psychology of Language: Formal and Experimental Approaches. New York: Plenum Press.

Chomsky, N. (1965). Aspects of the Theory of Syntax. Cambridge, Mass: MIT Press.

Clark, E. (1978). Awareness of language: some evidence from what children say and do. In A. Sinclair, R. J. Jarvella and W. J. M. Levelt (eds.) The Child's Conception of Language. Springerverlag.

Clark, E. V. and Andersen, E. S. (1979). Spontaneous repairs: awareness in the process of acquiring language. Papers and Reports on Child Language Development, Vol. 16. Stanford University.

Crystal, D., Fletcher, P. and Garman, M. (1976). The Grammatical Analysis of Language Disability. Edward Arnold.

Halliday, M. A. K. and Hasan, R. (1976). Cohesion in English. Longman.

Iwamura, S. (1980). The Verbal Games of Preschool Children. Croom Helm.

Karmiloff-Smith, A. (1979). A Functional Approach to Child Language. Cambridge University Press.

Leopold, W. F. (1949). Speech development of a bilingual child. Vol. 4. Northwestern University Press.

Quirk, R., Greenbaum, S., Leech, G. and Svartvik, J. (1972). A Grammar of contemporary English. Longman.

Rogers, S. (1978). Self-initiated corrections in the speech of infant school children. Journal of Child Language, 5, 365-371.

Savic, S. (1980). How twins learn to talk. Academic Press.

Schegloff, E. (1979). The relevance of repair to syntax-for-conversation. In T. Givon (ed.) Syntax and Semantics Vol. 12: Discourse and Syntax. Academic Press.

Schegloff, E., Jefferson, G. and Sacks, H. (1977). The preference for self-correction in the organisation of repair in conversation. Language, 53, 361-382.

Scollon, R. (1979). A real early stage: an unzippered condensation of a dissertation on child language. In E. Ochs and B. Schieffelin (eds.) Developmental Pragmatics. Academic Press.

Zakharova, A. V. (1973). Acquisition of forms of grammatical case by preschool children. In C. A. Ferguson and D. Slobin (eds.) Studies of Child Language Development. Holt, Rinehart and Winston.

"Don't interrupt!": Preschoolers' entry into
ongoing conversations.

Jacqueline Sachs
Department of Communication Sciences, U-85
University of Connecticut
Storrs, CT   06268

Abstract

Observations of natural interactions in a preschool
(18 children 3,4 to 5,6) yielded instances of children's
attempts to enter ongoing conversations between child-child,
adult-child, and adult-adult pairs. In this age range and
situation, there was little evidence of polite strategies
(e.g., waiting for acknowledgement) or verbal politeness
formulas for interruption. Adult-child pairs were more
frequently interrupted than adult-adult or child-child
pairs. Older children and girls tended to interrupt at a
closer distance than did younger children and boys. The
results are discussed in terms of the development of the
sociolinguistic rules and cognitive abilities involved in
entering ongoing conversations.

Introduction

We are all frequently faced with the difficult task
of bringing up a new topic to one or more people who are
already engaged in conversation. We must interrupt, but
attempt to do so politely, behaving in ways that follow
general rules of politeness such as "don't impose" and
"give options to the listeners" (Ervin-Tripp, 1973;
Lakoff, 1973). The previously participating members in the
conversation have the floor, and to interrupt politely we
may approach, wait for acknowledgement, and use a politeness formula (Ferguson, 1976) such as "excuse me" to indicate that we are introducing a new topic rather than simply joining the conversation. Furthermore, for an interruption to be perceived as legitimate, there must be a
valid reason for the topic change. Now imagine the following situation: Two people are talking quietly together.
A third person approaches them, and says in a loud voice,
"You know where I sleep? You know where I sleep? You
know where I sleep?" As you may easily guess, this third
person is a 3-year-old. In this paper, I will describe

344

some characteristics of interruptions in preschool children and discuss some reasons for the difficulty of interrupting gracefully.

The term "interruption" is applicable to two sorts of conversational events: the breaking into an utterance of one speaker by another and the breaking into an ongoing conversation by a non-participant. It is the first type of interruption--utterance interruption--that has received most attention thus far (see Sacks, Schegloff & Jefferson, 1974). For a conversation interruption to occur, there are two defining characteristics. The topic must be new and the person introducing the topic must be a nonparticipant. If a nonparticipant arrives and makes a comment on the established topic, this would simply be "joining the conversation." If a participant introduces a new topic, it is usually marked ("Oh, by the way? or "This is off the subject but") and, if it is not marked, it is perceived as a "non sequitur," not an interruption.

Researchers who have studied utterance interruptions by adults have noted that they reveal status or dominance relations in a group. For example, in cross-sex pairs, women are interrupted more by men than vice-versa (Bernard, 1968; Willis & Williams, 1976; Zimmerman & West, 1975). In parent-child dyads, Greif (1980) found that fathers interrupted children more than mothers did, and both interrupted girls more than boys. Since status affects utterance interruptions in two-party conversations, we might also expect status to be a factor in conversation interruptions, and everyday experience certainly suggests that there are different constraints on breaking into conversations depending on the status of the participants. Particularly relevant for this study, a conversation interruption has fewer constraints if the conversational participants are in a service role (e.g., one more freely would interrupt two salespeople talking). Constraints also vary according to the topic of the interruption, with the general rule being that more "pressing needs" have priority. Furthermore, an interruption that is based on the need of the addressee is more permissable than one based on the need of the interruptor.[1]

345

Various aspects of the interrupter's behavior would vary with such constraints: e.g., posture, distance, loudness of voice, length of waiting for acknowledgment before speaking, and politeness phrases used.

Children, of course, are notorious for interrupting. But even preschoolers are in the process of acquiring some relevant conversational skills. They learn how to initiate and join conversations by getting the attention of the addressee(s) (McTear, 1979; Shields, 1978), how to structure what is said so that the addressee can understand what is being said (Keenan & Schieffelin, 1976), and how to get a turn in a conversation (Ervin-Tripp, 1979).

Furthermore, though a polite preschooler may seem to some to be a contradiction in terms, recent work shows that young children are indeed learning some conversational graces. Gleason and Weintraub (1976) documented the explicit instruction that children receive regarding politeness routines, and their non-routine utterances such as requests also show some emerging sensitivity to not impose and to give options to the listener. Though preschoolers are more likely to use the less polite direct request forms than indirect requests (Garvey, 1975), the use of indirect forms increase in this age range (Bates, 1976a & b; Read & Cherry, 1978). In line with children's general sensitivity to age of listener as a determinant of conversational style (Ervin-Tripp, 1977; Sachs & Devin, 1976; Shatz & Gelman, 1973), 4-year-olds in role-play were most polite to dolls representing adults (Andersen, 1977; James, 1978). The familiarity of the listener and the probability that he/she will comply also affect request forms (Weeks, 1979). By school age (7 to 12 years), children use a variety of request forms and are aware of the factors that affect their choice (Mitchell-Kernan & Kernan, 1977; Gordon, Budwig, Strage & Carrell, 1980). Again, we might suppose that some of the factors influencing politeness in requests such as age of addressee would influence the probability and method of conversation interruption.

Another aspect of adult conversational behavior emerges early: sex differences in speech style. Most relevant to the topic at hand, Esposito (1979) found that in cross-sex dyads, boys were more likely to interrupt

346

utterances than were girls. In interrupting conversations, we might also expect to find evidence of boys' perception of their status as more dominant.

In this study, we collected natural instances of interruptions by preschoolers in the preschool setting, attending to variables such as the age and sex of the interrupting child, the status of those addressed, and the topics and manner of interrupting. The goal of the study was to determine whether preschoolers are acquiring some of the rules governing politeness in interrupting conversations.

Method

The data reported here consist of 73 observations of interruptions by 18 children (7 boys, ages 3,4 to 5,6 and and 11 girls, ages 3,6 to 5,3). The interruption episodes were hand-transcribed during 10 hours of observation, mostly in 1 to 1 1/2 hour blocks. Before the collection of these data, the observer had collected data for about 6 hours in the same preschool class, and the descriptive system used for coding the observations had been developed using the observations made during that time. Furthermore, the preliminary observation period insured that the children were very familiar with the observer and accustomed to the observation situation.

The observer sat or stood at various places in the room, attended to the ongoing conversations, and attempted to notice interruptions. An interruption was defined as an utterance by a child to two or more people who were already engaged in conversation, where the topic of the child's utterance was unrelated to the ongoing conversational topic. Obviously, with such a method, many interruptions would take place that the observer would not notice because she was attending elsewhere. However, when she did notice an interruption, she wrote down as much as she could recall about the child's nonverbal behavior, the interrupting utterance, and the reaction. On the same coding sheet, she made checks for the following variables: sex of interrupter, proximity, whether approaching, loudness, and status of people interrupted (adult-child, male-female). We are well aware of the limitations of the online observation method: e.g., incompleteness and in-

347

ability to recall exact wording. However, we hoped that we would obtain a general picture of the preschoolers' behavior which could lead to other methods of data collection in future research.

Results and Discussion

The major result of the observations is that we found essentially no politeness routines. Nonverbal signals for attention before actually beginning the interrupting utterance were almost nonexistent. In the 73 interruptions observed, there were two instances of waiting for acknowledgment and one of tapping a teacher on the leg. There were no verbal politeness formulas for interruption in these observations (e.g., "Excuse me"). It might be argued that either a nonverbal signal or politeness formula would make the interruption less disruptive and therefore less noticeable to the observer. Indeed, we do not know that such signals were never used, but we are confident that in this situation for this age group they are very rare.

Table 1. Percentage of interruptions to various addresses

Adult-Child	Adult-Adult	Child-Child
59%	36%	5%

Table 1 shows the percentage of interruptions to various addresses. Since there were no significant differences by sex or age of interrupter, these data are for all children. Most of the interruptions observed were interruptions of adult-child conversations (59%), with the target of the interruption almost always the adult. A significantly smaller percentage ($p < .05$) was addressed to adult-adult conversations (36%). Though it might appear that the children were differentiating between adult-child and adult-adult dyads in terms of their interruptability, to conclude this we would need to know that there were equal numbers of adult-child and adult-adult conversations to interrupt. This is in all likelihood not the case, and other procedures will be needed to see whether preschoolers view adult-adult and adult-child pairs differently.

A much smaller percentage of interruptions were addressed to child-child pairs (5%). Though this might initially seem surprising, we will see a bit later that the topics of the interruptions were usually bids for help or attention (which would be more reasonable from adults). When a child wishes to interact with or get attention from another child, it may be that quite different strategies from those used with adults are used. Corsaro (1979) studied the strategies used by children 2,10 to 4,10 for gaining access to ongoing child activities in a preschool. He found that children typically joined a group by simply placing themselves in the area (nonverbal entry) and/or producing a variant of the ongoing behavior. Only 7% of the access strategies observed were disruptive (a physical or verbal disruption of the ongoing activity). Since our interruptions would have been "disruptions" in Corsaro's system, the low percentage of child-child interruptions seems compatible with his results. Furthermore, he found that disruptive entry very rarely was successful in gaining the child a place in the activity. It may be that interruptions are more tolerated by adults in the preschool setting than they are by children.

Table 2. Percentage of interruptions that were proximal

	Boys	Girls
Younger	48%	50%
Older	72%	90%

Table 2 shows the results for proximity, with proximal meaning within a normal conversational distance. "Younger" is below 4 yrs, 6 mos. Girls interrupted significantly more proximally than did boys ($p < .01$) and older children interrupted significantly more proximally than did younger children ($p < .01$). Thus girls and older children are behaving more politely in their interruptions in terms of this variable. The interruptions were also coded as being at a conversational loudness (for preschool standards) or "yelled." Only 36% were at a conversation loudness and there were no reliable sex or age differences.

Therefore, the most typical conversation interruption would involve a child standing near a teacher-child pair and yelling the conversational initiation utterance. However, when the child was a boy younger than 4,6 it was just as likely that the initiation would be made from far away as near the addressees.

The reasons for the interruptions were classified as follows:

Needs-for action or intervention	E's not sharing; Will you play this with me?
for objects	P, can I have a pencil?
for help	I can't open it.
for permission	Can A sit with me?
for information	Hey P, where do I put this?
Requests for attention-- in context	I washed my hands; Look, I got raisins
out of context	Know what's on TV tonight? Zoom!
	I'm already living in my new house.
Greeting	Hi, D.
Uninterpretable or ambiguous	I don't need that other one.

The largest percentage of interruptions (50%) were of the sort that one would expect interruptions to be--indications of need of some sort--and rather evenly spread out over the various types. However, another 39% of the interruptions were requests for attention. Here there was nothing required of the addressee except to acknowledge and provide a conversational response such as OK, That's good, Right, etc. Such interruptions would almost invariably be perceived as a breach in adult interactions because there is no pressing need, but the fact that so many interruptions are requests for attention will come as no surprise to parents or others who deal with young children.

Why were there so many of these unnecessary (from the adult's point of view) interruptions? One contributing factor may be the preschool context. Interactions are extremely fluid, and though two people were talking together to fit our criterion for an ongoing conversation, the conversational partners do change frequently. Another, and in fact related, factor is the reactions of the teachers to the interruptions. When a child interrupted there was almost always a brief but positive response, whereupon the teacher resumed the earlier interaction. For example, two teachers were talking quietly. A child yelled to them I did it, I did it, I did it. One teacher turned to him and said Very good, S and then resumed her conversation. Recall that for adults, one variable affecting the interruptibility of talkers is whether they are in a service role. Teachers in a preschool presumably view themselves as being there to interact with the children rather than to interact with one another, so that it would not be seen as appropriate to prevent a child from having access to them. We observed only a few examples of teachers ignoring interruptions or redirecting the child to another teacher, and no occasions where a teacher used the phrase in our title, "Don't interrupt." In contrast, in family interactions, Ervin-Tripp (1979) found examples in which a younger child's attempt to interrupt was ignored by older children or adult-older child pairs.

One relevant question, then, regarding topics of interruptions is whether our results are unique to the preschool context. A study carried out by one of my students, Linda Schubert (1978), provides some evidence. She visited mothers of young children, and sat and talked with the mothers, recording any interruptions that happened to occur. Thus the situation was one with more constraints against interruption for the child. Two preschoolers provided 15 interruptions. Of these, 60% were requests for attention rather than expression of needs--an even higher percentage than in our preschool setting.

If it is indeed the case generally that children not only interrupt more than we think they should, without routines to signal politeness, but for topics that we consider inappropriate, then clearly there is considerable development in this aspect of conversational ability between preschool and adulthood. I find this change in interruption behavior interesting because I suspect that there are

351

at least two factors involved in the change: rule learning and changes in cognitive processing constraints.

We will first consider rule learning. There are a number of rules involved in appropriate conversation interruptions. One involves awareness of the turntaking nature of interactions. Turntaking in dyads seems to be relatively well controlled by the age we have observed here. In child-child conversations, utterance interruptions are not frequent (Garvey & Berninger, 1979) and are perhaps even fewer than one finds in adult conversations, where listeners come in early because they have made an incorrect prediction about the utterance end-point. Getting a turn in a conversation with 3 or more participants is more complex in terms of timing. Another category of conversational rules relevant to interruptions involves attending to the topic of the conversation. Children do show an increase in following the topic with age (Bloom, Rocissano & Hood, 1976; Chapman, Miller, MacKenzie & Bedrosian, 1981). However, throughout the preschool years there remains, even in dyadic interactions, some disconnectedness in topic that is quite atypical of adult-adult speech (Blank & Franklin, 1980). It may be that children sometimes attend to the topic and sometimes do not, and in the situation where they are interrupting an ongoing conversation, they may not be aware that they are initiating a topic change. In short, there are a number of rules to be learned in order to interrupt conversations appropriately, and future studies may reveal where the particular gaps in children's knowledge are.

The second factor that may affect children's ability to interrupt appropriately is a cluster of developmental changes I'll call "changes in cognitive processing constraints." For example, children may interrupt because they do not perceive the talking behavior of those they interrupt. Even more importantly, I suspect that problems in children's inhibition of behavior are quite central to the issue here. The child's intent to communicate takes precedence, even when he "knows" it shouldn't. For example, we are in the process of collecting data on interruptions in a different context, where the child is asked to approach two adults who are talking in order to make a request. In one case when so instructed a 3-year-old said to me "I have to wait until they stop talking." This 3-year-old <u>knows</u> something about interrupting, though not every-

352

thing since he does not know what to do when people do not simply stop talking. His mother and teachers would probably be very pleased. However, would we want to guess that this preschooler would behave differently from the ones we observed out on the preschool floor, or even when his mother is on the telephone? I think not, because his knowledge might very well be overridden by other factors. I would like to suggest that many aspects of conversational behavior, not just interruption, will be fully understood only by taking into account general developmental processes as well as conversational rule learning.

In summary, in naturalistic observation in the preschool, we found that preschoolers did not use politeness routines in interrupting conversations. Furthermore, they broke into conversations when there was no "pressing need," for reasons that would be inappropriate in adults. I have suggested that the child's development of appropriate interrupting behavior involves not only learning a number of conversation rules but also changes in the child's processing capacities to permit use of the rules that are known.

Notes

The author wishes to acknowledge the help of Maureen Maio, Linda Schubert, and the staff of the Preschool Laboratory.

[1] This discussion of constraints is not meant to be exhaustive. For example, the non-verbal behavior of talkers also influences how interruptible they are, with closeness and face-to-face stance indicative of "closedness" to a third party (Scheflen, 1972).

Bibliography

Andersen, E. Learning to speak with style: A study of the sociolinguistic skills of children. Unpublished doctoral dissertation, Stanford University, 1977.

Bates, E. Language and context: The acquisition of pragmatics. New York: Academic Press, 1976a.

353

Bates, E. Pragmatics and sociolinguistics in child language. In D. Morehead and A. Morehead (Eds.), Normal and deficient child language. Baltimore: University Park Press, 1976b.

Bernard, J. The sex game. N. Y.: Atheneum, 1968.

Blank, M. and Franklin, E. Dialogue with preschoolers: A cognitively-based system of assessment. Applied Psycholinguistics, 1980, 1, 127-150.

Bloom, L., Rocissano, L., and Hood, L. Adult-child discourse: Developmental interaction between information processing and linguistic knowledge. Cognitive Psychology, 1976, 8, 521-552.

Chapman, R., Miller, J. F., MacKenzie, H., and Bedrosian, J. Development of discourse skills in the second year of life. Paper presented at Second International Congress for the Study of Child Language, 1981.

Corsaro, W. A. "We're friends, right?" Children's use of access rituals in a nursery school. Language in Society, 1979, 8, 315-336.

Ervin-Tripp, S. Language acquisition and communicative choice. Stanford: Stanford University Press, 1973.

Ervin-Tripp, S. Wait for me, Roller Skate. In S. Ervin-Tripp and C. Mitchell-Kernan, (Eds.) Child Discourse. New York: Academic Press, 1977.

Ervin-Tripp, S. Children's verbal turn-taking. In E. Ochs and B. B. Schieffelin (Eds.), Developmental pragmatics. New York: Academic Press, 1979.

Esposito, A. Sex differences in children's conversation. Language and Speech, 1979, 22, 213-220.

Ferguson, C. A. The structure and use of politeness formulas. Language in Society, 1976, 5, 137-151.

Garvey, C. Requests and responses in children's speech. Journal of Child Language, 1975, 2, 41-63.

Garvey, C. and Berninger, G. Timing and turntaking in children's conversations. Paper presented at a meeting of the Society for Research in Child Development, 1979.

Gleason, J. B. and Weintraub, S. The acquisition of routines in child language. Language in Society, 1976, 5, 129-136.

Gordon, D., Budwig, N., Strage, A. and Carrell, P. Children's requests to unfamiliar adults: Form, social function, age variation. Paper presented at Boston University Conference on Child Language, 1980.

Greif, E. Sex differences in parent-child conversation. Women's Studies International Quarterly, 1980, 3, 253-258.

James, S. Effect of listener age and situation on the politeness of children's directives. Journal of Psycholinguistic Research, 1978, 7, 307-317.

Keenan, E. O. and Schieffelin, B. Topic as a discourse notion: A study of topic in the conversation of children and adults. In C. Li (Ed.), Subject and Topic. New York: Academic Press, 1976.

Lakoff, R. The logic of politeness of minding your p's and q's. Papers from the Ninth Regional Meeting of the Chicago Linguistic Society, Chicago Linguistic Society, Chicago, 1973.

McTear, M. Hey, I've got something to tell you: A study of the initiation of conversational exchange by preschool children. Journal of Pragmatics, 1979, 3, 321-336.

Mitchell-Kernan, C., and Kernan, K. Pragmatics of directive choice among children. In S. Ervin-Tripp and C. Mitchell-Kernan (Eds.), Child discourse. New York: Academic Press, 1977.

Read, B. K., and Cherry, L. J. Preschool children's production of directive forms. Discourse Processes, 1978, 1, 233-245.

Sachs, J., and Devin, J. Young children's use of age-appropriate speech styles in social interaction and role-playing. Journal of Child Language, 1976, 3, 81-98.

Sacks, S., Schegloff, E. A., and Jefferson, G. A simplest systematics for the organization of turn-taking for conversation. Language, 1974, 50, 696-735.

Scheflen, A. E. Body language and social order. Englewood Cliffs, N. J.: Prentice-Hall, 1972.

Schubert, L. A study of interruption behavior. Unpublished paper, University of Connecticut, 1978.

Shatz, M., and Gelman, R. The development of communication skills: Modification in the speech of young children as a function of the listener. Monographs of the Society for Research in Child Development, 1973, 38.

Shields, M. M. Some communicational skills of young children--A study of dialogue in the nursery school. In R. N. Campbell and P. T. Smith (Eds.) Recent advances in the psychology of language. New York: Plenum, 1978.

Weeks, T. Born to talk. Rowley, Mass.: Newbury House, 1979.

Willis, F., and Williams, S. Simultaneous talking in conversation and sex of speakers. Perceptual and Motor Skills, 1976, 43, 1067-1070.

Zimmerman, D., and West, C. Sex roles, interruptions and silences in conversation. In B. Thorne and N. Henley (Eds.), Language and sex: Difference and dominance. Rowley, Mass.: Newbury House, 1975.

An experimental investigation of children's comprehension of the locutionary verb <u>ask</u>

Christine Tanz
Department of Psychology
University of Arizona

ABSTRACT

The theoretical concerns of language acquisition research have expanded from an initial
focus on syntax, first to include semantics and
then also pragmatics. The same phenomenon in
children's language may undergo a series of
changing interpretations as theoretical foci
change. Here the datum of children's apparent
misunderstanding of the locutionary verb <u>ask</u> is
traced from its discovery in C. Chomsky's research on syntactic development, through its
interpretation in terms of E. Clark's theory of
semantic development, to a reinterpretation within the framework of pragmatic development.

Introduction

Carol Chomsky's (1969) well known research
on later developments in children's acquisition
of language was focused primarily on syntax. One
of the questions she investigated was how children
learn to interpret complex sentences in which the
subject of an embedded sentence does not appear on
the surface. Her experiments on <u>ask</u> and <u>tell</u> sentences fall into this category. The prototype
constructions were:

1. Tell John what to feed the doll.

2. Ask John what to feed the doll.

In sentence (1), the tell sentence, the unstated subject of "feed the doll" is John. In (2), the ask sentence, it is the addressee. Chomsky found that her younger subjects interpreted both subjects as John. On this basis she postulated that children initially operate according to a "minimum distance principle": the subject is the preceding noun phrase closest to the verb in question.

An unexpected finding, not directly relevant to the main syntactic issues, was that many children responded to the ask sentences by giving instructions about what the doll should be fed. For example, in response to the experimenter's "Ask John what to feed the doll," one child said cucumber. In other words, this child and others like her treated the ask instructions as though they were tell instructions.

E. Clark (1973), in a paper that was instrumental in directing attention toward questions of lexical semantics in children's language, assimilated their apparent confusion of ask and tell to her general model of semantic development. She postulated in general that children's lexical entries for words begin with an incomplete list of specifying features. Gradually features are added and differentiation of meanings proceeds. This analysis was applied most extensively to nominal errors recorded in diary studies of children's very early speech, (e.g., the use of the word cat for dogs, cows, sheep and horses) and to children's performance in comprehension experiments on relational terms having to do with space, time, and quantity, (e.g., the apparent confusion of less with more and after with before).

Clark extended the same type of analysis to ask and tell:

> If tell is interpreted in [contexts such as Sentence (2) above] as meaning roughly something like "I order you - you say to X - complement sentence," we can contrast it with the related analysis of ask: "I order you - you say to X - you request X - X say to you - complement sentence." This analysis contains the added information that this is a question that will need an answer, and not simply an assertion. From this rough performative analysis, it is clear that ask and tell overlap in meaning, but ask has some additional properties that are not found in tell. The meaning of ask involves learning the "request" feature and also the allocation of roles: the third person (X) and not the initial addressee is to supply the answer. One possible semantic interpretation of Chomsky's results, therefore, is that the meaning of tell is used for ask until the child learns the rest of the semantic information about the verb ask which will differentiate it in meaning from tell. (1973, p. 98)

According to this semantic perspective, the reason that Chomsky's subject proposed to feed the doll cucumber is that in her incomplete lexicon, ask "means" tell.

This paper presents an alternative interpretation of ask-tell "confusion." Instead of treating these data as evidence of semantic confusion, it treats them as evidence of pragmatic skill.

In ordinary discourse it is entirely normal
and legitimate to respond to instructions to ask
a question by providing direct information instead
of relaying the question. For example, if a speaker
says "Ask the captain when the ferry's leaving"
the literal message is a request to perform the
action of asking. But the speaker also conveys
a desire to know the ferry schedule. Under ordinary circumstances the speaker would express himself this way only if he assumes the addressee
isn't able to answer the question. If the addressee
does know the ferry schedule, then the cooperative
thing to do is not to comply with the literal request, (in this case-not to ask the captain), but
to come right out with the answer. Looking back
at the child in Chomsky's experiment who said
"cucumber" when requested to "ask John what to
feed the doll" - perhaps that child's problem was
simply that (in a Gricean sense) she was being
cooperative.

The current experiment tests this interpretation directly. The subjects are all requested
to ask someone else a series of questions. The
variable is whether they themselves know the answer to the question. Therefore the text is held
constant, and a pragmatic factor in the context
is varied.

The hypotheses are:

1. Children in the age range 5-10 (the range
    tested by Chomsky) do understand the
    literal meaning of the word ask.

2. When told to ask someone a question, they
    apply the rules of ordinary discourse.
    If they don't know the answer, they will
    relay the question. If they do know the
    answer, they will supply it.

Subjects

The subjects were 12 children age 5;5 to 9;9
attending kindergarten through 4th grade at a private school in Tucson, Arizona.

Recruitment for the experiment immediately
established a game context. Each child was first
asked: "Would you like to play a game?" All
who were approached said yes.

Method

To carry out the experiment it was necessary
to control children's knowledge about the subject
matter of the questions. This was done by showing them a playing board for an invented game.

Half of the subjects were placed in the condition of knowing the rules of the game. Children
in this group were shown the playing board, playing
pieces, dice, cards, etc. The rules for playing
and winning were explained to them. They were
then brought to a table where a second child was
seated. The subject was told: "Before you play,
I'd like you to ask Rachel (the other child) some
questions." The second group of subjects did
not receive any explanations but were brought over
to the second child immediately.

Subjects were given the following instructions:

1. Ask Rachel where to put the red cards.

2. Ask her where to put the blue chips.

3. Ask her where to put the playing pieces.

4. Ask her which piece to take.

5. Ask her how to start the game.

All subjects received the same questions in the
same order. Each child was examined individually.

Comparison of test materials with constructions used by Chomsky

The range of language materials used here
was more limited than Chomsky's in two ways. First,
instead of a mixture of ask and tell instructions,
only ask instructions were given. And second, the
ask instructions were all of a single syntactic

type, rather than the four types sampled by Chomsky.

Limiting the study to ask was considered sufficient, and even desirable, for several reasons. The claims about semantic confusion made by Chomsky and Clark were restricted to children's comprehension of ask. (Children were thought to comprehend tell fully). And the hypothesis offered here applies directly only to ask. These are both admittedly negative reasons for omitting tell instructions. In the face of such reasons, it might still seem preferable, for the sake of greater comparability with Chomsky's study, to include tell instructions as well. But there is also a positive reason for their omission. In language comprehension experiments where children are required to alternate rapidly and repeatedly between related responses there is always a risk of inducing confusion that is merely circumstantial and spurious. Such studies may unwittingly impose an additional level of "problem-solving" difficulty on top of ordinary semantic and syntactic processing as the child tries to keep straight which of two frequently repeated messages has been heard last. In some cases the desirability of within-subject comparisons outweighs these disadvantages. But in other cases, and especially where the groundwork has already been laid by previous research, it may be preferable to proceed by trying to tap comprehension of one thing at a time; in effect, "how does the child understand ask?", rather than "can the child discriminate between ask and tell in rapid succession?"

Chomsky's study, motivated as it was by syntactic concerns, sampled children's comprehension of ask in several different constructions, as in the following examples:

a. Bozo asks Mickey to go first in line.

b. Ask Laura what color this is.

c. Ask Laura the color of this book.

d. Ask Laura what to feed the doll.

362

Chomsky regards the sequence (a) - (d) as representing the order of difficulty of the four constructions. On theoretical grounds, item (d) is considered most difficult because the child "must refer outside of the complement clause to retrieve the subject" (1969; 47).

Chomsky's study confirmed the predicted order of difficulty. In fact, children who succeeded on items such as (d) always succeeded on (a), (b), and (c). Therefore in this study, all of the items are of type (d) (referred to in Chomsky as Case 3), the most difficult type. The complement consists of a wh-clause with subject omitted. If in an appropriate context, children are able to process these maximally difficult constructions, then presumably they can also comprehend the others.

Results

Responses were scored as ask responses if the child relayed, i.e., asked the question. They were scored as tell responses if the child provided the answer either verbally (e.g., "on the square") or by pointing. Table 1 shows the number of ask responses according to whether subjects knew or didn't know the answers to the questions.

Insert Table 1 about here

For children who knew the answers, the mean number of ask responses was .83 (out of a possible 5). For children who did not know the answers, the mean number of ask responses was 4.5. Knowing or not knowing the answer to the question was a highly significant determinant of whether children asked or told (t = 24.4, df = 10, p < .005, one-tail).

There was a strong tendency to be consistent in either asking or telling. Five children always asked questions in making their five responses; five always gave answers or "told"; only two subjects (age 7;10 and 8;8) gave a mixture of responses.

Of the children who had learned the rules of the game, all but one consistently "told." The single exception, who "asked" the questions despite the fact that he knew the answers, was located about midway in the age distribution, age 7;4. Among the children who didn't know the game, (including the youngest) four always asked the questions. The remaining two relayed the question at least some of the time.

Discussion

The fact that children in this experiment were able to construct appropriate questions in response to instructions to ask casts doubt on Chomsky's and Clark's interpretation of Chomsky's subjects' failure to do so. Perhaps those children also were able to interpret ask literally and to construct the corresponding questions but chose a different interpretation for contextual reasons.

The fact that it was possible to determine to a striking degree whether children asked or told by manipulating their possession of the information sought in the experimenter's question suggests that this may have been the contextual variable affecting children's responses in the Chomsky study as well.

Relation to other research on speech acts in children

Earlier research on pragmatic development (Holzman, 1972; Dore, 1977; Ervin-Tripp, 1977; Garvey, 1975; Shatz, 1975; Reeder, 1980, and others) has shown that very young children can go beyond a literal, compositional interpretation of utterances to make proper inferences about illocutionary force.

The current paper extends these findings in several ways. It broadens the range of speech acts considered, takes up 3-person conversational interactions, and raises the question of how children respond to infelicitous speech acts.

Research on pragmatic development in children has focused primarily on their comprehension and production of directives, especially indirect directives couched in question form. This study extends the focus by looking at almost the reverse situation: children's comprehension of utterances that are literally directives, but indirectly may convey a question.

Most theoretical discussions of speech acts and likewise most empirical investigations of children's pragmatic development focus on two-person interactions--those occuring between a single speaker and a single hearer. Little research has been conducted on three-person interactions and special patterns arising out of reported speech ("she said you should . . ."), quotation, and relayed messages ("tell him to . . . "). (In this regard it is interesting to note that no child in this experiment took the option of saying "She said to ask you where to put the red cards.")

In research that has been directed explicitly at issues of pragmatic development, the assumption has usually been made (and usually warranted) that the speaker has met the felicity conditions for a particular speech act. The question has been: given a well-formed, felicitous speech act, can the child interpret it correctly?

In the case investigated here a different set of conditions applies. Under the simplest and most straightforward circumstances, the speaker would ask the addressee to ask someone else a question only if he assumes that the addressee doesn't know the answer, but that the third party does. What happens if this assumption is incorrect because the addressee does know the answer? In such a case the infelicity must be known to the addressee since it is his own access to the answer that falsifies the speaker's assumption. The experimental question then becomes: given a speech act for which the felicity conditions have not been met, how does the child proceed?

The data presented here suggest that children

within this age range are able to skirt the infelicitous assumption. They make the inference
that the speaker who requests, literally and directly, that the child ask someone else a question, is trying indirectly to acquire information.[1]

The children who know and tell can be said to
apply Grice's conversational dictum (1975), "be
perspicuous." Instead of following the full
scenario that the speaker apparently intended,
(asking the question and waiting for someone else
to provide the answer), they skip one step and
hasten the arrival at the goal of getting an answer.

The relevance of the hearer's state of knowledge

When one applies the proposed pragmatic interpretation of ask-tell confusion to Chomsky's original data, some puzzles still remain. In Chomsky's
protocols there are examples such as the following:

Experimenter: Ask Linda what time it is.

Barbara (5;3): I don't know.

Experimenter: Ask Linda her last name.

Barbara: La Croix (1969, p. 63).

In this case the child fails to ask the question
even though she doesn't know the answer. This
type of example lends credence to Chomsky's and
Clark's interpretation that the child is making
errors at the lexical level and simply doesn't
understand the meaning of the word ask. In any
case one couldn't entirely rule out this possibility on the basis of the performance of a different set of subjects in a differently structured experiment. But the framework of speech-
act theory under which the present experiment
was conducted offers an alternative way of looking at this type of example. The child's response
does indicate confusion, but perhaps not on the
purely lexical level. The experimenter has requested the subject, in a series of non-sequiturs,
on the one hand to ask questions for some of which

366

he or the subject already knows the answer, and conversely, to tell things about which the subject may have no knowledge. If the child is trying to make sense of the interaction, he/she might simply get confused in general. It is hard to continue to make sense in situations like the following (if one is trying to make sense of them as interactions rather than treating them as senseless routines):

> Experimenter: Ask Susan what color this book is.
>
> Chris (5;1): Blue.
>
> Experimenter: And will you ask me my name.
>
> Chris: I don't know.
>
> (Susan interjects: What's your name?)
>
> Experimenter: It's Mrs. Chomsky. Susan just asked me what my name is. Can you ask me now?
>
> Chris: Mrs. Chomsky
>
> Experimenter: I think you told me what my name is. Will you tell me my name?
>
> Chris: Mrs. Chomsky.
>
> Experimenter: M-hm . . .

This particular fragment is admittedly an extreme example, but it reveals the existing potential for confusion. The experimenter after all is asking the child to ask her and tell her her own name.

An earlier fragment from the same interview shows a similar pattern:

> Experimenter: Ask Susan what time it is now.
>
> Chris: What time is it?

(Susan: I don't know).

Experimenter: It's ten o'clock (1969, p. 64).

Here the subject correctly asked the question,
only to discover that while the other child didn't
know the answer, the experimenter, who posed the
question, knew it all along.

The fact that the children in these "conversations" do consider the state of participants'
knowledge relevant to what is happening is shown
by other fragments from the protocols (in this
case from the same two children quoted above):

Experimenter: Ask Linda what's in this box.

Barbara: I don't know.

Experimenter: Could you ask Linda? Maybe
              Linda knows.

Barbara: Do you, Linda? (1969, p. 63)

              or

Experimenter: Ask Susan what's in this box.

Chris: I don't know.

Experimenter: Ask her. Maybe she knows.

Chris: Do you know? (1969, p. 64)

(The answer in both cases, incidentally, was no).

The pragmatic context of the language acquisition experiment

There is one additional catch in this treatment of children's linguistic performance. An
apparent semantic error has been re-interpreted
as a correct way of responding from a pragmatic
point of view by invoking rules that apply in ordinary conversational interaction. The catch
is that Chomsky's study, and the one reported here,

are not ordinary conversational interactions. They are language acquisition experiments. In this unusual context the experimenter's request for the subject to ask someone a question is not in fact a sincere attempt to get the information that the question pertains to, but rather a request for the subject to demonstrate linguistic knowledge.

In Chomsky's experiment the child was not supposed to apply ordinary rules for interpreting the speaker's intentions, but to behave, contrary to ordinary practice, as though speakers mean what they say, and exactly what they say. ("When I say ask, you ask.")

So, in effect, we have come full circle. The children who "tell" in response to the instruction to ask are still making an error. But the nature of the error has changed. Instead of reflecting a disparity between child and adult syntax and/or lexicon, it reflects a disparity between child and adult interpretations of the experiment as a discourse framework.

Children who actually relay the questions even when they know the answers to them demonstrate not only syntactic and semantic knowledge but a high order of pragmatic knowledge. They prove that they have realized that in this peculiar situation the rules of ordinary conversation have been de-activated.

Footnote

[1]The claim is not being made here that the speaker intends his utterance to pose a query to H_1. This would be a necessary condition for treating the utterance as having the illocutionary force of a question. Rather the utterance has the perlocutionary effect of making H_1 believe that the speaker seeks a particular bit of information.

References

Austin, J. How to do things with words. New York: Oxford University Press, 1962.

Chomsky, C. The acquisition of syntax in children from 5 to 10. Cambridge: MIT, 1969.

Clark, E. What's in a word? On the child's acquisition of semantics in his first language. In T. Moore (Ed.), Cognitive development and the acquisition of language. New York: Academic Press, 1973.

Dore, J. "Oh them Sheriff": A pragmatic analysis of children's responses to questions. In S. Ervin-Tripp and C. Mitchell Kernan (Eds.), Child Discourse. New York: Academic Press, 1977.

Garvey, C. Requests and responses in children's speech. Journal of Child Language, 1975, 2, 41-64.

Grice, H. P. Logic and conversation. In P. Cole and J. Morgan, Syntax and semantics, New York: Academic Press, 1975, 3.

Holzman, M. Use of interrogative forms in the verbal interaction of three mothers and their children. Journal of Psycholinguistic Research, 1972, 1, 311-336.

Reeder, K. The emergence of illocutionary skills. Journal of Child Language, 1980, 7, 13-28.

Searle, J. Speech acts. New York: Cambridge University Press, 1969.

Searle, J. Indirect speech acts. In P. Cole and J. Morgan, Syntax and semantics. New York: Academic Press, 1975, 3.

Shatz, M. How children respond to language: Procedures for answering. Papers and Reports on Child Language Development, No. 10, Palo Alto, California: Stanford University Press, 1975.

Table 1

Distribution of responses according to whether

subject knows the answers to the questions

Age (in months)	Subject knows answer			Subject doesn't know answer	
		Number of ask responses		Age	Number of ask responses
65		0		71	5
66		0		79	5
88		5		91	5
98		0		94	3
114		0		104	4
117		0		107	5
		$\overline{X}_1 = .83*$			$\overline{X}_2 = 4.5*$

*$\underline{p} < .005$, one-tail

A FUNCTIONAL ANALYSIS OF NATURAL LANGUAGE IN PRE-SCHOOL CHILDREN

Hans Vejleskov

The Royal Danish School of Educational Studies,
101, Emdrupvej. DK-2400 Copenhagen NV.

Preface

The research work presented here had not come into existence without the enthusiastic contribution
of colleages and students at my school and at The
Advanced Teacher College for Special Education in
Oslo, Norway.

I especially want to mention Palma Sjøvik who observed and analyzed the 3600 utterances of groups
No.'s 1-3 in Trondheim, Norway, and Liv Vedeler
who used and bettered the observation method as
part of a study of handicapped children in normal
kindergartens in Oslo, cf. group 4 in Table II below.

The observations

The research work presented here continues the one
presented at The Congress for the Study of Child
Language in Tokyo 1978.

Only data from communications like that in Fig. I
are discussed. They take place between three or
four 4-6 year old children. An adult person, i.e.
the pre-school teacher or the observer, may be either a rather active participant, or she may be
rather passive. One of the children may be a handicapped or disadvantaged child, e.g., with mental
retardation, with emotional disturbances, with delayed language development, or with a very bad
pronounciation.

The unit of recording and analysis is the individual utterance. Each utterance is characterized in
several respects:

372

THE UNIT OF ANALYSIS

- THE UTTERANCE PROVOKED BY/ DIRECTED TO/ ANSWERED BY ....?

- WHAT DOES IT TELL SOMETHING ABOUT?

- WHICH FUNCTION DOES IT HAVE?

- IS THAT FUNCTION EXPLICIT ?

- ARE OTHER EXPRESSIONS OF SIGNIFICANCE?

FIG. 1.   THE UNIT OF ANALYSIS

1) Its place in the communication pattern:
   - who, if any, did provoke it?
   - to whom, if any, was it directed? (Who is the intended listener(s)?)
   - who, if any, did answer it?

2) Its content:
   - what was the utterance a proposition about, - and how was this related to the content earlier in that communication sequence?

3) Its function:
   - what was the utterance intended to bring about?

4) Its "functional explicitness":
   - in which degree and in which way was the very function directly made explicit in the utterance?

5) Its dependence on other means of expression:
   - were gestures, mimics, glances, etc., of any significance?

Thus it appears that the task of the observers primarily is that of making interpretations of the children's motives or intentions, taking their activities and the whole context into consideration.

The data material

Table II presents the data material recorded and analyzed so far by means of the revised model that defers from the model for observation and categorization used in 1978.

For reasons of simplification, certain rather uniform situations (or sequences of communication) have been combined so that only the following types of situation are distinguished (left hand column in Table II):

374

- PLAY 1: The children mostly were engaged in family roleplay. However, the type of play might change in some periods.

- EATING: The children were sitting (or were supposed to sit) around a table having their lunch.

- DRESSING: The children were helped getting their outdoor things on or off.

- PLAY 2: The children mostly were constructing something of big toy bricks. Sometimes this activity was combined with role play. One child with language and social difficulties was usually keeping to himself.

- PLAY 3: This was one situation with a rather wild roleplay.

- PLAY 4: The children were sitting around a table working with plastcine.

The columns show the following figures:

1:      Number of the individual group of children.

2:      The total number of children in that group.

3:      The number of "handicapped" or "disadvantaged" children in the group.

4:      The total number of utterances in the various types of situation.

5:      The percent of utterances produced by adult persons (teacher or observer).

6:      The per cent of utterances which were 1) produced by one of the children, 2) directed to another child in the group and 3) adequately answered by that child.

375

COLUMN:	1	2	3	4	5	6
ˣ PLAY 1ᴀ				392	27	16
ˣ PLAY 1ʙ	1	3	1	351	6	31
EATING ᴀ				513	36	19
DRESSING ᴀ				332	46	6
PLAY 1ᴄ	2	3	1	250	8	29
DRESSING ʙ				118	46	0
ˣ PLAY 2				978	2	59
ˣ PLAY 3				185	1	22
EATING ʙ	3	3	2	228	19	36
EATING ᴄ				90	6	35
DRESSING ᴄ				207	24	28
				3644	-	-
				125	18	16
PLAY 4	4	3	2	57	26	-
				76	47	5
				70	0	13
				328	-	-
EATING ᴅ	5	6	0	170	17	28
				149	5	34
				319	-	-

TABLE II. DATA RECORDED AND ANALYZED USING REVISED MODEL

Some results concerning communication patterns.

The following tendencies are easily observed:

The teacher of group No. 3 is clearly less inclined to talk herself than the teacher of groups
No.'s 1 and 2 (which belong to the same kindergarten).

In general, when the adult persons are passive
(small figure in column 5), the children are more

376

frequently communicating in an effective way
(large) figure in column. 6).

The kind of activity obviously affects the frequency of proper communication among the children.

Studying more closely the four play situations
marked with an ⁕ in Table II, FIG III a-b shows
the pattern of communication in group No. 1.

The ⁕ at child No. 3 indicates that this 5;2 year
old girl is considered socially and linguistically
immature. The figures are the per cent of the total amount of utterances made in the particular
situation directed by each person to each of the
other persons. In addition is shown for each person the per cent of utterances that are not directed to any particular person, and - in brackets -
the per cent of utterances that are egocentric, i.
e., that are seemingly not intended to influence
any listener.

Fig. III a shows the distribution of the 392 utterances of group No. 1 in a play situation where
the teacher is rather active, whereas Fig. III b
deals with the 351 utterances of the same group
during the same kind of family role-play when the
teacher is absent or very passive.

It is observed that child No. 1 (a 4;0 year old
girl) to a certain extent substitutes the teacher
in the last situation as the one communicating
with the handicapped child No. 3. Furthermore, No.
1 and No. 2 do communicate more with each other
when the teacher is passive or absent. Finally, it
surprisingly appears that the amount of egocentric
speech increases in all children as the teacher
does not take part in the communication.

Fig. IV a-b shows in the same manner the per cent
distributions of utterances made by group 3 during
construction play mixed with role-play (IV a: 978
utterances) and during wild play (IV b: 185 utterances). Both child No. 1 and child No. 3 are considered having language or communication difficul-

377

Figure III. DISTRIBUTION OF UTTERANCES OF GROUP 1

a. Active Teacher
   392 utterances

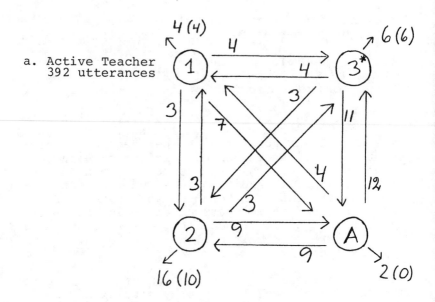

b. Passive or
   Absent Teacher
   351 utterances

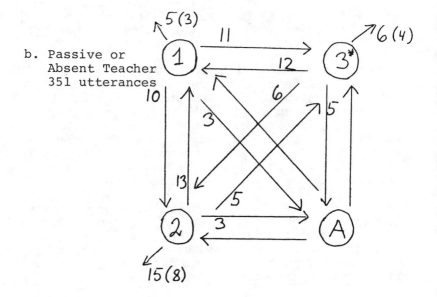

FIG. IV. DISTRIBUTION OF UTTERANCES OF GROUP 3

a. Construction
   and Role-Play

   978 utterances

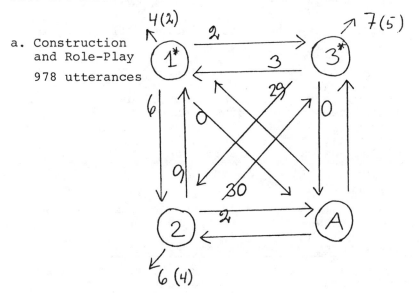

b. Wild Play
   185 utterances

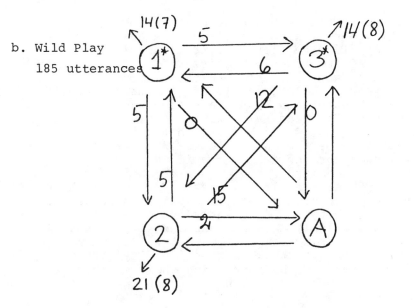

ties. However, only No. 1 is a rather isolated play mate; No. 3 frequently communicates with No. 2 despite his poor pronounciation. All the children are boys aged 5-5½ years.

Moving from the friendly atmosphere in the first type of situation to the wild play in the other, the frequency of utterances not directed to a particular person (including egocentric speech) significantly increases. On the other hand, the lively communication between No. 2 and No. 3 decreases, whereas No. 3 more frequently talks with (i. e., appeals to) No. 1.

It is mentioned that neither Fig. III nor Fig. IV show how often utterances from one person to another person are answered by that other person.

Some results concerning language functions

Due to lack of time and space, we will only consider group 3 in the type of situation shown in Fig. IV a, as we now proceed to exemplify the analysis of language functions (or motives).

To the left in Table V we present the per cent distribution of each child's utterances according to a simplified categorization, discriminating between 10 functions or motives. (Originally the utterances were put into one out of 23 categories). The rather isolated child No. 1 most frequently uses an utterance with the (often egocentric) function No. 2 and also with the No. 7-function to hold his own. Child No. 2 with the best language abilities is the one who most frequently expresses/provokes feelings (function No. 6) and states a fact for himself or for one of the other children. Finally child No. 3, who despite of his poor language does play and talk well with No. 2, is the one that most frequently produces utterances which seemingly have no function, i.e., word play, singing or play sounds. In that way he makes his contribution to the construction play with No. 2. So he also does by supporting their activity and by being eager to tell No. 2 something (functions No.'s 3 and 9).

380

SPEAKER INTENDS TO	CHILD NO. 1	2	3	1: 2	1: 3	2: 1	2: 3	3: 1	3: 2
1) PLAY/SING	6	6	13	0	0	1	1	0	2
2) SUPPORT/PLAN OWN ACTIVITY	17	10	8	10	19	6	8	3	7
3) SUPPORT/PLAN OWN GROUP'S ACT.	15	18	16	22	10	(20)	22	(6)	21
4) SUPPORT/INSTRUCT OTHERS	0	4	2	0	0	6	4	6	3
5) HAVE SMTH. (DONE)	7	6	5	3	5	6	7	18	5
6) EXPRESS/PROVOKE EMOTIONS	8	16	9	8	5	22	15	26	8
7) HOLD HIS OWN	16	8	7	15	28	5	11	15	8
8) STATE A FACT	16	21	16 }	32	24	(28)	29	(9)	34
9) TELL ABOUT SMTH.	11	6	12 }						
10) BE INFORMED	0	4	4	0	0	5	2	9	4
?	6	1	8	8	10	1	2	9	9
N:	119	462	282	59	21	85	294	34	280

TABLE V.   DISTRIBUTION (%) OF EACH CHILD'S UTTERANCES ACCORDING TO FUNCTIONAL TYPE

To the right in Table V we show the corresponding distributions of the same children's utterances in such a way that we distinguish according to listener. For instance, 59 of the 119 utterances produced by child No. 1 are directed to child No. 2 and only 21 to child No. 3 (The remaining 39 utterances are directed to the teacher or to the whole group, - or they are directed to nobody).

It is obvious that the use of language, i.e., the functions of the utterances or the motives of the individual speaker, vary significantly according to who is the receiver. For instance, child No. 2 is far more inclined to talk to the "weak" child no. 1 about the activities going on (function No. 3) and about certain facts (function No. 9) than is child No. 3, - c.f. the figures marked with a circle.

The functions also vary significantly according to type of situation as well as in correspondance with "the communicative status" of the utterance, - i.e., whether it is egocentric or "socialized", and whether it is answered or not.

THE CHILD INTENDS TO	UTTERANCES THAT ARE			N	% EXPLI- CIT MOTIVE
	TO SOMEBODY AND ANSWERED	TO SOMEBODY BUT NOT ANSWERED	EGO- CENTRIC		
1) PLAY/SING	1	2	61	30	0
2) SUPPORT/PLAN OWN ACTIVITY	7	14	23	46	15
3) SUPPORT/PLAN OWN GROUP'S ACT.	20	18	3	84	25
4) SUPPORT/INSTRUCT OTHERS	4	4	0	17	6
5) HAVE SMTH. (DONE)	7	6	0	27	37
6) EXPRESS/PROVOKE EMOTIONS	15	22	3	72	0
7) HOLD HIS OWN	11	3	0	37	3
8) STATE A FACT 9) TELL ABOUT SMTH.	30	27	10	126	0
10) BE INFORMED	5	3	0	19	0
?	1	1	0	4	0
N:	303	˙120	39	462	86

TABLE VI. DISTRIBUTION (%) OF CHILD 2's UTTERANCES ACCORDING TO THEIR COMMUNICATIVE STATUS

As an example we show in Table VI the per cent
distributions of child No. 2's utterances according to their "communicative status".

To the right in the same table is shown for each
functional category the per cent of utterances in
which this clever 5-year old child made his intention more or less explicite.

So far, this presentation is only a brief exem-
plification of some few analyses that can be performed on the basis of the data material described
above. A more detailed and complete - and yet
clear and understandable - presentation will hope-
fully soon be published.

Discussion

Although this research work has been carried out
during a period of several years, it is still considered a pilot study because of the obvious theoretical as well as practical problems one faces
when one tries to observe and describe what a
child means by producing a certain utterance in a
certain situation.

Even the terms "utterance" and "situation" give
rise to difficulties. For instance, it is by no
means easy to define a "situation", i.e., to determine the kind and amount of change that makes
one "situation" become another "situation". -
Neither is the term "free play" - which so frequently is used to describe situations observed
in pragmatic child language studies - an unambiguous one; on the contrary we found clear variations as to social structure and communication
pattern, and accordingly, also with respect to
language function, during a "free play situation".

With respect to function (or motive or intention),
it is equally clear that any categorization must
be arbitrary. As mentioned above, the observers
could choose among 23 different functions, and in
addition, they had the opportunity to record a
"secondary function" when they felt that a child
did aim at two things by his production of a cer-

tain utterance. In this **particular** presentation we
have combined several categories so that only 10
are distinguished. If however, other kinds of situations were observed, or if some specific problem were the object of our investigation, we
would probably make other combinations and so use
another series of function categories.

For example, if we want to focus upon the phenomena discussed by Susan R. Braunwald in her paper at
the Vancouver Congress 1981, a distinction should
be made between utterances by which the speaker
intends to help another person make himself understandable on the one hand, and on the other hand,
utterances by which he intends to support or in-
struct the listener with respect to his activity.
Further, one could also record utterances by which
the speaker intends to make himself more clear,
cf. the papers read by Judy Reilly and McTear at
the same congress.

The observations made so far have focussed upon
small groups of pre-school children occupied with
usual kindergarten activities. They have served
the general purpose of examine whether it is at
all possible to establish such categorizations and
so describe children's language pragmatically,
i.e., in terms of functions. A further, more specific purpose, has been to study language as an important aspect of the total interaction in such
groups of children with or without an active teacher, and with or without children with language
problems.

One future goal might be to define a set of rather
few, mutually exclusive functions to serve as a
conceptual apparatus for teachers (and parents)
that enables them to attend to this aspect of language, just as the concepts and categorizations of
traditional grammar enable them to characterize
the formal aspects of children's language. However, before such a simple and general classification can be tried, it is necessary not only to
analyze the existing data material in greater detail, but also to study other kinds of situation.

Obvious objects for such future investigations are the functions of utterances produced by one or more children when solving a kind of problem with or without guidance from an adult person, - or when being taught various kinds of subject by means of various kinds of teaching method.

The former may be a fruitful approach to the classical problem of the relationship between thought and language: To ask the question how children at various levels of cognitive development actually do use language when thinking. The latter may be a fruitful approach to the educational problems of one-way-communication dominating in the classroom and of certain "codes" used in teaching but not available to some children.

References

"Psycholinguistic Descriptions and their Relevance to Education I-III". Scand. Journ. Educ. Research, vol. 20, 1976 and vol. 21, 1977.

"Theory of Language Functions and Observations of Children's Use of Language".

a. Paper read at The First International Congress for the Study of Child Language, Tokyo, 1978.

b. More extensive, mimeographed version, The Royal Danish School of Educational Studies, 1978.

"Language, Acting and Personality". In: Auditory Training of Hearing Impaired Pre-School Children. (Proceedings from the 9th Danavox Symposium). Scand. Audiol. Suppl. 10. Ed. by Leo Marckmann, Copenhagen, 1980.

Different ways of explanation in two social classes:
story telling to children from 18 to 36 months

Maria Silvia Barbieri - Antonella Devescovi
University of Trieste - Italy

In the psychological research of the last
fifteen years a primary role has been given to
child-adult interaction as a means for the acquisition of a broad communicative competence (pragmatics), or as a means for the acquisition of a
more restricted linguistic competence (syntax,
semantics). In this perspective the complex relationships between maternal input and language development in the child have been investigated.

Less studied seems to be the mother's input
in a field of great relevance to a child's comprehension and use of language, i.e., discourse comprehension which implies the understanding of the
relationships between sentences or between sentences
and words of the discourse and the knowledge--more
or less organized--the child masters about the
world. Such knowledge allows him to decode and to
connect in a cognitive network what he hears.

In this direction cognitive models of discourse
comprehension offer stimulating suggestions:
they mainly stress the necessity of integration of
the meaning of the single sentence and maintain
that such an integration stems from the mastery of
what we call encyclopaedia by the listener. By
this term, we mean, with Castelfranchi and Parisi
(1980), a set of integrated knowledge socially
shared about the world and the language, allowing
the listener to reconstruct by inference also what
is not plainly stated.

But what happens when the two speakers do not
share the same competence? When the former is less
cognitively advanced than the other and his encyclopaedia is not yet complete, or in any way different from that of the adult partner? We assume that
a cognitive model of comprehension--qua cognitive--
presupposes the coincidence of two minds, i.e.,

the fact that the plan of the discourse and the connections of the events that are represented in the mind of the speaker are reconstructed in the mind of the listener. But when the two partners do not share the same competence, it becomes necessary for the more advanced partner to consider how structured the mind of the listener is and adapt to it (selecting or partially changing what is given in the text).

In a story telling situation, it is also possible that the effort of making himself understood elicits in the adult a true teaching behavior because, in the need to expose a sequence of events, the adult must use specific words or mention situations that, being unknown or only partially known to the child, must be clearly explained. In this context adapting to the child and teaching him are indistinguishable, as adaptation presupposes a more explicit language which imparts information about the world to the child and shows him the rules of usage of the acquired knowledge.

Furthermore we think that the different ways in which the adaptation appears and the explanations are given allow us to infer what the assumptions of the speaker are concerning the mind of the listener, by means of the cognitive meaning we assigned to the use of different kinds of explaining behavior.

In our study we chose a situation of story telling that we knew from previous research (Barbieri, Devescovi 1982) to fit quite well to our purposes. And as we hypothesized that the way explanations are given tell us something about the representation the speaker has of the mind of the listener, we tried to analyze the differences in the way the mother talked, according to the age of the child (18 to 36 months) and according to the sociocultural level of the mother (high or low).

It is a well known fact in developmental psychology that children from low socio-cultural backgrounds have a poorer linguistic development and that they show, both in comprehension and production, a narrower vocabulary and a limited mastery of syntactic devices. This phenomenon appears from the earliest ages: from two years in the lexicon and from three years in syntax (for Italian data, see Parisi 1977). More recent research has also pointed out that these linguistic difficulties do not concern only isolated sentences, as were those tested in the former research, but affect as well the understanding of full texts, i.e., short stories and plain discourses--the kind of competence most relevant for everyday life. Lumbelli and Salvadori (1977), for instance, tested the comprehension of short stories in three- to five-year-old children from two social classes and found that low social class children do not grasp the main cognitive nodes of the story and fail to distinguish facts that are important from unessential details.

In current research such a poor linguistic development is usually related to the mother's linguistic input and to her ways of interaction; and though we are conscious that the relationship between maternal input and the child linguistic development is not so direct and immediate as our proposition suggests, we nevertheless accept this hypothesis and consider maternal input one of the factors influencing the linguistic evolution of the child. We want now to go a little further and try to reconstruct from the behavior of the mother the representation of the mind of the child from which her behavior stems. We want also to try to define the possible consequences of her way of explanation (quantity and quality) for the child's construction of a representation of the world socially shared.

Types of explanation

We call explanation any kind of information given by the speaker which allows the listener to

understand any other information contained in the
discourse (i.e. the meaning of a linguistic expression or the linking of events in a sequence).

In the context of telling a story we consider two main categories of explanation: explanations linking together two events of the
story (between events) and explanations relating
to the connection between lexicon and encyclopaedia.

a) Explanations between events. The explanations of this type concern the events in the
story: the adult connects two events of the story
by a relationship of cause/effect or goal/mean.
In this way the occurrence of a certain event is
explained as a consequence of a previous one.
(Example: "Mummy is taking his temperature because he hurt himself"). This type of explanation can connect two events which occur in different pictures or in the same picture.

b) Explanations concerning the connection
between lexicon and encyclopaedia. These
are what we properly call explanations for integration (Castelfranchi, Parisi 1980) because the
speaker seems to give them with the goal of allowing the listener to set in his encyclopaedia what
he is told by the partner. They do not concern
the link between events in the story, but they
connect some entity of the story with the possible
knowledge the child has about the topics mentioned
by the mother. All the explanations belonging to
this class are the most important to our research
as they pertain both to the formation and to the
organization of the child's encyclopaedia, and to
the acquisition of rules and strategies for the
use of the encyclopaedia in the process of comprehension.

We divide this class of explanations into
three main categories, each one suggesting a different hypothesis about the progressive increase
of the child's encyclopaedia.

The first type (classifying) is useful for the construction of classes of knowledge that can be recalled by means of verbal labels with their corresponding definitions.

The second type (examples) has the aim of filling the classes with single entities possessing the defining characteristics of the class.

The third type (cues) gives the rules of access to the classes already defined.

- Classifying. These explanations promote the attribution of a defined linguistic label (name, verb, phrase) to an object, an action or an event of the story.

They can simply state--via the verbal label--one to one connections between the considered object and a class of knowledge consisting, in some cases, of one entity only (perhaps the one just seen in the story). In such a case we get a simple labelling, i.e. the statement that a certain entity belongs to a certain class, through a linguistic expression like "This is a..." (example: "This is a tree"). Such expression simply connects a sequence of sound (the name of the object) with the object examined: both the object and its name can be new for the child, i.e. the adult hasn't any presupposition about the possible previous knowledge of the child and behaves as if he had to form a new connection linking the object and his name in the child's mind.

But these explanations can also enlarge and semantically quality the verbal label attributed to the object considered.

In such a case they are true definitions, giving information about the peculiar characteristics of the entity labelled by a certain word (example: "This is a squirrel. It is an animal with a long tail").

They can also be <u>paraphrases</u>, i.e. substitution of a label or of an expression not familiar to the child with an easier one (Example: "It doesn 't hurt anymore, he doesn't <u>cry ouch, ouch, ouch</u>"). In this case the adult presupposes that the child knows, at least, an analogous object or situation, but that he doesn't know the linguistic label socially appropriate. Therefore the adult recalls the previous knowledge of the child and adds the correct name to it.

In conclusion, both in the case of naming and in the case of definitions and paraphrases the cognitive work carried out by the adult concerns the possibility of learning verbal labels referring to the various classes of knowledge. What changes, instead, in the two cases are the adult's presuppositions concerning the previous knowledge of the child. In this sense naming can be considered a more primitive strategy than the one implied with definitions and paraphrases.

-<u>Examples</u>. In this case the speaker compares the entity to be explained with another entity belonging to the same class and thought by the adult to be familiar to the child. The explaining link does not connect directly the object and its pertaining class, but connects the object that is mentioned and another object that is considered to be an example of that class (example: "<u>This is the bed. Look at this nice little blue bed just like yours</u>").

When we give examples to the child we assume: a) that he knows the relation between the object used as term of comparison and its name; b) that he can form classes containing more than one entity--no matter how different--if they all share the defining characteristics of the class. Therefore the new object is compared with the old one already familiar to the child and the class is, in this way, enlarged, while, in order to give paraphrases and definitions a single individual is sufficient enough for the constitution of the class of knowledge the speaker is referring to. In this sense the explanations via example can be considered as operations producing real improvement in the classes of knowledge included in the encyclopaedia.

-<u>Cues</u>. By means of these explanations the child is given information about the characteristics an object must have in order to be classified or labelled in a determined way; they are therefore rules of access to the classes of knowledge. They state the connection between the classes and the objects that show--in certain contexts--definite characteristics. (Example: <u>"This owl must be the doctor, look, this is a bandage"</u>). As we see by the example, the cues can be used as a basis for the inference that gives access to the encyclopaedia only if considered in the context they belong to: the fact that a certain character has a bandage in his hand is not sufficient--per se--to allow the attribution of the doctor's role to such an individual, but it can become sufficient if we consider this character in the context of a story where there is another character needing to be attended to, and that is represented in the same picture with a big bandage around his foot.

When we tell a child a story illustrating a book without a written text, it is very important to make explicit these kinds of rules, as the story, i.e. the series of events in which the characters play definite roles in definite places, must be entirely inferred from the cues given by individual pictures or by their order. By explaining clearly the rules through which the mother assumes a certain knowledge from a pictorial cue, she renders the child capable of reading the same book by himself at a later date.

More generally we think that the mastery of rules of inference of this kind promotes the appearance of autonomous processes of comprehension in the child; being rules, they are productive (every time you see an 'x' having, in the context 'y' the characteristic 'z', you can call it a 'q'), and can be used in many different situations. In

392

conclusion, while the two former types of explanation in this class seem to concern the construction of the encyclopaedia, this last type implies the presupposition, on the adult's part, that the child has an encyclopaedia already structured--at least partially--where there are classes of knowledge concerning the entities and their defining characteristics.

These classes are also assumed to be already linguistically labelled by the appropriate word. The adult teaches the child the cognitive task of scanning the object (or situation) in order to find out those features that, in the context examined, allow the recognition of the pertaining class of the object and the subsequent attribution of its linguistic label. This seems to be the most advanced cognitive strategy and the one which favours, in the child, the autonomous use of the acquired knowledge.

Subjects and methodology

Subjects of our research were 16 mother-child pairs. Eight pairs belonged to the middle upper class: both parents had high school or university education and their jobs were adequate to the cultural level (teachers, professionals, academic people). In this group we had four child-subjects, two males and two females, at two age levels: 18 to 24 months and 30 to 36 months.

The remaining eight pairs were from the low sociocultural class: both parents had the minimum level of education and were employed as unskilled workers. In this group we had the same age and sex distribution as in the former.

Every mother-child pair was videotaped in real time in an observation session. Mother and child, at home, sat on a sofa or at a table, as they were used to, and looked at the book. The tapes have been transcribed in a very detailed way and every subsequent analysis has been made from these transcripts.

The story

As in a previous research study (Barbieri and Devescovi 1982), the story was made out of seven drawings collected in a booklet. It is the story of a squirrel which, running through a meadow, stumbles on a stone. He hurts himself in the fall and is helped by a rabbit. He is healed by an owl and, after some time, recovers.

The fact that the story is without any written text and must be reconstructed inferentially allows the mother to tell it as she feels best for her child. She assigns roles to the characters and reconstructs their intentions according to the hypothesis she has of the comprehending possibilities of her partner.

Procedures of analysis and results

SPEECH ACTS

First we coded in every transcript the speech acts of the mother in order to distinguish between speech acts concerning the story (SSA) and speech acts concerning the interaction (SA). Such a distinction had two goals. Firstly it gave an idea of the way the mother used the situation. We attributed more or less cognitive emphasis on the mother's part depending on the proportion of speech acts concerning the story to the total of speech acts performed during the interaction. We treated this as an indication of how apt the mother considers the situation to the transmission of knowledge.

Secondly, as our main aim was the detection of the variations in the explanations depending on the age of the child and on the socio-cultural level of the mother, our distinction allowed a more reliable analysis of the data. We compared the number of different types of explanation to the number of other speech acts concerning the story performed by the mother. In fact, the more the mother spoke the more explanations linking the lexicon with the encyclopaedia were likely to be produced. Therefore it was

394

important to find a way of making comparisons between the different groups of mothers, no matter how long they talked.

As we said above we had two groups of speech acts; in the former group--speech acts concerning the interaction--we put those acts whose aim was to open or to maintain the interaction with the child: calling for attention, requesting actions (example: to turn the pages), requesting comments, assenting or denying the statements or the behavior of the child more or less appropriate to the situation, making requests relating to the situation itself, or vocalizing to the child.

In the second group--speech acts concerning the story--we put those acts whose aim was the construction and the explanation of the story: pointing to the pictures, naming objects or actions, repeating, expanding, describing events, making comments related to the story (example: "Look how long the ears of the rabbit are"), giving explanations both linking the events or pertaining to the relationships between lexicon and encyclopaedia, asking questions relating to the events or to the characters of the story, and moralizing.

In table 1 we can see the distribution of the two types of speech acts for younger (18 to 24 months) and older children (30 to 36 months) in the two socio-cultural classes.

Table 1 about here

As we can see ISA is found more in the Low Social Class (Low SC) (219 is 65% of 336), while the SSA are exactly divided between the two social groups (456 is 47% of 960). Inside the two groups this trend is even more evident. In the Low SC the ISA compose 32% of the total linguistic acts performed by the mother (219 is 32% of 674); instead, in the Middle SC the ISA compose only 18% of the total (117 is 18% of 262). The differences in the distribution of the two types of Speech Acts in the four groups considered are significant to the X^2 test (X^2 = 33,38; gl.3;

p < .001). We interpret these data as signifying a different emphasis given to the didactic situation in the two groups of status: more conspicuous in the higher one and less evident in the lower.

Looking now at the frequency distribution in every age group, interesting trends will appear. Mothers in the Low SC seem to consider it more worthwhile to speak to older childrena and less to the younger ones, but the ration of the ISA to the SSA remains unchanged in the two groups. We interpret these data in the sense that in this socio-cultural group older children are assumed to be more proficient in comprehending the language, and this assumption explains why the mother is talking more. Mothers however consider this greater comprehension in a very general sense, only as a greater mastery of the verbal medium, and this could explain the unchanged ratio between the two types of speech acts in the two age groups.

The Middle SC has a different distribution: here mothers speak more to the younger children and less to the older ones: furthermore ISA are 22% of the total for the younger group (84 is 22% of 378) and drop to 13% in the older. In our opinion mothers in this group give a different meaning to the situation and are more confident in the comprehending possibilities of the child. They think that children even if preverbal, or very scarcely verbal, can understand the mother's language provided the interacting devices are adequate to the communicative competence of the child, and this explains the need of speaking more both in respect to the situation itself and to the pictures. The older group then, is assumed to be acquainted with the story telling context and to master the language rules; this gives the mother the possibility of being more concise, focusing on the story and on the pictures and putting aside the interaction itself.

EXPLANATIONS

Overall explanations are 318: 152 (48%) in the Low SC and 166 (52%) in the Middle SC. They are exactly divided in the two groups of status and do not differ very much also in the two age groups. We have 139 (43%) for the younger children and 179 (57%) for the older ones. Therefore groups do not differ in the quantity of explanations, but in the quality of them, i.e. a different distribution of types of explanation inside the groups.

To emphasize this phenomenon we shall henceforth consider the distribution of the different types of explanations and of the remaining number of other SSA pertaining to each group. A X^2 test calculated on these data yielded a significant difference in the distribution of the different types of explanations in the four groups ($X^2 = 37, 69$; gl. 15; p < .001).

In order to understand these differences we considered separately each single type of explanation.

Explanations between events

As we can see from Table 2 this distribution does not present interesting differences. The percentage of explanations is about the same in all the age and the status groups and the only significant difference is between older and younger children in the Middle SC ($X^2 = 4, 52$; gl. 1; p < .05 > .02).

Most interesting in differentiating the four groups are the explanations linking lexicon and encyclopaedia; i.e. the real linguistic and cognitive work made by the mother, as we shall see.

Explanations relating lexicon and encyclopaedia

We remind you that this class of explanations is divided into three categories: a) classifying, b) examples, c) cues; each category has a different cognitive meaning, therefore we shall examine each of them separately.

397

a) Classifying

-Naming. Let us first consider naming, a very primitive strategy of explanation, usually reserved for younger children. Although simple naming drops in the older age groups, both in the Low SC and in the Middle SC, the ratio in the Low SC is always significantly greater. The differences among the four groups in the distribution of naming compared to the other SSA is significant to a X^2 test (X^2 = 20,47; gl. 3; p < .001).

-Paraphrases and definitions. Though the distribution in the four groups does not present any significant difference (X^2 = 2,71; gl. 3; n.s.), we notice that the greatest frequency is in the younger group of the Middle SC. We also stress the fact that 25% of expressions in this category are translations from baby talk to adult language (example: nanna=dormire-to sleep; bibi=male-pain). This implies that Middle SC mothers are ready to accept the language of the child, but they also want him/her to know a less idiosyncratic expression for the same meaning.

b) Examples

From the distribution of these explanations in Table 2, we can notice the insensitivity on the part of the Low SC's mothers to the aging of the child. The percentages do not change in the two Low SC age groups, while they increase in a significant way in the Middle SC (a X^2 test comparing the four groups for examples and other SSA yields a significant difference: X^2 = 16,13; gl. 3; p < .01 > .001). This means that the increase of explanations in the Middle SC group with the aging of the child allows the children to receive far more information than their peers in the other socio-cultural class.

c) Cues

Finally we shall examine the use of cues. As we can

398

see in Table 2, cues increase with age in both groups of status, but they are significantly more in the Middle SC than in the Low SC. The differences among the four groups for cues and other SSA are significant to a X^2 test (X^2 = 14,9; gl.3; p < .01 > .001). This means that the rules of inference given by the mothers are much more conspicuous in one socio-cultural group than in the other: the Middle SC child is taught to use his encyclopaedia, the other is not, and this happens from the earliest ages.

Comments and conclusions

If we assume, as we do, that "examples" have the function of increasing the quantity of data placed in the encyclopaedia and that "cues" give the rules of access to such data and of its use, we can then say that in the Middle SC such work on the mind of the child is carried out earlier and with much greater care. In the Low SC we observe a great deal of simple naming in both groups of age, in the other class the information given to the child, mainly in the older group, is more various and complex.

Concerning this it is important to notice some differences in the usage of cues and examples in the two socio-cultural groups. In the Low SC we only had examples referring to the individual experiences of the child (example: The rabbit takes the squirrel in his arms as mummy takes you) and cues directly relating to the visual context (example: And this owl must be the doctor. Look at the bandage in his hand). In the group of older children of Middle SC we can find more general expressions, both for examples (example: The rabbit helps the squirrel, he takes him in his arms and he puts him to bed; i.e. the mother mentions some ways in which it is possible to help a hurt friend), and for cues (example: The squirrel isn't feverish anymore. So he has recovered hasn't he?). We therefore say that the language spoken to the older Middle SC children is more abstract.

What do our data mean in respect to the mother's representation of the mind of the child? Two facts must be considered. Firstly the fact that the preferred linguistic behavior for explanation in the Low SC is naming, which we hypothesized to be the most primitive strategy, the one that does not imply any assumption about previous knowledge in the child. Secondly the fact that this occurs in both groups of age of this sociocultural level. According to us this means that the idea mothers have of the mind of the child is more undifferentiated than the one appearing in the other socio-cultural group. The lack of definite assumptions about the way the mind of the child is structured make the mothers feel that the more elaborated explanations are useless as they are unlikely to be grasped by the child.

Such interpretation could also be supported by the analysis of the distribution of ISA and SSA in the two groups of status. Nevertheless it requires some caution, especially for the kind of cognitive activity we studied. We should remind you of the different meaning of the book reading situation in the two social classes as it comes from the mother's spontaneous comments during the observation session.

In the Low SC book reading is an unusual activity (see also Parisi 1977) especially with younger children who are considered unable to understand even very simple series of events and unable to interpret the pictures. Books are considered boring, unsuitable pastimes and the mothers who actually give them to their children say that they leave the child alone to turn the pages. In their words their children are "too young to understand...". They are not very confident in the possibilities of their children, therefore they adopt more primitive strategies of explanation (naming) with the aim of building a list of labels, without caring to fill with examples the classes they have built and without giving the child the possibility of an autonomous use of his knowledge (cues). Also the activity of the construction of

the story is careless: four mothers out of eight
in this group called the same object or character--
both in the same picture or in two different ones--
in a very different and confusing way. One mother
illustrating picture 1 named the stone the squirrel
stumbled against once "ball" and shortly after
"stone"; another one called the meadow once "meadow"
and once "field of snow"; a third mentioned the
rabbit in the third picture as "mummy of the squirrel" and in the fifth picture as "a nurse", and
lastly a fourth mother answering to a child who
did not realize that the squirrel in the first and
that in the second picture were the same character,
said that "Yes, there are two of them".

        The behavior of the mothers in the Middle SC
is very different, as it is shown by the attention
and by the time devoted to the construction of the
story and by the number and types of explanations.
Children in the Middle SC are used to looking at
books together with the parents and enjoy this activity. Mothers adapt to their children using and
translating idiosyncratic words (paraphrases) or
seleecting words carefully in order to make themselves understood. A mother called the squirrel
"mouse" because her child did not know what a
squirrel was; another one explicitly stated that
she would not explain a certain passage because the
child could not understand. Mothers are conscious
that the encyclopaedia of their children is not
yet formed, and, even if partially organized, will
not coincide with the adult encyclopaedia. Therefore they act in a very sensitive way in order to
attain two aims according to the age of the child:
firstly constructing a set of cognitive nodes corresponding to the names of the things (naming),
secondly elaborating the nodes and linking them
with other nodes to achieve a very organic and
suitable representation of the world that could allow the reconstruction and the integration of the
events of the story.

        It is interesting to remind you that the to-
tal number of explanations do not differ in the
two social groups and that we are therefore focus-

401

ing on two strategies of socialization. So, if we remember the data on discourse comprehension in children quoted at the beginning of this paper, we can connect them with the explaining strategies of the mother via the cognitive representation she has of the mind of her child. In the light of this, our interpretation could agree with that put forward by Tulkin and Cohler (1973) in a different perspective, as they consider the representation of the child one of the main factors affecting mothers' behavior.

References

BARBIERI M.S., DEVESCOVI A. (1981)- Strategie per farsi comprendere: come gli adulti raccontano una storia a bambini dai 18 ai 36 mesi, (submitted to Giornale Italiano di Psicologia).

CASTELFRANCHI C., PARISI D. (1980)- Linguaggio conoscenze e scopi, Bologna, Il Mulino.

LUMBELLI L., SALVADORI M. (1977)- Capire le storie, Milano, EMME Edizioni.

PARISI D. (1977)- Sviluppo del linguaggio e ambiente sociale, Firenze, La Nuova Italia.

TULKIN S.R., COHLER B.S. (1973)- Child rearing attitudes and mother-child interaction in the first year of life- Merrill Palmer Quarterly, 19, 95-106.

Table 1 - Distribution of the two types of speech acts in the four groups considered.

	Low SC Younger	Low SC Older	Low SC Total	Middle SC Younger	Middle SC Older	Middle SC Total	GENERAL TOTAL
Interactive Speech Acts	77	142	219	84	33	117	336
Story Speech Acts	171	284	456	294	211	505	960
Total Speech Acts	284	426	674	378	244	622	1296

$X^2 = 33,38$; gl. 3; p<.001

403

Table 2 – Distribution of explanation and other SSA in the four groups considered.

	EXPLANATIONS										Other S S A		TOT.	
	Between Events		Naming		Definitions Paraphrases		Examples		Cues					
	N.	%	N.	%	N.	%	N.	%	N.	%	N.	%	N.	%
LOWSC Younger	12	7,0	32	18,7	6	3,5	6	3,5	1	0,5	114	66,6	171	100
Older	25	8,8	36	12,6	13	4,5	12	4,2	9	3,1	189	66,5	284	100
MIDDLESC Younger	20	6,8	25	8,5	20	6,8	5	1,7	12	4	212	72,1	294	100
Older	26	12,3	11	5,2	11	5,2	19	9,9	17	8	127	60,1	211	100
TOT	83		104		50		42		39		642		960	

$X^2 = 37,69$; gl. 15; $p < .001$.

<u>PROPER NAME USAGE IN MATERNAL SPEECH:</u>
<u>A LONGITUDINAL STUDY</u>

Kevin Durkin, D.R. Rutter,
  Susan Room and Patricia Grounds,
Social Psychology Research Unit,
University of Kent at Canterbury,
England.

INTRODUCTION

The use of proper names is one of the distinguishing features of talk addressed to babies. Commonly, names are used where pronouns (or pronouns plus auxiliaries) would be used in adult-adult interactions, in expressions such as 'Amy do it' or 'Edward want one?' This is so common a feature of (English) baby talk that Roger Brown (1977:2) has asserted that it can reliably be identified as peculiar to this register by testing against the investigator's intuition. (There are at least two other contexts in which similar phenomena seem to occur: speech addressed to pets and to lovers.) Although the style is familiar and commented on by a variety of investigators, there seems to be little systematic investigation of its place in the grammatical organisation of linguistic input, of how it develops as an aspect of parental speech over time, and of its implications for the language learning infant. This paper is concerned centrally with a longitudinal study of mothers' use of proper names during the early stages of language acquisition. In addition, some suggestions and some illustrations of the broader organisational implications and consequences of the speech style will be put forward.

The present paper extends an earlier cross-sectional investigation of maternal use of proper names that we have conducted (Durkin, Rutter and Tucker, in press). In that study, we investigated the use of the child's name and of 'Mummy' by mothers playing with their infants aged 12, 18 and 24 months. We investigated both structural and functional aspects of proper name usage and, for present purposes, three main points can be made about the findings:

(i) maternal utterances containing the child's name were found, variously, to be syntactically correct or syntactically deviant by the standards of adult grammar: several mothers used *both* types during the same (15-minute) play session;

(ii) no differences according to the age or sex of the child were found in the type or frequency of name usage: that is, names were used ungrammatically as frequently at 24 months as at 12 months;

(iii) independent scorers reached an acceptable level of agreement (74%) on the *functions* of name usage by the mothers: most often, the child's name was used in the context of an *Instruction to Act* or an *Attention-orienting* utterance.

We argued, following Newport, Gleitman & Gleitman (1977), that the speech modifications with which we were concerned reflected immediate functional goals of the parent in the course of everyday caregiving. Names appear to serve useful *control* functions, for example, in mother-infant interactions, as recognized elsewhere (Schaffer and Crook, 1979). However, the linguistic consequences are a complicated and inconsistent system of name and pronoun usage which, for several reasons (see Durkin, Rutter and Tucker, in press, for a more extended discussion), we argued do not facilitate language acquisition as such, though they may contribute very effectively to immediate communication.

That study was based on cross-sectional data, but such data are limited if we wish to study how parents adapt their linguistic behaviour as the child develops. Hence, the present paper reports an extension of the work, using a longitudinal sample. The data to be discussed are derived from the mothers' behaviour but, as the children were all normal infants during the age span 9-24 months, it can of course be taken for granted that their language develop-

406

ment in terms of both comprehension and production grew extensively during the period. The purpose of the investigation was to discover whether changes occurred in the organisation of maternal speech with respect to name usage during the infant's second year.

METHOD

Ten children, five boys and five girls, were selected at random from a larger sample currently under observation at our laboratories as part of a three-year study of mother-child interaction (for full details see Rutter & Durkin, 1982). All our subjects were initially selected at random from Health Visitors' Registers, and were invited to take part in a study of infant communication. They were filmed at monthly intervals from the baby's ninth month until his/her twenty-fourth month, and quarterly thereafter. Mothers were requested to play freely with their child for fifteen minutes, and both video and audio recordings were made. Relations with subjects were good, and this was reflected in a very low drop-out rate. Mothers were paid a nominal fee. The present study was concerned with maternal language at four points during the nine to twenty-four month span. Transcripts were made of all recordings taken at the children's ninth, twelfth, eighteenth and twenty-fourth month. Every use by the mother of the child's name or her own name (that is, 'Mummy') was identified, and classified as *Correct* or *Deviant* by the standards of adult grammar. *Correct* denotes usages which were judged to be both syntactically and pragmatically acceptable, by the standards of adult English. *Deviant* denotes usages which were either syntactically incorrect (e.g. 'Edward want one?') or pragmatically deviant (e.g. 'Give it to mummy', where the mother is the speaker), or both (strictly speaking, an utterance such as 'Give it to mummy' is syntactically acceptable, whereas 'Mummy try it', spoken by the mother, is deviant on both counts).

RESULTS

The main results were as follows:

1. All mothers used both their child's name and their own name several times.

2. All mothers used the child's name in both Correct and Deviant categories during the longitudinal period; usually, both types were used within each fifteen-minute session.

3. Use (by mothers) of 'Mummy' was *always* Deviant.

4. Mean frequencies of use of the three types are given in Table 1. Only the differences over

---

Table 1.

Mean frequencies of use of *Correct* and *Deviant* nominal styles by mothers.

	Using child's name				Using 'Mummy'	
	Correct		Deviant		Deviant	
	Mean	s.d.	Mean	s.d.	Mean	s.d.
9 mths.	3.00	2.29	4.00	6.98	5.67	7.42
12 mths.	11.30	6.49	6.60	13.17	8.20	8.52
18 mths.	9.90	6.87	6.80	8.28	12.90	11.32
24 mths.	5.30	4.16	2.70	2.95	5.90	4.31

Notes: 1. Figures for 9 mths. based on nine subjects due to unavailability of one subject for first observation.

2. 'Mummy' was only used in the Deviant style.

time in the Correct use of the baby's name were found to be significant (F $(3,24)$ = 6.19, $p < 0.01$, one-way repeated measures ANOVA) However, *post hoc* comparisons of means revealed that the differences between 9 and 12 months, between 9 and 18 months, and between 12 and 24 months were significant (all $p < 0.05$).

DISCUSSION

This longitudinal investigation has confirmed and
extended some of the main findings from our earlier study
(Durkin, Rutter and Tucker, in press).   All the mothers
in the longitudinal sample were found to use both the conventional adult style of proper names *and* the baby-talk
style, usually within the same session.   This supports
our earlier claims that young children are exposed to a
system of name usage which not only deviates from the adult
pattern but does so inconsistently.   The longitudinal
data indicate that such input is still more widespread
than our cross-sectional study had suggested (where a min-
ority of the mothers did not use names at all).

Although we find evidence of variation in the *frequency* of use of the different types over time, no clear
pattern emerges.   Significant differences were found only
in the use of the conventional (correct) form, which actually became *less* frequent from 12 - 24 months.   From
Table 1 it seems possible that the use of names in any
style is beginning to decrease by around 24 months, though
this does not reach statistical significance on every
measure.

More important than numerical differences, though, is
the fact that children appear to be confronted with both
types of name use throughout the second year, a major
period of early language acquisition.   The persistence of
the deviant style over such a lengthy period makes it an
unlikely candidate for a fine-tuning account of maternal
speech modifications.   There are a number of social and
functional reasons which help explain why mothers use names
in a deviant style (see Durkin, Rutter and Tucker, in press,
for a more extensive discussion) but, from a language instruction perspective, it seems difficult to explain why
the deviant style endures and why both styles are used
concurrently.

This is not to suggest that the use of names in the
deviant style has no *communicative* value, or that it has
no effect on the developing grammar as the child tackles
the complexities of the personal pronoun system.   In fact,

there is strong circumstantial evidence that at least some children adopt the same style in their own productions. To illustrate, we present two examples from the transcripts of one of our subjects, at 12 months and 24 months respectively. The first indicates some of the potential confusion that attaches to the maternal use of names and pronouns.

EXAMPLE 1 : Amy at 12 months.

(Taken from Hide-and-Seek game; Amy is 'hiding')

Mother: Where's that baby gone?   Where's that baby gone?   Amy, where's she gone?   Where's that baby gone?

Amy: Ther − er.   Oohoo.

Mother: Where is she, Amy?

Amy: Oo-ooh.

Mother: Amy, where's that baby?   Where's that (gasps) there she is!   You little rascal!

At this point, Amy's productions were very limited. A year later, however, she was able to engage in more substantial discourse and provide some indication of how the parental style might be reflected in her own speech.

EXAMPLE 2 : Amy at 24 months.

Amy: Mendid buttah.

Mother: Mend it.   Mummy mend it better or Daddy mend it better?

Amy: Mummy mend it better.

410

Durkin, Rutter and Tucker (in press) discuss further examples where use of names in place of pronouns *by the child* is seemingly endorsed by the parent even in the context of explicit attempts to modify or expand other aspects of the child's productions.

Charney (1980: 517) notes parenthetically the internal consistency of a two-year old's utterance about herself that *Karen ate yogurt and orange juice and she read a book.* Although Charney does not draw such an inference, phenomena such as these in children's productions are sometimes noted as odd, idiosyncratic (even cute) manifestations of early attempts at the personal reference system. In fact, the evidence is very strong that such structures may well have their origins in the speech addressed *to* the child. The child is tuning in to the input available (cf. Retherford, Schwartz and Chapman, 1981), but the structure of the input happens to reflect the social goals of the caregiver rather than the linguistic constraints of the adult grammar. Recent experimental evidence (Fee, in press) suggests that children exposed to a fairly high level of deviant name usage are more likely to exhibit difficulties with pronominal encodings in their own productions.

In conclusion, we suggest that any model of language acquisition which assumes some hypothesis formulation by the learner must take account also of the data against which those hypotheses may be tested. In the case of personal names, and hence of the personal pronoun system, the infant's data base is clearly quite different from adult grammar - and it may be more difficult.

REFERENCES

BROWN, R. (1977) Introduction. In C.E. Snow & C.A. Ferguson (Eds.) <u>Talking to Children: Language Input and Acquisition.</u> Cambridge: Cambridge University Press.

CHARNEY, R. (1980) Speech roles and the development of personal pronouns. Journal of Child Language, 7, 509-528.

DURKIN, K., RUTTER, D.R., and TUCKER, H. (in press) Social interaction and language acquisition: Motherese help you? To appear in: First Language.

FEE, E.J. (in press) Mother's pronominal modifications and the acquisition of personal reference . To appear in: Journal of Child Language.

NEWPORT, E.L., GLEITMAN, H., and GLEITMAN, L. (1977) Mother, I'd rather do it myself: Some effects and non-effects of maternal speech style. In C.E. Snow & C.A. Ferguson, (Eds.) Talking to Children: Language Input and Acquisition. Cambridge: Cambridge University Press.

RETHERFORD, K.S., SCHWARTZ, B.C. and CHAPMAN, R.S. (1981) Semantic roles and residual grammatical categories in mother and child speech: Who tunes into whom? Journal of Child Language, 8, 583-608.

RUTTER, D.R. and DURKIN, K. (1982) The development of turn-taking in mother-infant interaction: A longitudinal study. Final report to the Social Science Research Council of Great Britain.

SCHAFFER, H.R. and CROOK, C.K. (1979) Maternal control techniques in a directed play situation. Child Development, 50, 989-996.

ACKNOWLEDGEMENTS

This research was supported by grant number HR/5157/1 from the Social Science Research Council of Great Britain. We are very grateful to the mothers and children for their participation in the study.

An Examination of the Effects of Verbal and
Nonverbal Feedback on Maternal Speech to
Two-and-a-Half Year-Old Children

Karen L. Rembold

University of Wisconsin-Madison

Introduction

The quantitative and qualitative modifications made by mothers, and other individuals, in
their speech to language-learning children have
been well documented in the last decade. And yet
relatively little is known about how these modifications are elicited. Most of the research
attempting to unravel the elicitation process has
focused on the ways in which maternal speech is
related to the child's verbal behavior. The
present study examines the effect of the child's
nonverbal behavior on maternal speech.

Until the early 1970's it was assumed that
speech heard by language-learning children was
much the same as speech heard by adults. Upon
actual examination, however, researchers discovered that speech to children is qualitatively and
quantitatively different from speech to adults
(Broen, 1972; Remick, 1971; Phillips, 1973; Snow,
1972; Sachs et al., 1976). Much of this research
on speech modifications has involved mothers
(hence, the term "motherese", coined by Newport,
Gleitman, and Gleitman, 1975). And yet there is
evidence to suggest that not only mothers, but
a wide variety of individuals modify their speech
to language-learning children. For example,
Snow (1972) found that female adults who did not
have children of their own were only slightly
less skilled than mothers in modifying speech to
young children. In addition, several studies
indicate that fathers (and other men) modify
their speech to children in ways very similar to
those of mothers (Gleason, 1975; Kauffman, 1976;

Stein, 1973). Finally, Shatz and Gelman (1973)and Sachs and Devin (1976) have found that older children (4-5 years old) even modify their speech to younger children, so that it is significantly different from their speech to adults and peers.

In spite of the advances of the 1970's there remain critical, unanswered questions concerning how parental speech is elicited, apparently so universally, from those who converse with young children, and there remain questions of why this speech register even occurs in the first place. Although the questions of both how and why are fascinating, the present study focuses on the former. Perhaps if the questions concerning the "how" of elicitation can be answered, they will provide some insight into the "why."

A study by Snow (1972) first provided insight into the elicitation process by examining various conditions under which mothers altered, or did not alter, their speech to two-year-old children. Snow found that when mothers talked directly to their two-year-olds they made a greater number of speech modifications than when they talked to fictitious two-year-olds represented by a tape recorder. Although Snow's results are not unequivocal, they do strongly suggest that actual feedback from the child is responsible for at least some of the speech alterations that are made by mothers in conversations with their young children.

If this is indeed the case, the question arises as to what types of feedback provided by the child are most critical for eliciting parental speech modifications. The child's size and/or age? Degree of motor coordination? Linguistic production level? Linguistic comprehension level? Indications of cognitive ability? The child's nonverbal behavior? Some combination of all of these variables?

414

To date, most of the investigations of this question have centered on the child's level of linguistic production and comprehension (e.g. Cross, 1977; Snow, 1977; Chapman et al., 1978; Moerk, 1974; Phillips, 1973), although some have centered on the child's nonverbal behavior (e.g. Sylvester-Bradley & Trevarthen, 1978). Unfortunately, most of the studies examining the relationship between parental speech and child variables have failed to differentiate between the verbal and nonverbal responses of the child, and this has been the case for those focusing on nonverbal behavior as well as for those focusing on linguistic production and comprehension levels. As a result, not only has it been impossible to isolate the contribution of nonverbal behaviors to the mother-child linguistic interaction, but it has been impossible to get a clear measure of the linguistic variables themselves. It is only by separating these two dimensions of the child's response that the relative contribution of each to the complex structure of mother-child communication may be examined.

Aside from tragic situations in which parents cannot see their children, or in which children cannot verbalize to their parents, the only way to separate out the various contributions of verbal and nonverbal child input in a parent-child interaction is to artificially separate these communicative channels. The present study achieves this separation by having mothers and children communicate via television monitors, and by controlling the mother's access to auditory and visual input from the child. In one condition, the mothers are able both to see and hear their children over the monitor; in the other condition, the mothers are able only to hear their child. In both conditions, children are able to see and hear their mothers. A pilot study indicated that even in an unusual situation such as this, mothers still appear to modify their speech to children in contrast to their speech to adults.

The hypothesis of the present study is that when mothers have access to their child's verbal and nonverbal behavior as opposed to having access to verbal behavior alone, they will be more likely to alter their speech using the parental modifications. The best speech measures available to test this hypothesis are those which were found by Snow (1972) to alter as a function of both the age of the child (2 years old versus 10 years old), as well as the presence or absence of the child. These measures are: amount of speech, MLU, mean preverb length, and complete repetitions. For these measures, the alterations mothers made for 2-year-olds as opposed to 10-year-olds were the same as the alterations they made when the child was present as opposed to absent: quantity of speech increased, MLU decreased, mean preverb length decreased, and complete repetitions increased.

Since mean preverb length is basically a redundant measure with respect to MLU, and since a pilot study involving three subjects suggested that few complete repetitions in maternal speech would be found using the present experimental paradigm, the measures chosen to test the hypothesis in question are: MLU(mean number of morphemes per utterance; Brown, 1973) and amount of speech (mean number of utterances spoken per minute). The predictions for these measures are that MLU will decrease, and the number of utterances will increase, when mothers have access to both the verbal and nonverbal behavior of the child. MLU will be calculated for children, as well as mothers, for the purpose of estimating the children's linguistic level in the two experimental conditions.

Methods

Subjects

Nine white, native English-speaking 2-1/2-year old children and their mothers were randomly selected from a list compiled from newspapers, birth records and neighborhood listings. Four of the children were boys (average age 2 years, 6 months) and five were girls (average age 2 years, 7 months). In seven of the nine subject families the mother worked in the home and was the primary caretaker of the child, the father was employed in a white collar or professional position and both parents had some college education.

Design

Each of the mother-child dyads was tested individually and all 9 of the dyads participated in the same two experimental conditions: one in which the mother could both see and hear her child on a television monitor (V+ condition) and one in which the mother could only hear her child on the monitor (V- condition). Half of the mothers participated in the V+ condition first, the others participated in the V- condition first, and their ordering was determined randomly. The children could always both see and hear their mothers regardless of which condition the mothers were participating in.

Equipment

Video cameras and monitors were arranged in two rooms so that when a mother and child were each sitting alone in one of the rooms, they could technically see and hear each other on the television monitors. In addition, the arrangement of the equipment allowed the speech of both mother and child, as well as the child's picture, to be videotaped.

Procedure

For the mothers who participated in the V+, V- order of conditions, after a minute or two of warm-up the conversation continued for five more minutes with the mother able to see as well as hear the child. At the five minute point, the experimenter entered the mother's testing room and darkened the picture on her television set. The mother was then left alone again, for five minutes of conversation during which she could hear but not see the child.

For the mothers who participated in the V-, V+ order of conditions, the experimenter entered the mother's room to darken the television set immediately after the brief warm-up period. After five minutes of conversation during which the mother could hear but not see the child, the experimenter re-entered the room and brightened the television picture. Then the mother continued talking for five more minutes during which she was able to see as well as hear the child. As previously explained, the child was able to see and hear the mother at all times.

Transcription and Scoring

After all of the mother-child dyads were videotaped, the conversation between each mother and child was transcribed by the experimenter, using a standard English transcription. The average inter-rater agreement for the transcription process was .87.

Each transcript was then divided into V+ and V- segments to represent speech that occurred when the mother participated in either the V+ or the V- condition. The mother's utterances in the transcripts were scored for mean number of utterances per minute and MLU, and the children's utterances in the transcripts were scored for MLU.

The average inter-rater agreement for maternal MLU was .97. The average inter-rater agreement for child MLU was .94.

Analyses

Each of the three dependent measures (maternal utterances per minute, maternal MLU and child MLU) was analyzed using a repeated measures, split-plot analysis of variance (ANOVA) containing one within-subjects factor (condition) and one between-subjects factor (order of conditions).

Results

Maternal MLU

The raw scores for the dependent measure of maternal MLU are reported in Table 1. A repeated measures ANOVA (split-plot design) of the score reveals a significant treatment effect ($F_{1,7} = 8.77$, p <.05), a nonsignificant order effect ($F_{1,7} = .12$, p >.05), and a significant order-by-treatment interaction effect ($F_{1,7} = 10.42$, p < .05).

The significant treatment effect supports the hypothesis that maternal MLU decreases when mothers can both see and hear their child ($\bar{X}_{V+} = 4.49$) compared to when mothers can only hear their child ($\bar{X}_{V-} = 4.94$). The direction of this effect can be inferred from an examination of the raw and summary scores in Table 1.

The non-significant order effect indicates that maternal MLU did not alter systematically as a mere function of whether MLU was sampled during the mother's first five minute period or second five minute period of interaction.

The order-by-treatment interaction effect, however, indicates that the order in which the mothers received the V+ and V- treatments had a significant effect on how much their MLU varied

419

between the two treatments. As can be seen from
the cell means in Table 1, when mothers participated in Order A for the treatments (i.e. V+,
then V-), there was little if any difference between their MLU's in the two conditions. When
mothers participated in Order B (V-, then V+),
however, their V+ MLU's were much lower than
their V- MLU's.

Maternal Mean Number of Utterances Per Minute

The raw scores for the dependent measure of
maternal mean number of utterances are reported
in Table 2. A repeated measures ANOVA (split-
plot design) of the scores reveals a significant
treatment effect ($F_{1,7}$ = 20.63, $p < .05$), a non-
significant order effect ($F_{1,7}$ = .41, $p > .05$) and
a non-significant order-by-treatment interaction
effect ($F_{1,7}$ = .02, $p > .05$).

The significant treatment effect supports
the hypothesis that the maternal mean number
of utterances per minute increases when mothers
can both see and hear their child. ($\bar{X}_{V+}$ =20.65),
compared to when they can only hear their child
($\bar{X}_{V-}$ = 16.73). The direction of this effect
can be inferred from an examination of the raw
and summary data in Table 2.

The non-significant order effect indicates
that maternal mean number of utterances per
minute did not alter systematically as a mere
function of whether maternal utterances were
sampled during the mother's first five minute
period or second five minute period of interaction. And the non-significant order-by-treatment
effect indicates that the difference in mean
number of maternal utterances per minute in the
two conditions did not vary as a function of
the order in which the conditions occurred.

Child MLU

The raw scores for the dependent measure of
child MLU are reported in Table 3. A repeated

measures ANOVA (split plot design) of the scores reveals a non-significant treatment effect, ($F_{1,7}$ =1.71, p > .05), a non significant order effect [7] ($F_{1,7}$ = .43, p > .05), and a non-significant order-by-treatment interaction effect ($F_{1,7}$= .43 , p > .05).

The non-significant treatment effect indicates that the maternal treatments of V+ and V- did not systematically alter the MLU's of the children in the two conditions. The non-significant order effect indicates that the order in which the maternal treatments occurred did not systematically alter the MLU's of the children in the two orders of conditions. And, finally, the non-significant order-by-treatment interaction effect indicates that the difference in child MLU's in the two conditions was not systematically affected by the order in which those conditions occurred. In essence, the total effect of the maternal treatments on child MLU was null.

Discussion

The analyses of the present study have provided at least three pieces of useful information. First and secondly, they have supported the two primary hypotheses concerning maternal speech, i.e. that mothers conversing with their children via television monitors increase their number of utterances per minute and decrease their utterance lengths when they can both see and hear their children. Thirdly, they have demonstrated that children's average utterance lengths do not vary in the V+ and V- conditions, in spite of the treatment-related changes found in their mother's speech.

These results support the hypothesis that mothers are significantly more likely to modify the amount of their speech and its mean utterance length along the lines of the parental

speech register when they see as well as hear
their children, suggesting that some consistent
change takes place on the mother's side of a
mother-child interaction when the mother has
access to both visual and verbal feedback from
her child. What this change may represent, of
course, is open to alternative interpretations.
It is possible that the child's visual feedback
may merely help to clarify the child's verbal
feedback for the mother, and that it is primarily
this clarified verbal feedback to which the
mother responds when she lowers her MLU and raises
the number of utterances per minute in her speech.
It is also possible that one or more components
of visual feedback that are not immediately tied
to verbal interaction, such as gestures, facial
expressions, or eye movements, may be responsible
for mothers' shifts in communicative style. For
example, one of these components of visual communication may somehow indicate the child's lack
of comprehension to the mother, thereby influencing the mother's MLU and Amount of Speech, and
simultaneously provide her with feedback regarding the effectiveness of her alterations. A
third possible explanation is that it is the
number of communicative channels open to the
mother which influences the manner in which she
communicates with her child, such that the
critical factor is the total amount of information available to the mother, regardless of what
form it is in. For example, visual feedback plus
verbal feedback from the child may produce the
same effects on maternal speech as tactual feedback plus verbal feedback, or as tactual feedback plus visual feedback, because two communicative channels are available in each case.

Regardless of what mechanism is eventually
found to account for these shifts in register,
the present finding that mothers are more likely
to invoke the maternal speech register when they
can both hear and see their children sheds light
on at least two threads of research. First of

all, this finding provides additional evidence that some of the modifications in the parental speech register are indeed sensitive to feedback from the child, rather than being totally independent of the child's current status. And secondly, this finding provides an impetus to further examine the role of the child's nonverbal as well as verbal performance, in unraveling the mysteries of the parental speech register.

References

Broen, P.   The verbal environment of the language-learning child. <u>Monograph of American Speech and Hearing Association</u>.   No. 17, December 1972.

Brown, R.   <u>A first language: The early stages</u>. Cambridge, Mass.: Harvard University Press, 1973.

Chapman, R.; Hayes,D.; Retherford,K; Hayes,C. Early stages of language acquisition in hearing-impaired children: What mothers and children talk about.   Unpublished paper, University of Wisconsin, Madison, WI 1978.

Cross, T.   Mothers' speech adjustments: The contribution of selected child listener variables.   In C. Snow and C. Ferguson (Eds.) <u>Talking to children: Language input and acquisition</u>. Cambridge, Eng.: Cambridge University Press, 1977.

Gleason, J.   Fathers and other strangers: Men's speech to young children. <u>Georgetown University Round Table on Languages and Linguistics</u>, 1975, 289-297.

Kauffman, A. Mothers' and fathers' verbal interaction with children learning language. Unpublished Master's thesis, Rutgers University, New Jersey, 1976.

Moerk, E. Changes in verbal child-mother interaction with increasing language skills of
the child. Journal of Psycholinguistic
Research, 3, 101-116, 1974.

Newport, E; Gleitman, L.; Gleitman, H. A study
of mother's speech and child language acquisition. Papers and Reports on Child
Language Development, No. 10, Stanford
University, Stanford, California, 1975.

Phillips, J. Syntax and vocabulary of mothers'
speech to young children: Age and sex comparisons. Child Development, 44, 182-185,
1973.

Remick, H. The maternal environment of linguistic development. A Doctoral dissertation.
University of California, Davis,Cal. 1971.

Sachs, J.; Brown,R.; Salerno, R. Adults' speech
to children. In W. Von Raffler-Engel and
Y. LeBrun (Eds.) Baby talk and infant speech.
Lisse, Netherlands:Swets & Zeitlinger,1976.

Sachs, J. & Devin, J. Young children's use of
age-appropriate speech styles. Journal of
Child Language, 3, 81-98, 1976.

Shatz, M. & Gelman, R. The development of communication skills: Modification in the
speech of young children as a function of
listener. Monographs of the Society for
Research in Child Development, No. 152,
38(5), 1973.

Snow, C. Mothers' speech to children learning
language, Child Development, 43, 549-565,
1972.

Snow, C.   The development of communication be-
    tween mothers and babies.   Journal of
    Child Language, 4, 1-22, 1977.

Stein, A.   An analysis and comparison of mothers'
    and fathers' speech to children in a story-
    telling situation.   Unpublished paper,
    Boston University, School of Education,
    Boston, Mass. 1973.

Sylvester-Bradley, B. and Trevarthen, C.   Baby
    talk as an adaptation to the infant's
    communication.   In N. Waterson and C.Snow
    (Eds.), The Development of Communication.
    Chicester, England: John Wiley, 1978.

Table 1

Maternal MLU Scores in Two Conditions,
Grouped by Order of Conditions

Order	Condition		
	V+	V−	
A (V+,V−)	4.92	4.88	
	4.20	4.12	
	5.94	5.77	
	4.51	4.41	
	$\overline{X} = 4.89$	$\overline{X} = 4.79$	$\overline{X}_A = 4.84$
	SD = .76	SD = .72	$SD_A = .69$
B (V−,V+)	5.33	6.26	
	3.61	5.43	
	4.27	4.71	
	4.90	5.81	
	2.78	3.08	
	$\overline{X} = 4.18$	$\overline{X} = 5.06$	$\overline{X}_B = 4.62$
	SD = 1.02	SD = 1.24	$SD_B = 1.17$

$$\overline{X}_{V+} = 4.49 \quad \overline{X}_{V-} = 4.94$$
$$SD_{V+} = .93 \quad SD_{V-} = .99$$

Table 2

Maternal Mean Number of Utterances Per Minute
Scores in Two Conditions, Grouped by Order of
Conditions

Order	Condition		
	V+	V−	
A (V+,V−)	19.00	15.40	
	23.17	16.40	
	18.00	15.71	
	20.00	16.50	
	$\overline{X} = 20.04$ SD $= 2.24$	$\overline{X} = 16.00$ SD $= .53$	$\overline{X}_A = 18.02$ $SD_A = 2.63$
B (V+,V−)	20.00	19.20	
	17.50	11.67	
	20.22	16.33	
	28.17	20.55	
	19.75	18.80	
	$\overline{X} = 21.13$ SD $= 4.08$	$\overline{X} = 17.31$ SD $= 3.50$	$\overline{X}_B = 19.22$ $SD_B = 4.11$

$$\overline{X}_{V+} = 20.64 \quad \overline{X}_{V-} = 16.73$$
$$SD_{V+} = 3.25 \quad SD_{V-} = 2.59$$

Table 3

Child MLU Scores in Two Conditions,
Grouped by Order of Conditions

Order	Condition		
	V+	V−	
A (V+,V−)	1.29	1.50	
	2.15	2.93	
	1.81	1.97	
	2.77	2.77	
	$\overline{X}$ = 2.00	$\overline{X}$ = 2.29	$\overline{X}_A$= 2.15
	SD = .62	SD = .67	SD_A= .62
B (V−,V+)	1.87	1.23	
	2.55	3.17	
	1.64	1.92	
	1.51	1.80	
	1.63	1.59	
	$\overline{X}$ = 1.84	$\overline{X}$ = 1.94	$\overline{X}_B$= 1.89
	SD = .42	SD = .73	SD_B= .57

$$\overline{X}_{V+} = 1.91 \quad \overline{X}_{V-} = 2.10$$
$$SD_{V+} = .49 \quad SD_{V-} = .69$$

Ragnhild Söderbergh
Stockholm University
Child Language Research Institute

Linguistic effects by three years of age of extra contact during the first hour post partum

The background of the project. In 1977 I was asked to co-operate in a project headed by Professors Jan Winberg and Peter de Chateau, then at the University hospital in Umeå, now at Karolinska Hospital in Stockholm. The project is entitled "Long term effects on mother-infant behavior of extra contact during the first hour post partum" (Winberg – de Chateau in press, de Chateau 1980). My task was to seek possible linguistic effects stemming from the extra contact granted mother and child during the first hour after delivery. Similar projects have already been undertaken elsewhere (cf. Ringler et al. 1975).

How could early contact influence language? If one assumes a traditional, formal view of language as verbal language that may be given comprehensive description in terms of lexicon and grammar (semantics, morphology, syntax) with either a phonologic or graphematic representation – if such a view is assumed, the question of a possible connection between early contact and later language development may seem a bit far-fetched.

Recent trends in linguistic research, however, have focussed on language as communication and interaction. Research in child language acquisition now includes the study of non-verbal means of communication, and great progress has been made within the area of prespeech (e.g. Bullowa 1976, 1979; Lock 1978 et al.). The view that now prevails is that language acquisition essentially takes place in dialogue (Halliday 1977, Lock 1978). The precursors of dialogue may be found in the so-called protoconversation (Bateson 1971), first observed around three months of age. The child here takes his turns using nonverbal vocalizations in a "dialogue" with an adult. The principle of turntaking, however, seems to be learnt still earlier, during interaction in gazes between child and parent which can be traced back to the first few days after birth (Bullowa 1976).

In a series of studies from the second half of the 1970s, (Action, Gesture and Symbol; ed. Lock, 1978.) it has been shown how verbal symbols emerge out of pragmatically used prespeech which in turn develops out of movements and actions originally used without any communicative intentions. It is shown how this development comes about in close collaboration with speaking partners involved with the child in everyday situations of routine or play.

Given this background the question of a possible connection between early contact and later linguistic development may now be seen from a new perspective. With contact immediately after delivery the interaction between mother and child gets a chance to start directly during its very first hour, a time when the child is known to be more alert than he will ever be in later life. The child, having left the uterus, is also in need of warmth and bodily contact. Moreover, the mother, after having happily been delivered, is psychologically and emotionally highly motivated to seek contact with her newborn baby, to cuddle, feed and get to know her baby. With a separation after delivery, however, this mutual need is neglected, and the optimal chances for a beginning interaction are missed. In fact, the start of interaction may be postponed for several days if the short meetings during breastfeeding are not successful.

The linguistic project. I thus decided to concentrate on interaction when examining three-year-olds for possible linguistic effects of the extra contact during the first hour after delivery. A videotape was made for each of 38 different mother-child dyads, half of which had been granted extra contact, the other half constituting the control group. The videotaping was done by Peter de Chateau and Britt Wiberg. Each tape shows a halfhour's play in a doll house between mother and child when the child is approximately three years old.

To make it possible to follow the play on the tape, the doll house had been constructed without a roof. It contained a living-room, a bedroom, a bathroom and a kitchen, with standard modern Swedish furniture. The dolls were intended to represent the child's own family, and were chosen individually to suit each dyad: normally a Daddy doll, a Mommy doll, a child doll (male or female - representing the three-

430

year-old), and a baby doll if the child had a younger brother or sister. Occasionally there was also an uncle, aunt or grandmother, a cat or a dog. All the children showed great interest and were eager to play.

The mother and child sat on a mattress in a corner of a study, the doll house between them. The only instruction given to the mother was to relax and play with her child in the doll house, if possible as long as the tape lasted, i.e. for 30 minutes. This task may be said to have determined the character of the interaction.

Mother and child were supposed to play together. As far as playing is concerned this means that the mother had to make sure that the child cooperated with her in play. Linguistically it means that the mother had to maintain a dialogue, i.e. a linguistic interaction between the child and herself where both speak by turns and alternately act as listener and speaker, and where both talk about the same topic.

We decided to focus on this dialogue in our search for linguistic effects of early contact.

If a dialogue is to be maintained there must be a series of interesting topics and there must be a continuous shift of turns. In these videotapes the frames within which the topics may be chosen are set by the context of the here-and-now situation, the doll house. The adult's primary task here will be to be sensitive to the actions of the child and to choose topics in accordance with the child's already ongoing (silent) play or her own experience of the biases of her child.

As regards turnpassing and turntaking the mother must know how to pass the turn on to her child, and herself to take the role of the listener. She must also know how to listen actively and attentively, to be able to take her turn again at a convenient opportunity and in such a way that she really links up with what the child has just said.

The mother's task of passing the turn on often becomes a double one: to make the child take an active part both in the play and in the conversation. After having passed the turn on to her child she must not only be an attentive lis-

431

tener but also a good observer - to be able to give the child the best chance to contribute when it has something to say and/or be able herself to introduce new stuff at the right moment if the dialogue and play show signs of dying out.

The structure of a successful dialogue may thus vary considerably according to the personalities involved. If, for instance, the child is very active and very talkative, the role of the adult may be seemingly insignificant and not require much verbal contribution. If, on the contrary, the child is more passive and expectant (playing a "waiting game"), the task of the adult may become to inspire and persuade into action and talk. In that case the adult may be forced to use a considerable amount of both action and language to keep the play going and to maintain the dialogue.

The dialogue is dependent on the partners' ability to pass and to take turns. As said before, precursors of turntaking may be traced to the first postnatal weeks of the child's life. I thus decided to make turntaking and turnpassing the object of comparison between the dyads.

DEFINITIONS

Turn
The speaker is said to have his turn as long as the co-speaker does not take over. A turn may contain one or more utterances.

Utterance
An entity in spoken language with a status comparable to that of a sentence in written language. An utterance may contain one to several words (or vocal entities carrying content). Boundaries between utterances are signalled by intonation alone or by intonation combined with pause and/or syntactic structure.

Turnpassers
A turn may or may not contain a turnpasser, i. e. a signal to the listener that the speaker is willing to relinquish control. A turnpasser may be obligatory (Tobl) or potential (Tpot).After an obligatory turnpasser the listener is forced to take his turn, after a potential turnpasser he may or may not take his turn.

432

Obligatory turnpassers. Obligatory turnpassers are different kinds of question-formed utterances and certain tags which ask for information, persuade or coax the listener.

o Question-formed utterances with reversed word-order.

o Question-formed utterances introduced by vem, var, vad etc. (who, where, what etc.), i.e. corresponding to English wh-utterances.

o Question-formed utterances marked solely by intonation.

o Tags or one-word-utterances like va, da, visst, eller hur (roughly corresponding to eh, don't you, isn't it) and marked by emphatic and raising intonation.

o Potential turnpassers (see below) combined with direct eyecontact or gestures urging the partner to respond.

Potential turnpassers. After a potential turnpasser the listener may or may not take his turn. A good conversational partner, however, generally is very attentive to potential turnpassers and makes use of them to carry on a smooth conversation. Potential turnpassers are different kinds of appeals to the listener made by the speaker to show that he is not just talking to himself but expects an implicit or explicit approval (or disapproval), assertion or confirmation from the listener or otherwise wants the listener to take an active interest in what is said and/or done.

Some common potential turnpassers found in the mother-child dialogues are:

o Orders, often in the imperative. Primarily the order is supposed to be followed, but a verbal confirmation accompanying the action is not out of place and often found most natural: ja, mm (yes, o.k.) although it is not obligatory.

o Expressions of will, opinion, evaluation etc.: jag vill (I want to), jag tycker (I think), vilken fin säng! (What a nice bed) etc.

o Plans: vi ska (we shall/are going to), often in the weaker form of proposals: vi kan, vi kanske ska (we might, perhaps we might).

o Expressions of pretend-play: <u>vi kan låssas att</u> ... (we can pretend that ...).

o Attention-getters: <u>titta</u>! (look!), <u>den där</u> (that one) etc.

o <u>Statements</u>, <u>assertions</u>, <u>comments</u> or <u>information</u> expressed with emphasis and/or non-stressed words of appeal to the listener like <u>ju, du vet</u> (you know), or simply "tone of appeal" in its weak form: a certain rising tone at the end of the utterance. - If these verbal or tonal additions are lacking, statements etc. are free from any form of potential turnpassing.

o <u>Descriptions</u> and <u>stories</u> made/told in a certain <u>dramatic tone of voice</u> to keep the interest of the listener and to encourage him to contribute himself.

o "Emotional" tone added to utterances, expressing pity, love etc.

o "<u>Så</u>" (There) at the end of a commented action to mark that this action has been carried through.

<u>Observed and neglected turnpassers</u>. Turnpassers may be observed or neglected by the listener. Here we say that a turnpasser has been observed if the listener takes his turn and in doing so links up with what the former speaker has said

Ex. 1   Child: Where is the baby going to sleep?   <u>Tobl</u>
      Mother: But there may be room for the baby beside Maria.

Ex. 2   Child: And then she goes <to bed>
                <rising tone> <u>Tpot</u>
      Mother: Yes.

We say that a turnpasser has been neglected <u>either</u> if the speaker gets no response at all <u>or</u> if the listener takes his turn without linking up with the former speaker. In the first case the speaker after a pause (see below!) starts out again, either repeating his utterance - often making formal or semantic changes - to get a response, or else changing the topic completely

Ex. 3   Child: What is this?   <u>Tobl</u>
      Mother: (Does not answer)

434

| Child: | \<What is this> \<sulkily> | Tobl. |
| Mother: | That is a horsie | |

Ex. 4 Mother: What are we going to do? Tobl
        Child: (does not answer)
        Mother: Is this a telephone? Tobl

In the second case, the speaker whose turnpasser has been neglected may give in and join the partner's new topic, like in the following example:

Ex. 5 Child: Where is the baby? Tobl
        Mother: Where are we going to put the WC? Tobl
        Child: Into the bathroom.

In examples 1–5 above, every speaker makes only one utterance per turn. A turn, however, may consist of two or more utterances, <u>every</u> utterance containing a turnpasser, the last one obligatory or potential, the earlier ones potential, and yet the earlier potential turnpassers in the turn may not be considered as missed or neglected by the listener. This is the case when there is semantic and formal coherence between the different utterances, so that it is obvious that they are part of the same whole, often most skilfully planned by the speaker. Then only the last turnpasser in the turn counts when it comes to deciding if the turnpasser has been missed or observed by the listener. The earlier turnpassers then serve to keep the interest of the listener alive

Ex. 6 Mother: a) She (the mother doll) must take Kristina
                   and Anna out of the bath Tpot
                b) Perhaps Daddy is going to do that Tpot
                c) Then Daddy is going to take Kristina and
                   Anna out of the bath Tpot
                d) Won't he? Tobl
        Child: Yes

In Ex. 6 the end of the semantic and formal entity is marked by making the last turnpasser obligatory. But this may not always be the case. Compare the following example

Ex. 7 Mother: (describing what the child is doing)
                a) Take them and rub them so that they
                   don't \<get cold>. \<With emphasis> Tpot

435

```
Mother:   b) <Yes> <with "emotional" tone>    Tpot
Child:       Rub.
```

Analysis of turnpassers in this paper. In this paper ten
dyads of the 38 in the project have been randomly picked out
for analysis. Five were early-contact dyads, five control-
group dyads (the analyzer did not know which were which before the analysis).

15 minutes from each of the 38 videotapes had been transcribed beforehand (Strömqvist 1979) by assistants at Child
Language Research Institute. After going through each of the
videotapes two or three times, the transcribers then chose
"the best" coherent 15 minutes for transcription, i.e. a
section of the tape where the dyad seemed relaxed and naturally playing and talking together.

When the ten videotapes for this study had been picked out
(by Peter de Chateau), the first two minutes from each transcribed 15 minutes were chosen and a new detailed transcription was made, where every movement and gaze of mother and
child was recorded in the transcription (see Fig. 1 at the
end of this paper). From these new 2-minute-transcriptions
the first 25 turns in each were picked out. All turnpassers
were marked and classified as obligatory (Tobl) and potential (Tpot), observed and neglected. An evaluation of the
neglected turnpassers was then made, so as to compare and
rank the ten dyads. After that a count and comparison was
made and finally the code was broken.

Before the evaluation it was decided that:

o A high number of observed turnpassers should be considered as a mark of a good dialogue.

o If the mother neglected a turnpasser from the child, this
   should be considered as more serious than if vice versa.

o Neglected obligatory turnpassers should be considered as
   more detrimental to the dialogue than neglected potential
   turnpassers.

The result of the analysis is evident from the following
tables

436

Table I. Neglected turnpassers

Symbol of dyad	Neglected by mother		Neglected by child	
	Tobl	Tpot	Tobl	Tpot
No 2	–	–	–	–
4	4	1	–	2
5	1	–	1	–
8	–	–	–	2
12	2	–	5	4
23	–	1	–	2
25	–	–	–	–
29	–	–	4	–
32	–	3	2	–
35	–	3	–	1

Table I may be rewritten in such a way that the dyads are ranked according to the evaluation suggested above (the fewer misses the better the dialogue; non-observance by the mother more serious than non-observance by the child; non-observance of Tobl more serious than non-observance of Tpot). At the same time the code is broken in order to see if there is any correlation between good dialogue dyads and early contact dyads.

Table II. Neglected turnpassers related to early contact.

Neglected by mother		Neglected by child		Symbol of dyad		
Tobl	Tpot	Tobl	Tpot			
4	1	–	2	No	4	Control
2	–	5	4	No	12	Control
1	–	1	–	No	5	Control
–	3	2	–	No	32	Control
–	3	–	1	No	35	Control
–	1	–	2	No	23	Contact
–	–	4	–	No	29	Contact
–	–	–	2	No	8	Contact
–	–	–	–	No	25	Contact
–	–	–	–	No	2	Contact

From Table II it is evident that:

o Non-observance of obligatory turnpassers on part of the

mother is found only in three dyads. All of these belong
to the control group (No 4, No 12 and No 5).

In one of these dyads the child also has the highest number
of non-observed Tobl and the highest number of non-observed
turnpassers totally compared with the other nine children
(No 12).

o The two dyads where all turnpassers are observed both belong to the early contact group (No 2 and No 25).

o In one dyad where only the child misses turnpassers,these
   misses are two potential turnpassers (No 8). This dyad
   also belongs to the early-contact group.

o The remaining four dyads (32, 35, 23 and 29) stand out
   less clearly. Two of them are early contact dyads (23 and
   29), the other two are control dyads.

Early contact dyad 23 has the fewest non-observances totally
(3) of these four dyads, and these non-observances all concern potential turnpassers - only one by the mother.

Control dyad 32 has the highest number of non-observances
(5) of these four dyads, three on part of the mother. The
two on the part of the child concern obligatory turnpassers.

The remaining two dyads, 29 and 35, both have four non-observances. In early-contact dyad 29 the mother does not miss
any turnpassers from the child, but the child's four unob-
servances all concern obligatory turnpassers, which is serious. In control dyad 35 only potential turnpassers are
missed, three of these by the mother.

Summing up the result of this pilot study of linguistic effects at three years of age of early contact during the
first hour post partum the following may be said:

o The sought-for "linguistic effects" concern the art of
   carrying on a dialogue, as the dialogue is considered to
   be at the very core of language acquisition.

o The analysis has focussed on the observance of turnpassers i.e. taking one's turn after a turnpasser given by
   the dialogue partner and then linking up with what the

partner has just said. This choice has been made because:

a) observance of turnpassers is essential for the main-
   tainance of a dialogue

b) turntaking seems to be one of the earliest rules of
   interaction learnt by the child.

o The "linguistic effects" of early contact - if there are
   any - are assumed to be reciprocal.

o In the evaluation the dyad has been treated as an entity,
   with the mother as the more responsible partner, being
   the linguistically more mature of the two.

o In this pilot study of 10 dyads the three outstanding
   best dialogue dyads are early-contact dyads, the three
   unquestionably slightest are control dyads. Of the remaining four one of the early-contact dyads may possibly
   be assigned to the "better half", one of the control
   dyads to the less prominent half.

Although these results do not allow us to say anything definite about a correlation between early contact and dialogue
proficiency - and definitely not to draw any conclusions a-
bout direct linguistic effects of early contact - they are
interesting enough to motivate an analysis of the remaining
28 dyads and the subsequent choice of a greater number of
turns for analysis.

Fig. 1

Fam. 2

Ch	Ch/M	M
sitting beside doll house in the right half of the picture, turned towards camera (must turn right		kneeling in the left half of the picture, right side towards camera, looking at Ch and doll house
when playing in doll house) bends over the doll house and takes a stool(?) out of the bathroom with her left hand	Ch 1 : we may also build	observing what Ch is doing
puts it down at her right foot, takes another stool out of the bathroom and puts it beside the first one, her hand back to the bathroom moving things	M 2 : do [you think we may also build / Ch 3a: [yes / b: yes [and / M 4 : [rearrange the furniture / Ch 5 : \<yes\> \<happily\> / M 6 : \<yes\>\<rising tone\>	arranging the furniture in the bathroom / takes her hand away, observes what Ch is doing
arranging things in the bathroom, with left hand, takes the hand away, holds Daddy doll in her right takes child doll in her left	Ch 7 : W.C. / M 8a: and the W.C. / b: what a fine W.C. / Ch 9a: wants to [...] and / b: and	tilts her head right

440

References

Bateson, M.C., Epigenesis of conversational interaction, Paper presented to the Society for Research on Child Development, Minneapolis 1971.

Bullowa, M. et al. Infant vocalization: communication before speech. In Mc Cormack, W.C. &
Wurm, S.A. (eds.), Language and man. Anthropological issues. The Hague: Mouton 1976.

Bullowa, M. (ed.), Before Speech. Cambridge, Eng.:
Cambridge University Press 1979.

de Chateau, P., Perineonatal interaction - its long-
term effects. IN: Simmel, E. (ed.), Early
experience in early behavior; application of
social development. New York: Academic Press
1980.

Halliday, M., Learning how to mean. Explorations in
the development of language. London: Edward
Arnold 1977.

Lock, A. (ed.), Action, Gesture and Symbol: the
emergence of language. London: Academic Press
1978.

Ringler, N.M., Kennell J., Janella R., Wavojoski B.,
Klaus M. Mother-to-child speech at two years,
effects of postnatal contact. Journal of Ped-
iatrics 86: 141-144, 1975. Also in W. Von
Raffler-Engel (ed.), Child Language. London:
International Linguistic Association, 1975.

Strömqvist, S., Om kommunikation och transkribering -
with a brief English summary: On communication
and transcription. Stockholm: Child Language
Research Institute, Paper 1, 1979.

Söderbergh, R., En modell för beskrivning av dialoger
mellan barn och vuxna (summary in English: A
model for the description of dialogues between
children and adults.) In: Språkstimulering i
förskoleåldern. Stockholm: Child Language Research Institute, Paper 5, 1980.

Winberg, J., de Chateau, P., Mother-infant interaction and early social development. In Hartup,
W.W. (ed.), Rev Child Dev Res vol. VI. Chicago:
SCRD Press (in press).
441

Maternal Speech Patterns
and Differential Development

Lynn H. Waterhouse
Trenton State College

INTRODUCTION

A great deal of research has been done on the nature of the speech children hear as they acquire language, and from this research, arguments have been made for the existence of special adjustments of speech used to young children by adults and other children. While findings do suggest that children acquiring language do hear simplified speech (Phillips, 1973; Shatz and Gelman, 1973; Bellinger, 1980; Messer, 1980), the research which claims to show that specific features of mothers' speech correlate with their children's progress in language development (Cross, 1977; dePaulo and Bonvillian, 1978; Furrow et al., 1979) remains difficult to interpret.

The central assumption in interpreting any correlations between features of mothers' speech at time one and children's speech at time two is that significant, high, positive correlations reflect causality. Even when researchers themselves discuss the problems inherent in such an interpretation (Furrow et al., 1979), they often still resolve the issue in favor of a general causal interpretation.

The problem, of course, is that associational or correlational studies of mothers' speech and children's language development have at least three built-in causal confounds, each of which is simply the option for an alternate explanation of the association found to exist.

The central confound is the genetic/familial one. If there is a strong innate component to language acquisition, and to later language performance, there is likely to be greater between-family variation than within-family variation, both in mothers' features of speech, and children's stages of development. That means that the associative slopes on mothers' adjustments in speech and children's stages of acquisition (as measured in studies) will always be closer for mothers and children who are related, even when sampling for mother and child speech is done at different time periods.

Furthermore this confound is not obviated by findings of variation in correlations. If a study turns up some significant high positive correlations between mothers' speech variables and children's development amongst a large set of non-significant correlations, or negative correlations, it doesn't suggest that variation validates the notion of effect or causality. It may simply mean that those correlations are tapping some aspect of the basic language skill system which mother and child actually share.

Neither is this confound obviated by the finding of correlations which show a relationship between features of mothers' speech and children's development where measured skills in the children seem to be very different from the features of mothers' speech with which they are associated. If, for example, mothers' verb use were found to be correlated with children's later adjective use, it cannot be argued that, as it is not the same system aspect of language being tapped in both mother and child, therefore the association must be causal. Large scale correlational studies of features of both normal and developmentally delayed children's language acquisition suggest a strong intercorrelation of all language skills (Waterhouse and Fischer, 1976; Waterhouse and Fein, 1982). Thus the correlations between

443

mothers and children may reflect an association
between skill and feature measurements which best
tap some as yet unknown underlying general ability
or abilities for language which both mother and
child share.

The second major confound is that which is
provided by theories of the relationship of both
thought and language and social behavior and
language. Mothers speech adjustments may reflect
either a facilitation of content transmission to
the child--i.e., speaking that special way helps
her get her point across to the child, whatever
that point may be, or such special adjustments
may reflect an effort to engage in social facilitation, i.e., the adjustments a mother makes may
be a kind of ritual equilibrium, which serve to
(tacitly) show communicative respect for the
child. The motivations of getting a point across
and showing respect for the child as an interaction partner are alternate explanations for
found correlations between mothers and children's
speech and development patterns.

If the development of cognition and the
development of language are linked in the child's
course of development, then a mother adjusting
well to a child's cognitive skills,as displayed
in speech interaction situations, may have
features of her speech--as adjusted to the child--
which will relate to the child's linguistic
development at a later time. If the development
of social skills in interaction is linked to
actual language development, here too, a mother
adjusting her speech to a child's interaction
skills may have features of her speech at time
one which correlate with the child's stage of
language development at time two. Neither of
these explanations is causal, but both suggest a
real link, more of an ethological nature, between
mother and child language skills. Furthermore,
it is reasonable to assume that both explanations
may hold, and further, that there may <u>also</u> be a

444

genetic/familial basis for the relationships which
do appear in the data.

Unfortunately there is no real research plan
which can eliminate these possible confounds.
Even when the child's developmental stage is
partialled out of the correlation (Newport, et al.
1977), the residual association may reflect not
causation (mother's speech affecting child's
course or pattern of development), but may reflect
the expression of some genetic/familial association between mothers' language skills and their
children's rate of acquisition.

An adoption study, in which mother's speech
at time one is related to adopted child's stage
of language development at time two, offers the
promise of causal connection, but here too, it
may be that familial(and not "genetic")adjustments
alone offer enough variation from family to
family to make mother-child pairs within a family
--even where that mother and child are not
related to one another--show significantly greater
similarity in language features and skills than
would be expected by chance or random effect.

In addition to the two possible confounds
discussed above, there is the problem of the
statistical issues involved. In any data set,
where a great many correlations are run, it may
be expected that some subset of correlations
would be expected to reach significance by
chance. If several significant correlations are
found in a large set, then, it may be that these
do not represent real relationships, but merely
statistical artifacts. If then, researchers
attempt to present the most "positive" picture
they can by means of their data, they may reduce
the variable set of intercorrelations to those
which express significant findings. Beyond
this, discussions of correlations logically do
focus on those relationships for which a significant correlation has been found, and ignore

nonsignificant relationships among variables.
This unconscious shifting of emphasis takes place
in all sorts of papers in all fields, and it
represents the need for validating the beliefs of
the researchers.

TWIN RESEARCH

One research design which--though it cannot
resolve the basic confound problems of mother-
child speech associations--can shed some light on
the nature of adjustments mothers do make in
interaction with their children, is the twin
study method.

The twin situation offers a means of looking
at degree of adjustment to children whose development may be virtually identical (identical or MZ
twins) and at degree of adjustment to children
whose development may be only as similar as any
two siblings(fraternal or DZ twins). In cases
where mothers have misperceived the true zygosity
of their twins--thinking that identicals are
fraternals when they are infact identical--the
adjustment mothers make can be examined and
compared with speech adjustments made by those
mothers who have correctly perceived their twins
as fraternal, and as identical.

Where identical twins have been misperceived
as fraternals, and yet their actual development
in language is identical, mothers' patterns of
variation across co-twins--if found--might suggest
that mothers may at least be attempting to maintain their own perceptions of the two as different by treating them differently, or, more than
that, may be attempting to direct them differently. In any case, if mothers treat identicals
differently, they cannot be thought to be adjusting specifically to each child's developmental
level.

The present study of maternal speech to young
twins(1) was designed to investigate the following

questions: (1) Is there significant between-family maternal speech style variation?; (2) Do coded elements in maternal speech show correlation with children's performance on language acquisition measures?; (3) Are coded elements in mothers' speech to identical twins less variable than the same elements in mothers' speech to fraternal twins?; and (4) Where mothers have misperceived the zygosity of their identical twins, does their speech reflect more or less variation between co-twins?

THE STUDY

Methods

Subjects. The subjects were 21 same-sex, same eye-color twin pairs, aged 30-42 months old. Knowledge of the zygosity of the twin pairs was obtained by blood serum analysis of blood samples drawn from each of the children at the end of the study. Anti sera analysis using 12 separate tests established the presence of 11 monozygotic or identical twin pairs, and 10 dizygotic or fraternal pairs.

Zygocity estimates from the mothers, when compared with true zygocity as indicated by the blood anti sera analysis, were shown to be correct for all fraternal pairs, but incorrect for 5 of the 11 identical pairs. Data presented here is based on a subsample of 8 identical twin pairs, 4 pairs who were correctly perceived and 4 pairs who were incorrectly perceived, and 6 fraternal twin pairs, on whom complete language skill and maternal speech pattern data was collected.

Measures. The twin pairs were tested on a variety of language measures including the Peabody Picture Vocabulary Test, the Berko Wugs morphology test, Fraser's sentence comprehension task and a sentence repetition task (Mehrabian,

1970). The children's MLUs (mean length of utterance) were also determined, using Brown's scheme (1973).

Mothers were taped while in interaction with their twins--mother and each twin in a separate semi-structured picture-book examination situation.

Children's performances were coded correct or incorrect for each item on every test administered, and a total score for each test was obtained. This total raw score was changed into a transformed score by means of division of raw score by chronological age in months at the time of test administration.

Mothers' speech to each twin was coded for MLU, and for the presence of the following types of utterances: (1) questions; (2) answers; (3) exact repetitions of the child's utterance; (4) expansions; (5) assertions(declaratives); (6) criticisms (negative assertions about the child); (7) directions; (8) confirming conversational place-markers; and (9) labels for objects in the situation provided by the mother (deictic comments). This set of elements is derived from Cazden(1965). All coding was done by two coders. Reliabilities as per Scott's intercoder agreement coefficient ranged from .81 to .92, the high being found for the coding of questions in mothers' speech.

Results

The first research question was whether or not there was significant between-family variation in maternal speech styles. For the ten variables coded in maternal speech, the findings are split: there was significant between-family variation for only 5 variables--MLU, questions, expansions, assertions, and directions. For all mothers taken together, however, there was much greater between-family (i.e., between-mother) variation than there was within-family (i.e. twin-twin) on all ten coded variables. Thus the trend for all ten variables, and the findings of significance for 5 of the 10 variables suggest that there is generally greater variation in speech style from mother-to-mother than there is mother-to-twin A to mother-to-twin B.

The second question posed in this research was whether coded aspects of mothers' speech would correlate with scores of their children on tests of language development. While the full correlation tables have been presented elsewhere(2), the following summary may be considered here. When the ten coded variables in maternal speech were correlated with both children's test scores and an error coding of their spontaneous speech, out of 160 correlations (10 maternal speech elements x 16 separate test scores and error codings), 55 were significant--23 positive, and 32 negative. There was only one general pattern in these significant correlations: mothers' speech was positively associated with errors in production (8 maternal variables showed significant, positive correlations with children's errors in spontaneous speech-- mothers' MLUs, questions, answers, expansions, repetitions, assertions, directions and labels); and mothers' speech elements were negatively associated with children's test scores (8 maternal variables were involved here--mothers' MLU, questions, answers, expansions repetitions, criticisms, directions, and labels). Two-thirds of all significant negative and positive correlations (35/55) fit this pattern.

If this pattern of correlation can suggest anything, it suggests that mothers who do more questioning, repeating and the like have children who make more errors and have lower test scores. Not only are these findings distinct from other findings for such correlations, they hint at an almost negative role for aspects of maternal speech. As these findings were drawn from a very small population of twins, however, they cannot be generalized to any other population.

The third research question was whether there was greater within-pair variation for mothers' speech to fraternal twins than to identical twins. There was greater variation between fraternals than between identicals for all but two maternal speech variables--assertions and confirmations-- which suggests that, in general, mothers do use a speech style to their identical twins which is similar, and use a speech style to fraternals which, at least, shows greater variation between twins than that shown by the mothers of identicals.

Given that the children in this sample are all same-sex, same-hair-color, same-eye-color twins and given the fact that fraternals in this sample have been shown to have significantly greater variation in language development than the identi- cals (3), this suggests that mothers may un- consciously do some pretty fine adjusting of their speech styles to their children at different developmental stages.

The fourth research question was whether there was greater variation in maternal speech variables directed by mothers to identicals thought to be fraternals. Consider the following table:

Table One
Within-pair variation in Maternal Speech
to correctly perceived identicals (CMZ),
incorrectly perceived identicals (IMZ), and
correctly perceived fraternals (DZ)

	CMZ n=4prs	IMZ n=4prs	DZ n=6prs
MLU	0.32	0.13	1.99
questions	22.15	215.46	528.53
answers	2.60	7.46	12.40
expansions	0.90	3.00	0.95
repetitions	2.60	75.46	30.53
assertions	40.39	674.33	641.95
criticisms	0.35	1.00	6.40

Table One, cont.

	CMZ n=4prs	IMZ n=4prs	DZ n=6prs
confirmations	52.90	79.67	25.88
directions	54.80	87.00	70.48
labels	35.46	159.67	96.62

For every variable but MLU,mothers of identicals they believe to be fraternals are showing much greater variation in their speech styles to each twin than are mothers of identicals who believe they are identicals. It is hard to believe that mothers have such speech style elements under conscious control, or believe that mothers are using speech variation to try to differentiate their children. It may be that those mothers who believe they have fraternal twins are also those mothers who would show greater speech style variation in interaction with all their children. While the sample is small, the findings are dramatic, and suggest that maternal speech style may be more "creative" than causal or reactive.

CONCLUSION

Evidence from the present study suggests that maternal speech patterns (1) are variable across families(mothers), (2) are reflective of the child's developmental state, and (3) are reflective of the mother's perception of her child. These findings do not offer specific support for any particular theoretical point of view, but they are consonant with the ethological position in general.

The ethological viewpoint argues that many maternal and child behaviors are interlinked, and that the nature of the interlinking is genetically programmed, but that variation in specific patterns should be great, with greater style variation to appear in mothers' behaviors.

In terms of the rather lengthy discussion of confounds in interpreting mother-child speech correlations, the present finding of significant between-family variation for half of all variables coded in mothers' speech to her twins does offer support for the presence of possible confounds to any causal interpretation. If strong between-family variation in maternal speech provides a base for mother-child correlations, then covariance rather than causality might explain significant relationships found between mothers' and children's language performances.

What is most likely however is that real source of significant correlations is an inter-mixture of many sources: significant correlations may represent covariance, causality, and coincidence working at the same time in the same population. Clearly more research needs to be done.

Reference Notes

1. These data were collected as part of the author's dissertation research, which was done jointly with Dr. Karen Fischer, and which was funded by NIMH 21422 to Dr. Sandra Scarr.

2. The complete table of correlations is present in the author's dissertation, Genetic and Sociocultural Influences on Language Development, University of Pennsylvania, 1972, unpub.

3. Waterhouse and Fischer, 1976.

References

Bellinger, D.(1980). Consistency in the pattern of change in mothers' speech: some discriminant analyses. J. Ch. Lang., 7, 469-487.

Brown, R. (1973). A first language: the early stages. Cambridge, Mass: Harvard University Press.

Cazden, C.(1965). Environmental assistance to the child's acquisition of grammar. Unpublished doctoral dissertation. Harvard University.

Cross,T.B.(1977). Mothers' speech adjustments: the contributions of selected child listener variables. In C.E. Snow & C.A. Ferguson (eds.) Talking to children:language input and acquisition. Cambridge: Cambridge University Press.

DePaulo, B.M. & Bonvillian, J.D. (1978). The effects on language development of the special characteristics of speech addressed to young children. J. Psycholing. Res.,7, 189-211.

Furrow, D., Nelson, K. and Benedict, H. (1979). Mothers' speech to children and syntactic development: some simple relationships. J. Ch. Lang., 6, 423-442.

Messer, D. (1980). The episodic structure of maternal speech to young children. J.Ch. Lang., 7, 29-40.

Munsinger, H. & Douglass, A. II (1976). The syntactic abilities of identical twins, fraternal twins and their siblings. Ch.Dev.,47,40-50.

Newport, E., Gleitman, L. & Gleitman, H. (1977). Mother, I'd rather do it myself: some effects and non-effects of maternal speech style. In Snow and Ferguson,(eds.), Talking to children: language input and acquisition. Cambridge: Cambridge University Press.

Phillips, J.(1973). Syntax and vocabulary of
mothers' speech to young children: age and
sex comparisons. Ch.Dev., 44, 182-185.

Shatz, M. & Gelman, R.(1973). The development of
communication skills: modification of the
speech of young children as a function of the
listener. Monogr.Soc.Res.Ch.Dev., 38,No.5.

Waterhouse, L. & Fein, D.(1982). Language skills in
developmentally disabled children. Brain.&
Lang., 15, 307-333.

Waterhouse, L. & Fischer, K.(1976). Genetic
contributions to variability in preschool
linguistic skills. In W. von Raffler-Engel
and Y. Lebrun,(eds.) Baby Talk and Infant
Speech. Amsterdam: Swets and Zeitlinger.

Development in Realization of Story Structure in Written Productions of School Children

Aviva Freedman

In recent years, there has been a great deal of important work analysing discourse structure, specifically story schemata, with special reference to the role of such schemata in discourse comprehension and recall.[1] The role of such schemata in discourse production, however, has received less attention, and, with the notable exception of the work reported on by Bartlett (in press) and Bereiter and Scardamalia (1981), the ability to realize conventional schemata in written discourse has hardly been investigated at all.

The study reported on here involves an attempt to describe the development in children's ability to incorporate story schemata in their written productions. Specifically, I chose to analyse and compare stories written by children in grades 5, 7, and 8, using an instrument of analysis based on the kind of story grammar that has been articulated in recent work on discourse comprehension and recall.

Research Design

The students whose work was analysed represent a one percent sample of the entire grade 5, 7, and 8 population of the Carleton Board of Education, Ottawa (some 9,000 students in all). The scripts were elicited as part of two other projects,[2] each involving a ten percent sample of the Board's population; one involving the grade 5 students; a second, the grades 7 and 8. For this study, I randomly selected a further ten percent as a subsample of the larger sample, in order to obtain 23 grade 5 papers, 28 grade 7's, and 28 grade 8's.

The students in both projects had been given the same assignment: to write a story about a terrible

455

event or an event where something had gone wrong. In each case, the students were given only this verbal prompt; as opposed to the Bartlett experiment (in press), they were not provided with any more directive stimulus, such as a picture or movie or sequence of cartoons.[3] The children were asked to produce their narratives in a 40 - 60 minute class period. The only difference in procedure between the two assignments was that the grade 5 pupils were given a later opportunity to revise their writing, an opportunity very few took.

The Subjects

Given what we know about the impact of culture on discourse patterns (see, for example, Chafe (1981) and Kaplan (1966), etc.), a description of the cultural background of the student population whose work was elicited is in order. The Carleton Board of Education is one of two major public boards in Ottawa; it represents urban, suburban, as well as some rural children. The Board has relatively few E.S.L. students and, for both studies, all children for whom English was a second language were excluded. Furthermore, although Ottawa has a large French population, French students typically go to a separate school system; so the students whose work we were investigating were typically from homes where the dominant language and culture is English.

Furthermore, as a whole, Ottawa is an upper middle class city: there is no heavy industry, very little poverty, and undoubtedly an exceptionally high and uniformly high educational level among its population. In several research studies investigating writing development among Carleton Board students, and looking specifically at syntactic maturation (1979, 1980), my colleague Ian Pringle and I have found that these students score very high on all the usual tests of syntactic maturity when compared to the North American norms: the students ON AVERAGE displayed a higher degree of syntactic sophistication (in terms of words per T-unit, clauses per T-unit, T-units per sentence), than the high groups in what has become accepted as the status study, Loban's work in California (1976).   Performance according to other measures has also led us to believe that this is an extraordinarily literate group.

The Analysis

Since the objective of this study was to determine the degree to which writers at different stages of development were able to realize the conventional schema for story structure in their narratives, we needed, for our analysis, some way of operationally defining story structure.   The various story grammars developed in recent work on discourse comprehension and recall provided the basis for such an instrument.   Grammars of this kind have been put forward by researchers such as Propp (1968), Rumelhart (1975), Meyer (1975), Mandler and Johnson (1977), Thorndyke (1977), Kintsch (1977), and Stein and Glenn (1979).   A survey of these various models reveals, as Bartlett (in press) points out, that there is considerable agreement in substance; consequently, our criteria for selecting a specific model on which to base our instrument were these: first, that the instrument be easily applicable on a large scale by different raters: and second, that minimal criteria for success in realizing the schema be defined as part of the model. For these reasons, we chose to base our instrument on the model developed by Stein and Glenn (1979), (which is, in itself, an elaboration of that put forward by Rumelhart (1975), whose own origins can be found in Propp (1968)).

The Stein and Glenn model first defines the basic units of a story by classifying the basic categories of information which can recur; these categories are further subdivided into subunits; and rules for their interrelationship are defined.

457

Specifically, then, a story consists of a setting category and an episode system. The setting "introduces the main character(s) and describes the social, physical or temporal context in which the remainder of the story occurs" (Stein and Glenn, 1979, p. 59). The episode system consists of one or more episodes or behavioural sequences related in certain specified ways. Each episode consists of an intiating event, a response to that event and a consequent plan sequence, which includes an internal plan, the application of that plan, and a resolution (that is, a direct consequence and a reaction). And each of these broad categories can be further subdivided in terms of kinds of information so that, for example, the initiating event can be either a natural occurrence, a human action, or an internal event, say a decision or a feeling. See Table 1 for a specification of the kinds of basic units and subunits possible within each episode.

Table 1 - Episode Structure

Initiating Event
  Natural occurrence
  Action
  Internal event
Internal Response
  Affective
  Goal
  Cognition
Internal Plan
  Cognition
  Subgoal
Plan Application
  Attempt
Direct Consequence
  Natural occurrence
  Action
  End state
Reaction
  Affective
  Cognition
  State

Episodes vary, however, so that in many cases the internal response, say, is not specified, nor perhaps the internal plan. However, for an episode to be considered complete, it must contain at least some reference to:

> (1) the purpose of the behavioral sequence, (2) overt goal-directed behavior, and (3) the attainment of nonattainment of the character's goal. Therefore, an episode must contain (1) an initiating event or an internal response which causes a character to formulate a goal-directed behavioral sequence, (2) an action, which can either be an attempt or a consequence, and (3) a direct consequence marking the attainment or nonattainment of the goal. If these three criteria are not met, the behavioral sequence is defined as an incomplete episode.
>   (Stein and Glenn, 1979, p. 72)

On the basis of the Stein and Glenn formulation, the minimal criteria for success in incorporating story structure were defined as follows. Each attempted story must contain (1) some setting information and (2) at least one complete episode as defined above.[4]

For our analysis, all the information in each story was classified according to the categories and subcategories specified in the above grammar, and the interrelationships between categories were defined. Further each episode was identified as complete or incomplete, and the total number of complete and incomplete episodes per story was tabulated.

Pilot Work

To pilot the study, this scheme was used to analyze a number of short stories written by professional writers -- mainly, although not exclusively contemporary; mainly, although not exclusively English. Specifically, the following stories were analysed: Alice Munro, "How I Met My Husband"; Robert Kroetsch, "That Yellow Prairie Sky"; Claire Martin, "Springtime"; Randy Brown, "Heil"; Elizabeth Brewster, "Silent Movie"; Ken Mitchell, "You Better Not Pout"; Jean-Paul Sartre, "The Wall"; Alberto Moravia, "Bitter Honeymoon"; Heinrich Boll, "My Melancholy Face"; Abraham Cahan, "A Ghetto Wedding"; Dorothy Parker, "The Standard of Living"; Isaac Bashevis Singer, "Fate"; Gabrielle Roy, "Wilhelm"; Elizabeth Wilson, "Mrs. Golightly and the First Convention".

There were several reasons for this analysis. First, I wished to train the raters and test the ease of applicability of the model. Second, since both the Rumelhart and the Stein and Glenn models are derived from an analysis of folk-tales, myths and/or children's stories, I was concerned to test the universality of the model by applying it to mature adult writing, especially because the students whose work we would be examining included 12 and 13-year-olds whose literary experience presumably extended beyond folk-tales and children's stories. Third, many of the tales previously analysed were oral tales. Since I was interested in the students' production of written discourse, I wanted to see whether adult models of written discourse embodied the same structure. (A priori, there might be good reason to suspect that this would not be the case.) Finally, I wished to test our minimal criteria.

This pilot study confirmed that the model could be applied, with relative ease, to professional short stories aimed at an adult audience. Furthermore, our minimal criteria were satisfied by all the stories: 100% of these stories included some setting information and at least one complete episode, although 33% also contained one or more incomplete episodes that depended on a complete episode.

460

Results

The first point to note is that the differences between the 7's and 8's using this instrument were slight, and not consistently in one direction.[5] Taking the 7's and 8's as one group, however, there were interesting and significant differences between that group and the 5's, and it is these that will be reported on.

The first and most striking difference has to do with the criteria set for realizing story structure: that is, the inclusion of some setting information and one complete episode. As to setting, almost all the stories at both levels (with only one exception at the grade 5 level) included some setting information. The difference lay in the presentation of complete episodes. While 94.6% of the 7 and 8 stories included at least one complete episode, some 34.8% of the grade 5's did not; that is, only approximately two thirds of the 5's fulfilled the criteria we had stipulated as essential to the realization of the story schema we had developed, although almost all the grade 7 and 8 stories realized these criteria. (See Appendix A for a typical grade 5 story which did not fulfil the minimal criteria.)

As to incomplete episodes, both sets of stories included some incomplete episodes, as did the professional writing; for the 7's and 8's and those of the 5's which included a complete episode, these incomplete episodes were dependent upon the complete episodes contained in the stories. Nevertheless, there is a difference in terms of the number of incomplete episodes as well: while 75% of the 7's and 8's have no incomplete episodes; only 47.8% of the 5's have none, and while 12.9% of the 5's have more than 2, only 1.8% of the 7's and 8's have more than two.

As to setting information, an interesting difference emerges as well. While both groups were comparable in terms of their presentation of what Stein and Glenn call minor setting information (identifying physical context, that is, place and time), more of the 7 and 8 group present information concerning the characters (83.9% vs. 69.6%).

Focusing more closely on the elements comprising the episodes, we find important differences between the two groups as well. Both sets of stories always include initiating events, and as initiating events, comparable proportions of natural occurrence, actions, and internal events. (See Table 2.) Although the percentage of the grade 7 and 8 stories including at least one instance of each item is somewhat higher for each of the three categories, the real difference seems to be that the older students simply present more of such events, with a mean of 5.695 initiating events for the grade 5 stories, and 7.713 for the 7/8's.

The situation is different for the presentation of internal responses: in this case, the 7/8's differ not just in the number of items presented but in their inclusion of such items at all. More specifically, a higher percentage of the 7/8's included at least one affective response (60.7% vs. 30.4%) and at least one cognition (53.6% vs. 34.8%). Neither group included goals. Nor were internal plans presented to any extent by either group of students.

Far more of the 7/8 stories included plan applications, and among those which included a plan application (i.e., excluding the 0's), there were more instances. At the same time, more of the 7/8 stories included direct consequences, although, in this case when we exclude the 0's, there were no more direct consequences per story.

Moreover as Table 2 shows, there is a striking difference between the percentage of stories which include reactions, especially affective reactions

Table 2

Percentage of Papers Including at Least One Instance

	Grade 5	Grade 7 and 8
Setting	95.7	100
Character	69.6	83.9
Physical Context	95.7	94.6
EPISODE STRUCTURE:		
Initiating Event	91.3	100
Natural Occurrence	39.1	43.2
Action	87.0	98.2
Internal Event	43.5	46.4
*Internal Response	52.2	82.1
*Affective	30.4	60.7
Goal	4.3	5.4
*Cognition	34.8	53.6
Internal Plan	17.4	21.4
Cognition	17.4	19.9
Subgoal	0	1.8
*Plan Application	60.9	89.3
*Direct Consequence	69.6	94.6
Natural Occurrence	13	10.7
Action	69.6	80.4
*End State	17.4	35.7
*Reaction	30.4	62.5
*Affective	26.1	44.6
*Cognition	8.7	32.1
State	0	1.8

*indicates that difference is significant when measured by a chi-square test.

and cognitions, with the 7/8 students again predominating. Further, the mean number of reactions for the 5's was .3578 as compared to 1.0356 for the 7/8's.

To sum up then, both sets of stories include setting information and initiating events; neither set includes much in the way of internal plans or descriptions of states as reactions. Where they differ is in the number of grade 7 and 8 stories including internal responses to the initiating events (especially affective responses and cognitions) as well as overall reactions to the episodes (again in terms of affective reactions and cognitions). More of the grade 7/8 stories also tend to include plan applications and direct consequences. And further, for all these categories (except direct consequences) as well as for initiating events, if we exclude those stories which had no instances of a particular item, we find that the 7/8 narratives have more instances of each item -- more initiating events, more plan applications.

The grade 7 and 8 stories, then, are richer, contain more events in general, and contain more emphasis on affective and cognitive responses to events within the story as well as reactions to the episodes themselves.

One further distinction is the following: we categorized as well the kinds of connections linking episodes: the possible connections for this set of papers were the following: and, cause, then (temporal sequence) and nested (one episode contained within another). For both sets of papers, the predominant relationship between episodes was "then" signifying temporal sequence. In each case 75% of the total links were of this kind. 14% of the grade 5 links were causal, while 22% of the grade 7 and 8 links were causal. There were, furthermore, somewhat suggestive differences among the untypical cases: 9.5% of the grade 5 episodes were linked by an "and" relationship;

there were no instances of such a connection in the grade 7 and 8 papers. In contrast, we did have two instances of nested episodes in the 7 and 8 papers -- a phenomenon that was simply absent in the 5's.

Discussion

To sum up the major implications of our findings: first, the Stein and Glenn story grammar (or at least our modified version) is a useful instrument for measuring both crude and somewhat finer changes in the production of written stories between grades 5 and 7, although not for describing differences between grades 7 and 8, which may mean that there are no changes within that time frame or that a more subtle instrument or a different kind of analysis entirely is necessary.

Secondly, there is a striking growth between grade 5 and grade 7 in the ability to realize the ideal schema for story structure. Broadly, then, the grade 7 an d 8 children were able to realize the ideal schema for story structure in a way that was possible only to about 66% of the grade 5 students. A reading of the stories, however, pointed to a further distinction, which we pursued with the following results. The instructions were simply to write a story, and the students wrote what we have called "real" and invented stories in roughly equal proportions at all grade levels. However, further analysis showed that for the grade 5 studies, 88.9% of the invented stories conformed to the criteria for story structure while only 50% of the real stories did. And interestingly, for the grade 7 and 8's, the one story which did not conform to our criteria was a real story; furthermore, of the 25% of the stories which included one or more incomplete episodes (which depended upon complete episodes within the story), all were real stories.

The difficulty which the grade 5 students experienced, and which the grade 7 and 8 students had almost overcome, then, was in writing stories that both conformed to story structure as well as to the sequence of reality. The point is that, in order to write a story based on real experience which also conforms to the norms of a story schema, certain elements of the real experience must be heightened, and others ignored: only those which are consistent with the "initiating event - plan attempt - resolution" schema can be selected. Furthermore, it is possible that not all sequences of experience can be packaged to fit such a schema at all; some experiences may simply not provide material for "stories" in this sense, and must be rejected in toto. It is this negotiation between the demands of story structure and the actuality of life's experiences that seems difficult for the grade 5 students. (Again, the essay in Appendix A is illustrative.)

Thirdly, some of the differences we found are parallel to those discovered by both the Mandler and Johnson (1977) and the Stein and Glenn (1979) studies investigating story recall by young children. In the Stein and Glenn experiment, first and fifth grade children are compared and there were significant differences by grade, first in terms of the number of units of information recalled (and we found comparable differences in the number of units of information produced for most categories and as a whole); and second, by category: Stein and Glenn found a significant difference by grade in the recall of internal responses, just as we found such a difference in the written production of this category.

There are similar parallels with the Mandler and Johnson experiment which compares first and fourth grade children. Their fourth grade children differed from their first in their improved recall of what they call "attempts" (which is roughly comparable to the Stein and Glenn "plan application".) We found in our study that the older children produced significantly more plan applications than the younger. Thus there seem to be similar developmental patterns with respect to realization of this schema for story structure in both the retrieval and the construction tasks. Further, and what is even more interesting, the rank order of frequency of the categories either realized or constructed (comparing in our cases, percentage of stories with at least one instance and, in the Mandler and Johnson and Stein and Glenn studies, mean proportion of propositions and clauses recalled) is roughly the same in all three experiments at both levels, except that responses and reactions are sometimes reversed. In other words, the relative salience of these categories is highly consistent not only across grades, but across tasks. All this seems to suggest that the same schema operates 1) in the retrieval from memory of stories that have been encoded; 2) in the selection from memory of experiences for the construction of "real stories"; 3) and in the generation of "invented stories."

Fourthly, research into the spontaneous construction of oral narratives bears interesting parallels and interesting differences with our findings. At first glance studies such as those by Applebee (1978), and Botvin and Sutton-Smith (1977) suggest that the patterns of development are the same between the oral and the written conditions except that the whole process is delayed for writing so that, assuming fundamental similarities across the different schemata used, all of the 7-year-olds in the Botvin and Sutton-Smith experiment were achieving orally what only 2/3 of our 10-year-olds were able to achieve in writing in general and what only 50% were able to achieve in the production of "real stories."

However, since all the studies on the construction of oral narrative seem to involve invented stories, comparisons are not possible, and we have no real indication of how writing affects the construction of stories except to say that by

467

grade 5 on the whole pupils can write invented
stories that conform to the schema for story
structure and that between grades 5 and 7 they
develop the ability to reconstruct from their life
experience stories that accord to this structure
following a developmental pattern similar to that
followed by younger children developing the
ability to produce oral narratives conforming to
story structure. There remain many unanswered
questions concerning the effects of the written
versus the oral conditions in story production.
Thus, the relationship between the construction of
narratives orally and in writing remains to be
explored.

Finally, there were interesting differences
between grade 5 and grades 7/8 in the richness of
the stories (the older children presented far more
dense and elaborated stories) and in terms of the
presentation of affective and cognitive responses
to events both by characters within the story and
by the narrator. The stories included far more
internal responses to initiating events as well as
far more evaluations, to use a term employed by
Labov and Waletsky (1967). Along with this
increased ability to reflect on experiences rather
than simply to report on them came another
indication of decentredness. More of the 7/8
stories, although still less than one quarter, had
invented protagonists: 23% vs. only 4% of the
grade 5's. The two movements are parallel - the
ability to decenter and to center empathetically
into a protagonist who is not "I" and the ability
to distance oneself and reflect on events and
experiences.

Conclusion

This study is most usefully seen as a pilot,
indicating directions for further research
investigating both development in the realization
of story structure in written narratives as well
as the relationship between such developmental
patterns and development in, first, oral

468

story-telling; second, discourse comprehension; and third, story recall. In the course of this study, the importance of distinguishing "real" from "invented" stories in future investigations of story production (and, perhaps, story comprehension) became clear. And finally, the necessity for a more finely callibrated instrument of analysis was revealed by the indistinguishability of the grade 7 and 8 papers.

Notes

[1] For a review of this work, see Bartlett (in press).

[2] The grade 7 and 8 writing was elicited as part of a holistic evaluation project. Students in 18 classes were asked to write one story and one argument each; these scripts were used in several training sessions where teachers were taught holistic evaluation. The grade 5 stories were elicited as part of a Board-wide writing evaluation.

[3] This contrasts with the procedure in the Bartlett (in press) experiment where students were provided with a sequence of scenes in cartoon form and asked to compose a story in response. I was interested in seeing how children would perform without such directive prompting. This difference in stimulus undoubtedly accounts for the different results.

[4] In insisting on these as minimal criteria for success in incorporating story structure, I went further than Stein and Glenn, whose aims in this regard were descriptive rather than prescriptive. However, the results of the analysis of professional short story writing, which is discussed further within, seemed to justify the setting of such criteria.

[5] That there was little to distinguish the 7's and 8's may indicate a number of things: there

may be a ceiling effect in terms of story structure; or, and I'm rather inclined to this position, the Stein and Glenn instrument is too crude to measure the kinds of changes that take place at that level.

References

Applebee, A.N. The child's concept of story. Chicago: University of Chicago Press, 1978.

Bartlett, E.J. Learning to tell a story. In A. Freedman, I. Pringle and J. Yalden (Eds.), Learning to write: First language/second language. London: Longman, in press.

Bereiter, C., and Scardamalia, M. From conversation to composition: The role of instruction in a developmental process. In R. Glaser (Ed.), Advances in instructional psychology (Vol. 2). Hillsdale, N.J.: Erlbaum, 1981.

Botvin, G.J., and Sutton-Smith, B. The development of structural complexity in children's fantasy narratives. Developmental Psychology, 1977, 13, 377-388.

Chafe, W. (Ed.) The Pear Stories. Norwood, N.J.: Ablex, 1981.

Kaplan, R.B. Cultural thought patterns in inter-cultural education. Language Learning, 16 (1966), 1-20.

Kintsch, W. The representation of meaning in memory. Hillsdale, N.J.: Lawrence Erlbaum Associates, 1974.

Labov, W., and Waletzky, J. Narrative analysis: Oral versions of personal experience. In J. Helm (Ed.), Essays on the verbal and visual arts. Seattle: University of Washington Press, 1967.

Loban, W.D. Language development: Kindergarten through grade twelve. Urbana, Illinois: National Council of Teachers of English, 1976.

Mandler, J.M., and Johnson, N.S. Remembrance of things parsed: Story structure and recall. Cognitive Psychology, 1977, 9, 111-151.

Meyer, B. The organization of prose and its effect on memory. Amsterdam: North-Holland, 1975.

Pringle, I., and Freedman, A. The writing abilities of grade seven and eight students. Report prepared for the Carleton Board of Education, October, 1979.

Pringle, I., and Freedman, A. An analysis of the syntactic maturity and writing skills of grade five, eight, and twelve student writers. Report prepared for the Carleton School Board, May, 1980.

Propp, V. Morphology of the folktale. Austin: University of Texas Press, 1968.

Rumelhart, D.E. Notes on a schema for stories. In D.G. Brown and A. Collins (Eds.), Representation and understanding: Studies in cognitive science. New York: Academic Press, 1975.

Stein, N.L., and Glenn, C.L. An analysis of story comprehension in elementary school children. In R. Freedle (Ed.), New Directions in discourse processing (Vol. 2). Norwood, New Jersey: Ablex, 1979.

Thorndyke, P.W. Cognitive structures in comprehension and memory of narrative discourse. Cognitive Psychology, 1977, 9, 77-110.

471

APPENDIX A

The Story at my Camp

This past summer at Echo Bay there was a very bad
storm. I was there when the storm occured.
Twelve trees fell down. Eight trailers were hit
with trees. Some of the telephone wires were
down. Some of them weren't. We were lucky to
phone the telephone companie to come out and fix
the telephone wires. My Aunt, Uncle, and cousin
came to visit us. They left just before the storm
came. Nobody was hurt thank goodness! Somebody
was up the lake and didn't even know the storm was
there! They were only a little bit up the lake
when the storm came.

A Linguistic Analysis of Hyperlexia

Rosa Needleman, Ph.D.
Dept. of Linguistics/Dept. of Psychiatry
Neuropsychiatric Institute, UCLA

A paradoxical linguistic ability in otherwise language impaired children was noted by Kanner (1943), Itard (1962) and others; several reports of children with early infantile autism indicated that the children demonstrated a highly developed ability to read in spite of severe impairment in other linguistic and cognitive functioning. Case studies of psychotic and other language disordered children have mentioned the presence of this precocious ability but there has been little systematic research into the finding and its prevalence is still unknown. In 1968 Silberberg and Silberberg (1971) coined the term "hyperlexia" to "describe children lacking the ability to abstract and conceptualize well, but who are able to recognize words at levels much higher than prediction." The same authors emphasized the disparity between the children's other language abilities (usually very poor) and the reading ability, the spontaneity with which the recognition of words developed (there was usually no formal teaching) and the lack of comprehension of what the children read. Mehegan and Dreifuss (1972) described 12 hyperlexic children, not at all of whom were autistic but who were all "brain damaged", as having other characteristics in common: little spontaneous language, echolalia, a compulsive and indiscriminate attraction to written material, reading in a "compulsive and ritualistic" fashion, and the abrupt emergence of the ability - usually before the age of 5 and occasionally before 3. Mehegan and Dreifuss considered hyperlexia to be a "unique disturbance of language development" and they speculated that the neurologically and perceptually handicapped may acquire reading by different means than the normal population. Huttenlocher and Huttenlocher (1973) reported on 3 hyperlexic children who could

473

communicate to some extent and concluded that the basic language defect in these children appeared to be "in the association between speech symbols and meaning". None of these reports on hyperlexic children give details of their receptive and expressive language abilities nor of their other visual abilities. (Cobrinik (1974) does examine this latter dimension but his children were adolescents.)

The phenomenon of hyperlexia is still virtually unexplored and certainly unexplained. Research has ignored the specific nature of the reading ability: do the children employ a "whole-word" approach or do they employ sight-sound correspondence; do they have a memorized list of words or is this ability productive; how much comprehension of written material is present. This latter is exceptionally difficult to assess in non-communicative children. Standardized reading comprehension tasks are likely to be well beyond their cognitive capacities and merely making the nature of the task clear to them presents a problem. The reason for the emergence of such spectacular ability to read in otherwise language impaired children has also been cause for speculation. Cain (1969) associates the "special abilities" of psychotic children with "deep need or conflict" and asserts that other variables include "heavy environmental reinforcements and lack of meaningful human relations." Cobrinik (1974) relates hyperlexia to a highly developed visual ability and calls it an extension of pattern recognition. None of these speculations have sufficient power to account for this syndrome. The population of hyperlexic children includes non-psychotic individuals as well as autistic and schizophrenics; from parental reports and my own observations it has been noted that when given a choice of toys and objects usually appealing to children, these very young developmentally deviant subjects (as young as 2 years old) will invariably choose to play with (i.e. scrutinize, handle) alphabet blocks or magnetized letters, ignoring all other stimuli around them.

Later, as they grow older, these children will look at books to the exclusion of other objects in spite of considerable discouragement from parents and therapists who are distressed by the inappropriateness of the behavior.

My own interest in hyperlexia was first engaged by the case of a 5 year old female patient at the UCLA Neuropsychiatric Institute who had a total oral apraxia (an articulation disorder which resulted in muteness), undifferentiated brain damage and who was hyperlexic. Over the subsequent 5 years I encountered approximately 3 dozen such children at the NPI and extensively studied ten of them to date. My research has centered around two questions: first - to what extent do these children comprehend what they read? It has often been stated -without substantiation- that the reading is "merely by rote", "name-calling" or simply memorized lists; however, those few studies which examined this issue generally used tasks which were too difficult or which presented too many stimuli. The second question involves the degree to which this reading ability is truly linguistic and not merely a visual trick.

To recapitulate, there appears to be general agreement that the syndrome of hyperlexia has these defining characteristics:
   -occurs in a developmentally disordered
    population
   -has a very early manifestation (possibly
    by age 2)
   -emerges suddenly and is self-generated
   -has a driven, compulsive, ritualistic and
    indiscriminate quality
and I would add-
   -is in advance of cognitive and other
    linguistic abilities.

Subjects
   Nine children are being reported on here, all between the ages of 3 years and 9 years. Several were patients at the UCLA Neuropsychiatric Insti-

tute and some lived at home and came only for
evaluation and research. All had been referred
to the NPI for diagnosis by an inter-disciplinary
team consisting of a psychiatrist, psychologist,
linguist and social worker. Diagnoses were
autism (6 children), pervasive developmental disorder (2 children), oral apraxia (1 child). All
were diagnosed additionally as hyperlexic by
virtue of parental or staff report of an early
attraction to written material and by a demonstrated ability to "recognize" words from the
Wide Range Achievement Test (spelling sub-test)
and the Gates-McKillop Reading Diagnostic Test.

Evaluation
    Each child was given either the Merrill-
Palmer, Stanford Binet or the WISC-R depending
upon age and developmental level and each child
was also given a language evaluation utilizing
standardized tests: the Peabody Picture Vocabulary Test, The Carrow Test of Auditory Comprehension for Language or the Test of Language Development. A language sample was obtained to assess
expressive language.

To test the reading and spelling ability of the
child these additional tests were administered:
    a) subtests of the WRAT
    b) the reading recognition and reading
       comprehension sections of the Gates-
       McKillop Reading Diagnostic test were
       adapted by putting individual words
       on separate cards rather than presenting
       a list of words in order to minimize
       distracting stimuli
    c) the Porch Index of Communicative Ability
       in Children adapted in similar fashion
       where necessary.

Additional experimental measures were the following:
    a) the children were asked to spell aloud
       foreign and nonsense words
    b) from an array of five phonologically and

476

graphically similar words they were asked to select a word on being given the auditory stimulus (e.g. from "contemplate, contempt, contact, contract, content" pick "contempt")

c) the children were required to match written words to pictures using words and pictures from the PPVT and to objects
d) written commands were presented for the children to follow
e) a task involving Chinese ideographs to be matched to pictures was taught to each child.

Results

Table 1 presents the chronological age, IQ, language age and reading scores.

1. The two youngest children were unable to respond to any reading recognition or reading comprehension tests.

2. Each child's score on Merrill Palmer puzzle assembly and form board or block design and object assembly from the WISC was obtained for comparison with reading level. These particular tasks require comparatively less abstraction but do require recall and manipulation of visual stimuli. The children diagnosed as autistic scored well on these tasks-as would be expected of autistic children - but only one child scored at or above age level. All the non-autistic children scored poorly on visual-spatial and visual memory tasks.

3. None of the children reached levels better than chance in a recognition task of Chinese ideographs, standard road signs and other non-linguistic visual stimuli.

4. Spelling was by consistent rules of sight-sound correspondences; that is, on being asked to spell foreign or sophisticated words

Table 1

		C.A. mos.	I.Q.	Lang.Age mos.	Read. Recog.	Read. Comp.
E.M.	autistic	33	54	22	?	?
L.C.	autistic	36	52	24	?	?
J.K.	P.D.D.	48	46	24	2nd gr.	begin. level
P.J.	autistic	48	52	28	1st gr.	begin. level
V.C.	apraxic	60	50	36	6th gr.	4th gr.
G.D.	P.D.D.	72	58	36	6th gr.	3rd gr.
M.B.	autistic	72	68	48	6th gr.	3-4 gr.
R.B.	autistic	84	58	40	7th gr.	4th gr.
D.C.	autistic	108	74	92	5th gr.	3-4 gr.

presumably unfamiliar to them, they would, for example, consistently spell the sound [k] with a "k" (as in [kabayero]). Reading new words aloud was also done by "sounding out" but once read this way, on subsequent occasions the word was recognized and spoken instantly.

5. One unusual result was the discovery that several of the children could read as quickly backwards as forwards. For example "KROF" was read as "fork" if the child already knew that word.

6. Initially only one 6 year old (G.D.) and the 2 older children were able to follow written directions and respond to written questions about reading material. Some time was spent in training the remaining children and once they understood what was expected, the 5 year old, the second six year old and one four year old (J.K.) were able to follow one-part written commands but only sporadically responded to very simple written questions about what they read.

Discussion:

From my research it appears that there is a developmental aspect to hyperlexia in language disordered children; in the youngest children there is minimal comprehension of written material and minimal awareness that the written words refer to real world objects. As the children grow older the growing awareness leads to true comprehension of words (not merely within the limits of cognitive and specific deficits) and then to comprehension of longer structures. It is only the oldest and most competent of the children, however, who read for information and this has most probably been fostered by the schools they attend. For most of the children examined to date there appears to be a plateau effect at the 4th grade level in reading comprehension. Moreover, both parental and school reports indicated that the driven, compulsive and exclusive quality of the reading tends to diminish in many hyperlexic children as other skills develop. One might well speculate that the initial impetus toward reading is purely self-stimulatory but it is certainly a potentially useful behavior.

Evidence that the nature of the reading is based on a cross-model associative ability, i.e. that the children haven't simply memorized lists of words nor are they using purely visual strategies or visual recall alone, comes from their spelling errors in particular and from the "sounding-out" process with which even the youngest confronted new words. They quite clearly use productive and self-induced rules to read and spell. It is also highly significant that they did not learn either non-linguistic visual nor non-alphabetic linguistic tasks.

There is little doubt that these children are both cognitively and linguistically impaired and that they have many of the deficits seen in retarded populations as well as specific deficits associated with autism and other developmental disorders along with unusual abilities sometimes associated with such deviant development. Overall their symbolic language ability is invariably very poor (especially in the case of the autistics). Nevertheless comprehension of written language - although considerably below reading recognition levels - was present at levels higher than predictable given such deficits and often at levels better than comprehension of auditory language. This argues strongly that this is a specific and isolated linguistic ability.

This work was supported by USPHS Grant MH-30879 and the Solomon and Rebecca Baker Foundation.

BIBLIOGRAPHY

Cain, A. Special Isolated Abilities in Severely Psychotic Young Children. Psychiatry 1969, 32, 137-149.

Cobrinik, A. Unusual Reading Ability in Severely Distubed Children. Journal of Autism and Schizophrenia, 1974, 4:163-175.

Elliott, E. and Needleman, R. The Syndrome of Hyperlexia. Brain and Language 1976, 3, 339-349.

Gates, A.I. and McKillop, A.S. Gates-McKillop Reading Diagnostic Tests. Western Psychological Services, 1962.

Itard, J.M.G. The Wild Boy of Aveyron. New York; Appleton-Century-Crofts, 1962.

Kanner, L. Autistic Disturbances of Affective Contact. Nervous Child, 1943, 2, 217-250.

Mehegan, C. and Dreyfuss, M.B. Hyperlexia. Neurology, 1972, 22, 11, 1105-1111.

Porch, B.E. Porch Index of Communicative Ability in Children. Palo Alto, CA: Consulting Psychology Press, 1978.

Silberberg, N. and Silberberg, M. Case Histories in Hyperlexia. Journal of School Psychology 1969, 7,3-7.

Silberberg, N. and Silberberg, M. Hyperlexia: The Other End of the Continuum. Journal of Special Education, 1971, 5, 3, 233-241.

JAPANESE/CHINESE KANJI -
WHAT THEY CAN TELL US ABOUT NONVERBAL
CHILDREN AND EARLY SYMBOLIC LANGUAGE

Mary Rees Nishio

Department of Psychology
University of Toronto
Toronto, Ontario, M58 1A1

Introduction

Those new to the field of neuropsychology and apha-
siology are often surprised to find that the capacities which they have always considered to be uni-
tary are, in fact, composed of many different abilities, each of which can be affected by brain damage
singly or in combination. One facet of this phenomenon is the phonetic versus the visual-gestalt
processing of written words.

A clue to this differential phonetic and visual-
gestalt processing is provided for us in the example
of Monsieur C in France in 1887. Due to a stroke,
this patient had completely lost his ability to read
letters of the alphabet and words and could not read
the letters "R" and "F" if presented individually.
If, however, a circle was drawn around them, he
would immediately reply "Republique Francaise" (Gardner, 1973). Though having lost the ability to process discrete letters of the alphabet, he still re-
tained the capacity to process visual symbols associated with whole auditory words.

English, due to its primarily phonetic character,
has not often provided us clues to this dual character of written language processing, but evidence
from aphasics in Japan where the language has three
distinct systems - two syllabic systems, katakana
and hiragana, and one logographic system, Chinese/

Japanese kanji, has shown that cerebral injury may result in the loss of understanding of the phonograms while the understanding of many of the kanji may be left intact. There is, in addition, evidence to indicate that kanji may involve both hemispheres in processing to a greater extent than the individual kana.

Reading instruction in Japan does not begin until the age of six or seven, and during the first year, the emphasis is primarily on the phonetic kana with only seventy-six kanji taught in the first year. The generally held opinion in Japan is that the kana are easier to learn than kanji. This belief more than likely originated in the fact that the kanji are visually more complex and more difficult to write.

Given the evidence from adult Japanese aphasics and the success of visual alternative communication systems with various populations, it was hypothesized that very young, prelingual, language disabled children might be able to learn kanji words if they showed good ability in visual discrimination.

Subjects

The evidence to be presented is based on four subjects. The first, Takeshi, was three years four months old at the beginning of the study. He had no eye contact or evidence of creative play. Receptive vocabulary was reported to be a few words in the home but none was evident in the testing situation. He had one word in his expressive vocabulary ("this"). Takeshi demonstrated good ability in matching colors, shapes, and sizes (Nishio, 1981).

Koichi, the second subject, was three years three months old, had fairly good receptive speech but not one word of expressive speech. Unlike Takeshi, he showed evidence of creativity in play and his visual matching ability was good.

483

Makoto, five years seven months old at the beginning of the study, had been diagnosed as autistic.
At the time he began, he had some limited receptive ability for short words, phrases and commands, but his expressive speech was predominantly
echolalic with only a few meaningful words and
short phrases (e.g. "juice" when he wanted to be
given juice; or "MacDonald" when he wanted to go
for a hamburger). Makoto could draw and had some
normal play. He also showed high ability in
matching shapes and colors.

Four years four months old at the beginning of the
study, Toshiaki had been diagnosed as autistic.
He had a very limited receptive vocabulary and no
expressive speech. His only play behavior consisted of lining up objects. He was able to match
complex shapes of various colors and sizes.

Method

Training materials consisted of four or five different pictures of the same object, with each
differing in color, size, and abstractness. During
training a picture and the word in three or four
centimeter kanji were inserted into a plastic case
with magnetized plastic attached to the back. The
individual kanji words were also placed in magnetized cases. Many Japanese children's words that
are ordinarily written in kana were sometimes written by us using Chinese characters while some were
improvised. Words of the same length were always
tested together. In the training task, a picture
with the kanji showing was placed on the board and
the subject chose the matching kanji from those in
front of him. The pictures were left on the board
until all were matched. Scoring was done for four
major tasks: 1)Picture with Kanji to Kanji (PK →
K)- this was the pattern matching task done with
the kanji showing 2)Picture to Kanji (P → K)- this
testing was usually done the following week after
the child had taken the pictures home to supposedly
practice. A picture with no kanji showing was
placed on the board and the subject had to choose

484

the correct kanji from the four in front of him.
3) Speech to Picture (Sp → P) - the experimenter
pronounced the word and the child chose the correct picture from the seven to fifteen in front
of him. 4) Speech to Kanji (Sp → K) - the experimenter said a word and the subject chose the
correct kanji from the seven to fifteen kanji words
before him.

Results

Appendix I shows the results of all subjects by
task including two otherwise normal but profoundly
deaf children aged three and a half and five and
a half at the time of the study. In summarizing
the general results, it can be said that Takeshi
acquired visual recognition for meaning for a large
number of kanji words, and demonstrated some ability to process these words in sentences. He spontaneously wrote the kanji for "ear" and "mouth"
while patting his own ear and mouth and wrote the
kanji for "dog". Many of these kanji words were
used to request desired things in the home and the
experimental situation. Excellent ability in the
highly complex pattern matching of kanji was observed and the few errors which occurred were mainly on words where the concept could not be grasped
by the child. Early training when the child was
still not processing auditory input showed that the
visual symbol was as effective (though not as con-
veniently available) as auditory words in helping
the child form concepts of unfamiliar words. Later
training with this subject showed him capable of
learning phonetic kana words though the same word
in kanji was consistently easier for him. There
was evidence to show that kanji word training contributed to improvement in emotional, social, and
language behavior.

With near-normal interpersonal relationships, better receptive speech ability, and creative play
behavior, Koichi was considered less impaired than
the autistic-tendencied Takeshi. Interestingly
enough, though he did learn many kanji words for

485

meaning, he did not perform as well as Takeshi.
What did distinguish him from Takeshi and the other
two children was his frequent demonstration of
creative and symbolic understanding of the kanji
in his spontaneous play, some examples of which
were: 1) He placed the kanji for "stand" on the
board and made everyone stand 2) He held the kanji
for "mirror" in front of his face as though he were
using a mirror 3) He brought a cup of water and the
kanji for "lake" together as if to say "they are
both water" 4) Put a "whistle" kanji to the recorder's mouth 5) Held the "mother" kanji up to his
mother's face 6) Walked the kanji for "walk"
7) Put the "sugar" kanji in his mouth 8) Gave his
sister's kanji some sugar 9) Grabbed the kanji for
rabbit and began to hop. This child was also taught
sign language signs.   In one month's time he
learned approximately ninety signs, many of which
he could use both on command and spontaneously to
request things and comment on his environment. A
few examples of this are: 1) Saw a standing pig
and used the "stand" sign 2) Did the "water" sign
for the "faucet" picture even though no water was
shown in the picture 3) When the picture of a
sleeping dog was placed on the board, Koichi used
the "sleep" sign 4) During the teaching of the word
"policeman", the picture of two policemen and a po-
licebox was put up. Seeing this, Koichi signed the
sign for "house" 5) The picture of an ambulance
also contained the picture of a stretcher; seeing
this, Koichi produced the sign for "sleep" 6) Saw
the picture of an aquarium and did the "water" sign.

In addition to the three hundred and eight recorded
incidents of spontaneous signs at home for Koichi,
there were various incidents involving kanji:
1) Kanji words found on his toys or in newspapers
were pointed out and his understanding of their
meaning was made evident by his actions or use of
signs. These words were "mouth", "money", "car",
"bicycle", "airplane", and "big" 2) On six different occasions, Koichi brought the "eat" kanji
to the table when everyone sat down to eat. He
then placed it next to everyone's mouth 3) Even

though able to correctly match the kanji to the correct picture, he would put the kanji for "flower"("hana" in Japanese) to his nose (also pronounced "hana" in Japanese) as if to say "they have the same pronunciation". 4) He would correctly imitate the actions on seeing the kanji for "walk", "run", "cry", "baseball", "crawl", and rabbit" 5) Though the Picture to Kanji task was correctly performed for the words "strawberry" and "mother", he pointed to his mother (母) upon seeing the kanji for "strawberry" (苺) 6) Upon seeing the kanji for "cry" (泣), he pointed to the (立) part which read alone means "to stand" and stood up from a sitting position 7) He pinched his sister to make her cry and then held the "cry" kanji to her face 8) Imitated driving upon seeing the "car" kanji 9) Pointed out that the first kanji in the word for "sugar" (砂糖) was the same as that in "sandpile" (砂場) 10) Expressed a liking for the "sweet" kanji.

There were three other tasks which illustrate even more clearly the richness of association of Koichi's mind. When studying words of people in various occupations and the things they commonly use (e.g. doctor-stethoscope; fireman-hose; mailman-letter), we would put a picture of, for instance, a mailman on the board and then ask, "What does a mailman carry?", to which Koichi had to choose the kanji word for "letter" from the five kanji in front of him. Of six trials of this sort, all were correct. In a more difficult variation on this task, the experimenter placed only the kanji word on the board and asked "Who carries this?". The task would be for the child to read the kanji word for "gun" and then choose the kanji word for "policeman". Of the seventy-three trials of this kind, sixty-four or 88% were correct.

In order to test whether the kanji learned generalized to the other senses, Koichi was taught the words for "sugar" and "salt" and then given a taste of each with no other clues provided. In five trials where he had to choose from among four kanji, he responded correctly four times (80%).

487

Though not as dramatic as the evidence from Koichi and Takeshi, the evidence from the two "autistic" children, Makoto and Toshiaki, can tell us several things. The first of these is that though some authors have held that autistic children are not capable of symbolic language behavior, results with these two children with high visuo-motor ability showed them to be capable of learning to attach meaning to ideographic language symbols (kanji). In learning these words, the children proved themselves capable of extracting essential information about the words and developing a generalized concept. They did not respond to isolated features but seemed to synthesize information from a variety of pictures to create their concept. Observation of these two children seemed to point to their being impaired in different ways with one having a more sensory-auditory problem than the other. Makoto and Toshiaki also demonstrated a difference in the processing of different types of words and this would appear to point to a cognitive deficit over and above primary visual and auditory processing problems. This type of visual training is felt to have played a role in the increase in meaningful speech observed in the echolalic child. The visual teaching method (unclear if the symbols or pictures were responsible) appeared to help the child retain the auditory word. It was observed that the echolalic child responded more consistently with the visual symbol than with the auditory word. There was also some evidence to indicate that this child may have had difficulties with face recognition and may possibly have had mirror vision.

Both children showed generalization of the words learned to other situations. There were, however, clear differences in the ability to handle various word classes (i.e. concrete nouns, adjectives, verbs, names of people, foods, etc.), and this type of training may prove useful in investigating the minds of children of this kind.

One interesting incident deserves mention as it may prove of use in assessment. Excessive difficulty with the kanji for colors raised the question

of whether Toshiaki might be colorblind. Color-
blindness test pictures composed of very abstract
dot drawings of a flower, an elephant, and a dog
were placed on the board one at a time with the
usual four kanji to choose from. No training was
done for these, but to our great surprise, Toshiaki
chose the correct kanji for each of the three pictures without error in three successive trials.
His problem with color was clearly not due to color-
blindness.

Research with these children does not support recent
claims that autism is due only to a language impairment. It would appear that these children have a
variety of problems, one aspect of which is the
language disability. Even so, the two children appear to be different in the exact nature of their
language impairment with the echolalic child having
fewer problems of a sensory auditory kind and for
some reason not performing as well as the younger
child on visual memory tasks. This may be a memory
deficit, an overall cognitive (associational) deficit, a visual learning deficit, etc., but it does
not appear to be related to the reception of sound
only.

Conclusions

There are a number of generalizations which can be
made based on the work with all four children. The
first of these is that the difficulty in learning
a kanji word did not seem to depend on its visual
complexity, but rather on the child's ability to
grasp the concept behind the word. Though the
children usually grasped the concept of the words
learned, it was observed that the child could sometimes make the auditory-visual association between
voice and kanji words even when he did not yet
understand the meaning of the word. Overall kanji
words learned showed generalization and could be
matched to pictures seen for the first time. Another observation was that if the child was first
trained using large kanji words, these could then
be reduced by as much as 75% or more with no loss
of comprehension by the child.

Results from all children taught would seem to indicate that children aged three (and probably
younger) can learn to read if a visual, whole word
method is emphasized. It is also clear that kanji
and probably other whole word or gestalt symbols
can be matched to pictures even when the subject
is not capable of speech. Though not true of all,
some mute children appear to be capable of assigning the qualities of an object to the abstract kanji symbols. Results indicate that both kanji and
kana might be taught earlier in Japan if a highly
visual technique is used.

All the evidence taken together underscores the
problem of the specificity of the modality of input.
Though not advocating this type of static word
training as the sole form of language therapy, it is
believed that it can be helpful in pinpointing and
capitalizing on the preserved abilities of the language delayed or disabled child.

BIBLIOGRAPHY

Gardner, Howard, 1973 , Developmental dyslexia: the for-
gotten lesson of monsieur c. Psychology Today, 7(3):
62-67.

Rees, Mary A., 1979 , Alternative modes of communication
for the language disabled - evidence from brain function and neuropathology, Thesis presented as partial
requirement for an M.A. in psychology at the University of Tokyo, Tokyo, Japan.

Nishio, Mary Rees, 1981 , Kanji reading by a prekinder-
garten language-disabled child: a pilot study, Brain
and Language, 13: 259-289.

NAME	AGE	PK→K*	# of TRIALS	P→Kˣ	# of TRIALS	SP→P*	# of Trials	SP→K*	# of Trials	ALL TASKS	# of Trials	DISABILITY
TAKESHI	3 1/2	93%	940	79%	1084	74%	574	83%	521	83%	3119	Devel.delay/ autistic tendencied
KOICHI	3 1/2	67%	618	74%	456	77%	254	91%	181	74%	1509	Devel.delay
YASUAKI	3 1/2	79%	448	73%	375	72%	123	55%	109	73%	1055	Deaf (Profoundly)
KAZUKO	5 1/2	99%	466	94%	474	91%	203	82%	367	92%	1510	Deaf (Profoundly)
MAKOTO	5 1/2	88%	292	72%	428	89%	249	66%	248	78%	1217	Autistic/ echolalic
TOSHIAKI	4	97%	216	92%	150	78%	145	79%	107	88%	618	Autistic/ mute

*This score represents the percent correct of all trials on this task.

APPENDIX I. AVERAGE SCORES OF ALL SUBJECTS BY TASK.

CHILD LANGUAGE AND FAILURE IN READING ACQUISITION: A TWO-WAY
RELATIONSHIP   By P.G. Patel, University of Ottawa

It is at some point during the period of middle childhood,
the age range between five and seven that most of the children in literate societies begin to read (Gibson and Levin
1975; Doehring 1976). The eye joins the ear at a certain
level of psycholinguistic development and orthographic and
speech processes become interdependent. A significant
proportion of the child population, except in Japan (Makita
1968, 1975) and China (Kuo 1978), remains different in this
regard for a variety of reasons. The children who cannot
acquire orthographic processing at a rate commensurate with
their mental age even though they have no apparent psychosocial disadvantages are placed in a clinical category called
'dyslexia' or 'specific reading retardation'. Since this
concept has no scientific content (Rutter 1978), I shall use
terms like 'failure in reading acquisition' and 'deficient
reading acquisition' in this paper.

When these children are studied, mostly in clinical neurology
or neuropsychology, it is found that deficient reading acquisition is usually correlated with a large number of symptoms.
As Critchley (1970) suggests, most of these correlates are a
part of the epiphenomenon which is characteristic of brain
problems. In other words, these deficits cannot be directly
responsible for reading acquisition disorders. Interestingly,
most of these symptoms occuring with persistent reading
problems seem to involve different aspects of language development. Perhaps the study of these children within the
framework of child language development would help understand
the real genotypic basis of failure in reading acquisition.
I would like to present a theoretical argument and the partial results of a study in this direction.

The psycholinguistic organization and processing in children
before the age of four-five are closely tied to objects,
people, and events in specific situations. Initially, auditory images of words and utterances are stored episodically
and these phonetic gestalts are recognized as such only in
conjunction with specific events (Menyuk and Menn, 1979).
Even toward the end of early childhood and the beginning of
middle childhood the storage seems to be mainly iconic.
Anglin's (1977) large-scale study shows that preschool children's knowledge of verbal concepts appears to be
"instance-oriented", and seems to be based on the ability to
recall specific encounters with specific instances. How do

preschool children then interpret utterances? There is a great deal of evidence to indicate that most of the children around the age of four deal with utterances in terms of their increasing knowledge of the world.

Strohmer and Nelson (1974) suggest that young children do not process word order, but consistently follow "probable event strategy", while 4-5-year-olds show evidence for a word order strategy. The absence of any critical use of syntactic information in utterance processing during early child-hood seems to be reflected in the acceptability judgements. Several studies indicate that the 4- and 5-year-olds judge acceptability on the basis of pragmatics and meaning; this tendency disappears after the age of six or so (Gleitman and Gleitman 1979; Hakes, Evans and Tunmer, 1980). It is not until the end of middle childhood that syntactic information can critically influence psycholinguistic performance. Scholes (1978) has been able to tap the developmental course of the ability to process utterances in terms of syntactic structure per se.

The studies by Scholes show that 5-year-olds perform like adolescents and adults on sentence-picture matching on the basis of lexical semantics. However, when the use of syn-tactic structure is critically necessary, the five-year-olds perform only at a chance level (50% correct). Cromer's (1976: 347) observations on the intermediate stage throw a great deal of light on the ongoing developmental changes:

> "...At about 6 years old, however, they enter what can be called the "intermediate stage". At this stage they no longer always treat the surface subject as the actor, but they do not yet per-form correctly. They get some structures right and others wrong. Furthermore, they are not simply acquiring the semantic markings or syn-tactical understanding of the particular words like "happy", "glad", "fun", and "tasty" which indicate which deep structure to recover when they are used in this structure. Rather, they are inconsistent from day to day in their answers, and this intermediate period lasts for about three years. Finally, about 9 to 10 years old, they fairly rapidly become capable of performing correctly in the adult manner..."

493

How does this confusion clear up? I should like to offer an explanatory perspective, albeit a speculative one.

At some point in time toward the end of early childhood and/ or the beginning of middle childhood, depending upon indivi- dual differences, most of the children show changes related to the organization of lexical memory. Petrey (1977) argues that the so-called syntagmatic-paradigmatic shift is an effect reflecting the separation of 'semantic memory'. As Menyuk and Menn (1979: 63) put it, the proto-words become words as they are untied from specific situations and intona- tion contours.

The three stage process of vocables first becoming words and then the lexicon postulated by Werner and Kaplan (1953) to explain conceptual development supports the logic of the present perspective. Involved in this organizational process, perhaps causally, is the development of what has come to be known as 'linguistic awareness' or 'metacoding' ability, that is , the ability to decompose utterances into phrases, words, morphemes, syllables, and phonemic segments. Karpova's (1977) study of Russian children indicates the trend in the segmental hierarchy: utterances as "unified semantic wholes", intonational-semantic groups of subjects and predicate", syllables, words, and finally phonemic units. There are many North American replications of this developmental trend involving different experimental tasks and procedures (Fox and Routh, 1975; Liberman, Shankweiler, Fischer, and Carter 1974; Rosner and Simon 1971; etc.). In spite of the method- ological issues involved in the study of linguistic awareness operationalized as segmental ability; there is no doubt that the phenomenon is natural in that it seems to be at the core of speech play. The different types of speech play indulged in by children, especially in middle childhood, involve phonological perception and recoding without any association with meaning. Sanches and Kirshenbalt-Gembeltt (1976) show how young children relish phonological gibberish. Interest- ingly, Francis (1972: 956) suggests that it is the "abili- ties to isolate words from sentences and to make comparisons across related constituents" that are responsible for "the lengthy reorganization of the mental filing system of the preschool child". Consequently, the process of auditory discrimination of minimal pair words becomes completely phonological. During the early stages of the development of the ability for auditory discrimination of minimal pair words, the process operates on a lexical basis. (Menyuk and Menn 1979); in other words, initially children recognize only familiar words when they are asked to make the same-different judgement (Barton 1976). It may very well be that the segmental ability is developmentally related to the ability for auditory discrimination on a phonological, that is, non-lexical basis. Ollila, Johnson, and Downing (1974) have reported that training kindergarten children for six weeks with an Elkonin type of phonemic segmentation program resulted in significantly higher Wepman scores for the experimental group than for a control group which received an auditory discrimination program stressing attention to environmental sounds and initial consonants, (cf. Helfgott 1976).

As the mental lexicon is acquiring the phonological and semantic representations, children also begin to store visual-images of words, given the climate of literacy. Children "grow into reading" (Monroe 1951: 125) "amalgamating ortho-graphic images into their growing lexical memory (Ehri 1980). As phonetic images of words get phonologically analyzed in the mental dictionary, so do the visual gestalt, for words get analyzed in terms of orthographic patterns involving graphological units corresponding to morphemes, syllables and phonemes. Thus develops the ability to decode the spelling patterns into sound patterns and lexical access and retrieval in response to printed words, especially in sentence and more so in discourse processing become efficient.

It seems that the acquisition of reading also facilitates a realignment of language functions (Olson 1972, 1975). The processing of written language involves an internal recoding which cannot be completed without syntactic information. Olson and Nickerson (1978: 134) suggest that during middle childhood "children come to operate upon sentences, rather than merely acting upon the meanings" as preschoolers do. There are also speculations and data to indicate that the process of internalizing orthographic representation furthers the acquisition of complex morphophonemic patterns (Moskowitz 1973), phonological discrimination (Jung 1977 cited in Valtin 1980), and higher syntactic-semantic structures (Greenfield 1972; Olson 1972).

495

The development of language after the age of five necessarily involves orthographic processing, especially in relation to the organization of internal lexicon and the higher syntactic-semantic processing. The emergence of reading depends upon a certain quality of language development along with literate ecology and also changes the course of further psycholinguistic maturation. In this perspective, the deficient language processes found in association with failure in reading acquisition or dyslexia include the causes as well as the consequences. The separation of the two is an exciting challenge waiting for the attention of many more students of child language. I shall now report a few selected aspects of a study in this direction. This study was done in collaboration with D. G. Doehring, R. L. Trites, and C. Fiedorowicz, (Doehring, Trites, Patel, and Fiedorowicz 1981).

Eighty-eight children and young adults within the age range of 8-14, with three older than 20 were selected from the referrals to the Neuropsychology Clinic at the Royal Ottawa Hospital. The majority of the IQ's were within the range of 90-110, the PIQ being higher than VIQ in most cases. There were more VIQ's below 90 and more PIQ's above 110. All the subjects were at least two years behind their school counterparts in reading acquisition which was assessed on the basis of standard tests, the WRAT and the Durrell Analysis of Reading Difficulty. There was increasing amount of retardation with increasing age uniformly on oral reading, silent reading, word recognition, word analysis, etc.

The language battery included Sound Deletion, Pig Latin, and Ubby Dubby as measures of segmentation-recoding (blending), morphophonemics at the intermediate level, and Ask-Tell, and Token Test for syntactic-semantics relational processing, Semantic Fields for lexical organization, Immediate Recall of Acceptable, Anomalous, Related Words, and Unrelated Word Strings for short-term verbal memory, and Cartoon Description for syntactic morphological generation. Sound Deletion requires taking out a given sound from words and regular non-sense syllables, for example: plate - p = late; lant - n = lat. Semantic Fields asked for two word associations.

All except the Cartoon Description were scored in terms of latency of response when the error rate was sufficiently low. The criterion of low error rate was based on the distributions of errors of a sample of normally-achieving children.

For normative trends, the battery was administered to ten
normal children per grade from Kindergarten through grade
six, a total of 70 children. Estimates of grade levels for
accuracy and for stable speed of response were first calculated. The accuracy limit was defined as the highest grade
where two or fewer subjects exceeded the criterion of errors
for a test; the latency limit was defined as the grade where
the latency of accurate responses approached a lower limit.
Grade 3 was important for the accuracy limit, and Grade 5
for the latency limit.

Centrally important in terms of the interpretation of the
results on the problem sample is the finding about individual
differences. The variability within grades and the overlap
of scores from grade to grade suggested that there was a wide
range of individual differences.

The scores of the subjects with reading disorders were expressed in terms of percentiles based on the performance of
the normal sample. A single distribution of error and
latency scores of the 70 children was made for each language
test, with the highest percentile assigned to the shortest
latency and the lowest to the largest number of errors.

To look at some findings, the subjects with reading problems
were about as impaired in language processes as they were in
reading processes. The worst performance was on morphophonemics and syntactic-morphological complexity in spontaneous
use where they all were at about the level of normal first
grade children. The same was the case for semantic fields
and segmentation-recoding, and repeating randomly arranged
word lists, while about two years on ask-tell, parts of
Token-Test, and repetition of acceptable anomalous strings.
The total pattern suggests one finding clearly: the higher
level language processes are almost normal, while the lower
level processes involving short-term verbal memory and
segmentation-coding are uniformly deficient. It can be
said that the linguistic deficits associated with failure in
reading acquisition tend to involve, in most children, the
processes at and below the lexical level.

In contrast to the results on reading component abilities,
where there was less than 50% overlap on the majority of the
tests, the reading problem and normal groups overlapped at

least 50% on all language tests. Within the 8 to 11 age
range, over half of the subjects with reading problems had
language abilities comparable to those of normally-achieving
children.

The conventional R Factor analysis yielding Four Factors
gave the most information about correlational trends. Factor
1 involved Ask and Tell and the Token Test; Factor 2 involved
short-term verbal memory, and Factor 3 involved phonemic
segmentation-blending. When 3, 4, and 5 Factor solutions
were used to analyse the percentiles of the 88 subjects by
the Q technique, each solution yielded only two stable
factors, which suggested two different profiles or subgroups.
Both the profiles involved low scores on phonemic segmentation-
blending, morphophonemics, and semantic fields, and relatively
good scores on Ask and Tell. It was the performance on the
repetition task that differentiated the two subgroups:
Type 1 was poor on both syntactic and unrelated word strings;
the scores on the unrelated word strings were worse than those
on the acceptable and anomalous strings, obviously due to
syntactic structure. Type 2 was characterized by relatively
good scores on both the syntactic and unrelated word strings.
The factor differentiating the two types seems to involve
short-term verbal memory; clearly the deficient performance
cannot be attributed to syntactic-semantic knowledge.

The stability of the Q technique classification was evaluated
by analyzing subsamples of different ages and also by cluster
analysis. The 88 subjects were divided into groups of 31
subjects 8 to 20 years old, 28 subjects 11 to 13.5 years old,
and 29 subjects 13.6 to 17 years old. The language test
scores were factor analyzed by a 3 Factor solution. The
factors defining the two subgroups emerged very clearly in
each age group as either Factor 1 or Factor 2, with the
third Factor not revealing any clear pattern. The majority
of subjects, that is, 78% were classified into the same types
in the smaller samples. Thus, the patterns of psycholinguistic deficit did not change with age.

A critically relevant question not yet explored asks whether
the children who were reported to have delayed and/or deviant
speech production in their developmental histories would fall
in one of these two subgroups. Out of the 88 subjects, as
many as 42 of them were reported by their parents to have
ontogenetic irregularities. It is now being increasingly

498

accepted that both deficient language development and deficient reading acquisition are not homogeneous entities. It
is only logical to expect some interlinks between the subgroups in the two areas.

In conclusion, the developmental perspective from child
language is critically important in the study of reading
acquisition failure. The reverse is equally productive in
understanding the developmental course and conditions necessary for language maturation. Further work along the line
suggested in this paper is likely to reveal the role of
orthographic structure in child language representation and
processing.

REFERENCES

Anglin, J.M. 1977. Word, Object and Conceptual Development. New York: W.M. Norton & Co. Inc.

Barton, D. 1976. Phonemic discrimination and the knowledge of words in children under 3 years. Papers and Reports on Child Language Development. Department of Linguistics, Stanford University.

Barton, D. 1980. Phonemic perception in children. In G. Yeni-Komshian, J.F. Kavanagh, and C.A. Ferguson (Eds.), Child Phonology, Volume 2, pp. 97-116. New York: Academic Press.

Critchley, M. 1970. The Dyslexic Child. London: Heinemann Medical Books Ltd.

Cromer, R. 1976. Developmental strategies for language. In V. Hamilton and M. Vernon (Eds.), The Development of Cognitive Processes. London: Academic Press.

Doehring, D.G. 1976. Acquisition of rapid reading responses. Monographs of the Society for Research in Child Development, No. 165.

Doehring, D.G., R.L. Trites, P.G. Patel, and C. Fiedorowicz. 1981. Reading Disabilities: The Interaction of Reading, Language, and Neuropsychological Deficits. New York: Academic Press.

Ehri, L. 1980. The role of orthographic images in learning printed words. In Kavanagh, J.F. and Venezky, R.L. (Eds.), Orthography, Reading, and Dyslexia. Baltimore: University Press.

Fox, B. and Routh, D.K. 1975. Analyzing spoken language into words, syllables, and phonemes: a developmental study. Jounal of Psycholinguistic Research 4, 331-342.

Francis, H. 1972. Toward an explanation of the paradigmatic-syntagmatic shift. Child Development 43, 949-559.

Gibson, E. and Levin, H. 1975. The Psychology of Reading. Cambridge: the MIT Press.

Gleitman, L. and H. Gleitman. 1979. Language use and language judgement. In Individual Differences in Language Ability and Language Behavior, ed. by C.J. Fillmore, D. Kempler, and Wm. S-Y Wang, 103-126. New York: Academic Press.

Greenfield, P.M. 1972. Oral and written language: The consequences for cognitive development in Africa, the United States and England. Language and Speech 15, 169-178.

Hakes, D., Evans, J. and Tunmer, W. 1980. The Development of Metalinguistic Abilities in Children. New York: Springer-Verlag.

Helfgott, J. 1976. Phonemic segmentation and blending skills of kindergarten children: implications for beginning reading acquisition. Contemporary Educational Psychol. 1, 157-169.

Karpova, S.N. 1977. The Realization of the Verbal Composition of Speech by Preschool Children. The Hague: Mouton.

Kirshenbalt-Gimblet, B. (Ed.) 1976. Speech Play: Research and Resources for Studying Linguistic Creativity. Philadelphia: University of Pennsylvania Press.

Kuo, W.F. 1978. A preliminary study of reading disabilities in the Republic of China. Collection of Papers by National Taiwan University 20: 57-78.

Liberman, I., Shankweiler, D., Fischer, F.W., and Carter, B. 1974. Explicit syllable and phoneme segmentation in the young child. Journal of Experimental Child Psychology 18, 201-212.

Makita, K. 1968. The rarity of reading disability in Japan. American Journal of Orthopsychiatry 38: 599-614.

Makita, K. 1975. Dyslexia and orthography. In D. Moyle (Ed.), Reading: What of the Future? London: Ward Lock Educ.

Menyuk, P. and Menn, L. 1979. Early strategies for the perception and production of words and sounds. In P. Fletcher and M. Garman (Eds.), Language Acquisition. London: Cambridge University Press.

501

Monroe, M. 1951. Growing into Reading: How Readiness for Reading Develops at Home and at School. New York: Greenwood Press, Publishers.

Moskowitz, A. 1973. On the status of the vowel shift in English. In T. Moore (Ed.), Cognitive Development and the Acquisition of Language. New York: Academic Press.

Olson, D.R. 1972. Language use for communicating, instructing, and thinking. In J.B. Carroll and R.O. Freedle(Eds), Language Comprehension and the Acquisition of Knowledge. John Wiley & Sons, pp. 139-167.

Olson, D.R. 1975. Review essay on Toward a Literate Society (J.B. Carroll and J. Chall, Eds.). Proceedings of the National Academy of Education 2, 109-178.

Olson D.R. and Nickerson, N. 1978. Language development through the school years: Learning to confine interpretation to the information in the text. In K.E. Nelson (Ed.), Children's Language, Vol. 1. New York: Gardner Press, Inc., pp. 117-169.

Ollila, L., Johnson, T. and Downing, J. 1974. Adapting Russian methods of auditory discrimination training for English. Elementary English 51: 1138-1145.

Petrey, S. 1977. Word associations and the development of lexical memory. Cognition 5, 57-71.

Rosner, J. and Simon, D.P. 1971. The auditory analysis test: An initial report. Journal of Learning Disabilities 4, 384-398.

Rutter, M.L. 1978. Prevalence and types of dyslexia. In A. Benton and D. Pearl (Eds.), Dyslexia: An Appraisal of Current Knowledge. London: Oxford University Press.

Scholes, R. 1978. Syntactic and lexical components of sentence comprehension. In A. Caramazza and E. Zurif(Eds), Language Acquisition and Language Breakdown:Parallels and Divergencies, Baltimore: The Johns Hopkins University Press.

Strohner, H. and Nelson, K.E. 1974. The young child's development of sentence comprehension: Influence of event probability, nonverbal context, syntactic form and strategies. Child Development 45, 567-576.

Valtin, R. 1980. Deficiencies in research on reading deficiencies. In J.F. Kavanagh and R.L. Venezky (Eds.), Orthography, Reading, and Dyslexia. Baltimore: University Park Press.

Werner, H. and Kaplan, B. 1963. Symbol Formation. New York: John Wiley & Sons, Inc.

A Developmental Analysis of Spelling Pattern Abstraction

in

Learning Disabled Spellers

Sybil Schwartz Ph.D.

McGill-Montreal Children's Hospital Learning Centre

It is far more difficult for Learning Disabled children to learn to spell than to read. Most children continue to have problems in spelling long after they have learned to read. We have little understanding of the nature of the difficulty or the underlying deficits when a child fails to learn to spell.

Our knowledge of the normal acquisition process is limited as well. Until fairly recently it was believed that beginning spellers use the same strategies as adults and that learning to spell involved a change in the number of words that could be spelled and the speed of execution (Horn, 1964).

Modern linguistic investigation has led to the view that spelling is a language-based skill with developmental stages. This developmental view assumes that there are qualitative differences between the strategies used by younger children at the early stages of learning to spell and those used by older proficient spellers (Marsh, Friedman, Welch, and Desberg, 1980).

Spelling depends to a large extent upon an intuitive mastery of a rule system and a collection of facts. What a child learns depends on the cognitive and linguistic maturity at the time. Investigation of spelling ability in pre-school and elementry school children indicate that spelling and reading are separate language systems whose acquisition processes do not necessarily interact (Read,

1974; Chomsky, 1971). Read (1971, 1973) found tht preschool children derived similar ways of spelling sounds.
Sounds were classified on a phonetic rather than an
auditory basis.

Another study of the early development of spelling
by Beers (1974) confirmed the existance of nonstandard
spelling patterns in the the misspellings of children in
Grades 1 and 2. He found that spelling skills are acquired
by following a predictable sequence from a basically
syllabic representation to a method which reflects an
awareness of each sound in the syllable. At first, children
spell by the phonemic feature that is emphasized in the
alphabetic letter-name. The next stage is the emergence
of an awareness that letters represent sounds rather than
being sounds. Patterns begin to emerge, e.g. long vowels
which were spelled by a letter-name are accompanied by a
marker. Before the correct form is mastered there is a
transitional stage where the markers are not yet used
correctly .

The four stages postulated by Beers (1974) can be
summarized as follows:

1. No attempt or omission of the vowel element,
i.e. BK/bake.

2. Letter-name strategy, i.e. BAK/bake

3. Transitional strategy, i.e. BAEK/bake

4. Correct form, i.e. BAKE

Similar stages have been described in the acquisition of
reading (Gibson and Levin, 1975). First the child must
master phonemic segmentation and the ability to use
standard grapheme-phoneme correspondences. The next
stage is the abstraction of principles. The child must find
the invariants in the system and learn the rules. Children
must move away from the notion that the relationship
among letters in a word is the sole indicator of

pronunciation.

Hanna, Hanna, Hodges and Rudorf (1966) examined children's knowledge of sound-symbol correspondences for the spelling process, but few studies have looked at how or when spelling patterns are learned. One study by Schwartz examined children's knowledge of spelling patterns at each grade level from 2 to 5 (Schwartz, 1975; Schwartz and Doehring, 1977). She studied the ability of Good Spellers (the top third of a normal distribution) and Poor Spellers (the bottom third of a normal distribution) to abstract and encode two types of patterns: (1) Orthographic patterns, such as the alternation of single and double consonants to mark the quality of the preceding vowel, e.g. coma versus comma; and (2) Morphological patterns, such as the formation of the plural or the past tense. Both groups showed the same developmental trends but Good Spellers were about 2 years ahead of the Poor Spellers in abstracting the two types of patterns. Schwartz concluded that pattern abstraction is part of the process of learning to spell.

Even fewer studies have looked at the spelling ability of the learning disabled population or at which aspects of the spelling process or developmental sequence they find difficult to master. Several classification studies have suggested that those learning disabled spellers, who are able to spell phonetically, are less disabled and more linguistically advanced than those who cannot (Boder, 1971; Naidoo, 1972; Nelson and Warrington, 1975; Sweeney and Rourke, 1978). As yet there has been no systematic developmental study of the acquisition of spelling skills by learning disabled children. The present study was designed to investigate age-related changes in the ability of learning disabled children to abstract spelling patterns and to assess the strategies they use in the learning process.

506

Subjects:

A total of 80 Learning Disabled Spellers were studied, 20 at each age level from 8 to 11. The Learning Disabled Spellers were all diagnosed as having learning problems by the staff of the McGill-Montreal Children's Hospital Learning Centre. Criteria for this diagnosis were significant difficulties in learning to read and spell in the absence of mental retardation, primary emotional problems or major neurological or sensory deficits.

Tests:

Three tests designed by Schwartz (1975) were used. Test I was a multiple choice test of nonsense words. The words were embedded in a carrier phrase spoken by the examiner. The subject had to choose one of three printed nonsense words. Test II was a multiple choice test of familiar, real words which were given in the same manner as Test I. On Test III the subject had to write nonsense words from dictation. The nonsense words differed from those used in Test I. Here again the words were embedded in a carrier phrase.

Each test contained 30 items exemplifying two types of patterns, Morphological and Orthographic. Morphological patterns are used to convey grammatical information. The 13 Morphological items comprised five sub-patterns related to the spelling of the plural, three to the past tense, two to the possessive and three to adjectival items (the comparative, the superlative, and adjectival y). The Orthographic patterns investigated concern visual information that is not derived directly from the spoken language but represents the internal stucture of the orthograpy. Of the 17 Orthographic items, ten related to vowel correspondence, four related to consonant correspondence, and three dealt with syllabic consonants. The same sub-patterns were used in each of the tests. It was hypothesized that the two patterns might be abstracted differently, as suggested by Gibson's theory that different features of words are processed independently and sequentially (Gibson, 1971).

Procedure

The subjects were tested in small groups or individually. Tests were always given in the same order - Test I, Test II, and Test III, with a 15 to 20 minute break interspersed between Tests I and II, and a 45 minute to one hour break between Tests II and III. Tests I and II required about 10 to 15 minutes each to administer. The time required for Test III varied with the skill of the subject, ranging from 10 to 25 minutes.

Results

Table I shows the percentage correct scores for Tests I, II, and III for 20 Learning Disabled Spellers at each age level from 8 to 11. A comparison of percentage correct scores for each of the tests indicates that for all age levels the highest percentage of correct scores was obtained on Test II (multiple choice, real words) and the lowest on Test III (written, nonsense words). It should also be noted that chance performance on the multiple choice tests (Tests I nd II) would produce 33% correct answers, so that the Test I mean percentages for the 8 and 9 year old subjects (36.8 and 37.5 respectively) are just slightly above chance.

Insert Table I about here

A two-way analysis of variance was performed separately for each of the three tests. The independent variables were Age (8, 9, 10, 11), and Patterns (Morphological and Orthographic). For all three tests performance improved with age ($p < .001$).

Newman-Keuls Tests were used to determine the direction of the difference in performance for each of the three tests. In each instance, it was found that both the 10 and 11 yeart olds' performances differed significantly from the 8 and 9 year olds'; however neither the 8 and 9

508

Table 1

Mean percent correct scores for Tests I, II, and III as a function of Age and Spelling Patterns

Age	Test I			Test II			Test III		
	M	O	M&O	M	O	M&O	M	O	M&O
8	38.0	34.7	36.8	41.6	48.8	45.2	14.2	10.6	12.4
9	36.2	38.8	37.5	53.1	52.1	52.6	17.3	8.8	13.1
10	56.1	54.4	55.3	71.1	77.1	74.1	33.8	30.9	32.4
11	54.4	49.8	52.1	67.3	73.1	70.2	38.8	31.6	35.2
Pooled	46.4	44.4		58.3	62.8		26.0	20.5	

509

year olds', nor the 10 and 11 year olds' differed significantly.

There was a Pattern effect for Test II (multiple choice, real words) F (1,76)=9.50, p <.001 and III (written, nonsense words), F (1,76)=14.18, p<.001. On Test II Orthographic scores were higher than Morphological scores, and on Test III Morphological scores were higher than Orthographic scores. There were no significant interactions.

Error Analyses

To investigate the strategies used by Learning Disabled Spellers individual error analyses were carried out on eight of the items from Test III, the written test of nonsense words (see Table 2). These eight items were chosen for analysis to investigate the presence of nonstandard spelling patterns noted by Read (1973) and later by Beers and Henderson (1977) in the spelling of pre-schoolers and beginning spellers, and to see if the four stages of spelling development noted by Beers (1974) would be followed by the Learning Disabled Spellers. The nonstandard patterns investigated were the use of a vowel letter-name to code a vowel (Items 8 and 9), a consonant letter-name to code a syllable (Item 26), T to code the past tense (Item 15), and a syllabic consonant to code a syllable (Items 18,21,22, and 27). Responses were coded as Correct (C), Transitional (T), Nonstandard (NS), and Other (O), all other incorrect answers, corresponding approximately to Beer's four stages. It was hypothesized that Learning Disabled Spellers would persist in the use of nonstandard spelling patterns characteristic of younger children.

Insert Table 2 about here

The percentage of spelling responses classified as Correct, Transitional, Nonstandard, and Other for 20

Table 2

Examples of Responses Classifed as
Transitional (T), Nonstandard (NS), and
Other (O) for Items used in the Error Analysis

	Item	T	NS	O
8.	gabe	GAEB	GAB	GIB
9.	vike	VIEK	VIK	VK
26.	rundy	RUNDE	RUND	RON
15.	mished	MISHD	MISHT	MISH
18.	juffle	JUFFEL	JUFL	JUF
21.	raffom	RAFME	RAFM	RAF
22.	gadden	GADNE	GADN	GAND
27.	vister	VISTRE	VISTR	VEST

Learning Disabled Spellers at each age from 8 to 11 for the eight items analyzed can be seen in Table 3. In all instances and at all ages the persistance of nonstandard spelling patterns is evident. The older Learning Disabled Spellers (ages 10 and 11) used fewer Nonstandard Patterns that the younger Learning Disabled groups (ages 8 and 9). However, Nonstandard Patterns were still used 26.3% of the time by the 10 year olds and 22.5% of the time by the 11 year olds. Other responses were used less by the 10 and 11 year old Learning Disabled Spellers than the 8 and 9 year olds, but here again, were still quite prevalent in the older subjects (25% for the 10 year olds and 25.6% for the 11 year olds). A small percentage of Transitional responses was found at all age levels.

Insert Table 3 about here

Discussion

At ages 8 and 9 the Learning Disabled Spellers showed little ability to abstract patterns on the two hardest tests, I and III (nonsense words), while on Test II scores were only minimally above chance. On all three tests there was no significant change from age 8 to 9. However, from age 9 to 10 there was considerable improvement in performance. There was no significant improvement in pattern abstraction from age 10 to 11. This may indicate a slow rate of growth in the ability to abstract spelling patterns or a cessation of development. Clinical experience would suggest the former. Testing with older Learning Disabled Children would be necessary to determine if and when development in pattern abstraction ability continues .

The hypothesis that the two patterns would be abstracted differently was supported to some extent. On Test II (the easiest test) scores for Orthographic Patterns were higher than those for Morphological Patterns, while on Test III (the hardest test) scores were higher on Morphological Patterns than Orthographic Patterns. There may be some indication that Orthographic Patterns are

512

Table 3

Percentage of Spelling Responses Classifed as
Correct (C), Transitional (T), Nonstandard
(NS), and Other (O) in Error Analysis of 8
items from Test III.

Age	C	T	NS	O
8	18.5	5.0	33.8	42.5
9	12.5	6.3	42.5	38.8
10	42.5	6.3	26.3	25.0
11	46.9	5.0	22.5	25.6

abstracted with greater ease as spelling ability improves.

The hypothesis that the Learning Disabled Spellers would persist in the use of Nonstandard Patterns was supported. This would indicate functioning at a stage of spelling acquisition similar to that of pre-school and begining spellers. The persistance of Other responses in the older subjects, indicating an even lower level of functioning, was unexpected. These responses correspond to non-phonetic spelling. Forty-two and one half percent of the responses of the 8 year olds, 38.8% of the responses of the 9 year olds, 25% of the responses of the 10 year olds, and 25.6% of the responses of the 11 year olds were non-phonetic. One cannot determine from the data whether the difficulty lies in the ability to segment words into phonemes or in the use of sound-symbol correspondences .

The results of the present study support the clinical observation that Learning Disabled Spellers are delayed in the ability to abstract spelling patterns but do not indicate if spelling pattern abstraction continues in these children after the age of 11. Further testing of older Learning Disabled Spellers is needed. It would be interesting to compare the development of spelling patterns abstraction in those Learning Disbled Spellers who have difficulty with phonemic segmentation with those who do not.

REFERENCES

Beers, J. First and second grade children's developing orthographic concepts of tense and lax vowels. Unpublished doctoral dissertation. Univeristy of Virginia, 1974.

Beers, J. & Henderson, F. First grade children's developing orthographic concepts. Research in the Teaching of English, Fall, 1977.

Boder, E. Developmental dyslexia: Prevailing diagnostic concepts and a new diagnostic approach. In H.R.

514

Myklebust (Ed.). Progress in Learning Disabilities (Vol. II). New York: Grune and Stratton, 1971.

Chomsky, S. Invented spelling in the open classroom. In special issue, "Child Language, 1975", reprinted from Word, 1971, 27, 1,3.

Gibson, E. Perceptual learning and the theory of word perception. Cognitive Psychology, 1971, 2, 351-368.

Hanna, P.R., Hanna, J.S., Hodges, R.E. & Rudorf, E.H.Jr. Phoneme-grapheme Correspondences as Cues to Spelling Improvement (Bureau of Research, U.S. Department of Health, Education and Welfare) Washington, D.C.: U.S. Government Printing Office, 1966.

Horn, T.D. Spelling. In R.L. Ebels, (Ed.) Encyclopedia of Educational Research (4th edition), New York: Macmillan, 1969.

Marsh, G., Friedman, M., Welch, V. & Desberg, P. The development of strategies in spelling. In U. Frith (Ed.). Cognitive Processes in Spelling. London: Academic Press Inc., 1980.

Naidoo, S. Specific dyslexia. New York: Wiley & Sons, 1972.

Nelson, H.E. & Warrington, E.K. Developmental spelling retardation. In R.M. Knights and D.J. Bakker, (Eds.). The neuropsychology of learning disabilities: Theoretical approaches.Baltimore: University Park Press, 1975.

Read, C. Pre-school children's knowledge of English phonology. Harvard Educational Review. 1971, 41, 1-34.

Read, C. Children's judgements of phonetic similarities in relation to Eglish spelling. Language Learning. 1973, 23, 17-28.

Schwartz, S. A developmental study of children's ability to acquire knowledge of spelling patterns. Unpublished doctoral dissertation. McGill University, 1975.

Schwartz, S. & Doehring, D. A developmental study of children's ability to abstract spelling patterns. Developmental Psychology, 1977, 13, 419-420.

Sweeney, J.E. & Rourke, B.P. Neuropsychological significances of phonetically accurate and phonetically inaccurate spelling errors in younger and older retarded spellers. Brain and Language, 1978, 6, 212-228.

This is publication no. 82019 of the McGill University - Montreal Children's Hospital Research Institute.

SPELLING ERRORS IN THE COMPOSITIONS OF NORMAL CHILDREN

Christopher M. Sterling
and
Philip T. Smith

(University of Reading)

INTRODUCTION.

English spelling has a reputation for idiosyncrasy, and this reputation is founded on the existence of large numbers of irregularly spelled words. The problem with these words is that their spelling is not predictable from the alphabetic correspondences and rules of English spelling. For example tnere seems to be no coherent reason why <u>yacht</u> is spelled the way it is and not as <u>yot</u> (as in <u>cot</u>, <u>dot</u>, <u>not</u> etc.). Not surprisingly, irregularly spelled words pose problems for both adults and children.

The distinction between regularly spelled words and irregularly spelled words has been the basis of a great deal of research into reading and spelling (e.g. Coltheart 1977, Frith 1981). The fundamental notion of this research is that there are two basic strategies available to readers and spellers and that these strategies are differentially applicable to the two kinds of word : firstly there is what may be referred to as the Phonological strategy, which is concerned with the use of the regularities of English spelling to covert print to sound (reading) and sound to print (spelling) and which can only be applied successfully to regularly spelled words; secondly, there is the Direct or Visual strategy, which in both reading and spelling is dependent on the graphemic or visual representation of the word in long term memory and which can be applied equally to regular and irregular words. So, in spelling, the phonological strategy (or phonetic transcription strategy) relies on the sound of the word and knowledge of various sound-to-spelling rules for its success while the Direct strategy relies on the ability to remember the visual identity and configuration of the letters.

Now even though there are a large number of errors in this corpus which suggest extensive use of a phonetic transcription strategy, issues pertaining to this will not be discussed here. This paper is concerned with errors that the traditional, "two channel" approach to spelling does not address. It argues that to understand these errors, which are often on simple common words, we must stop thinking of spelling as an isolated psychological process and begin thinking of it as part of writing and language production, processes which are likely to generate errors of their own.

METHOD.

Subjects and Materials.

Essays were collected from two classes of 28 children (56 in all). One class had written an essay entitled "The Haunted House", the other an essay entitled "The Most Exciting Day of My Life". They were approximately 12 yrs. old (precise information was not available), were of mixed ability and spoke in the Scottish Dialect.

RESULTS.

Mean essay length was 337 words with a mean of 7.2 errors per essay. Errors per subject ranged from 1 to 27. As a preliminary analysis revealed no major differences between the two sets of essays, the results are pooled and treated as one set.

	S	N
A. MORPHEMIC ERRORS.		
1) Inflections *	40	92
2) Derivations	25	42
3) Compounds	8	9
B. NON-MORPHEMIC ERRORS.		
1) Articulatory *	20	32
2) Terminal omissions *	21	30
3) Other	52	20
C. SPLITS. *	34	72

Table 1
Major categories of error. Those asterisked are discussed in this paper. S : number of subjects committing an error. N : number of erors in that class.

We can see from table 1 that the major partition of errors is into the classes Morphemic, Non-morphemic and Splits. Morphemic errors are errors occurring in inflected, derived or compound words that may have been due to the morphemic structure of the items involved. Thus for example, a misspelled suffix such as finalley (finally), or a failure to apply a particular spelling rule when spelling an inflected form (e.g. a failure to drop final

e in <u>move</u> when spelling <u>moving</u>, to produce
<u>moveing</u>) would result in the error being
assigned to this category. An error unrelated to
morphemic structure, regardless of whether it
occurred in a morphemically complx word or not,
would be classed as a non-morphemic error e.g.
<u>fienally</u> (<u>finally</u>), or <u>mooving</u> (<u>moving</u>). The
third major class, Splits, consists of errors
where an inappropriate gap has been left between
two parts of the same word e.g. <u>to gether</u>
(<u>together</u>), <u>down stairs</u> (<u>downstairs</u>).

Only those categories of error in table 1
that are marked with an asterisk will concern us
directly. Those categories not so marked can be
accounted for by the kind of phonetic
transcription strategy discussed earlier. That
is, the majority of errors on derived words and
compounds, and on non-morphemic words in the
"other" category are most accurately described
as being attempts to produce phonetically
appropriate spellings. In some cases the items
involved are regular words, in other cases
irregular words; in some cases the error is due
to an ignorance of or misapplication of a
particular spelling rule, in others to
interference from a homophonic alternative, and
so on. A full discussion of these errors is to
be found in Sterling (1982); for the present it
need only be said that they provide general
support for the notion that phonetic
transcription is a principal strategy of
children's spelling.

Articulation Errors.

The category of errors in P1 of table 2
enables us to say with some precision what we
mean when we say that the sound of the word to-
be-spelled is the basis of phonetic
transcription.

520

ARTICULATION ERRORS.   S   N

P1. Conson. sound change   19   25
    e.g. remeber (remember)
P2. Conson. distinctive   6   7
    feature change.
    e.g. avoin (avoid)

Table 2
Frequency of articulation errors.
S : Number of subjects, N : Number
of errors.

        All the errors in P1 involve consonantal
letters, and their inferential value is only
evident if we consider the sounds that they
represent. In 23 of the errors the consonant
involved occurs within a consonant cluster, and
in 22 of these 23 cases the effect of the error
is to reduce the cluster. This reduction occurs
principally as a result of the omission of the
consonant (16 cases) and secondarily as a result
of the phonological process of fronting (5
cases). Examples of reduction by omission are
harly (hardly) (glottalisation) and remeber
(remember), while menacinly (menacingly) is an
example of fronting. If we look more closely at
the omissions we find that in 11 cases the less
or least obstruent member of the cluster is the
one that is omitted e.g. of a nasal/stop pair it
would be the nasal that would be omitted.
Another feature of the omissions is that 9 of
the 16 cases involve nasals and liquids,
producing errors such as accounter (encounter)
and Tillicoutry (Tillicoultry).

        All these features, cluster reduction,
the relative obstruency of the omitted
consonants, and the prevalence of nasals and
liquids relative to other sounds, are all also
features to be found in the speech errors of

521

children between the ages of 2 and 4, whose speech has yet to be fully developed (see Ingram 1976). This similarity between these speech errors and our spelling errors suggests that the latter are, in the first instance, articulation errors. That is, they are not so much incorrect spellings of correct sounds as correct spellings of incorrect sounds.

A smaller set of errors, P2 in table 2, also seem to have articulatory origins. They are similar to the errors in P1 in that they involve consonantal sounds, but they differ in several features : they occur in short words (mean lenth 4.1 letters as opposed to 8.2 letters) in which single consonants, not in clusters, have been substituted by others that differ from the target by one distinctive feature of articulation (either voicing or nasality) e.g. avoin (avoid), differend (different). It is not very clear why these errors occur. At least some of them are the product of the environment (e.g. avoin an old cat), but others don't seem to be (all differend places on our bikes). In any event, they have in common the feature of a distinctive feature relationship between the error and the target and as such are best construed as phonetic errors.

In summary : These articulation errors support the informal but common observation that children's writing is accompanied by subvocal articulation and suggest that this articulation is the basis of phonetic transcription i.e. that the children use their articulation of the word in deriving its spelling.

Inflection Errors.

Psychological evidence from a number of sources (e.g. Van de Molen and Morton 1979) suggests that inflected words such as the plural forms of nouns or the present participle form of verbs are not morphemic units but are morphemically complex. That is, the morphemic description of an inflected word as root + inflection is not just a linguistic description but also a psychological one.

Note firstly that some errors in table 3 support the notion that phonetic transcription is a major spelling strategy. The errors in I1 of table 3 are phonetic in that they consist of phonetically appropriate spellings, occurring on items which have viable alternative spellings.

INFLECTION ERRORS.	S	N
I1) Phonetic	10	12
e.g. <u>blose</u> (<u>blows</u>)		
I2) Concatenation	16	24
e.g. <u>moveing</u> (<u>moving</u>)		
I3) Inflection Omissions	22	30
e.g. <u>look</u> (<u>looked</u>)		
I4) Residue	17	26
e.g. <u>windining</u> (<u>winding</u>)		

Table 3
Frequency of Inflection errors.
S : Number of subjects, N : number of errors.

Evidence for the morphemically complex structure of inflected words comes from the class of errors I2 in table 3. In English some inflected words are formed by simple concatentaion e.g. <u>jumped</u>, <u>wanted</u>, but a number require an adjustment to be made first. In some cases this is to drop the final e of the root e.g. <u>waste</u> - <u>wasting</u>, in others it is to double the final consonant of the root e.g. <u>stab</u> -

<u>stabbed</u>, and in still others the adjustment
produces an abnormal form e.g. <u>bet</u>- <u>bet</u>, <u>say</u> -
<u>said</u>. (Fuller discussions of these rules are to
be found in Sterling 1981). What has happened in
these errors is that the root and the inflection
have been concatenated without the necessary
adjustment having been made to the root.

Evidence for the morphemic complexity of
inflected words also comes from errors in I3. In
these errors the inflection has been omitted. If
we compare the frequency of omission of the -<u>ed</u>
morpheme with that of another pair of non-
morphemic final letters we find that -<u>ed</u> was
omitted by significantly more children (S(-<u>ed</u>) =
10, S(other) = 2; X^2= 5.33; d.f. = 1; p < 0.05).
Also if we compare the relative omission
frequencies of inflected -<u>s</u> and non-inflected
-<u>s</u>, expressing each as a proportion of frequency
of occurrence of that type of -<u>s</u> in the
children's essays, we find again that inflected
-<u>s</u> is omitted proportionately more often (sign
test, p < 0.003). (This more elaborate
comparison was made necessary by the high
frequency of omission of non-inflected, single,
terminal letters, a phenomenon to which we shall
return shortly). These comparisons indicate that
it is the morphemic status of these final
letters that stimulates their omission and that
the inflected words in which these morphemes
occur are therefore morphemically complex.

More precise information is available as
to what is happening when these inflected words
are spelled. One source of such information is
that all but three of the omissions involved
non-syllabic inflections e.g. it was the non-
syllabic /t/ and /d/, as in <u>jumped</u> and <u>called</u>,
that were omitted and not the syllabic /id/
(<u>waited</u>). This supports the general notion of
phonetic (articulatory) transcription. It
indicates that the transcription is of units the
size of a syllable.

A second source of information is that in a large number of instances of concatenation (14 that are unambiguous) the sound of the word does not enable one to predict the spelling. e.g. phonetically, _moving_ and _cutting_ could well be spelled _moveing_ and _cuting_; it is a spelling rule that is being violated. This feature suggests that these concatenation errors are not the product of simple phonetic transcription; the errors occur because of a concatenation of the graphemic forms of the root (_move_) and the inflection (_ing_) without application of the appropriate adjustment rule. Inflected words are not spelled by merely retrieving their graphemic forms from memory, but are spelled by a process of generation or construction : the graphemic forms of the root and inflection being retrieved separately from memory and put together at the time of spelling.

Terminal Omissions.

The omission of terminal letters is not confined to inflections.

TERMINAL OMISSIONS	S	N
T1. Lexical Remainder e.g. _the_ (_them_)	21	30
T2. Non Lexical Remainder e.g. _crep_ (_crept_)	8	10

Table 4
Frequency of terminal Omissions. S : number of subjects, N : number of errors.

The errors comprising T1 in table 4 are errors on short, common words such as _them_ and _every_ in which the final letter has been omitted. The striking feature of the errors is that in a significant majority of cases the remainder left by the omission is a word in its own right. e.g. the (them), ever (every). (S(lex. rem. only) = 14, S(non-lex. rem. only) = 3; x^2 = 7.1; d.f. = 1; p < 0.001).

What have these terminal omissions in common with the inflection omissions? In both cases the final letter(s) has been omitted and in both cases the remainder is a word in its own right. It therefore seems plausible that the former is contingent on the latter. What sort of mechanism could account for this? One possibility is that they are both the indirect product of a lexical monitoring device, whose function in writing is to check that what has been written is a bona fide lexical item (or rather what the child believes to be a bona fide lexical item). What may be happening is that even though terminal letters are being omitted from a variety of words (for a number of "performance" reasons such as inattention), those leaving non-lexical remainders are detected by the lexical monitor and appropriate corrections made, while those leaving lexical remainders are undetected because they satisfy the lexical identity criterion.

Splits.

Evidence for the existence of a lexical monitor also comes from a third source, that of errors consisting of the inappropriate splitting of an item into two parts. e.g. loud speaker (loudspeaker), be sides (besides). See table 5.

526

SPLITS.		S	N
Splits		34	72

e.g. <u>be sides</u> (<u>besides</u>)
    <u>to gether</u> (<u>together</u>)

Table 5
Frequency of Splits. S : Number of
subjects, N : number of errors.

The first feature of interest is that in all the items involved the first component is a word in its own right, and in 61 of the 72 cases the second component is also a word. Once again the contingency of the error on the lexical identity of the first component suggests that the lexical monitor is responsible for the error. The gap that is left between words in the course of normal writing is here being left in the inappropriate place (e.g. after the <u>to</u> of <u>together</u>) because of information being fed back to the writing system by the monitor that a word has been completed; the error is occurring because the monitor is not waiting for the whole sequence to be finished before sending this information.

The second feature of these splits is that in the majority of cases the split is syntactically compatible with its environment. That is, the components resulting from the split are as syntactically compatible with the environment as was the single word they replaced. e.g. the noun in <u>on the loudspeaker</u> is replaced by <u>on the loud speaker</u>. This suggests that the lexical monitor is sensitive to syntactic information and that it tends to supply inappropriate information only when syntactic constraints are not violated (S(syntactically compatible splits only) = 23, S(syntactically incompatible splits only) = 2; X^2 = 13.59; d.f. = 1; p < 0.01).

527

In summary : the Lexical Monitor is a
device that operates on the basis of lexical and
syntactic information and its function is to
check on the lexical identity of what is being
written.

CONCLUSION.

The major results of this paper are
firstly that children's subvocal articulations
are a component in their spelling; secondly that
inflected words are spelled by a process of
construction rather than direct retrieval from
memory; and thirdly that their writing involves
use of a lexical monitoring device.

What general conclusions can we draw from
these results.

The first is that if we wish to understand
spelling errors that occur in situ, that is , in
the spontaneous writings of children, then we
need to look beyond the traditional two channel
model and the analyses that it spawns. This is
not to deny the value of the traditional
analyses, for large numbers of errors can only
be understood by reference to strategies such as
the phonetic transcription strategy and the
visual strategy. The point is simply that the
traditional model is insufficient, and that to
understand a number of errors that it doesn't
address we need to look elsewhere : to other
cognitive processes that are an essential part
not just of the spelling of individual words but
also of the production of the coherent text that
comprises a piece of spontaneous, creative
writing.

The second major conclusion is the
complement of the first. Spelling errors have a

value beyond that which they can tell us about
how children spell and what their problems are;
they can also tell us about a number of other
psychological processes involved in writing and,
indeed, language production. In this respect
this paper is not unique. The value of speech
errors to the understanding of speech production
has long been recognised (e.g. Garrett 1975),
and more recently, the value of writing errors
to an understanding of writing processes has
also been appreciated (Hotopf 1980). This paper
has contributed to this body of knowledge.

Acknowledgements : To the Social Science
Research Council under whose auspices this paper
was prepared.

REFERENCES.

Coltheart M., Davelaar E., Jonasson J.T., &
Besner D. (1977). Access to the Internal
Lexicon. In Dornic S. (ed). Attention and
Performance VI. Hillsdale, Erlbaum.

Frith U. (1981). The Similarities and
Differences Between Reading and Spelling.
(Manuscript).

Garrett M. F. (1975). The Analysis of Sentence
Production. In Bower G.H. (ed) The Psychology of
Learning and Motivation. Vol. 9. New York :
Academic Press.

Hotopf N. (1980). Slips of the Pen. In Frith U.
(ed) Cognitive Processes in Spelling. Academic
Press.

Ingram D. (1976). Phonological Disability in Children. London : Edward Arnold.

Sterling C. M. (1981). The Nature of Representation in the Internal Lexicon. Unpublished Ph.D. thesis. Stirling University.

Sterling C. M. (1982). Spelling Errors in Context (manuscript).

Van de Molen H. and Morton J. (1979) Remembering Plurals : Unit of Coding and Form of Coding During Serial Recall. Cognition, 7, 35-47.

CONSTRAINTS IN THE PHONOLOGY
OF A CHILD WITH DOWN'S SYNDROME

KEN BLEILE
University of Oregon, Eugene

This paper explored one aspect of the phonology of a 4-yr-old child with Down's Syndrome. This child had a phonological constraint that ordered his consonants from those produced at the front of the mouth to those produced at the back of the mouth. This meant that in a CVC word, C^1 could either be produced at the same place in the mouth as C^2, or at a place more forward than C^2. It is argued in this paper that this Consonant Ordering Strategy (COS)-which is equivalent to Ingram's fronting strategy (Ingram, 1974a)-motivated all the consonant substitutions found in the subject's attempted pronunciations of CVC words. The paper concludes by showing the value of an analysis that recognizes phonological strategies and larger-than-phoneme units.

During the last decade, child phonologists have shown an increased interest in the avenues available to children acquiring the phonology of their parent language. Their work has consistently shown that normal children are constrained along genetic and environmental lines, but are free within these confines to construct generalities and develop strategies that facilitate the reception, organization, and production of speech (Ferguson and Macken, 1980; Macken, 1978; Menn, 1976a, 1976b; Kiparsky and Menn, 1977; Ingram 1974a, 1974b, 1976; Vihman, 1976, 1978.) This paper seeks to extend the "child strategist" paradigm from the study of children with Down's Syndrome. This is being done for two interrelated reasons: (a) Down's Syndrome children hold interest for the child phonologist because they may show fragments of language behavior that are not easily isolated in normal children (Lenneberg et al., 1964); (b) by learning more about the language options available to children with Down's Syndrome, speech pathologists may be able to design more effective therapy programs.

Subject and Method

The subject is the third child of an American father and a German mother. He is the only retarded member of the family. Like many children with Down's Syndrome, he suffers from frequent colds and ear infections. He was sick twice during the period of the investigation. No data were collected at these times. On visual inspection, the subject's oral structure appears relatively normal, except for a large tongue and a moderate underbite.

The subject was 4 yr old at the beginning of the study and 4 yr, 7 mo when the last data point was taken. Using the method outlined in Dale (1976), the subject's mean length of utterance at 4 yr was measured at 1.25, which places him in Brown's (1973) Stage I. The McCarthy Scales of Children's Abilities was administered when the subject was 4 yr, 1 mo. The results of this test are reported in Table 1.

TABLE 1
McCarthy Scores

Chronological Age	4 yr., 1 mo.
McCarthy Mental Age (Kaufman Tables)	2 yr., 6 mo.
McCarthy General Cognitive Index (Harrison-Naglieri Extrapolated)	43 (est.)

All the observations were made in relatively quiet rooms at the Preschool, Center for Human

Development, University of Oregon. For the first
observation, a student speech pathologist used
objects to elicit one-word responses. The objects
were chosen to represent a quasi-random variety of
consonants, vowels, and simple syllable shapes. I
transcribed during the session, using a modified
version of the IPA (Ingram, 1976). Context notes
were also made. The session was recorded on a
high-quality Panasonic audio cassette.
Originally, the subject's responses were divided
into three categories: spontaneous, delayed
imitation (over a 2-sec pause between the model
and the subject's response), and imitation. These
distinctions proved unnecessary, however, so the
data were later collapsed. All together, 52
forms and 33 words were collected. The observation lasted approximately 20 min.

The second series of observations, which
lasted from October 1980 to March 1981, were made
in response to questions raised by the first
observation. For this series, I acted as elicitor
and transcriber. Audio tapes were made during
selected sessions. Each session lasted from 4 to
7 min, during which time between three and six
forms were elicited. For these observations
nonsense forms were used in order to remove as
many semantic variables as possible. (The chief
problem associated with nonsense forms is that
children tend to take these forms as instances of
words already in their vocabulary. Barton 1976
contains a full discussion of nonsense forms, both
positively and negatively.) For each nonsense
form a blockman or a simple drawing of a man was
presented. The eliciting phrase was, "his name is
X. Can you tell me his name?" In all, 52
instances of 18 forms were collected in this way.

Reliability

There was no second transcriber available
during either the first or second series of
observations, so I was forced to settle for
intraobserver reliability. For the first
observation this procedure included five steps:

533

1. A transcription was made during the session
2. As soon as the session ended, a transcription was made fromthe audiotape, while referring to the first transcription as necessary,
3. Three days later, another transcription was made from the audio tape, this time without referring to previous transcriptions,
4. Two days later another transcription was made from the audio tape, again without referring to any previous transcriptions,
5. All the transcriptions were compared and all the conflicting data was removed.

Since a fairly broad transcription was being used, the discarded list consisted of only two diacritics and three vowels.

The second series of observations presented fewer problems, since I was only interested in distinguishing three broad regions (labial, alveolar, and velar), and I could always recheck questionable segments. All questions were resolved in this way.

Results and Discussion

First Observation

The subject was 4 yr old at the time of the first observation, but his surface phonology resembled that of a much younger "normal" child. In rank order, his predominate syllable shapes were CV, V, and CVC. The C^1 was dominated by two processes, Stopping and Voicing. The V was simple and generally lax. The C^2 was also dominated by two processes, Devoicing and Final Consonant Deletion. (See Donegon and Stampe (1979) for a discussion of processes; see Hooper (1979) for a theoretical framework within which Devoicing might be considered a step in the process of Final Consonant Deletion.)

Out of 17 opportunities, the subject maintained C^2 five times, Table 2 lists these five items. The number sequences refer to consonant productions.

1 the general region of the lips

2 the general region of the alveolar ridge

3 the general region of the back of the mouth

Each region, then, represents an area dominated by a single "active articulator", the lips, the tongue tip, and the back of the tongue (see Williamson, 1977, for an interesting discussion of articulators). If this child truly has a CO constraint, his outputs should be 1 + 1, 2, or 3; 2 + 2 or 3; and 3 + 3. His outputs should not be

TABLE 2
First Observation-CVC Words

Input		Sequence		Output
1. faɾm	(farm)	1-1	1-1	mam
2. goʊt	(goat)	3-2	2-2	dot[+]
3. tʃ ik	(cheek)	2-3	2-3	di·k
4. ip	(sheep)	2-1	1-1	bip
5. trɔk	(truck)	2-3	2-3	dɔːk[+]

[a]+ = released; : = lengthened;
· = half-lengthened.

2 + 1; or 3 + 2 or 1. All of the subject's productions fall within the CO constraint.

The subject generally achieved CO by adjusting C^1 to match the position of C^2, though there are exceptions to this pattern, such as when g t d k (e.g., Table 5, No. 16) by metathesis. However, CO should not be identified with any particular feature-changing process or processes,

535

unless we wish to assume the complicating notion that each process that achieved CO represented a different CO. This would be a strange assumption if all the processes were found to be achieving the same end. Instead, it seems better to hold with Ingram that CO is a conspiracy-a functional unity operating through a number of individual processes-and should not be equated with any particular process (Kisseberth, 1970, is the original work on conspiracies).

Second Series of Observations

Tables 3-5 list the pertinent forms. Table 3 shows the realization of various consonants when C^2 is not present. Table 4 lists those input words (adult models) that fall within the CO constraint. Table 5 lists those input words that fall outside the CO constraint. It should be noted that in Table 4 the first consonant in CVO output words has not altered in place of articulation, whereas in Table 5 the first consonant in CVO output words has undergone a place movement that has the effect of putting the CVC sequence within the CO constraint, even though C^2 happens not to appear on the surface. This finding can be explained if it is assumed that the processes

TABLE 3
CV Realizations

Input	Output
1. pə	bə
2. bə	bə
3. tə	də
4. də	də
5. ʃə	də

Table 3, cont.

6.	kə	də
7.	gə	də

TABLE 4
Nonsense Words Within the CO Constraint[a]

	Input	Sequence		Output
1.	pəp$^+$	1-1	1-1	bə:b$^+$
2.	bɔp$^+$	1-1	1-0	bə
3.	bəp$^+$	1-1	1-1	bəp
4.	pəb	1-1	1-0	bə·
5.	bəb$^+$	1-1	1-1	bəwb$^+$
6.	pət$^+$	1-2	1-2	pət
7.	pət$^+$	1-2	1-0	bɔ
8.	bət$^+$	1-2	1-2	bət$^+$
9.	bət$^+$	1-2	1-2	bət
10.	bɔt^o	1-2	1-2	bət$^+$
11.	wət+	1-2	1-2	wət$^+$
12.	pəd$^+$	1-2	1-0	pə
13.	pəd$^+$	1-2	1-2	bət$^+$
14.	bəd$^+$	1-2	1-2	bə::d
15.	pɔk$^+$	1-3	1-3	bɔk$^+$
16.	pək	1-3	1-3	bə:k$^+$

Table 4, cont.

17.	bək$^+$	1-3	1-0	bə
18.	bək	1-3	1-3	bək$^+$
19.	bək$^+$	1-3	1-3	bək$^+$
20.	bəg	1-3	1-3	bə·k$^+$
21.	tət$^+$	2-2	2-2	dət
22.	dət$^+$	2-2	2-0	də
23.	dəd$^+$	2-2	2-0	də
24.	tək$^+$	2-3	2-0	də
25.	tək^o	2-3	2-0	də
26.	tək$^+$	2-3	2-3	də⦂dək
27.	tək$^+$	2-3	2-0	də
28.	dək$^+$	2-3	2-3	də:k$^+$
29.	dək$^+$	2-3	2-0	də
30.	dək$^+$	2-3	2-0	də
31.	təg	2-3	2-3	də·g
32.	dəg	2-3	2-3	dək
33.	gək$^+$	3-3	3-3	gək
34.	gəg	3-3	3-3	gə$gə

^{a}Instances of the same form were collected on different days.

^{b}+ = released   o = unreleased;   ∅ = not controlled for release

TABLE 5
Nonsense Words Outside the CO Constraint[a]

	Input	Sequence		Output
1.	tэp	2-1	1-1	bэp[+]
2.	tэp[+]	2-1	1-1	bэp[+]
3.	dэp[+]	2-1	1-1	bэp[+]
4.	dэp[+]	2-1	1-0	bэ
5.	tэb[+]	2-1	1-1	bэp
6.	dэb[+]	2-1	1-1	ba$bэ
7.	kэp	3-1	1-1	bэ·p
8.	kэp	3-1	1-1	bэp[+]
9.	gэp	3-1	1-1	bэp[+]
10.	gэp[+]	3-1	1-1	bэp[+]
11.	gэp[o]	3-1	1-0	bэ
12.	kэb[+]	3-1	1-0	ba::
13.	kэt[+]	3-2	2-2	dэ::t[+]
14.	kэt[+]	3-2	2-2	dэt[+]
15.	kэt[+]	3-2	2-2	dэt[+]
16.	gэt	3-2	2-3	dэk[+]
17.	gэt[+]	3-2	3-3	gэk[+]
18.	kэd[+]	3-2	1-2	bэd

[a]Instances of the same form were collected on different days.

Table 5, cont.

b_+ = released; o = unreleased;
∅ = not controlled for release.

that enact the COS occur prior to Final Consonant Deletion.

Correct order: dəp (Table 5, no. 4)
                 bəp CO processes
                 bə   Final Consonant Deletion

Incorrect order: dəp
                  də   Final Consonant Deletion
                 *də   CO processes do not apply

Table 6 summarizes the results of the previous
two tables. It is noted that CO occurs without
exception. Table 7 shows that the subject's COS
applies to real as well as nonsense words (this
is the complete list of real words collected
during the period of the study).

TABLE 6
Nonsense Words Summary

	Input	Change	Output Within CO	Output Outside CO
Number of words within CO constraint	34		34	0
Number of words outside CO constraint	<u>18</u>		<u>18</u>	<u>0</u>
Total	52		52	0

TABLE 7
Real Words Collected During
The Second Observation

	Input		Sequence		Output
1.	kɔp	(cup)	3-1	1-1	bəːp
2.	fʊt	(foot)	1-2	2-0	duː
3.	goʊt	(goat)	3-2	2-2	də·t[+]
4.	bʊk	(book)	1-3	1-3	bʊk[+]
5.	dək	(duck)	2-3	2-0	də
6.	tʃik	(cheek)	2-3	2-3	dik
7.	dɔg	(dog)	2-3	2-0	dɔ·
8.	kɛn	(Ken)	3-2	2-2	dɛn

Conclusion

The data presented in Tables 2 through 7 clearly indicates that the subject does not allow CVC words to fall ourside the CO constraint. Somewhat less clearly, the data indicates that CVC words in which C^1 and C^2 agree in place are favored over CVC words in which C^1 is more forward than C^2. The reason for positing two degrees of allowability has to do with the fact that the vast majority of input words that violated the CO constraint underwent changes that caused their consonants to agree in place. The three sequencing possibilities can be represented as a scale.

A	B	C
words in which consonants are made at the same place	words in which C^1 is more forward than C^2	words in which C^2 is more forward than C^1

Words in column A are the most favored, for the reason given above. Words in column B are allowed. Words on column C are not allowed, and so they undergo changes that have the effect of putting most of their members in column A.

The effect of this scale is to give the subject's speech an appearance of randomness. For example, the subject realized word-initial /g/ as /g/ in CVC words that contained a word-final velar (Table 4, No. 33), as /d/ or /g/ in CVC words that contained a word-final aveolar (Table 5, No. 16, No. 17), and as /b/ in CVC words that contained a word-final labial (Table 5, No. 9). This meant that word-initial /g/ could be realized as a labial, alveolar, or a velar-not a common substitution pattern. Still, this paper contends that, common or not, these substitutions are patterned, lawful, and describable. To demonstrate this, I have utilized two simple notions. First, children-including children afflicted with Down's Syndrome-actively impose structure on the sounds they produce. Second, sound substitutions that appear inexplicable at the level of the single segment can sometimes be explained if a larger unit of organization is taken into account. Only future research will tell how many more notions will be needed to capture the strategies of other children with Down's Syndrome.

I wish to thank the following people for their encouragement and criticism during the course of this study: Palmer Curtis, Edith Bavin, Diane Bricker, Mary Beth Bruder, Patti Wade, Karen Pollack, and Valerie Young.

References

Barton, D. (1976). Phonemic discrimination and the knowledge of words in children under 3 years. Pap. Rep. Child Lang. Dev. 11: 61-102.

Bodine, M. (1971). A phonological analysis of the speech of two mongoloid (Down's Syndrome) children. Unpublished doctoral dissertation.

Brown, R. (1973). <u>A First Language</u>. Cambridge, Mass.: Harvard University Press.

Dale, P. (1976). <u>Language Development</u>. New York: Holt, Rinehart, and Winston.

Dodd, B. (1975). Recognition and reproduction of words by Down's Syndrome and non-Down's Syndrome retarded children. <u>Am. J. Mental Deficiency</u> 80: 306-311.

Dodd, B. (1976). A comparison of the phonological systems of mental age matched normal, severely subnormal, and Down's Syndrome children. <u>Br. J. Dis. Comm.</u> 11: 27-42.

Donegan, P., and Stampe, D. (1979). The study of natural phonology. In D. Dinnesen (ed.), <u>Current Approaches to Phonological Theory</u>. Bloomington: Indiana University Press.

Ferguson, C., and Macken, M. (1980). Phonological development in children: play and cognition. <u>Pap. Rep. Child Lang. Dev.</u> 18: 138-177.

Hooper, J. (1979). Substantive principles in natural generative phonology. In D. Dinnesen (ed.), <u>Current Approaches to Phonological Theory</u>. Bloomington: Indiana University Press.

Ingram, D. (1974a). Fronting in child phonology. <u>J. Child Lang.</u> 1:233-241.

Ingram, D. (1974b). Phonological rules in young children. <u>J. Child Lang.</u> 1:49-64.

Ingram, D. (1976). <u>Phonological Disability in Children</u>. New York: Elsevier.

Karlin, I., and Strazulla, M. (1952). Speech and language problems of mentally deficient children. <u>J. Speech Hear. Dis.</u> 17: 286-294.

Kiparsky, P., and Menn, L. (1977). On the

Bibliography, cont.

acquisition of phonology. In J. MacNamara
(ed.), Language Learning and Thought. New
York: Academic Press.

Kisseberth, C. (1970). On the functional unity
of phonological rules. Linguistic Inquiry
1: 291-306.

Lenneberg, E., Nichols, I., and Rosenberger, E.
(1964). Primitive stages of language development in mongolism. In D. Rioch and
E. Weinstein (eds.), Disorders of Communication. Baltimore: Williams and Wilkins.

(1972) McCarthy Scales of Children's Abilities.
New York: The Psychological Corporation.

Menn, L. (1976a). Pattern, control, and
contrast in beginning speech: a case study in
the development of word form and word function.
Unpublished doctoral dissertation. University of Illinois, Urbana.

Menn, L. (1976b). Evidence for an interaction-
ist-discovery theory of child phonology.
Pap. Rep. Child Lang. Dev. 12: 169-177.

Menn, L. (1978). Phonological units in beginning
speech. In A. Bell and J. Hooper (eds.),
Syllables and Segments. New York: Elsevier.

Stoel-Gammon, C. (1980a). A longitudinal study
of phonological processes in the speech of
Down's Syndrome children. Paper presented at
the Symposium on Research in Child Language
Disorders, Madison, Wisconsin.

Stoel-Gammon, C. (1980b). Phonological analysis
of four Down's syndrome children. Appl.
Psycholing. 1:31-48.

Vihman, M. (1976). From pre-speech to speech:
on early phonology. Pap. Rep. Child Lang.

Bibliography, cont.

Dev. 12: 230-242.

Vihman, M. (1978). Consonant harmony: its
scope and function in child language. In
J. Greenberg (ed.), Universals of Human
Language, V. 2: Phonology. Stanford:
Stanford University Press.

Williamson, K. (1977). Multivalued features for
consonants. Language 53: 843-871.

Zisk, P., and Bialer, I. (1967). Speech and
language problems in mongolism: a review of
the literature. J. Speech Hear. Dis. 32:
228-241.

A STUDY OF INTENTIONAL VOCALIZING IN HANDICAPPED, INSTITUTIONALIZED INFANTS

Sandra Bochner,
Special Education Centre,
Macquarie University.

The study reported here was derived from an interest in two related problem areas: one was concerned with the difficulties that are often experienced by mentally retarded children in learning to talk, while the other resulted from evidence that these problems in language acquisition can be exacerbated by early institutionalization. The object of the study was to document the vocal development of preverbal infants resident in a hospital for sick babies. It was hypothesized that infants, between birth and their first words, communicate their intentions through a range of vocal behaviours that function as increasingly complex communicative acts. Results are reported on the emergence of such vocal acts in five handicapped, institutionalized infants.

THEORETICAL BACKGROUND

Following Morris (1946) language was conceptualized as comprising three main elements: pragmatics, semantics and syntax. The focus of this study was on the pragmatic aspect of early communication. Austin (1962) and Searle's (1969) Speech Act model of language seemed to provide the most appropriate theoretical framework for the study, with its emphasis on the communicative function of language for the speaker. The concept of perlocution derived from the Speech Act model was of particular relevance since it referred to vocal communicative acts that carried a message but were not expressed in a conventional speech form. It was argued that as an infant acquired control over the sounds he produced, and developed a desire to cause an effect on a listener and elicit a response, so his vocalizing became increasingly regulated. Such sounds could be classified as perlocutionary, since they conveyed some intended meaning for the infant but were not embedded in a conventional form. The study reported here documented the emergence of such communicative acts in the vocalizing of five infants.

A number of studies have been reported that examined specific aspects of infant cries. For example a group of researchers in Sweden (eg. Wasz-Hockert, Lind, Vuorenkoski, Partanen and Valanne, 1968) attempted to use spectograph analysis to identify abnormal cries among newborn babies and studies using spectograph techniques were described by Ostwald, Phibbs and Fox (1968), Wolff (1969) and Lester (1976). Another series of reports explored the extent to which infant cries could be consistently differentiated by adult listeners. Morsbach and Murphy (1979) demonstrated that midwives and adults with and without families could successfully discriminate between the cries of individual babies. Ricks (1975) showed that by eight months, parents could identify both the sounds of their own child from a set of four, and the message (request, greeting, surprise or frustration) in sounds produced by their own and a small group of other babies. Such research suggested that from birth the infant's sounds were closely tied to his emotive state and over time were used consistently, with intonation and prosodic patterns, to carry a message (Dore, 1973).

A major issue which arose in studies that inferred meaning from infant cries was identification of the precise point at which the infant's communicative acts, vocal or non-vocal, moved from random or not consciously controlled to purposeful, controlled and potentially carrying a more accurate message. Lock (1976) suggested that much infant activity that adults interpreted as intentional was in reality the production of originally chance acts which caused an effect that the child attended to and over time learned to repeat. Lock cited the example of David, who learned to wave his arms to cause an event to recur (eg. blocks fall down). While initially David's actions were a "natural generalization from previous secondary circular reaction experiences" (Flavell, 1963, p.106, cited by Lock, 1976) the actions were interpreted as having a communicative intent by David's caretakers, who therefore responded appropriately. Over time the child learned that he could cause things to happen by reproducing the action schema of arm-waving. He gradually learned to discriminate situations in which agents could cause an event to occur, from situations which occurred without an agent and were thus not potentially repeatable. However his action schema were still directed at the situation, rather than at an agent who could be instrumental in the recurrence of the desired effect. Evidence of conscious use of the schema, with communicative intent, was only observed at a later date, when David waved his arms and looked at the adult agent before looking at the ball that was out of his reach.

A second issue of relevance to this study was concerned with the transition of the child's vocalizations from non-linguistic to language-specific patterns. Crystal (1976) raised this issue in his comments on a paper by Ricks (1975) which reported that mothers were unable to identify the vocalization of a non-English child from a set of four cries. Crystal suggested that a fruitful cross-cultural study was to identify the point at which infant vocal patterns departed from those that were biologically determined. However, this study was concerned with the emergence of vocal acts that were capable of interpretation by adult caretakers in the infant's social setting. The extent to which these sounds were non-linguistic as opposed to being language-specific was not explicitly examined though judgements were made by adult listeners (non-linguists) about the purpose or intent of the sounds (as judged from the viewpoint of standard English-speaking adults). The use of such adults to assess and classify the sounds was justified on the grounds that all infants were exposed from birth to close dyadic relationships with caretakers who interpreted and responded to their vocalizations in much the same way as the adult coders used in this study.

The procedures used in the study for collection and subsequent analysis of the infant cry

data evolved following a review of the relevant
literature (particularly Bates, 1976; Dore, 1973;
Greenfield and Smith, 1976; Halliday 1979) and a
series of trials of appropriate techniques. Data
was collected during weekly recording sessions over
a fifteen month period, with time and day held
constant. Vocalizations were coded using a system
based on elements of Jacobson, Fant and Halle's
(1952) speech analysis system and from Halliday's
classification of early meanings expressed at the
one- and two-word stage (Halliday, 1979). This
latter classification system was found to be
inappropriate for the limited range of meanings
that could be recognized in the sounds produced by
the infants studied and it was gradually modified
to include classifications that appeared to be
appropriate for the data. New categories were
introduced as the need became apparent. It is
conceded that the classification system which
eventually evolved may have been relevant only for
the particular group of infants studied, since the
tapes made in this hospital setting were all
distinguished by a low rate of adult-child interaction. In this they differed markedly from most
studies of infant communication which are designed
around observations of mother-infant pairs, often
in a home setting.

In the remaining sections of the report the method
of the study will be described, results are reported
and some conclusions drawn regarding the early vocal
development of handicapped, institutionalized infants.

METHOD

The study was longitudinal and observational
in method with data collected from five institutionalized handicapped infants aged from 3-6 months at the
beginning of the study:

Dianne (Hydrocephalic), Blake (Spina
Bifida) and three Down's Syndrome infants, Grant
Michelle and Matthew.

Tape recordings were made of individual

infants at regular intervals in their natural
setting, supplemented by a written record of events
that occurred during observation sessions. Samples
of infant tapes were analysed using a fixed interval
procedure (30 second intervals). Infant sounds
were analysed in terms of amplitude, mood, pitch,
type and length of sound, intent and intended
listener. Only data on the variable Intent will
be reported here. The categories used to code this
variable included the following:

Intent Categories

1. None apparent - sound seems accidental - no
   reason behind it.
2. Self-stimulation/entertainment - self directed
   vocalizing, voice play with teeth, tongue, lips
   that produces a sound.
3. Combination.
4. Self commenting - sounds like talking to self.
5. Interactional - response to another's voice,
   interactional turn-taking, conversational
   vocalizing with pauses from child to allow
   other person to reply.
6. Personal - assertion of self - demanding -
   projection of voice to call attention - loud
   and often rising intonation.
7. Protest - cry - complaining - clearly negative
   in mood - expressing distress, sobs, falling
   intonation.
8. Uncertain of intent expressed in child's sounds,
   but the sounds do not appear random or
   accidental.

Analysis of data was completed in two
phases: in Phase I, at least 30 minutes of all the
tapes for one infant (Dianne) were coded by the
investigator. Both environmental and infant sounds
were coded at this stage. In Phase II, ten-minute
samples of vocalizations only from the tapes of all
five infants were analysed by the investigator and
an assistant, using a consensus method (Sackett,
Gluck and Ruppenthal (1978). Results obtained from
the ten-minute samples will be reported here. The
decision to limit the consensus coding to ten-minute
samples was based largely on the length of time

taken to analyse each tape. However it was further
justified by the impression (confirmed in the
comparison of the thirty-minute and ten-minute data)
that the behaviour of the infants studied showed
little variation during observation sessions that
usually lasted up to 45 minutes. This is supported
by McDade (1981) who cited studies suggesting that
samples of 3-5 minutes adequately represented the
interactions taking place in a thirty-minute mother-
infant interaction sample. A major disadvantage in
the use of short rather than long tape segments in
the analysis was in the reduction of opportunities
in which an infant could produce a particular vocal
behaviour.While it is acknowledged that data
collected in analysis of ten-minute tape samples
does not provide a complete and accurate picture of
the vocal behaviour of the five infants during the
study period it may be claimed that it does provide
some indication of the range of vocal behaviours
that they were able to produce at that stage in
their development.

RESULTS

        Results of the data analysis are reported
in terms of frequency counts and percentages.
Initially, the data for individual infants is
examined, and a comparison is made between results
reported for the two non-Down's and the three
Down's Syndrome infants. Finally, information is
reported on the level of language development
achieved by the five children in mid 1981, three
years after the study was completed.

        To facilitate comparison of results between
infants, data from individual sessions were combined
into selected time periods according to the age of
the infant at each recording session. Four time
periods were used: 1 (2-5 months); 2 (6-8 months);
3 (9-13 months); 4 (14-20 months). The decision
to group the data in terms of infant age was a
practical solution to overcome problems associated
with infant illnesses, absences from the hospital
and equipment failures. It also helped to minimize
the effect of chance events on infant vocalizing.

Changes in infant behaviour occurred relatively
slowly, so it was unlikely that significant
information was obscured with the grouping of data
across more than one observation session. Not all
infants were observed during all four time periods.
Dianne had no tapes recorded in the 2-5 month period
and none of the Down's Syndrome infants were
observed after 13 months. Otherwise each infant
had 3-4 tape samples for each time period.

1. Results for individual children
A. Dianne. In her first six months, Dianne
appeared to have used her voice largely to
protest. During the 6-13 month period, it was
difficult to discern any meaning in her
vocalizing, though by 9-13 months she was
beginning to use her voice in social interaction.
By 14-20 months, this function was firmly
established, with a high proportion (around 60%)
of her vocalizing during observation sessions
directed to this usage. No instances of request
or self commenting were observed at any stage in
Dianne's tapes.

B. Blake. As with Dianne, the intent of a
large proportion of Blake's early sounds could
not be recognized, though in the final time
period (14-20 months) the number of sounds with
uncertain meaning diminished dramatically and
Blake began to use his voice in social interaction. Blake was also observed to comment to
himself in the final months but showed little
evidence of self stimulation after the first
time period. His rate of protest was never more
than 17% (2-5 month stage) and almost disappeared
after 7 months. The personal function was
observed twice in Blake's tapes - (in the second
and fourth time periods).

C. Grant. Grant did not show evidence of
beginning to use his voice to express any
function other than protest or self stimulation
during the study period. His early protests
appear to have been louder and more continuous
than the protests observed in the early cries
of Dianne and Blake. From 6 months his sounds

were almost equally divided between protest, self-stimulation and uncertain meaning, but from 9 months, 62% were self stimulatory, while the rate of protest had reduced to 7%. There was no evidence of the expression of social interaction or the personal function in any of Grant's vocalizing.

D.   Michelle.   Initially more than half Michelle's vocalizing had no clear meaning, though she also expressed protest (29%) with a few instances of self-stimulation and personal sounds observed. However, by 6 months, over half the sounds were for self-stimulation, with the rate of uncertain meaning reduced to 38%. The rate of protest was now very low (2 instances in a total of 21 time intervals in which vocalizing occurred). The relative proportion of instances of self-stimulation and uncertain meaning continued into the third time period (47% and 32% respectively), and during this period Michelle was observed to produce some socially interactive sounds (3 instances) and one instance of the personal function.

E.   Matthew.   Between 2-5 months, Matthew's sounds were mainly interpreted as protest (42%), uncertain meaning (36%) and no meaning apparent (19%). One instance of social interaction was also observed at this time. Between 6 and 8 months, the rate of uncertain meaning increased (50%) as the rate of protest diminished (29%). At this stage 18% of Matthew's sounds were self-stimulation, with a single instance of social interaction observed. By 9-13 months, 98% of the sounds were self stimulatory. The rate of use of social interactive sounds did not appear to have increased and there was no evidence of the personal use of vocalizing. The rate of vocalizing across time intervals increased with the increase in self-stimulation -- 60% in the first observation period to 70% and finally to 84%. Apparently Matthew vocalized more as the range of meanings expressed in his sounds diminished.

2. Comparison of non-Down's and Down's Syndrome infant results

The major trends that distinguished the non-Down's and Down's infant groups related to the categories of self entertainment, social interaction, protest and uncertain meaning. The initial difference in the rate of protest between the two groups was considerable (17% and 61%) but this could have resulted from the ages of the infants at the time of observation. Blake was in his 5th month when the initial tape recordings were made, while Grant, Michelle and Matthew were aged from 2-4 months at the first observation session. In the second time period both groups reduced their rate of crying (3% and 30%) and by the third time period there were few instances of protest observed. Possibly factors within the institutional environment mitigated against the infants protesting very often.

The rate of production of vocalizing with uncertain meaning was much greater for the non-Down's than for the Down's infants across the first three time periods (44%, 82% and 75% compared with 33%, 40% and 11%). Apparently it was easier to recognize meaning in the sounds produced by the Down's infants than in the sounds of the non-Down's infants.

An increasing proportion of the Down's infants sounds were interpreted as self-stimulation, (4%, 30% and 77%, compared with 25%, 3% and 0% for the non-Down's infants over the first three time periods).

In contrast with the increase in the rate of vocalizing for self entertainment from the Down's infants, the non-Down's infants increasingly used their voices in social interaction. This trend became evident in the 9-13 month period (5%) but increased dramatically (67%) in the final time period. During these months, both Dianne and Blake actively sought vocal contact with adults - by moving close to a seated adult (Blake) or calling out to someone in the room (Dianne). Michelle showed some evidence of having early skills in social interaction - possibly because she had opportunities for such experiences during visits with her parents. Matthew also demonstrated socially interactive vocalizing on a few occasions during the study but Grant appeared to lack even the skills that underlie this activity - attention and some form of response to adult stimulation.

Overall, the major differences observed between the use of vocalizing in the two groups of infants were:

1. The high rate of "uncertain meaning" in the non-Down's infants under 14 months.
2. The increasing use of sounds in "social inter-action" in the non-Down's infants from around 12 months.
3. The sharp increase in sounds that appeared to be produced from self-stimulation in the Down's infants from 6 months.

Follow-up Reports

It was not possible to directly assess the language level that had been reached by the infants by the age of 4½, but contact was made with two of the families concerned (Grant and Matthew) and information was obtained on the development of two other infants (Dianne and Blake). Michelle could not be traced.

Dianne, fostered at 16 months, was reported to be functioning within the normal intellectual range, with adequate language skills.

Blake returned to his family soon after the study ended. His speech was at first difficult to under-stand, but he was now talking normally for his age.

Grant, fostered at 13 months, had no speech and was attending a school for mentally handicapped children.

Matthew, fostered at 3 by a teacher, began to produce a few words following his enrolment in a normal pre-school at 4 years.

None of the children had hearing problems.

DISCUSSION

In the study reported here, the early vocal behaviour of five infants was monitored to document the emergence of intentionally communicative vocalizing, using adult judgements about aspects of infant sounds sampled over an extended time period to identify the point where such vocal communication began. In this the adult listeners attended to the potential perlocutionary act inherent in the infant's vocalizing, rather than to the form of the sound or its propositional content. Two criteria were identified by which infant sounds could be classified as perlocutionary acts in this study:

1. The sound was produced with the intention of eliciting a response in a listener.

2. The sound was regulated in its production according to rules that were recognized by a listener. This regulation could refer to the form of the sound (pitch, mood) or to the procedures that surrounded its production (during turn-taking with an adult).

In developing a plan for coding the intent recognized by adults in the infant sound samples, eight categories were selected of which only one (No Meaning Apparent) did not qualify as a perlocutionary act on either criterion. Self-stimulation failed to satisfy one criterion for perlocutionary acts in that the sounds were randomly patterned; there was moreover no clear communicative effect implicit in their production though they may have satisfied the target listener criterion in that the sounds appeared to be produced for their own stimulation by the infants. Self commenting, on the other hand, satisfied both the criteria for a perlocutionary act. These sounds were self-directed (low in amplitude) and they appeared to be regulated in the procedure in which they were produced, presenting in a conversational form, with variation in the sounds, intonation, number of separate sounds and length of pauses involved.

556

Socially-interactive vocalizing was classifiable as a perlocutionary act in that it comprised an interactive mode and included sounds that were procedurally regulated, with some constraints on the manner of production - eg. moderate amplitude and limited vocalization time. Similar sounds classified within the category of Personal were perlocutionary acts, in that they were projected at a listener (it was not always possible to identify the target listener) and were regulated productively - short, loud sounds, often apparently produced to attract attention.

Protest sounds, if produced to elicit a response in a particular listener, would be examples of perlocutionary acts. However the early protest cries observed in this study did not satisfy the criterion of other-directedness. More than half (68%) of the intervals in which Protest was observed occurred when the infants were under six months of age, so it could be asserted that few of the instances of Protest were likely to be classifiable as perlocutionary acts.

With more comprehensive data-collection techniques (eg. video-tape recorders) it may have been possible to classify as instances of perlocutionary acts many of the intervals that were coded as Uncertain Meaning in this study: 34% of all intervals in which vocalizing occurred were coded in this way. This category was used in many instances where the most parsimonious interpretation of a vocalization was used; many sounds coded thus carried some indications of regulation and other-directedness in their production. In fact two trends evident in the data lent support to the assertion that during the period in which the infants were acquiring perlocutionary skills, an initially high, but diminishing percentage of their sounds were difficult to interpret. For Dianne and Blake, there was a consistent increase (58%, 62%, 78%) in the percentage of intervals with vocalizing coded as Uncertain Meaning for the first three time periods (0-13 months) with a rapid decrease in such intervals (16%) in the final 14-20 month period, when the perlocutionary categories (Self Commenting, Social Interaction, Personal) increased rapidly. The total percentages recorded for these three categories were 0%, 8%, 5% and 78%, for each of the four time periods. On the other hand, while a similar trend was evident in the percentage of intervals coded Uncertain Meaning for the three Down's Syndrome infants over the first two time periods (27% and 43% between 0-8 months), the decline in the rate of Uncertain Meaning sounds occurred earlier (11% between 9-13 months). In this case, the reduction in instances of Uncertain Meaning was associated with an increase in the production of non-perlocutionary sounds (Self-Stimulation) between 9 and 13 months; the percentage occurrence over the three time periods (0-13) months) was 4%, 30% and 77% for these infants.

The results reported here suggested that from around 9 months, both Dianne and Blake began to produce with increasing frequency, sounds that had the potential to function as perlocutionary acts, with the rate of success of these vocal acts increasing with infant age. This pattern was not evident in the sounds of the three Down's Syndrome infants, whose vocalizing was increasingly non-communicative in function. It must be acknowledged that if longer-term data had been collected from these infants, an increasing rate of production of perlocutionary acts may have been observed. However, the follow-up reports on the later language development of these infants suggested that the rate of communicative vocalizing may not have changed significantly in Grant, who at four was not yet using words to communicate, though it may have begun to increase in Michelle and Matthew who showed signs of acquiring the early skills that may have contributed to the development of skills like speech.

CONCLUSION

Overall, it may be claimed that the two more able infants in the study did show evidence of using their voices to communicate intentionally before they learned to talk. Between 9 months and 20 months, the percentage of their observed sounds that could be classified as perlocutionary acts increased dramatically, with this skill demonstrated most explicitly during social exchanges with care-taking staff. However these meanings were probably relatively difficult to recognize and in the early stages were more often included in the general cate-gory of Uncertain Meaning than in any other classifi-cation. While this evidence does not confirm that such intentional vocalizing is an essential pre-requisite for the acquisition of speech, it does suggest that prior to the production of their first words, the proportion of sounds in which some meaning can be inferred may increase. It is also possible that the failure of such perlocutionary vocalizing to emerge at a time when most children begin to produce such sounds may be a strong indication that the infant is delayed in the acquisition of critical skills that precede speech.

REFERENCES

AUSTIN, J.L. How to do things with words. The William James Lectures delivered at Harvard Univer-sity in 1955. Edited by F.O. Urmson, 2nd Edition, 1975. Clarendon Press, 1962.

BATES, E. Language and context, the acquisition of pragmatics. Academic Press, N.Y., 1976.

CRYSTAL, D. Developmental intonology. In Y.Lebrun and W. von Raffler-Engel (eds.) Baby talk and infant speech. Swets and Zeitlinger, Lisse, 1976.

DORE, J. The Development of Speech Acts. Phd Dissertation, 1973. Reproduced by University Microfilms International, London, 1978.

FLAVEL, J.H. The Developmental Psychology of Jean Piaget. D. van Nostrand. Princeton. 1963.

GREENFIELD, P.M. & SMITH, J.H. The structure of communication in early language development. Academic Press, N.Y., 1976.

HALLIDAY, M.A.K. One child's protolanguage. In M.Bullowa (Ed.) Before Speech: The beginning of inter-personal communication. Cambridge University Press, Cambridge 1979.

JACOBSON, R. FANT, C. & HALLE, M. Preliminaries to Speech Analysis. M.I.T. Press Cambridge Mass., 1952.

LESTER, B.M. Spectrum analysis of the cry sounds of well-nourished and malnourished infants. Child Development. 47 (1976) 237-241.

LOCK, A.J. Acts not sentences. In Y. Lebrun and W. von Raffler-Engel (Eds.) Baby talk and infant speech. Swets and Zeitlinger, Lisse, 1976.

McDADE, H.L. A parent-child interactional model for assessing and remediating language disabilities. British Journal of Disorders in Communication 16. 3. 175-183 1981.

MORRIS, C. Signs, Language and Behaviour. Prentice-Hall, Englewood Cliffs, New Jersey. 1946.

MORSBACH, G. & MURPHY, M.C. Recognition of individual neonates' cries by experienced and inexperienced adults. Journal of Child Language 6 (1979) 175-179.

OSTWALD, P.F., PHIBBS, R. & FOX, S. Diagnostic use of the infant cry. Biology of the Neonate 13 (1968) 68-82.

RICKS, D.M. Vocal communication in preverbal normal and autistic children. In N. O'Connor (Ed.) Language, Cognitive Deficits and Retardation. Butterworths, London 1975.

SACKETT, G.P., GLUCK, G. & RUPPENTHAL, G.C. Introduction. In C.P. Sackett (Ed.) Observing behaviour vol.11. Data collection and analysis methods. University Park Press, Baltimore, 1978.

SEARLE, J.R. Speech Acts. Cambridge University Press, Cambridge, 1969.

WASZ-HOCKERT, O., LIND, J., VUORENKOSKI, V., PARTANEN, T.J. & VALANNE, L. The Infant Cry : A spectographic and auditory analysis. Heineman Medical Books, New York, 1968.

WOLFF, P.H. The natural history of crying and other vocalizations in early infancy. In B.M. Foss (Ed.) Determinants of Infant Behaviour IV, Methuen, London. 1969.

FRICATIVES AND AFFRICATES IN THE SPEECH OF CHILDREN
WITH PHONOLOGICAL DISABILITY

Pamela Grunwell, School of Speech Pathology, Leicester Polytechnic, U.K.

The acquisition of fricatives and affricates has
always been an interesting aspect of phonological
development for a variety of reasons. Fricatives
and affricates are regarded as 'difficult' sounds
from the point of view of their perception and production. Phonetically, they tend to show gradual
development in their articulatory production. Phonologically, and especially in English, they form
a complex sub-system of the inventory of consonant
contrasts. In this regard, as a natural phonemic
class they also exhibit a pattern of gradual development. They have therefore understandably been
the focus of attention of a number of studies of
normal development, most notably Ferguson(1978) and
most recently those of Ingram and colleagues(1978;
1980). It is also not surprising that they are
often the focus of attention in clinical practice,
since they frequently appear to present specific
problems for linguistically delayed/deviant children.

In his recent papers, Ingram has proposed 5 stages
for the development of the production of fricatives
and affricates in the speech of normal English children. He has supported these stages with a carefully controlled cross-sectional study(1980); though
in the conclusion of this study the necessity of
looking in detail at children's speech patterns on
an individual basis is emphasised, since much individual variation was apparent in the production of
the children studied. Ingram(1978) examined data
from 'linguistically deviant' children and found
evidence from word-initial fricatives and affricates
to support the general characteristics of phonological disability he had proposed in his earlier
monograph on the subject(1976). These characteristics are, in summary, the occurrence of Persistent
Processes, Unusual and/or Idiosyncratic Processes
and Chronological Mismatch. My own research(1977;
1981) has in general supported these findings when
considering the overall characteristics of phonological disability. This paper presents the results
of an examination of data from children with phono-

logical disability with particular regard to the
word-initial fricatives and affricates.

These investigations fall into two parts :
Part I examines the data of 12 children, focussing
on the following questions :
1. Is there evidence for the normal stages proposed
by Ingram in the patterns of these children?
2. Do these data support Ingram's findings with
reference to 'deviant' children?
3. Is it appropriate to consider fricatives and
affricates as an isolated class of sounds showing
particular developmental patterns, or is it necessary to refer to other aspects of the children's
speech patterns to gain a full appreciation of
fricative and affricate development?
Part II examines the data of 5 children over a fifteen-month period and addresses these questions :
1. Do these children pass through the proposed normal stages in their development of these sounds?
2. Are there any continuing indications during development that these children are not developing
normally; i.e. have a phonological learning disability ?
3. Is it appropriate to consider this class of
sounds in isolation from general trends and patterns
in phonological development?
Ingram's point about individuals is of course a sine
qua non in the investigation of children with delayed or disordered language development.

Methodology
It should be borne in mind throughout that the investigation is concerned only with the production
of fricatives and affricates. As a point of information, however, it should be noted that all of the
children were able to perceive and appeared to discriminate adequately between the sounds investigated.
They were all assessed as having 'normal hearing for
speech', and in auditory discrimination tasks demonstrated the ability to use auditorily differences
they were not producing in their own speech to distinguish between minimally different word pairs.
Their perceptual phonology would thus appear to be
in advance of their phonological production system.
This delay in the development of production could

not, however, be attributed to any major articulatory difficulties. As is evident from some of the
data examined in these investigations and confirmed
by examination of the whole of the speech samples,
the children were capable of pronouncing almost all
of the types of consonants which occur in adult
English pronunciation and were certainly able to
produce spontaneously or in imitation all of the
fricatives and affricates.

The first seven children investigated in Part I
were the subjects of a detailed synchronic study
during 1974-75, which was the basis of a Ph.D.
thesis, (Grunwell 1977; 1981). Each child was observed over the period of approximately one month,
involving minimally three and usually four or five
recording sessions, during their regular speech
therapy clinics. All were diagnosed as having a
'severe functional articulation disorder'/phono-
logical disability.

The other five children were the subjects of a
diachronic study over a fifteen-month period in
1979-80. They were seen approximately once a month
during school term-time in the language unit which
they attended daily. This unit was attached to a
normal first school, but the children received all
their education in the unit, which was staffed by
a full-time qualified nursery/primary teacher, a
full-time speech and language therapist and a full-
time nursery assistant. Over the fifteen months
there were between ten and twelve children attending the unit, all of whom had some language and
language-associated learning difficulties. The
five children included in this study had developmental language delay with a phonological disorder;
i.e. a specific phonological problem was identifi-
able as well as their general language difficulties.
It should be noted that although receiving special
education for their linguistic disabilities, they
did not receive any direct articulatory or phonological therapy for their speech disorder on a
regular or programmed basis. However, the methods
for teaching reading and writing skills, which were
used jointly by the teacher and the therapist, were
designed to facilitate spoken language development;
a combined phonic and linguistically-influenced

sentence building approach was employed.

The data for all the children are detailed phonetic transcriptions of their spontaneous speech in response to picture-naming activities and free conversation. For all twelve children the same procedures were used for the first sample : the picture-naming was obtained by administering a standardised articulation test(Edinburgh Articulation Test. Anthony et al 1971); a matched set of words elicited using pictures(see Grunwell 1981); an auditory discrimination test(see Grunwell 1981); and a fairly lengthy sample of free conversation. For the five children studied longitudinally subsequent data collection sessions were much shorter and involved spontaneous picture-naming using an articulation test and up to about five minutes of free conversation. All the sessions were transcribed 'live' by the author and tape-recorded. The transcriptions were checked against the recordings within 24 hours of the session. A narrow phonetic transcription was made at all times.

Because of the relatively unstructured nature of the recording sessions not all of the fricatives and affricates were always sampled in word-initial position. Initial /z/ occurred so infrequently that it has been excluded entirely from this study. The absence of data on other fricatives and affricates from some of the recordings does not appear substantially to hinder the discernment of the trends in development.

Part I
It is necessary to consider each child individually since every one of the 12 children has different patterns in the production of the sounds(Table 1).

Joanne(J.) would appear to have reached Stage 4 Type /θ/ but as indicated in these data there was excessive variability in this child's speech with both stopping of fricatives and the frication of plosives. It was this co-occurrence of patterns from several different stages of development and their extreme instability that characterised this disordered phonology.

TABLE 1 Word-initial fricatives and affricates of the 12 children in Part I of the study

	f	v	θ	ð	s	ʃ	tʃ	dʒ
J. 5;0	f p	v b	f	ð d	s ʂ ʃ tʃ	ʃ ʃ tʃ	tʃ ʃ ʂ	dʒ
M. 6;3	f	v ʋ	f	ð d v ?	f	f	f	f
D.1 6;3	f θ	v b ð d	f θ	β ð	f θ	f θ	t	d
P.1 6;11	f	f	f	ð v n	ʂ θ	ʂ θ	t	t
T. 8;0	f	b p	f	ð d n	ɕ ʂ	ɕ ʂ	t d tɬ	t dɮ
D.2 5;8	d t b	w d f	θ p t d	d	d t	d t k	d t k	d t
P.2 7;2	f ɓ pf ɓ	β ɓ	f b	ð n pf 8	t d	t d	t d	d
S. 4;7	w	w	w j	d	j	j	t d	d
C.1 4;9	d	b β	n m	d	d t θ	d t w	d ƫ	d
C.2 5;8	f	b	f	d ð	ʂ h	h	ƫ h	h
A. 4;6	h	b	h	ð	h s t	h	d	d
D.3 5;9	f	v	f	n v ð	ʂ t	ʃ	tʃ tʒ̥	dʒ

Martin(M.) is not comparable with any of Ingram's stages, but as there is widespread occurrence of one continuant [f], this could be regarded as a deviant type of Stage 3. Martin's realisations of the fricatives and affricates were very stable; he also realised target initial /tr; dr/ as [f]. None of Ingram's deviant speech samples show a similar pattern; this is therefore an idiosyncratic pattern using a 'favourite articulation'.

Darren(D.1) appears to be in transition from Stage 2 to Stage 3, since there is widespread occurrence of continuants, but unlike normal patterns there is no [s]-type fricative nor any frication of the target affricate realisations. The patterns here are, however, most remarkably different from normal development in that the variability in the place of articulation of the fricatives is consistent, being determined by a pervasive consonant-vowel harmony process affecting plosive, fricative and approximant targets in stressed syllable-initial position; another idiosyncratic pattern.

Paul(P.1) can more easily be identified as a Stage 3 type of pattern, except that there is no frication of affricates and no appearance of any palato-alveolars. In addition, the fricative and affricate realisations are subject to a pervasive 'voicing' process which is contrary to normal trends.

Tanya(T.) is also at Stage 3, but again deviates from the norm in evidencing very few instances of the frication of target affricates. Here there is furthermore an unusual alveolo-palatal fricative being used for the majority of /s;ʃ/ targets. The variable voicing pattern here is also counter to the normal trend.

David(D.2) provides an example of a deviant Stage 2 pattern, in that while 'Stopping' predominates, there is extreme variability in the place of articulation of the realisations of fricatives and, to a lesser extent, affricates. The most frequent place of articulation is alveolar, a pattern which Ingram(1976) also found in deviant data and called tetism. There were no fricatives in David's speech patterns and the variability seen here was pervasive.

Pamela(P.2) is also at Stage 2, but conforms to the normal pattern 'Stopping'. It should be noted however, that [s - ʂ] were used frequently in word-final position for target lingual fricatives and affricates, as well as inappropriately for non-fricative targets, such as /t/ and /k/. The confused variability in the realisations of /f/ and /v/ also affected /p/ and /b/ and appeared to be consequent upon intervention designed to teach /f/.

Simon(S.) could be described as conforming to Stage 3; there are however no fricatives whatsoever in this child's patterns. He is using a pervasive process of gliding of fricatives, which is occasionally observed in normal children. This would appear to be a classic instance of the characteristic of the overuse of unusual processes(Lorentz 1974; Ingram 1976). In relation to the implications of these target fricative realisations, it is relevant to note that Simon also used an unusual process of reducing clusters to the second element, /tr/→[w], thus rendering his extremely simple speech patterns even more difficult to understand.

Christine(C.1) is somewhat similar to David(D.2), in that she is clearly at Stage 2 and also exhibits the unusual pattern of tetism. However, she differs from David in that she does not show such extreme variability; most of her variable realisations of all types of targets, including fricatives and affricates could be accounted for by unusual types of assimilatory processes, though none of these were of a regular pattern.

Clive(C.2) has a pattern which is difficult to classify; it could be regarded as a deviant type of Stage 3, with normal realisations for / f ;v;/ and /θ; ð/ and an unusual pattern with the [h] re-alisations of the other targets in this class. In fact [h] was pervasive in initial position, occurring also for target clusters and occasionally for single plosives. In contrast, [s] and [z] were used consistently and correctly in final position for phonemic and morphemic targets including when required in clusters.

Anthony(A.) shows a pattern similar to Clive and is arguably another deviant type of Stage 3. However, Anthony only uses [h] for fricative targets; affricates are consistently stopped and his cluster reduction patterns were normal,(cf. Oller 1973; Ingram 1976). Another point to note about Anthony's overall pattern is that word-final sibilants are consistently realised as [s;z].

David(D.3) is clearly approaching Stage 4 Type /θ/, though there are occasional lapses into earlier stages with stopping patterns occurring; these are by no means as marked as in Joanne's data, which is superficially comparable to David's(D.3). David shows the characteristic immaturities of this stage [ʂ;ʃ]. The confusion of [tʃ] and [tɹ] is also a common immaturity; in David's instance however this involves a different pattern from the normal type, in that [tɹ] is the pervasive realisation of all non-nasal clusters involving lingual targets,(in initial position).

Part I Summary
While most of the 12 children have patterns which conform to a greater or lesser extent to 4 of the 5 stages proposed by Ingram, there are clear indications of some deviance in their production of initial fricatives and affricates. A pattern that is common to the speech of the majority of the children (9/12; 75%), at whatever stage they might be, is the absence of affricates, and indeed of any palato-alveolars,(cf. Anthony et al 1971, who also found these types of sounds to be 'good discriminators between normal and 'speech-retarded'children).

All of the children evidence characteristics of phonological disability, with persistent processes and unusual or idiosyncratic processes. There is no clear evidence of chronological mismatch from these data alone; where there was variability between stopping and fricative realisations these are probably better interpreted as indications of a transitional stage. If however other aspects of the child's speech patterns are considered, there is clear evidence of this characteristic too; e.g. Clive's(C.2) word-final sibilant clusters co-occurrent with the pervasive use of [h] initially.

It is evident from the discussion of many of the children that it is often appropriate to take other aspects of their speech patterns into consideration in evaluating the realisations of the word-initial fricatives and affricates.

Part II
In this diachronic study it is also necessary to focus on each child individually. The data is presented for three-monthly intervals as these adequately reflect the general trends in developmental change.

Simon(S.) (Table 2) In the first three months Simon makes major advances and moves from Stage 3 to Stage 4, and his realisations begin to conform entirely to the normal pattern. Then, no further major developments occur; there are however major changes in other aspects of his phonology from 1/80 with the establishment of velar consonants, initial clusters and word-final fricatives. The appearance of affricates at 12/80 was probably promoted by active intervention. Nevertheless, to all intents and purposes Simon is still at Stage 4.

Christine(C.1) (Table 3) Christine has moved into Stage 3 at 1/80 and is giving evidence of transition into Stage 4 by 3/80, a trend which continues throughout the sampling period. A major advance in Christine's speech overall, and seen here in the fricative and affricate realisations,is a reduction in variability. There are many other changes in Christine's speech during this period, including a precocious advance in the realisations of clusters. By 12/80 she has the phonetic constituents of a normal complete adult system; their phonological value remains in question because there is still considerable variability in her speech. Christine is now reminiscent of Joanne.

Clive(C.2) (Table 4) Clive achieves a normal type

TABLE 2 Simon(S.) (in 9/79, age 4;7)

	f	v	θ	ð	s	ʃ	tʃ	dʒ
9/79	w	w	w j	d	j	j	t d	d
1/80	f	v	s̩	NR	s̬	s	t	t
3/80	f	NR	tθ̬	ð	s̩	s̩	t	d
6/80	f	NR	θ	ð	s̩	s̩	t	d
9/80	f	v	θ	ð	s̩	s̩	t̬	NR
12/80	f	NR	θ	N̈R	s̩	s̩	tj	dʒ̣

TABLE 3 Christine(C.1) (in 9/79, age 4;9)

	f	v	θ	ð	s	ʃ	tʃ	dʒ
9/79	d	b β	n m	d	d t θ	d t w	d t̬	d
1/80	f b w	b β	w	dz	s ʃ w h	ʃ tʃ	tʃ ts	dʒ̣
3/80	f	NR	θ	d	s j ç ts	ᵗʃ s̩	tʃ w	NR
6/80	f	NR	θ	ð v	s t ts	ʃ	tʃ ts dʒ	dʒ
9/80	f	NR	θ	NR	s̩ ʃ	ᵗʃ	ʃ s	dʒ
12/80	f	v	θ	NR	s̩ ʃ ts	s̬ tʃ	tʃ tj	NR

TABLE 4   Clive(C.2)   (in 9/79, age 5;8)

	f	v	θ	ð	s	ʃ	tʃ	dʒ
9/79	f	b	f	d ð	ʂ h	h	d	d
1/80	f	b	f	NR	s	ʂ ʃ	tʃ ts s	s͡ʃ
3/80	f	NR	f	ð	ʂ	ʂ	θ ts	ḍ̣
6/80	f	v	f	ð	ʂ	ʃ	ʂ	dʒ
9/80	f	NR	θ f	ð	ʂ	s	tʃ s	dʒ
12/80	f	NR	f	ð	ʂ	s	tʃ	dʒ

TABLE 5   Anthony(A.)   (in 9/79, age 4;6)

	f	v	θ	ð	s	ʃ	tʃ	dʒ
9/79	h	b	h	ð	h s t	h	d	d
1/80	f	b	ʂ	ḍ̣	ʂ	ʂ	k	d
3/80	f	NR	f	d	ʂ	ʂ	t	NR
6/80	f	NR	f	d	s	ʂ	t ts	d
9/80	f	NR	f	d	ʂ	ʃ s	tʃ tj	NR
12/80	f	v	f	ð	s	s	t	dʒ

TABLE 6 David(D.3) (in 9/79, 5;9)

	f	v	θ	ð	s	ʃ	tʃ	dʒ
9/79	f	v	f	n v ð	ʂ t	ʃ	tʃ tʂ̥	dʒ̧
1/80	f	v	p	ð	s	ʃ	tʃ	dʒ
3/80	f	NR	f	ð	s	ʃ	tʃ	dʒ
6/80	f	v	θ	ð v d ·	s	ʃ	tʃ	dʒ
9/80	f	NR	θ f	Ø	s	ʃ	tʃ	dʒ
12/80	f	NR	θ f	NR	s	ʃ	tʃ	NR

NR   not recorded in the data sample

Ø   omitted

572

of Stage 3 by 1/80. It should be noted, however,
that the newly introduced [ş] is overgeneralised to
clusters that were previously realised as [n]. He
slowly progresses in the direction of Stage 4 Type
/θ/, although he does not actually achieve this
stage. There are other changes occurring concurrently during this period, with the development of
initial clusters being the most significant. By
6/80 Clive's speech patterns can be described as
typically immature. Palato-alveolars are occasionally evidenced after 6/80, but are very unstable.
In fact in the last six months of the period there
are hardly any changes in Clive's speech, except
for the emergence of affricates.

Anthony(A.) (Table 5) In the first three months
Anthony shows a major advance and achieves a normal Stage 3; the newly introduced fricatives are
used appropriately. The realisation of /tʃ/as [k]
is an over-generalisation of the velar consonants
which are also being established in his speech.
During the rest of the period there are no major
developments that are brought to completion. The
final sample contains the occurrence of affricates
which have been introduced by direct intervention.
These twelve months are not however an entirely
fallow period in phonological development as velars
are now used consistently correctly and clusters
of all types have been established.

David(D.3) (Table 6) No changes are evident in
David's fricatives and affricates until 6/80 and
this transitional stage continues for this class
of sounds until the end of the sampling period.
However, changes have occurred in other aspects
of David's speech patterns : by 1/80 velar consonants, previously absent, are established; by
6/80 initial clusters are established and are
almost correct, except for immature lengthening
and occasional epenthesis, which disappear by 12/80.

It should be noted that the 'direct intervention'
that apparently promoted the development of affricates was the occasion of the Christmas concert,
which featured a Nativity Play(Jesus ; Joseph) and
'Jack and the Beanstalk'.

Part II Summary
This diachronic study of 5 children with phonological disability reveals certain common trends.

There is a rapid advance in <u>fricative</u> (nb. not in
affricate) development to Stage 3, if the child is
at an early deviant or extremely simple stage, and
progress is generally maintained to Stage 4. Thus
these deviant children are to a certain extent now
more similar to normal children in the speech patterns they use for this class of sounds. Yet, none
of the children reach Stage 5, and many continue to
exhibit restrictions at Stage 4 in the use of palato-alveolars and affricates; a characteristic that
was noted in Part I.

Having achieved Stage 4, fricative development is
apparently arrested, or persists for an abnormally
long time at this stage, so that there may be instances of chronological mismatch, as some patterns
may have lagged behind, such as velar fronting in
David's(D.3) speech, or other patterns may advance
more rapidly, such as clusters in Christine's(C.1)
speech. The children's speech patterns thus continue to exhibit some of the characteristics of
phonological disability.

In order to evaluate the changes or lack of them in
the word-initial fricatives and affricates, it is
important to consider what is happening in other
aspects of a child's developing phonology. This
leads to what is perhaps the most interesting finding of this diachronic study - developments only
appear to be introduced in one aspect of the phon-
ologies of these 5 children at a time. This finding lends further substance to the characterisa-
tion of phonological disability as a linguistic
learning disability.

References
Anthony,A., Bogle,D., Ingram,T.T.S. & McIsaac,M.W.
(1971) <u>Edinburgh Articulation Test</u> Edinburgh :
Churchill Livingstone
Ferguson,C.A. (1978) Fricatives in child language
acquisition. in Honsa,V. & Hardman-de-Bautista,M.J.

(eds.) Papers on linguistics and child language
The Hague : Mouton
Grunwell,P. (1977) The analysis of phonological disability in children Unpublished Ph.D. thesis. Univ.
of Reading
 Grunwell,P. (1981) The nature of phonological disability in children London : Academic Press
Ingram,D. (1976) Phonological disability in children
London : Edward Arnold
Ingram,D. (1978) The production of word-initial
fricatives and affricates by normal and linguistically deviant children in Caramazza,A. & Zurif,E.B.
(eds.) Language acquisition and breakdown - paral-
lels and divergencies Baltimore : John Hopkins
University Press
Ingram,D., Christensen,L., Veach,S. & Webster,B.
(1980) The acquisition of word-initial fricatives
and affricates in English by children between 2
and 6 years in Yeni-Komshian,G.H., Kavanagh,J.F.
& Ferguson,C.A. (eds.) Child phonology Vol.I -
Production London ; Academic Press
Lorentz,J.P. (1974) A deviant phonological system
of English Papers and Reports on Child Language
Development, 008, 55-64 Stanford,Ca. : Stanford
University Press
Oller,D.K. (1973) Regularities in abnormal child
phonology Journal of Speech and Hearing Disorders,
38, 36-47

Phonological Processes: Within or Across Phoneme Class Generalization in Articulation Training

Leija V. McReynolds, Ph.D.
University of Kansas Medical Center

Mary Elbert, Ph.D.
Indiana University

The purpose of our presentation today is to report experimentally obtained data on the breadth and depth of the phonological processes attributed to children with articulation disorders.

Operation of phonological processes in normally developing children is an accepted fact. The processes are said to function to simplify adult forms which are difficult for children to produce during phonological acquisition. A number of processes have been identified and agreed to in regard to young normal children. Operation of processes has been extended to disordered speech and language populations, mainly children hitherto labelled children with functional articulation disorders. There is a movement to relabel these children as phonologically disordered, primarily because their errors evidence patterns which might be attributed to presence of phonological processes.

The concept appeals to speech pathologists for several reasons. First, it provides a systematic framework for analyzing errors, but perhaps most important, it offers a promise for improving the effectiveness and efficiency of the training children need to correct their articulation errors. The promise is inherent in the description of phonological processes as general processes by phonologists. General processes affect several sounds or classes of sounds, not single sounds alone. Thus a process is responsible for several error sounds because it is not confined to specific instances. That, too, is an accepted fact. The speech pathologist has been encouraged to extend this general process concept to remediation. By identifying a process and the sounds affected by the process, remediation can be directed to elimination of the process in all the sounds affected by it. But even more attractive is the linguistic notion of rules, general processes or operation of a system. It is a well established truism that a child need not learn each specific instance to which a rule applies individually. Indeed, a few exemplars suffice and the rule is extended to other instances without specific learning occurring in each instance. The same concept should apply to elimination of processes in children with articulation problems. Although a number of sounds in error are attributed to the operation of one process it may not be necessary to eliminate the process in all affected sounds individually. Instead, by eliminating the process in a few error sounds, the process disappears in the remaining error sounds without additional training on each. After all, processes are general - cutting across sounds and sound classes. The generality should be maintained when processes are eliminated during intervention.

The purpose of the two studies to be reported was to examine just how general the processes are.

The two processes explored were Cluster Reduction and Final Consonant Deletion. Before reporting the results, I will explain the design of one study because the same design was used for investigating both processes.

Method

Our question in both studies addressed the issue of generality of processes. That is, for example, if plosive and fricative sound classes are affected by the same process, and a child is trained to eliminate the process in a few exemplars of one class, would the process be eliminated:

1) just in sounds within the sound class trained (within class generalization).

or

2) in sounds in both classes; sounds within the class trained and also in sounds of the class not involved in the training (across class generalization).

The first study was directed to exploring within and across class generalization in errors described as errors resulting from a Cluster Reduction Process. More explicitly, - if Cluster Reduction occurs in /s/ clusters and /r/ clusters and a child is trained to produce /s/ in a few exemplars of /s/ clusters, will correct production transfer only to remaining /s/ clusters or to both /s/ and /r/ clusters. Conversely, if Cluster Reduction occurs in both /s/ and /r/ clusters and a child is trained to produce /r/ in a few /r/ clusters will cluster reduction disappear in only /r/ clusters or both /s/ and /r/ clusters? We asked if a process is limited to within a sound class or if it extends across classes during acquisition when it affects sounds in more than one class.

Subjects

For both studies children ranging in age from 3.6 to 7.8 years with moderate to severe articulation problems participated in the study. All children were functioning normally in preschools or public schools and had normal hearing.

The design for both studies consisted of a single subject multiple baseline design across behaviors. The Cluster Reduction Study design is shown in Table 1.

Table 1 here

The design was developed for the purpose of evaluating effects of treatment variables experimentally. It is a within subject design in which each subject serves as his own control. Originally the response of interest is measured as in assessment to determine that it is not occurring prior to introduction of treatment, the phase is labelled the A phase, baseline phase. In a multiple baseline the two behaviors are treated in sequence. While behavior 1 is treated, behavior 2 continues in assessment (Baseline). Behavior 2 serves as a control to demonstrate that it does not change until treated. That is, the effect of extraneous variables is ruled out. Then, when training on Behavior 1 is completed, the second behavior is administered the same treatment to demonstrate the effectiveness of the treatment. When 2 behaviors are involved, they are counterbalanced across subects to rule out order effects.

In the Cluster Reduction study the two behaviors were the /s/ and /r/ clusters and for one child, the /s/ and /l/ clusters. Three of the subjects were trained on /s/ clusters first and /r/ clusters second; the reverse was true for the other 3 subjects except for Child 6 who received training on /s/ and /l/ clusters.

Procedures

The /s/ clusters represented in the study consisted of /sl, sp, st, sk, sm, sn and sw/ clusters in nonsense syllable contexts with a variety of vowels. The children were trained to produce /s/ in the context of only the /st/ cluster; the training items consisted of /sti, stæ, stu and sta/.

Table 2 here

The /r/ clusters included /tr, pr, kr, br, dr, θr, gr, and fr/, but the training items were limited to /tri, træ, tru and tra/. The /l/ items are also listed in Table 2.

Training

The children were trained to produce /s, r or l/ in a nonsense syllable context through imitation. When they reached criterion on each nonsense syllable they were tested to determine if Cluster Reduction had been eliminated in items which were in the sound class not being trained as well as in the sound class receiving training. For example, when /s/ clusters were trained, generalization was tested to all remaining /s/ clusters and to all /r/ clusters, and when /r/ clusters were trained generalization to both /r/ and /s/ clusters was tested.

Procedures for the Final Consonant Deletion study were the same except that the two sound classes were different and consisted of plosives and fricatives. The plosives were the /p, b, t, d, k and g/, and the fricatives were the /s, z, f, θ and ʃ /. The generalization words are shown in the next table.

Table 3 here

The plosives were trained in the context of the vowel /a/ and consisted of the syllables /ab, at, ag/ while the training items for the fricatives were /as, az and af/. Production of plosive and fricative final consonants was trained through imitation for children who deleted all plosives and fricatives in the final position in words.

Results for Cluster Study

Results for the Cluster Reduction study are presented first. Results for the three subjects trained first on /s/ clusters and second on /r/ clusters are presented in the table. (Remember that Subject 6 was trained on l clusters).

Table 4 here

Before training, the children produced no /s/ or /r/ clusters correctly or only rarely. When /s/ clusters were tested after /s/ training all children generalized (75 - 85 - 82% correct), but only one child generalized to the /r/ cluster. Generalization to /r/

clusters occurred only after /r/ cluster training. So, within class generalization was obtained but not across class generalization.

Table 5 here

Similar results were obtained with the other 3 children as shown in Table 5. They were trained on /r/ clusters first and /s/ clusters second. Again, few correct responses were produced before training. When /r/ was trained, correct responses to /r/ generalization items ranged from 16 to 72%, but the /s/ items remained at about the same level as in baseline. Not until /s/ cluster training did generalization to /s/ items occur at a high level -70 -70 - 80%.

We concluded that if Cluster Reduction was a process, it was not general enough to operate across sound classes, rather, it appeared to be limited to specific classes. Note that the child trained on /l/ clusters exhibited the same generalization pattern - transfer to within class clusters but not across class clusters.

Similar results were obtained for the Final Consonant Deletion study. Here, as can be seen in Tables 6 and 7, the children generalized very little either within or across class. Essentially, it is reasonable to say that child 2 and child 3 did not generalize at

Tables 6 and 7 here

all. When final plosives were trained the process was continued in words with final fricatives and final plosives. Similarly, when final fricatives were trained the children seldom produced final fricatives or for that matter, plosives in the probe words either imitatively or spontaneously. Subject 4 did slightly better, he generalized, but substantially within and across class only after both classes had been trained. The first child was the only one to exhibit reasonable generalization but it was within, not across class generalization. Thus, when final plosives were trained he generalized to final plosive items but not to final fricative items. Final fricatives began to appear only after fricatives were trained. From the Final Consonant Deletion Study it is possible to question whether processes always operate even within classes.

Discussion

The results of the two studies can be interpreted in a number of ways. For speech pathologists they are not surprising. Studies of articulation generalization conducted without recourse to the concept of phonological processes have demonstrated the same kind of in-class generalization without across class generalization. Calling articulation error patterns phonological processes has added little to the understanding and treatment of articulation disorders. If these patterns reflect processes, the processes are limited, not general, thus precluding the opportunity to make our articulation intervention strategies more efficient and effective than they are presently. We cannot, of course, deny that processes are present, but we can encourage a more careful examination of the definition of processes in the speech pathology literature and the usefulness of the definition for children with articulation disorders.

Table 1. Cluster Reduction Study
Multiple Baseline Across Behaviors

Subjects 1-3-6*   Subjects 2-4-5

Beh. 1

/s/ Cluster | Baseline A | Training B |

Beh. 2

/r/ Cluster | Baseline A | Training B |

Beh. 2

/r/ Cluster | Baseline A | Training B |

Beh. 1

/s/ Cluster | Baseline A | Training B |

*#6 Trained on /l/ instead of /r/

Table 2. /s/, /r/ and /l/ cluster training and generalization items

1) Training items for /s/ clusters: /sti, stæ, stu, sta/.
   Items for testing /s/ cluster generalization:
   /sl, sp, st, sk, sm, sn, sw/ with
       Vowels: /i , I, ε , æ, a, u, ʌ and oʊ/.

       TOTAL: 56 TEST ITEMS

2) Training items for /r/ clusters: /tri , træ, tru, tra/
       Items for testing /r/ cluster generalization:
       /tr, pr, kr, br, dr, θr, gr, fr/.

       TOTAL: 72 ITEMS

3) Training items for /l/ clusters: /pli , plæ, plu, pla/
       Items for testing /l/ cluster generalization
       /sl, pl, gl, kl, fl, bl/

       TOTAL: 48 ITEMS

Table 3. Forty-eight words used as probe items both in imitated and spontaneous production in Final Consonant Deletion Study

Plosives		Fricatives	
/p/	rope	/s/	bus
	cup		juice
	stop		dress
	sheep		goose
/b/	crib	/z/	cheese
	tub		rose
	web		peas
	robe		hose
/t/	cat	/f/	leaf
	boat		calf
	hat		roof
	kite		knife
/d/	sled	/v/	stove
	bed		glove
	road		sleeve
	slide		five
/k/	milk	/ʃ/	fish
	bike		mustache
	rake		splash
	lock		toothbrush
/g/	pig	/θ/	bath
	frog		teeth
	dog		mouth
	flag		tooth

Table 4.　Percent correct performance in baseline and probes in /s/ and /r/ or /l/ clusters for subjects trained on /s/ clusters first and /r/ or /l/ clusters second.

Subject	/s/ and /r/ or /l/ Baseline			Probe after /s/ training		Probe after /r/ or /l/ training	
	1	2	3	/s/	/r/ or /l/	/s/	/r/ or /l/
S 1							
/s/	0%	0%	0%	75%	90%		
/r/	0%	0%	0%			–	–	–
S 3							
/s/	10%	1%	3%	85%	2%		
/r/	1%	0%	0%			78%	29%
S 6							
/s/	3%	0%	0%	82%	6%		
/l/	0%	0%	0%			98%	94%

Table 5. Percent correct performance in baseline and probes in /s/and /r/ clusters for subjects trained on /r/ clusters first and /s/ clusters second.

Subject	/r/ and /s/ Baseline			Probe after /r/ training		Probe after /s/ training	
	1	2	3	/r/	/s/	/r/	/s/
S 2							
/r/	0%	0%	1%	16%	10%		
/s/	1%	5%	0%			11%	70%
S 4							
/r/	0%	0%	0%	70%	0%		
/s/	0%	0%	0%			91%	70%
S 5							
/r/	0%	3%	0%	72%	7%		
/s/	0%	0%	0%			75%	80%

Table 6. Results for S1 and S2 trained on final plosives first and final fricatives second.

	Percent Correct					
	Baseline (Average)		After Plosive Training		After Fricative Training	
S1	Imit.	Spont.	Imit.	Spont.	Imit.	Spont.
Plos.[1]	1%	1%	60%	33%	100%	83%
Fric.[2]	0%	0%	0%	0%	33%	25%
S2						
Plos.[1]	1%	0%	25%	0%	25%	25%
Fric.[2]	0%	0%	0%	0%	0%	0%

Table 7. Results for S3 and S4 trained on final fricatives first and plosives second.

	Percent Correct					
	Baseline (Average)		After Plosive Training		After Fricative Training	
S3	Imit.	Spont.	Imit.	Spont.	Imit.	Spont.
Fric.[1]	0%	0%	0%	0%	6%	6%
Plos.[2]	0%	0%	8%	0%	8%	6%
S4						
Fric.[1]	4%	1%	25%	0%	75%	21%
Plos.[2]	2%	5%	8%	0%	62%	8%

The Use of Melodic Intonation Therapy and Signing In Language Training of Autistic Children

Frances O. Pappas

The case studies presented were children with speech and language handicaps secondary to autism. Review of the medical, educational, and communication literature reveals unquestionable support for the probability of communication disorders as a result of autism. Furthermore, the use of Melodic Intonation Therapy has been well documented with the adult aphasic populations and recently with aphasic children. Likewise, sign language has also been accepted as the teaching modality for hearing-impaired, deaf, and autistic children. The purpose of this paper was not to add to this documentation, but to expand on a preliminary report by Miller and Toca on a combination of these techniques (Journal of Clinical Psychiatry, vol. 40, no. 4, April 1979).

Facility

Presented will be a summary of case studies of six autistic preschoolers who participated in the Louisiana State University Therapeutic Nursery School program, a state-funded special education program for emotionally-disturbed children. The school is 12 years old. Enrollment could theoretically be from the time of identification (birth to 2½ years) until mainstreaming into other nursery programs or public schools (at 5 years).

Program/Personnel

Average enrollment in the four-day a week morning program was two years. Total enrollment in the school is usually 8 to 12 children. An ongoing multidisciplinary approach is utilized, involving the psychiatrist, neurologist, ENT, speech pathologist, audiologist, psychologist, psychotherapist, occupational therapist, drama therapist, music therapist, and the parents.

587

The amount of time the child spent in individual therapies was determined by the severity of the autistic involvement. Parental involvement is a prerequisite to acceptance into the program, including the parents' participation in the classroom, in each of the therapies, in the mothers' and fathers' groups, and in carryover home activities.

All children were scheduled for two to four ½hour individual language therapy sessions weekly, and four ½hour group sessions. Language therapy was provided by speech pathology graduate students enrolled in the LSU Medical Center Master of Communication Disorders program.

Patient staffings occurred weekly. Each child's progress was reviewed by the respective specialists. Cooperative decisions were then made to revise and/or coordinate goals. Throughout the academic year children could be recommended for placement in other settings. Decisions were made in consideration of PL 94-142 and its mandating of the "least restrictive educational environment." Semi-annual reevaluations were used to document status changes in each area.

Population
The six boys were referred at ages ranging from 20 months to 4 years. All were diagnosed as autistic using the National Society for Autistic Children's working definition of autism, i.e. identification before thirty months of age and disturbances of (1) developmental rates and/or sequences; (2) responses to sensory stimuli; (3) speech, language, and cognitive capacities; and (4) capacities to relate to people, events, and objects.

Testing
Delays were documented cognitively, with functioning in the Educable Mentally Retarded and

Trainable Mentally Retarded ranges (three children
in each range). Instruments used were the <u>Stanford-
Binet</u>, <u>Cattell Infant Intellignece Scale</u>, and the
<u>Kaufman Developmental Scale</u>. Gross motor skills
were within six months of chronological age. With
regard to fine motor skills, many displayed "virgin
hands" problems and were one year delayed.

Audiological results were initially obtained
through sound field, and yielded suspected normal
hearing. However, five of the six children had
histories of chronic middle ear problems. Brain-
stem Evoked Response results showed dyssynchrony
between ears. Follow-up audiological testing after
vigilant conditioning training revealed document-
able normal sensitivity.

Social development was deviant (as defined
by autism).

Communication Skills
The range in communicative delays was 14 to
27 months - moderate to severe impairments.
Assessment instruments used were the <u>Receptive-
Expressive Emergent Language Scale</u>, <u>Sequenced
Inventory of Communication Development</u>, and an
in-depth analysis of an expressive language
sample (including pragmatics, prosody, semantics,
syntax, and morphology). Four children were
functioning between the 6 to 12 month level, one
at the 18 month level, and one at the 2½ year level.

Language Program
Developmental language programs were used,
e.g. Stremel and Waryas' Language Training Sequence,
Fokes' <u>Sentence Builder</u>, or Lee's <u>Interactive
Language Development Teaching</u>, but with the special
addition of the simultanteous usage of signing and
MIT. The signing system used was Signing Exact
English and the predominant melody was the opening
melody of Beethoven's Fifth Symphony ♪♪♪ o.
The vowel's duration was usually prolonged.

An example of an early therapy session might be the following: Child and clinician would be seated at a table with a tray of snacks (raisins, pieces of cookie and cracker, and a drink). The clinician's introduction would be, as follows:

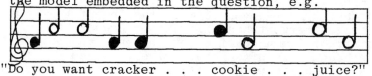

"Look at the raisins, cookies, crackers, and drink."

Then she would pause, allowing the child to process the visual and auditory images. She would follow with the question:

"What do you want?"

again, allowing him time to process. She could then prompt him, if he made no response, with the model embedded in the question, e.g.

"Do you want cracker . . . cookie . . . juice?"

The clinician might also prompt with

"Tell me 'I want raisin·'". or "I want more raisin."

or "Do you want more drink?"

Initially, 100% signing and MIT were used.
As the child gave a signed or verbal response, the
MIT was faded for that item. The initial responses
given by the children were in MIT or sign, but not
both. When response failures occurred, MIT was
reintroduced. Each new activity or language
structure to be taught was introduced with both MIT
and signing. This was true even as the child
progressed to the verbal level, using the
techniques as facilitators. As the child's spontaneous productions increased, the amount of MIT
used was decreased proportionately. The staff
attempted to use both of these techniques in all
therapies at school, but most parents used
neither technique.

The communication goals incorporated pragmatic skills, as well as semantic and syntactic ones,
specifically, turn-taking, greeting, and topic
maintenance (gesturally, vocally, or verbally).
The reinforcement was intrinsic to the activity,
e.g. being allowed to swing, climb, play ball, or
eat when the appropriate response was obtained. One
hundred percent verbal and signed reinforcement
accompanied performance of the motor task. Social
reinforcement was added as the child's eye contact
and affect improved. Secondary reinforcers were
selected that tended to assist in reducing tactile
defensiveness, e.g. blowing bubbles.

Results

Following 1½ to 2½ years of therapy, one child
was communicating at age level, two made 2½ years
of improvement (representing mild delays pragmatically and syntactically), two made 18 months of
progress (maintaining mild to moderate delays), and
one made no significant improvement in functional
usage.

Cognitive abilities, when retested, were also
improved: two children were in the normal range of

591

intelligence, two remained in the Trainable Range, and two tested in the Educable Range.

Four children are currently placed in autistic classrooms and two are in regular kindergarten classes. Reevaluations are scheduled at this center in one year.

Rationale/Conclusions

In conclusion, the reasons for success are also the rationale for simultaneous usage:

(1)   appeal to the visual channel strength (through signing),

(2)   redirection of bizarre hand movements by manipulating the child's hands to make the signs,

(3)   circumvention of the impaired auditory channel (Condon's reverberation time, slow processing time, and slow response time) (through both techniques),

(4)   appeal to the right hemisphere strength (documented by the children's interest in music, jingles, commercials, rote memory skills) (through MIT), and

(5)   modification of the suprasegmental features of normal conversation (additional pauses, slower rate) (through MIT).

At present, the center is pursuing further controlled studies to better establish the validity of the simultaneous usage of these techniques.

Bibliography

Condon, William S., "Multiple Response to Sound in Dysfunctional Children," *Journal of Autism and Childhood Schizophrenia*, 1975, 5, 37 - 56.

Creedon, Margaret. *Appropriate Behavior Through Communication: A New Program in Simultaneous Language*. Chicago: Dysfunctioning Child Center at Michael Reese Medical Center, 1973.

Ritvo, Edward R., editor. *Autism: Diagnosis, Current Research and Management*. New York: Spectrum Publications, Inc., 1976.

Rutter, Michael. "Concepts of Autism: A Review of Research," *Journal of Child Psychology and Psychiatry*, 1968, 9, 1 - 25.

Sparks, Robert, M. Albert, and Nancy Helm. "Melodic Intonation Therapy for Aphasics," *Archives of Neurology*, 1973, 29, 130 - 131.

Sparks, Robert, Nancy Helm, and M. Albert. "Aphasia Rehabilitation Resulting from Melodic Intonation Therapy," *Cortex*, 1974, 10, 303 - 316.

Sparks, Robert and Audrey Holland. "Melodic Intonation Therapy for Aphasia," *Journal of Speech and Hearing Disorders*, 1976, 41, 287 - 297.

Riddles and Rhymes: The Importance of Speech Play for Blind and Visually Handicapped Children

Sally M. Rogow
University of British Columbia

How children acquire semantic knowledge reflects the complex inter-relationships between language and experience. The constant association that words have with their referents provides a perceptual basis for word knowledge. (Brown, 1958) The language development of blind and severely visually handicapped children, for whom the perceptual basis may be somewhat different or diminished, focuses attention on the role of criterial attributes in semantic development. But vocabulary is not built one word at a time, nor is the full meaning of the word acquired all at once. (Crystal, 1976) The strategies of over-extending and over-restricting the meaning of words seems to be characteristic of young children as they build their word concepts. (Crystal, 1976)

The ambiguity of language itself contributes to the complexity of building word concepts as it also gives language its flexibility and creative potential. As the child becomes aware of word meaning he begins to use his knowledge in non-instrumental ways. The interest in nonsense rhymes and verse emerges between the ages of three and five, the age at which the child becomes aware of meaning and the nature of relationships in the real world. Nonsense seems to strengthen his sense of the real; the child who is unaware of the real order of things does not engage in play which reverses that order. (Chukovsky, 1968) Nonsense seems to play an important role in the child's understanding of ambiguity and incongruity. McGhee (1979) noted that incongruity is at the heart of the humour of young children.

The purpose of the present study was to explore how blind and other visually handicapped children regard the ambiguity of lexical items. It was of particular interest to explore the possible relationship between the child's semantic understanding of the ambiguous word and his ability to consider alternate meanings. Visually handicapped children are believed to have difficulty in establishing a perceptual basis for many words, especially those that have a visual reference. (Tobin, 1972) Research on the subject, however, is sparse and reflects a marked difference in points of view between those who regard blindness as an insurmountable cognitive handicap and those who consider that early education and a wholesome environment can successfully prevent psychological handicaps from developing. (Lowenfeld, 1981) Tobin (1972) summarizing the literature on vocabulary development, concluded that blind children have an inadequate grasp of word meaning. Lenneberg (1967) draws a very different conclusion and argues that blind children do not demonstrate any major deficit in vocabulary development. It should also be noted that visually handicapped children differ from one another in regard to family background, attitudes, expectations and linguistic environments.

How blind children handle ambiguity may reveal the nature of their word knowledge. Recognition of ambiguity seems to require a conscious knowledge of the word as separate from its referent. (Cazden, 1976) Attention to form and surface features seems to also be linked to metalinguistic awareness, which in turn, is associated with more complex language skills, such as reading. (Cazden, 1976), (Lundberg, 1978)

Lexical riddles were chosen as the medium of the present study because these riddles are based on words that have more than one meaning or on words that have the same surface structure (e.g. "bear" and "bare"). The appreciation of riddles is in itself evidence of the ability to "detach"

595

the word or phrase from its context. This is why
the lexical riddle is so appropriate a medium in
which to explore the competence of children in
making judgments about word meaning or ambiguity.
(Hirsh-Pasek, Gleitman and Gleitman, 1978)

Riddles are conventionalized in their treatment of ambiguity. Comprehension and resolution
of the riddle depends upon the child's ability to
recognize the riddle's "trick" question. The
ability to recognize and enjoy the humour of riddles has been associated with the attainment of the
Piagetian stage of concrete operations. (Sutton-
Smith,1976), (McDowell, 1979), (McGhee, 1968),
(Whitt and Prentice, 1977). Interest in riddles
seems to peak at the same time as conservation
tasks are mastered.

An earlier study of riddle comprehension by
blind and visually handicapped children between
the ages of seven and eight years demonstrated that
blind children are able to recognize and resolve
riddle ambiguity at the same ages as sighted
children. (Rogow, 1981) The present study is an
examination of the explanations of lexical riddles
given by visually handicapped children.

Method

Subjects

Fifteen legally blind subjects between 6.6 and
ten years of age were the subjects of the present
study. Six children were totally blind from birth
and eight were severely sight impaired. Seven
children were between 8 and ten years and eight
children were between 6.6 and 7.11 years. All the
subjects were enrolled in regular classes in public
schools; all receive specialized assistance from
either a resource room or itinerant teacher. None
of the subjects had English as a second language.
Two subjects were in Grade One, four in Grade Two,
four in Grade Three, three in Grade Four, and two

in Grade Five.

Procedure:

Fifteen lexical riddles were told to each
subject by the writer. After each riddle was told
to each subject individually (and the answer
supplied), the riddle was discussed. Each subject
was asked to explain the riddle and the meaning of
the "trick" word.

The Riddles:

Three types of lexical riddles were used: the
first type is based on a word that has more than
one meaning. The second type is based on words
that have the same phonetic structure, but connote
different meanings. This is illustrated by the
riddle: When is a boy most like a bear? (when he
is barefoot). The third type of lexical riddle is
illustrated by the riddle: "What did one wall say
to the next?" ("I'll meet you at the corner" or
"Pleased to meet you.")

Scoring Procedure:

The subject's explanations were only scored if
they were: Type A: In this type of explanation,
the riddle was explained in terms of the alternate
meaning of the trick word. This type of explanation
is free of the context described by the riddle and
focuses on the word itself.

Type B: In this type of explanation, the
riddle was explained in terms of the context of the
riddle. The meaning of the trick word was extended
to cover the situation described in the riddle. A
Type B response is an extended analogy while a
Type A response provides a meaning of the trick word
that is independent of the riddle proposition.

For example, an illustration of a Type A
response to the riddle "Why do farmers feed their
pigs all day long?" (So they can make hogs of
themselves). A Type A response is "A hog can be a

597

greedy person as well as a pig." A Type B response
was "If pigs didn't eat so much,they wouldn't be
called pigs."

Explanations which did not meet the criteria
of Type A or Type B were not scored. In other words,
any response which did not address the trick word or
phrase was not counted.

Results

The percentage of Type A responses was smaller
than the percentage of Type B responses. Twenty-
three percent of the explanations were of Type A
and 77% were Type B. Type A and Type B responses
were given 39% of the time. The younger subjects
gave many fewer Type A explanations than the older
(8-10 year olds). Thirty-seven percent of the
explanations of the older subjects were Type A
while 9% of the responses of the younger (6-8 years)
were Type A. (It is interesting to note that when
these same riddles were given to a group of sighted
children from 6 to 8 years, 13% of their explanations were Type A and 87% were Type B. There were
only seven children in this sample.)

The most interesting aspect of the study was
the explanations themselves. Those riddles which
were based on words which had the same surface
structure but connoted different meanings provoked
the most discussion. To the riddle "Why is the
center of a tree trunk like a dog's tail?" (Both
are furthest from the bark) the following comments
were made. "A dog barks at his mouth. A tree has
a different kind of bark; it doesn't bark. You
know how tree trunks get skinnier as they go up,
except for palm trees." Another totally blind
child remarked, "A tree just shakes quietly in the
wind and the dog barks a lot louder. They're made
different."

To the riddle "How do you know the ocean is

friendly?" (Because it waves), one child remarked that it was the wind that made the waves. "The ocean doesn't really wave at you; it just has waves. Once there was a windstorm outside of my house. I could hear it outside. I thought it was going to be a tornado."

"Why is a boy called a horse when he has a cold?" asked another blind subject when discussing the riddle, "When is a boy most like a pony?" (When he is a little hoarse.) This same subject asked "Why would a boy be like a bear if he is barefoot?" when discussing the riddle "When is a boy most like a bear?" (When he is barefoot). "A bare foot is not the same as having a real bear's foot" this subject declared.

The chart below shows Type A and Type B responses to a sample group of lexical riddles.

Type A and Type B Explanations

Riddle	Type A	Type B
Why did the farmer feed his pig all day long? (So he could make a hog of himself.)	A hog can be a greedy person.	If pigs didn't eat so much, they wouldn't be called pigs.
		A pig needs food.
		A pig has to eat.
What is the hardest thing about ice-skating? (The ice.)	The ice is hard.	When you don't know how to skate.
	Hard, hard, it's hard on your head.	Keeping steady.
	Hard is also difficult.	When there's no ice.

Riddle	Type A	Type B
Why is a moody man like a tea kettle? (One minute he whistles, the next he steams.	A moody man is one who's happy and grumpy. You never know when he's mad. He whistles when he's happy.	Steam comes out of his ears. He's mad and steam pops out of him.
When is the ocean friendly? (When it waves.)	The ocean has waves. A person waves to say "Hello".	Because it can be calm or rough. It's only friendly if you go in the shallow part. It's not friendly in the deep part.

Discussion

Type B explanations derive from comparisons of perceptual or criterial attributes and can be described as extended analogies. In contrast Type A explanations derive from knowledge of an alternate meaning and ability to detach the word from its context. The older subjects provided many more Type A explanations than did the younger subjects. Totally blind children seemed able to detach the word from its context, but seemed to need more verification of their own perception of the word.

Visually handicapped children demonstrated a keen awareness of words as a source of humour. They understood the pun as a "play on words" and defined riddles as "trick questions" at the same time as they expressed uncertainty about their understanding of the ambiguous word and its usage. This was particularly true of those words which had the same surface features such as "bear" and "bare" or "bark" (of a tree) and "bark" (of a dog). They seemed concerned with why the words should be alike since in their understanding they connoted different "meanings". The totally blind subjects in this study seemed less willing to "play" with word concepts and thus less able to enjoy the pun. They seemed to want assurance about the performance of word meanings. Ambiguity was simultaneously recognized, comprehended and questioned. Incongruity was appreciated and perceived as humorous, but it was also queried.

Summary and Conclusion

Recognition of incongruity itself may be a condition of metalinguistic awareness. Incongruity is at the heart of children's humour. Nonsense rhymes and verse are derived from incongruous relationships. Insufficient experience with what is real may narrow the blind child's appreciation and enjoyment of incongruity. Incongruous labeling of objects and events derives from experience with objects. Calling a "shirt" a pair of "trousers" or a "brush" a "comb" helps to achieve a sense of mastery over the word. Chukovsky (1968) noted that mastery of the word is a critical factor in determining when a child begins to find it funny to change the names of objects. This type of non-instrumental play with language is the sort of language experience that should be encouraged with children whose variety of experience is necessarily narrowed by the presence of handicap.

The basis of incongruity recognition are (1) mastery over the linguistic components of the riddle and (2) attendance to the workings of language as a source of humour. (Fowles and Glanz, 1979) Blind and other visually handicapped children demonstrated both these abilities. Attention to

the surface properties of the riddles existed side
by side with literal interpretation. The single
most important strategy of the totally blind subjects was the use of extended analogy to account
for the incongruity of the riddle. This was most
frequently the case with the younger subjects.

Hirsh-Pasek, Gleitman and Gleitman (1979)
noted that reflective skills appear later in life
and show more individual variation than do skills
related to language perception and production.
The reflective skills of visually handicapped
children are associated with the quality of their
interaction in the real world. It is important
for educators to appreciate the quality and variety
of language experience children need before they
are truly able to reflect upon language. This is
particularly true for blind children for whom access to experience is necessarily narrowed.
Language play is one means of enriching and expanding the child's enjoyment and participation
in the development of ideas. The didactic model
of instruction needs to be complemented by a
strong emphasis on all forms of play with language
and ideas.

References

Brown, R. Words and things. New York: Free Press, 1958

Cazden, C. B. "Play with language and metalinguistic awareness." In Bruner, J.P., Jolly, A. and Sylva, K. (eds.) Play - Its role in development and evolution. New York: Penguin, 1976.

Chukovsky, K. From two to five. California: University of California Press, 1968.

Crystal, D. Child language, learning, and linguistics. London: Edward Arnold, 1976.

Fowles, B. and Glanz, H.E. "Competence and talent in verbal riddle comprehension", Child Language, 4, 433-452, 1980.

Hirsh-Pasek, K., Gleitman, L.R. and Gleitman, H. "What did the brain say to the mind? A study of the detection and report of ambiguity by young children." In Sinclair, A. et al (eds.) The child's conception of language. New York: Springer-Verlag, 1978.

Lenneberg, E. H. Biological foundations of language. New York: Wiley, 1967.

Lowenfeld, B. On blindness and blind people: Selected Papers. New York: American Foundation for the Blind, 1981.

Lundberg, I. "Aspects of linguistic awareness related to reading." In Sinclair, A. et al (eds.) The child's conception of language. New York: Springer-Verlag, 1978.

McDowell, J.H. Children's riddling. Bloomington, Indiana: Indiana University Press, 1979.

McGhee, P.E. Humor, its origin and development.
     San Francisco: W.H. Freeman, 1979.

Rogow, S.M.   "The appreciation of riddles by blind
     and other visually impaired children".
     Education of the Visually Handicapped, 1981
     (in press).

Sutton-Smith, B.   "A developmental structural
     account of riddles". In Kirschenblatt-Gimblett
     (ed.) Speech play: Research and resources for
     studying linguistic creativity. Philadelphia:
     University of Pennsylvania Press, 1976.

Tobin, M. J.   "The vocabulary of the young blind
     schoolchild". Great Britain: College of
     Teachers of the Blind, 1972.

Whitt, J.K. and Prentice, N.M. "Cognitive pro-
     cesses in the development of children's enjoy-
     ment and comprehension of joking riddles."
     Journal of Developmental Psychology, 13:
     129-136.

Wills, D.M. "Problems of play and mastery in the
     blind child." British Journal of Medical
     Psychology, 41, 213-222, 1968.